MVS TSO

Mike Murach & Associates, Inc.

4697 West Jacquelyn Avenue
Fresno, California 93722
(209) 275-3335

MVS TSO

CONCEPTS • COMMANDS • ISPF • CLIST

Doug Lowe

Other books by Doug Lowe from Mike Murach & Associates, Inc.

MVS JCL
OS Utilities
VSAM: Access Method Services and Application Programming
CICS for the COBOL Programmer, Part 1: An Introductory Course
CICS for the COBOL Programmer, Part 2: An Advanced Course
The CICS Programmer's Desk Reference

Production director   Ed Gallock
Text designer   Steve Ehlers
Editor   Judy Taylor

Thanks to IBM for permission to reprint the material in figures 1-1, 1-10, and 1-11.

Library of Congress number: 84-061126
ISBN: 0-911625-19-4

20   19   18   17   16   15   14   13   12   11   10   9   8   7

Contents

Preface

If you're involved in any kind of program development on an IBM mainframe computer running under OS/MVS, you're probably using some type of time-sharing system. If that time-sharing system is TSO, this book is for you.

What this book does

In this book, you'll learn how to use TSO facilities to perform the everyday tasks of program development: editing (that is, creating and changing) source programs; compiling, link-editing, and executing programs; displaying file contents; allocating, copying, and scratching data sets; and much more. And you'll learn how to do those tasks using either basic TSO commands or SPF, a full-screen menu-driven version of TSO. You'll also learn how to create and use command procedures (CLISTs) of considerable complexity.

Of course, this book isn't the only way you can learn how to use TSO. One alternative is to use the IBM manuals. But reading an alphabetical list of commands along with complete details of each command's syntax isn't my idea of an efficient way to learn any programming subject, particularly one as complex as TSO.

Another option is to take one of the self-instructional TSO courses currently available. Unfortunately, my experience has been that the "basic" courses are too basic, while the "advanced" courses dwell on trivial aspects of TSO like how to use abbreviation in a TSO command. Rarely does one of these courses actually teach you what you need to know to use TSO effectively.

Because TSO has a rather extensive help facility, it's often tempting to ignore training and let the new user learn as he or she goes. Here, though, the problem is becoming satisfied with

1

an incomplete knowledge of TSO and its facilities. In other words, once a new user learns enough to get by, the help screens are rarely consulted again. As a result, the user never learns any but the most basic of TSO's facilities.

Unlike those approaches, this book is designed to help you do your job well right away. That means it teaches you how to use the most essential features of TSO almost immediately. It emphasizes the important aspects of TSO instead of the trivial ones. It shows you how TSO relates to MVS so you can make better use of your system's resources. And it teaches you to treat the IBM manuals and help facility as the references they're supposed to be.

In short, this book helps you go beyond a basic understanding of TSO towards a complete mastery of it.

Why this book is effective

I believe this book is effective for two reasons. First, I spent a great deal of time planning its content before I wrote one word. Though it's tempting to cover every possible aspect of a subject in a single book, the result is usually a loss in educational effectiveness. So for this book, I've carefully chosen and presented a practical subset of TSO facilities that will let you do most everything you need to. When and if you want to go beyond that subset, the background you've gained will make it easy for you to use other TSO references.

Second, I've placed a heavy emphasis on illustration in this book. In fact, you'll find more than 220 illustrations— illustrations that show not just *how* to code a TSO command or operand, but also *when* and *why* you should code it.

Who this book is for

As I mentioned before, this book is for anyone who needs to use TSO. That includes college students enrolled in a programming course, beginning programmers, and experienced applications or systems programmers. The only prerequisite is a familiarity with basic computer concepts. A basic knowledge of OS job-control language is also helpful but not essential.

How to use this book

The organization of this book gives you, as a student or teacher, many choices as to the sequence in which you cover the TSO facilities. Here's the general plan of the book:

Part	Chapters	Title	Prerequisite parts
1	1	Required background	—
2	2-7	How to use SPF	1
3	8-11	How to use TSO commands	1
4	12-14	How to use command procedures (CLISTs)	1,3

This means that after you've read part 1, you can read part 2 (chapters 2-7) or part 3 (chapters 8-11), depending on whether you'll be using SPF or native TSO commands. And once you've studied part 3, you can move on to part 4 (chapters 12-14).

Within the parts, the chapters are generally organized sequentially. In other words, you should read them in order. However, there are certain topics or chapters you can skip. For example, chapter 6 explains how to compile a program in foreground mode under SPF. If you'd rather do all your compilations in background mode, you can skip chapter 6 and go directly to chapter 7. I'll be sure to give specific instructions whenever such considerations apply.

One last word of advice on using this book. Although I explain various TSO facilities as carefully as possible, with many supporting illustrations, the best way to learn how to use a particular TSO feature is to actually use it. If you have access to a TSO system as you study this text, you'll be able to apply what you've learned immediately by trying out each TSO feature as I present it. By comparing the results of your experimentation with the examples in this book, you'll come to a deeper understanding of how each TSO feature works. As a result, your study will be much more rewarding.

Conclusion

I'm confident that this book will teach you how to use TSO effectively. And I know you'll use this book often as a desk reference once you've learned the TSO fundamentals. In fact, I guarantee it: You must find this book to be worth many times its purchase price, or you can return it for a full refund...no matter how long you've had it.

As with all our books, we welcome your questions, comments, criticisms, and suggestions. Is this book as useful as I've promised? Is there a way we can make it more effective? Have you found any inaccuracies or technical errors? If so, please let us know by using the postage-paid comment form at the back of this book. With your help, we can serve you better by improving not only this product, but future products as well.

Doug Lowe
Fresno, California
June, 1984

Part 1

Required background

Chapter 1

Preliminary
concepts and terminology

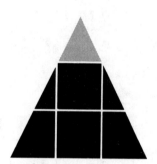

Before you can start using IBM's Time-Sharing Option (TSO), you need to understand some basic concepts. So this chapter provides the background you need.

In topic 1, I give you an overview of the operating system that supports TSO: MVS. In topic 2, I present an introduction to TSO: what it is, how it relates to MVS, and how you access it. And in topic 3, I show you how to use a 3270 terminal.

If you're already familiar with any of these subjects through previous experience, feel free to skip one or more of the topics in this chapter. A quick review of the terminology list at the end of each topic will help you decide whether you need to study the topic.

TOPIC 1   An introduction to MVS

An *operating system* is a collection of programs designed to control the operations of a computer system. Two major operating systems are available for the System/370: DOS and OS. DOS (including DOS/VSE) and earlier versions of OS (like OS/VS1) don't support TSO. So in this book, I cover only the current version of OS, called *OS/VS2-MVS*, or just *MVS*.

In this topic, I first describe three important operating system concepts: virtual storage, multiprogramming, and spooling. Then, I explain how MVS controls program execution. And finally, I explain an important MVS feature called data management services.

You're not going to become an MVS expert simply by reading this topic. Fortunately, you don't have to be an MVS expert to use TSO. All I expect in this topic is that you become familiar with many of the terms and concepts of MVS. In later chapters, I'll come back to the elements you control through TSO and explain them in more detail.

VIRTUAL STORAGE

The idea of *virtual storage* is simple: a small CPU simulates a larger CPU. For example, a CPU with 8 million bytes (abbreviated 8MB) of virtual storage can be simulated on a CPU with only 2MB of *real storage*. To accomplish this simulation, MVS uses disk storage as an extension of CPU storage.

During processing, only small portions of the programs being run are actually present in real storage. MVS stores the parts of the programs that aren't currently in use on disk. As additional portions of programs are required, the parts no longer needed are written out to disk and the new ones replace them in real storage.

Figure 1-1 shows the relationship between virtual storage and real storage. Here, real storage consists of a fixed area plus a *page pool*. The fixed area consists of programs that do *not* participate in virtual storage for performance reasons. The page pool consists of portions of the programs currently executing. These program portions are fixed-size blocks, 4K (about 4000 bytes) in length, called *pages*. The 4K blocks of real storage they occupy are called *page frames*.

As a program executes, MVS transfers required program pages to real storage from a special disk file called the *page data set*. If a page in real storage is changed during its execution, it's written back to the page data set (otherwise, it remains unchanged on the page data set). This shuttling of pages back and forth between real storage and the page data set is called *paging*, or *swapping*. The result of paging is that the 8MB system in figure 1-1 appears to have 16MB of storage instead.

MULTIPROGRAMMING

Few—if any— programs require all the resources of a machine as large as virtual storage provides. Instead, the computer's virtual storage is shared among several programs at once. That's where multiprogramming comes in.

Multiprogramming means the simultaneous execution of more than one program in a single CPU. Actually, though, that's misleading, because even though multiple programs are present in separate parts of virtual storage, only one program executes at any given time. The others wait for input or output operations to complete, or simply wait to be given control by MVS.

The intent of multiprogramming is to make better use of a system's resources. In general, those resources fall into three categories: CPU storage space, CPU time, and I/O devices. Multiprogramming effectively manages all three.

Managing CPU storage space

MVS tries to maximize storage space utilization in two ways. First, only the space actually required for a program is

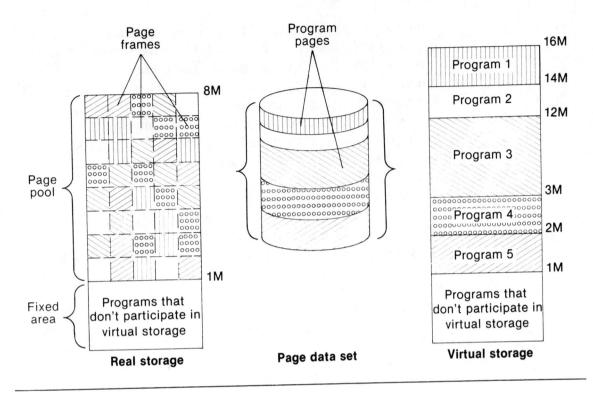

Figure 1-1   The concept of virtual storage

allocated to it. For example, a program that requires 48K of
virtual storage is assigned a 48K *region* (or *address space*). The
remaining virtual storage of the system can be assigned to
other programs. In a non-multiprogramming system, all of a
computer's available storage is allocated to each program as it
executes.

The second technique MVS uses to maximize storage
utilization is sharing program segments. For example, only one
copy of commonly used routines—like I/O routines—is stored
in virtual storage. Then, the programs currently in virtual
storage share those segments of code. If it weren't for shared
program segments, each program would require its own copy
of those routines.

Managing CPU time

Besides optimizing storage usage, multiprogramming makes
better use of CPU time by cutting down on the amount of time

the CPU is idle. Typically, the CPU becomes idle whenever an I/O instruction is issued because I/O device speeds are slow when compared with CPU speeds. But under multiprogramming, while one program waits for an I/O operation to finish, MVS branches to another program. When that program issues an I/O instruction, MVS branches to yet another program. Since the CPU doesn't have to wait for I/O operations to finish, a lot more processing gets done in the same amount of time.

But effective management of CPU time goes beyond just minimizing CPU idle time: the available CPU time must be allocated to the most important jobs first and the least important jobs last. To do this, MVS uses a priority scheme that permits distribution of processing time according to the users' needs. Users assign *job classes* and *priorities* to MVS jobs based on what work is most or least important. Then, as several programs are placed into storage for execution, MVS applies the priority scheme to decide which program gets control of the CPU.

Managing I/O device usage

You can also see the effects of multiprogramming at the I/O device level. Since several programs are running at once, more I/O devices are used at a time; they aren't sitting idle so often. In addition, certain devices—such as disk drives—can serve more than one program. For instance, instead of a disk drive spinning idly while a program processes a record just retrieved from it, the drive can be reading a record from another file on that disk for a second program.

SPOOLING

As I just said, multiprogramming increases I/O device utilization by allowing several programs that use different I/O devices—or sharable devices like disk drives—to execute at the same time. Unfortunately, a conflict results when two or more programs try to access a device that can't be shared, such as a printer.

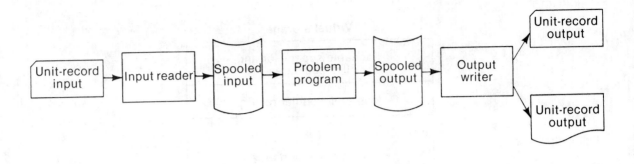

Figure 1-2   The concept of spooling

Spooling eliminates this problem by acting as an interface between programs and non-sharable devices. For example, when a processing program tries to print a line on a printer, spooling causes the line to be written as a record to a disk file instead. Later, under control of the spooling program (one of the programs of MVS), the output is written to the printer.

Figure 1-2 illustrates spooling. Quite simply, input data from a unit-record device (such as a card reader) is read by the input reader and converted into a disk file. Then, the application program processes the data by reading it from the disk file. For output, lines intended for a printer or other unit-record device are written instead to a disk file for later processing by the output writer.

OS JOB MANAGEMENT

Job management refers to the MVS function that routes jobs through the system. In MVS, a *job* is a set of one or more related *job steps*, each of which invokes a program. To understand job management, you must understand job scheduling, job control, and the job entry subsystem (JES).

Before you can understand these concepts, however, you must understand how MVS manages its virtual storage. Figure 1-3 presents a simplified map of virtual storage for an MVS system. Here, virtual storage is divided into five areas: the MVS nucleus, the non-pageable dynamic area, the dynamic region area, the master scheduler region, and the pageable supervisor and link-pack area.

Virtual storage

Pageable supervisor and link-pack area
Master scheduler region
Dynamic region area
Non-pageable dynamic area
MVS nucleus

Figure 1-3 Storage map for an MVS system

The first two storage areas in figure 1-3—the MVS nucleus and non-pageable dynamic area—are fixed in main storage. That means they're not subject to the normal operation of virtual storage. Instead, they're always *resident* in main storage.

The MVS *nucleus* resides in the lowest area of fixed storage. This critical element consists of the most heavily used parts of the operating system and controls—among other things—the operation of virtual storage. Obviously, the nucleus itself cannot be paged.

The *non-pageable dynamic area* (sometimes called the $V = R$ *area*, for virtual equals real) provides for additional programs that must operate in real storage. Typically, time-dependent programs such as telecommunications access methods (TCAM or VTAM) are executed here.

The *dynamic region area* contains virtual storage allocated to job steps as they execute. I'll explain how this area is used in just a moment.

The *master scheduler region* contains the *master scheduler program*, which is responsible for communication between MVS and the system operator.

The highest address portion of virtual storage is used for the pageable supervisor area and the link-pack area. As I mentioned a minute ago, only the most heavily used parts of MVS are kept in the nucleus area of real storage. Because the operating system is so large, the less frequently used parts are kept in the *pageable supervisor area* and swapped in and out as needed.

The *link-pack area* is for heavily used I/O routines or other system subroutines. Since these routines are placed in the link-pack area, they can be shared by many programs. (Actually, MVS maintains two link-pack areas: one within the pageable supervisor area and the other in the non-pageable dynamic area.)

Job scheduling

A special MVS program called the *job scheduler* selects jobs for processing. Figure 1-4 illustrates *job scheduling*. First, the job scheduler selects a job from the job queue (the *job queue* is simply a list of jobs waiting to be executed). For each step in the job, the job scheduler starts an *initiator/terminator task* that allocates the devices and main storage needed to run the program in that step.

It's the initiator/terminator task that decides how to allocate the storage in the dynamic region area. For example, if a job step invokes a 32K program, 32K of storage from the dynamic region area is allocated to that job step. Then, if the job's next step requires 48K, a 48K region is allocated, and so on until all of the job's steps have been executed. Then, the initiator/terminator returns to the job scheduler so another job can be processed.

Job-control language

To tell MVS which jobs to execute, which programs to execute for each job step, and which devices and how much storage to allocate for each program, you use a special language called *job-control language*, or *JCL*. Although you don't have to know JCL to use TSO, you won't last long in an MVS environment without a good knowledge of it. To get that knowledge, I recommend you read my book, *MVS JCL*. It's available from Mike Murach & Associates, Inc.

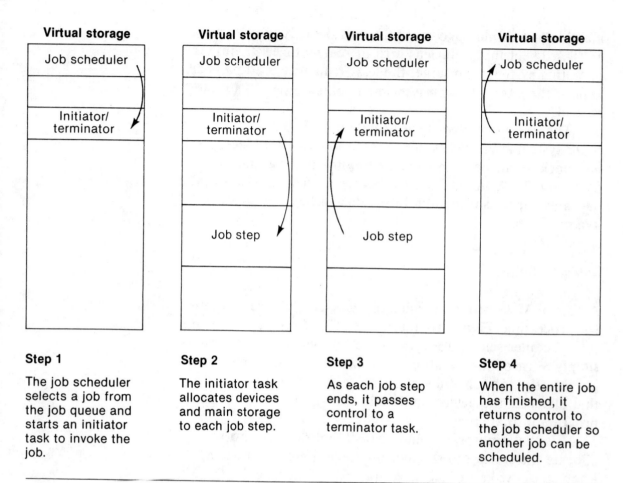

Step 1

The job scheduler selects a job from the job queue and starts an initiator task to invoke the job.

Step 2

The initiator task allocates devices and main storage to each job step.

Step 3

As each job step ends, it passes control to a terminator task.

Step 4

When the entire job has finished, it returns control to the job scheduler so another job can be scheduled.

Figure 1-4   Job scheduling in an MVS system

Job entry subsystem

The *job entry subsystem*, or *JES*, combines the functions of job scheduling and spooling to provide a comprehensive facility for processing jobs through an MVS system. Actually, it's the job entry subsystem that reads and processes JCL statements. There are two versions of JES, called *JES2* and *JES3*. JES2 is designed for single-processor systems, which don't have serious job scheduling problems. In contrast, JES3 is designed for large, multi-processor systems, in which job scheduling is highly complicated.

Both JES2 and JES3 provide basic job scheduling functions. Using JES2 or JES3 commands, you can submit a job for processing, specify a job class to control how long the

job remains in the job queue before being executed, or cancel a
job. But JES3 provides additional job scheduling functions not
available under JES2. For example, under JES3, you can
specify that a job must be executed every day by 10:00 a.m. Or
you can say that a job should not be started until another job
has finished.

JES2 and JES3 also provide many options for the final
disposition of spooled output data (called *SYSOUT data*),
based on the one-character *SYSOUT class* that was assigned to
the data when it was created. This SYSOUT class specifies
what type of device to use for the output. Normally, the
SYSOUT class and JES2/JES3 cause SYSOUT data to be
printed automatically along with the rest of the job output at a
default printer. But you can also change the SYSOUT class
and use JES2 or JES3 commands to route SYSOUT data to a
specific local or remote printer or to delete the output without
printing it.

DATA MANAGEMENT SERVICES

MVS provides automatic *data management services* for file
handling. You activate these services whenever you invoke a
function that processes a file. When you use TSO, you invoke
data management services often—usually without realizing it.
Four categories of data management services are important
when you use TSO: (1) data set storage control; (2) cataloging;
(3) space allocation; and (4) security.

Incidentally, in MVS terminology a file is called a *data set*.
Thus, I use the terms "file" and "data set" interchangeably
throughout the rest of this book.

Data set storage control

The service called *data set storage control* is the cornerstone of
data management services. This function, through which all
files are accessed, consists of a number of subfunctions.
Among the OS facilities managed by this group of
subfunctions are data set labeling, data control block
generation, and data set organization.

Data set labels   Under MVS, a storage entity such as a reel of tape or a disk pack is called a *volume* and may contain many files. MVS uses data set labels to identify the files on a volume. The volume itself is identified by a *volume serial number* (or *vol-ser*).

For direct-access volumes, a special area called the *volume table of contents,* or *VTOC*, contains the data set labels for each file on the volume. Each label in the VTOC gives the file name, the file's physical characteristics (block length, record length, organization, and so on), and its location on the disk.

One of the most important pieces of file information in a data set label is the file's *data set name*. Under MVS, a data set name consists of one or more *qualifiers*, each a maximum of eight characters long. The qualifiers are separated by periods, and the maximum length of a data set name including the periods is 44 characters (that allows for five eight-character qualifiers and four separating periods). Here are some examples of valid data set names:

```
MASTER
MASTER.DATA
TEST.MASTER.DATA
```

The first qualifier in a data set name is called the *high-level qualifier*. You'll be assigned a high-level qualifier to use whenever you create a data set. MVS uses special high-level qualifiers—like SYS1 and SYS2—for its system files. For example, SYS1.LINKLIB is the name of the system link library.

Within a single volume, all data set names must be unique. However, the same data set name can exist on more than one volume. In that case, you must provide the vol-ser as well as the data set name to uniquely identify the file.

Data control block   When a program opens a file, MVS creates a *data control block* (*DCB*) for the file based on information taken from the program statements and the data set label for the file. Each DCB is a table in storage used by various routines to control I/O operations. Normally, you code

JCL parameters to supply some of the information for the DCB. As a result, each file processed by a job step has its own DCB.

An MVS feature called *dynamic allocation* lets a program create a DCB without specifying any file information in the JCL. Instead, the program itself supplies the DCB information before it opens the file. It can also reuse a DCB by closing the file, changing the DCB information, and opening another file using the same DCB. As a result, a single DCB can serve many files. Although it's uncommon to write application programs that use dynamic allocation, TSO itself uses dynamic allocation for many of the data sets you access during a TSO session.

Data set organization   MVS provides several methods of organizing data sets. Only two of them are important to TSO: sequential and partitioned.

Sequential organization means the records of the file are written in processing sequence, one after the other. As a result, when a program reads the file, the records are always retrieved in the same order. To process a record in the middle of the file, you have to read all of the preceding records. Under TSO, most of the sequential files you'll use will be spooled JES output—compiler listings, program output, and so on.

A *partitioned data set*, often called a *PDS* or *library*, consists of a *directory* and one or more *members*. A PDS directory is simply a list of the members in the library. Each member is functionally the same as a sequential data set. In fact, you can process an individual member of a partitioned data set as if it were a sequential data set. But the advantage of partitioned organization is that you can also process the entire library as a single file.

In a partitioned data set, each member has a one- to eight-character *member name*. To refer to a member, you specify the member name in parentheses following the data set name. For example,

```
TEST.SOURCE.COBOL(REORDLST)
```

refers to the member REORDLST in the library named TEST.SOURCE.COBOL.

Cataloging

MVS maintains a structure of *catalogs* to store the names and other information of commonly used files. To access a *cataloged data set*, you specify only the data set name. MVS locates the file by searching its catalogs. To access a file that isn't cataloged, you must supply the data set name and the vol-ser for the volume that contains the file.

An MVS catalog structure consists of one *master catalog* and a number of *user catalogs*. In general, the master catalog contains catalog entries for system files (files that begin with SYS1 or SYS2) and user catalogs. User catalogs contain catalog entries for users' data sets.

Space allocation

The allocation of direct-access space is an important function of data management services. It lets you specify how much space your file will need and, optionally, which volume the file will go on. If you specify the volume, you're responsible for making sure it has enough empty space for the file. Otherwise, MVS will choose a volume for you that has enough space.

Security

In most TSO installations, *security* is a major concern. MVS provides for data set security by allowing you to set *passwords* for sensitive files. Then, only users who know the correct password can access the file.

Installations that need more security than standard MVS provides often use a special security system called *RACF* (*Resource Acquisition Control Facility*). RACF provides a multi-level password scheme that has different levels of access authority for different users. In addition, RACF provides for automatic cycling of passwords. For example, you can set up RACF so that you have to change your password every 10 days.

DISCUSSION

As I mentioned at the outset of this topic, I don't expect you to be an MVS expert at this point. The only way to really understand many of the concepts in this topic is through experience. The topic's purpose, then, is simply to introduce you to the terms and concepts you'll frequently encounter as you use an MVS system. As you continue through this book and start to work with TSO, you'll gain a fuller understanding of those terms and concepts.

Terminology

operating system
OS/VS2-MVS
MVS
virtual storage
real storage
page pool
page
page frame
page data set
paging
swapping
multiprogramming
region
address space
job class
priority
spooling
job management
job
job step
resident
nucleus
non-pageable dynamic area
V = R area
dynamic region area
master scheduler region
master scheduler program
pageable supervisor area
link-pack area
job scheduler
job scheduling

job queue
initiator/terminator task
job-control language
JCL
job entry subsystem
JES
JES2
JES3
SYSOUT data
SYSOUT class
data management services
data set
data set storage control
volume
volume serial number
vol-ser
volume table of contents
VTOC
data set name
qualifier
high-level qualifier
data control block
DCB
dynamic allocation
sequential data set
partitioned data set
PDS
library
directory
member
member name

Terminology (continued)

catalog
cataloged data set
master catalog
user catalog
security
password
RACF
Resource Acquisition Control Facility

Objectives

1. Briefly describe how virtual storage, multiprogramming, and spooling affect the operation of a computer system.

2. Briefly describe the function of these elements of MVS job management:

   a. job scheduling
   b. job-control language
   c. job entry subsystem

3. Briefly describe the intent of these features of MVS data management services:

   a. data set storage control
   b. cataloging
   c. space allocation
   d. security

TOPIC 2   An introduction to TSO

TSO stands for Time-Sharing Option. And that's exactly what TSO is: an optional feature of OS/MVS that provides time-sharing capabilities.

TSO has many advantages over traditional batch systems. For example, under TSO you communicate with the system using a terminal device rather than a card reader. TSO provides easy-to-use commands and menus rather than complicated JCL. And when you use TSO, response time is measured in seconds rather than hours.

In this topic, I introduce you to TSO. First, I explain how time-sharing works. Then, I describe how TSO relates to MVS. Next, I present an overview of what you can do using TSO. And finally, I describe some of the basics of using TSO—file name formats and access procedures. When you've completed this topic, you'll be ready to start learning how to use TSO.

TIME-SHARING

Quite simply, *time-sharing* is just what it says: sharing computer time among many users. In a time-sharing system, computer time is divided into *time slices*. Each terminal user is allocated a time slice in turn. Because each time slice is very short (in human terms), the users don't notice that they don't have complete control of the computer system.

To illustrate the concept of time-sharing, consider figure 1-5. Here, a computer's CPU time is divided into 12 time slices, one for each of 12 users. Currently, the CPU is allocated to user 5. When the time slice for user 5 expires, user 6 gains control of the system.

Time-sharing is similar in concept to multiprogramming. However, there are two significant differences. First, multiprogramming generally operates on a smaller scale than time-sharing. A typical multiprogramming system processes six to

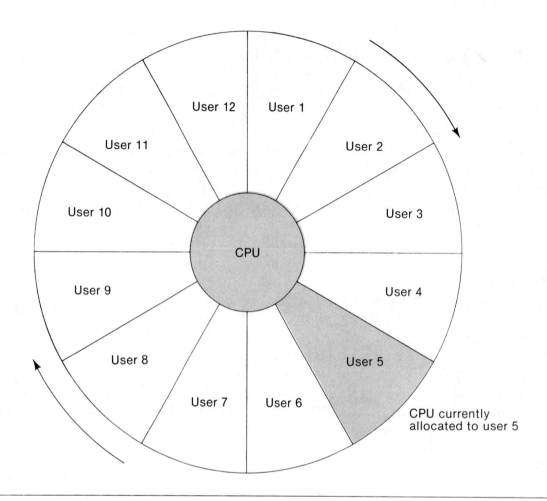

Figure 1-5   Time sharing and time slices

ten jobs at once. In contrast, a time-sharing system may support hundreds or even thousands of users.

The second difference between time-sharing and multiprogramming is how CPU time is allocated among tasks. As I just said, a time-sharing system allocates time to users in fixed-length intervals called time slices. In a multiprogramming system, however, once a program obtains control of the CPU, it generally keeps it until the program issues an I/O command.

HOW TSO RELATES TO MVS

Although you don't have to understand exactly how TSO operates in an MVS environment, it does help to understand

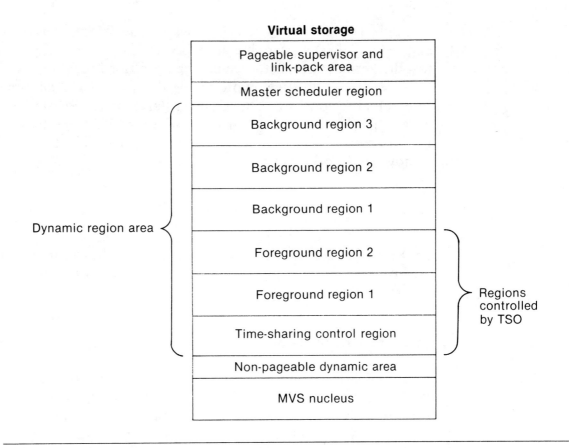

Virtual storage

Figure 1-6   TSO in an MVS system

the general relationship between TSO and MVS. Figure 1-6 illustrates this relationship.

As you can see, the dynamic region area contains several regions (a typical MVS installation might allow five to ten regions to be active at any one time in the dynamic region area). Some of the regions in figure 1-6 are *background regions*, used for typical MVS batch jobs. TSO executes in the *time-sharing control region* and, from it, controls user jobs in one or more *foreground regions*.

TSO implements time-sharing by allowing multiple jobs to execute simultaneously in each foreground region. TSO allocates jobs to each foreground region using a time-slice algorithm. Each job is allowed to execute in the foreground region for a short period of time. Then, TSO copies the job to an *external page data set* and swaps in another job. This cycle continues until all jobs have been processed. Then, the first job

is swapped in and the cycle begins again. The external page
data set and TSO's swapping are separate from—and subject
to—the normal virtual storage paging operations of MVS.

As you can imagine, coordinating the user jobs in multiple
foreground regions is a complex task. Fortunately, you don't
have to understand how all of it works to use TSO effectively.
I've presented this background just so you'll have a better idea
of how TSO works as you use it.

TSO CAPABILITIES

TSO provides many useful features. I've divided them into two
categories: standard features of TSO and features of related
system products.

Standard TSO features

Figure 1-7 lists the most helpful of TSO's standard features.
I've divided them into four types: program development
functions, data set management functions, the batch job
facility, and other useful features. Now, I want to give you a
brief overview of each type. You'll learn the details of how to
use these features in later chapters.

Program development functions   Under TSO, you can
create and edit program source files using either a line editor or
a full-screen editor. You can compile and link-edit programs
immediately by invoking the compiler or link editor in your
foreground region. You can view the compiler output at your
terminal or send it to a system printer. And you can test your
programs on-line.

Data set management functions   TSO provides powerful
features for data set management that make it unnecessary to
use the standard OS utility programs. Under TSO, you can
dynamically create (allocate) data sets. And you can easily list,
copy, scratch, or rename them. In addition, you can list
catalog or VTOC information.

One other useful feature of TSO is that any AMS (VSAM
Access Method Services) command can be processed on-line by

Program development functions

Create and edit program source libraries.
Compile a source program.
Link-edit a compiled program.
Test a link-edited program.
View compiler and linkage-editor output.
Route output to a printer.

Data set management functions

Dynamically allocate data sets.
List data sets.
Copy data sets.
Scratch data sets.
Rename data sets.
List catalog entries.
List VTOC entries.
Use VSAM AMS commands.

Batch job facility

Submit a job for background processing.
Monitor the progress of a background job.
View output from a background job.
Route output to a local or remote site.
Cancel submitted jobs.

Other TSO features

Help facility
Message broadcast
CLIST

Figure 1-7   Functions available under TSO

TSO. As a result, you can manipulate VSAM data sets on-line. (Since AMS commands are beyond the scope of this book, I won't say any more about them.)

Batch job facility   This TSO feature lets you communicate with MVS' job entry subsystem (JES2 or JES3) to submit background jobs. You can monitor the status of each job you submit to determine if it's awaiting execution, executing, or awaiting output. And you can view the job output at your terminal, print it, delete it, or route it to a remote site.

Other useful features of TSO   Besides the program development, data set management, and batch job features, TSO provides a variety of other features, three of which are listed in figure 1-7.

The *help facility* provides on-line reference information for all TSO commands. I describe how to use it in chapter 8.

Message broadcast is a TSO feature that lets you send short messages to other TSO users. You can send a message to a specific TSO user, a specific terminal, or all active TSO users. Normally, you don't use this feature. So I won't cover it in this book.

A *CLIST* (often called a *command procedure*) is simply a list of TSO commands that are executed together. CLIST

provides many of the features of a high-level programming
language: symbolic variables, conditional logic, branching, and
so on. I cover CLIST in chapters 12 through 14.

Related system products

A number of separate system products are often used with
TSO. Though these products are not actually a part of TSO,
most installations have one or more of them. Four that are
commonly used are DSPRINT, the TSO session manager, ISPF
(or just SPF), and SCRIPT/VS.

DSPRINT   *DSPRINT* is a TSO extension that lets you
direct TSO output to an on-line printer. Figure 1-8 shows how
DSPRINT works. Basically, TSO users running in foreground
regions invoke DSPRINT to copy a data set to a print file on
disk. Then, the DSPRINT print processor running in a
background region copies the print file to a printer. You'll see
examples of how to use DSPRINT throughout this book. And
I'll show you how to invoke the DSPRINT command in
chapter 9.

TSO session manager   TSO was first released in 1969. At
that time, terminal devices such as the 2741, a hardcopy
terminal that looked much like an IBM selectric typewriter,
were popular. The major characteristic of these terminals was
that input and output were processed one line at a time. As a
result, TSO was designed to interact with users one line at a
time.
    Two years later, IBM came out with the 3270 Information
Display System, the system on which TSO is now most popular.
Unlike earlier devices, the 3270 terminal can display a whole
screenload of data at a time. So when the 3270 was announced,
TSO was modified slightly to allow for the new type of
display. As a result, TSO causes 3270 terminals to display data
one line at a time, starting at line 1 and moving down the
screen until the display is filled. Then, the screen is erased and
the next line starts again at the top.
    The problem with this line-by-line display is that whenever
the screen is cleared, the data that was displayed is lost. The

Virtual storage

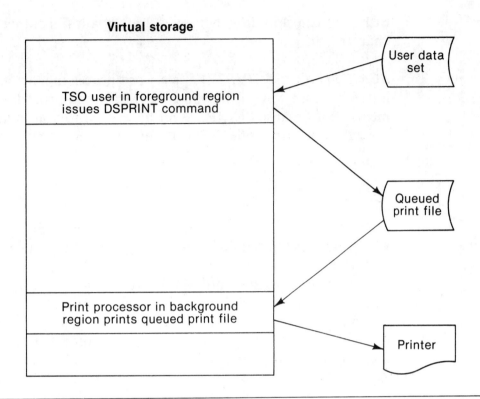

Figure 1-8   How DSPRINT works

main purpose of the *TSO session manager* is to make it easy to
recall data that has been cleared from the screen. As a result,
the session manager records all line-oriented terminal activity in
a special journal and provides simple commands to display
journal entries on the terminal. I'll describe the session
manager in chapter 8.

ISPF   *ISPF*, which stands for *Interactive System
Productivity Facility*, provides a menu-driven, full-screen
interface to most of TSO's features. With *SPF* (as it's
commonly called), you invoke TSO's functions by selecting
menu options and answering system prompts. Without SPF,
you invoke TSO functions using commands.

This book is designed to teach you SPF as well as standard command-driven TSO (called *native TSO*). Since most
installations today use SPF, I present the SPF features first, in
part 2. I present native TSO in part 3. If you won't be using

SPF, you can skip directly to part 3 after you finish this chapter.

SCRIPT/VS   *SCRIPT/VS* is a word-processing system that interfaces with TSO to let you create, edit, and print documents. But because SCRIPT/VS isn't crucial to your ability to use MVS facilities under TSO, I don't cover it in this book.

TSO DATA SETS

Many TSO functions create or modify data sets. For example, when you edit a program source file, you modify a member of a partitioned data set.

In addition to standard MVS data set naming conventions, TSO uses naming conventions of its own. Normally, any data set you create or modify in a TSO session is named according to these conventions. As you will see in a moment, however, these conventions are not absolute requirements.

In TSO, a data set name generally follows this format:

```
user-id.name.type
```

User-id is the TSO user identification number assigned to each user. *Name* is the name you create to identify the data set. And *type* is one of the values in figure 1-9 used to identify the type of data stored in the data set.

To illustrate this naming convention, suppose your user-id is TSO0001 and you want to create a COBOL source library named SOURCE. In this case, the TSO data set name would be TSO0001.SOURCE.COBOL.

Normally, TSO supplies the user-id component of a data set name. For example, you could refer to TSO0001.SOURCE.COBOL simply as SOURCE.COBOL. TSO would automatically add your user-id to the name.

Incidentally, the name component of a TSO data set name can be qualified. For example, you can create a data set name like this:

```
TSO0001.SOURCE.TEST.COBOL
```

Type	Meaning
ASM	Assembler-language source code
CLIST	Command procedure containing TSO commands
CNTL	JCL job stream used for batch job facility
COBOL	COBOL source code
DATA	Uppercase text data
FORT	FORTRAN source code
OBJ	Executable object module
PLI	PL/I source code
TEXT	Upper and lowercase text data

Figure 1-9   Common data set types

Here, the name component is SOURCE.TEST. The only restriction on this kind of qualification is that the total length of the data set name—including the periods used to separate its components—can't be longer than 44 characters.

Partitioned data set members are specified in the usual way—the member name is enclosed in parentheses following the data set name, as in this example:

```
TSO0001.SOURCE.COBOL(ORDRENT)
```

Here, the member name is ORDRENT. Again, you can omit the user-id. In that case, you would specify the data set name as SOURCE.COBOL(ORDRENT).

Remember that these conventions are just that—conventions. They are not absolute requirements of MVS or TSO. In fact, TSO allows you to bypass these conventions by specifying a data set name—using any format you desire—in apostrophes. As a result, you can refer to a data set named AR.MASTER like this:

```
'AR.MASTER'
```

When you use apostrophes like this, TSO doesn't add the user-id component to the data set name.

HOW TO ACCESS TSO

Accessing a TSO system involves two steps: connecting your terminal to TSO and entering a LOGON command. You use a related command, LOGOFF, to end a TSO session.

How to connect your terminal to TSO

The procedures for connecting your system depend on your specific configuration: whether your terminal is local or remote, which telecommunications access method your system uses, and how your installation has tailored your network configuration. In any event, find out from your supervisor what procedures to follow.

The LOGON command

Once you've connected your terminal to TSO, you must enter a LOGON command to use TSO. The format of the LOGON command is this:

```
LOGON user-id/password ACCT(account-number)
```

For example, if your user-id is TSO0001, your password is DAL, and your account number is 1234, you enter the LOGON command like this:

```
LOGON TSO0001/DAL ACCT(1234)
```

If you omit the parameters and just enter the word LOGON, TSO prompts you for the missing information. Usually, though, it's easier—and faster—to enter all the information in the LOGON command.

In response to your LOGON command, TSO may display a number of messages. These messages, called *notices*, are created by systems programmers or operators and may contain information about new releases of software products, scheduled interruptions in the system's operation, and so on.

Usually, it's a good idea to scan these messages. But if you wish, you can suppress the notices by specifying

NONOTICE on your LOGON command, like this:

```
LOGON TSO0001/DAL ACCT(1234) NONOTICE
```

In this case, the notices aren't displayed.

When you issue a LOGON command, TSO submits a JCL procedure to JES2 or JES3. This procedure includes statements that describe the data sets to be used in your session and that indicate whether the session manager or standard TSO is in effect. As a result, the procedure starts a foreground job to process your TSO session.

But you don't have to worry about writing this procedure yourself. Normally, a systems programmer creates and maintains the logon JCL.

The LOGOFF command

The LOGOFF command has a simple format:

```
LOGOFF
```

When you enter a LOGOFF command, your TSO session is ended. In other words, your TSO foreground job is terminated. Before you can do more work, you must enter another LOGON command.

In many installations, TSO is set up so that you'll automatically be logged off if your terminal is idle for a certain period of time—for example, 15 minutes. That's because it generally costs more to sit idle for 15 minutes or more than it does to logoff and logon again later.

DISCUSSION

So far in this chapter, I've tried to give you a deeper level of understanding than most introductory courses on TSO do. That's because I think you'll be better able to exploit your system's resources if you understand how you're using them.

Unfortunately, the drawback of my approach is that I've given you more information than you absolutely need to begin using TSO. So if you're confused about the relationship between TSO and MVS, don't be frustrated. The relationship is complex, and you'll understand it better as you work with TSO.

In the next topic, I describe the 3270 Information Display System. To be more specific, I introduce you to the 3270 terminal and show you how to use the keyboard. If you already have some experience working with a terminal device, you can skip topic 3 entirely. But in that case, you must now decide whether you're going to use SPF or native TSO.

Because SPF is easier to use, I recommend you go on to part 2 and study it first if SPF is available on your system. Then, when you need to do something SPF doesn't provide for or when you need to create and use a command procedure (CLIST), you can go to parts 3 and 4 to study TSO commands and CLIST. If, on the other hand, you're not going to use SPF at all, you can skip part 2 and proceed directly to part 3, the part that covers TSO commands.

Terminology

time-sharing
time slice
background region
time-sharing control region
foreground region
external page data set
help facility
message broadcast
CLIST
command procedure

DSPRINT
TSO session manager
ISPF
Interactive System Productivity
  Facility
SPF
native TSO
SCRIPT/VS
notices

Objectives

1. Briefly describe the meaning of the term *time-sharing*.

2. Explain how TSO relates to MVS.

3. Describe the functions available through TSO.

4. Describe the data-set naming conventions used under TSO.

5. Describe the procedures for logging on and off TSO.

TOPIC 3   The 3270 information display system

Although you can use a variety of terminal devices with TSO,
by far the most common is the 3270. In this topic, I first
describe the various components of the 3270 Information
Display System. Then, I show you how to use a 3270 terminal.
If you've used 3270-type terminals before, feel free to skip this
topic.

Components of a 3270 system

The 3270 Information Display System is not a single device,
but rather a system of *display stations* (commonly called
terminals) and printers connected to a piece of equipment
called a *controller*. The controller, in turn, communicates with
a host computer system either remotely over phone lines or
directly by being attached to a CPU. In other words, the
terminals and printers use the resources of the host system,
whether or not they're located in the same place. Figure 1-10
illustrates the components of a typical 3270 system.

3270 display stations   3270 display stations are available in a
variety of configurations, offering anywhere from 12 lines of
40 characters each to 43 lines of 80 characters, with one model
that displays 27 lines of 132 characters. One of the most
common 3270 display stations is the 3178. This terminal
displays 24 lines with 80 characters in each, plus a special
status line at the bottom of the screen.
    3270 display stations can be configured with many
options, including alternate keyboard configurations for special
applications and foreign languages. Less common options
include: a selector light pen that allows an operator to
communicate with the host system without using the keyboard;
a lock and key to prevent unauthorized use; displays in four or
seven colors; extended highlighting capabilities that let you
underscore characters, cause them to blink, or have them

Figure 1-10   Components of a 3270 Information Display System

display in reverse video (dark characters against a light background); and graphics.

3270 printers   In addition to display stations, printers can be attached to a 3270 system. Many 3270 systems have a local-print feature that allows the data on the screen of a 3270 display station to be transferred to the terminal controller and then printed by one of the 3270 printers. Since this operation doesn't involve transmission of data between the 3270 system and the host, it's an efficient way to print.

3270-compatible devices and emulators   Because of the enormous popularity of the 3270 system, many manufacturers besides IBM offer compatible terminals, controllers, and printers. And most manufacturers of minicomputers and microcomputers offer *emulator programs* that allow their computers to behave as if they were 3270 devices. As a matter of fact, many of the examples in this book were tested using an emulator program running on an IBM Personal Computer. Because of cost advantages and additional benefits, it's becoming more and more common to see such products in use in 3270 networks.

How to use a 3270 display station

To use TSO effectively, you need to know how to use a 3270 display station effectively. If you've used a terminal device of any type in the past, this should present no special problems. Your main tasks are to learn how the 3270 display works and how to operate the 3270 keyboard.

Characteristics of the 3270 display screen   As I've already mentioned, most 3270 terminals display 24 rows of 80 characters. To control the way data is displayed, the 3270 treats its screen as a series of *fields*, each of which has various characteristics. For example, some screen fields allow the operator to key data into them, while others are protected from data entry.

Data-entry fields are called *unprotected fields* because they are *not* protected from operator entry. As a result, an operator can key data into an unprotected field. In contrast, display-only fields—such as captions and data displayed by a program—are called *protected fields* because they're protected from operator entry.

Functions of the 3270 keys   The 3270 display station's keyboard is similar to a typewriter keyboard, with the addition of a few special keys. Although 3270 keyboards are available in many different configurations, the keyboard layout shown in figure 1-11 is typical. The keyboard contains five types of keys: (1) data-entry keys, (2) cursor-control keys, (3) editing keys, (4) attention keys, and (5) miscellaneous keys. Each keyboard in figure 1-11 highlights one of the five categories of keys.

The data-entry keys include the letters, numerals, and special characters (#, @, and so on) normally found on a typewriter keyboard. You use these keys for normal text and data entry. The shift and shift-lock keys work just as they do

Data-entry keys

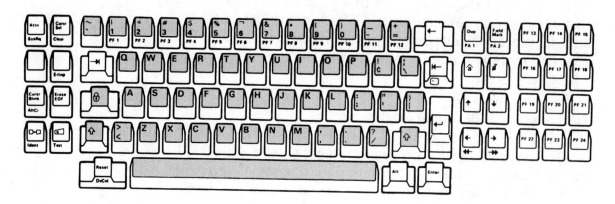

Cursor-control keys

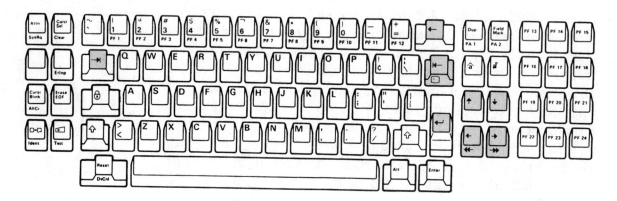

Editing keys

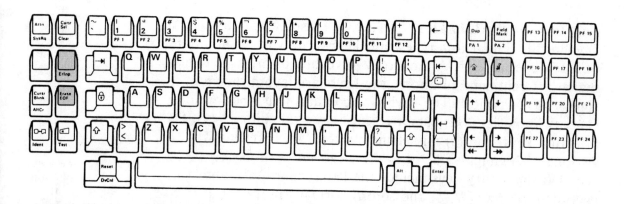

Figure 1-11 A typical 3270 keyboard arrangement (part 1 of 2)

Attention keys

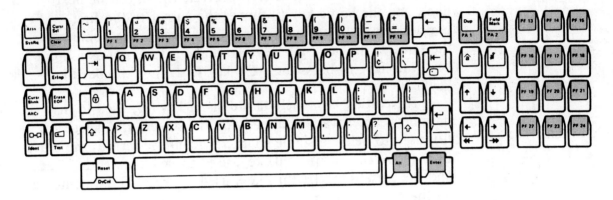

Miscellaneous keys

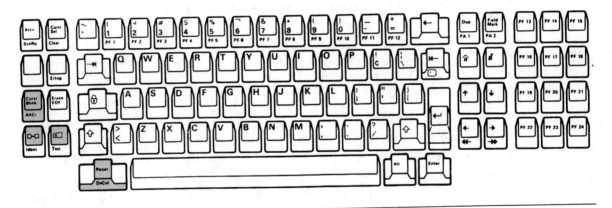

Figure 1-11 A typical 3270 keyboard arrangement (part 2 of 2)

on a typewriter. On some keyboards, a special numeric keypad is included to speed entry of numeric data.

The cursor-control keys are used to change the location of the cursor on the terminal's screen (the *cursor* is a special character—an underscore or a solid block—that shows the screen location of the next character entered at the keyboard). The cursor keys include four keys with arrows that move the cursor in the direction of the arrow—up, down, left, or right. Other cursor-control keys include the tab key (it moves the cursor to the next unprotected field), the back-tab key (it moves the cursor to the previous unprotected field), the backspace key (it moves the cursor one position to the left and erases the character at that position), the new-line key (it moves the cursor to the first unprotected field on the next line), and the home key (it moves the cursor to the first unprotected field on the screen). Incidentally, the home key is the same as the back-tab key. To make it function as a home key, you have to press the ALT key first, then the back-tab key.

The editing keys include the insert key (ⓐ), used to insert data between characters already on the screen; the delete key (ⓢ), used to delete a single character from the screen; the erase-EOF (erase to end-of-field) key, used to delete an entire field; and the erase-input (ErInp) key, used to erase all data entered on the screen.

The attention keys allow you to communicate with the system. For example, when you press the enter key, TSO processes the data you've entered on the screen.

The *program function keys* (or *PF keys*) are attention keys you use to invoke pre-defined TSO functions. A 3270 display station can have up to 24 PF keys; most have 12. The PF keys are labelled PF1, PF2, and so on up to PF24.

If you study the PF keys in figure 1-11, you'll see that the PF1 through PF12 keys are located along the top row of the keyboard, on the same keys as the numerals. To use PF1-12, you must first depress the ALT key, then press the correct PF key. For example, to use PF8, you press ALT and 8.

In contrast, the PF13-24 keys in figure 1-11 are separated from the main keyboard. Because you don't have to use the ALT key, the PF13-24 keys are easier to use than the PF1-12 keys. But as I said, not all 3270 keyboards have all 24 PF keys. As a result, many TSO functions use both sets of PF keys. In other words, PF1 and PF13 have the same function, as do PF2 and PF14. This isn't true for all 3270 applications, but it generally is for TSO. To show that you can use both sets of keys, in this book I usually refer to the keys in pairs. Thus, PF1/13 means PF1 or PF13.

A 3270 keyboard also has two or three *program access keys* (or *PA keys*), labelled PA1, PA2, and PA3. (Note that the keyboard in figure 1-11 doesn't have PA3.) The PA keys work like the PF keys except that no data is sent to the system when they are used. Instead, just an indication of which PA key was pressed is sent. PA1 is used as an *interrupt key* for many TSO operations. In other words, when you press PA1, the TSO operation currently processing is immediately interrupted. PA2 allows you to redisplay the screen, ignoring any changes you may have made.

The *clear key* works like a PA key, except that it causes the screen to be erased and any data that was on the screen is lost. As a result, you shouldn't normally use the clear key.

As you can see in figure 1-11, there are several other keys on a 3270 keyboard. But with the exception of the *reset key*, you don't use them often. You use the reset key whenever the terminal "locks up"—that is, when you make an entry error and the terminal freezes the keyboard to prevent further data entry. In this case, the keyboard is released when you press the reset key.

Discussion

I included this topic just as a brief overview of how to use a 3270 terminal. As you might guess, the best way to learn how to use a 3270 is to use it for a while. It doesn't take long to master. And you'll get plenty of experience as you now go on to part 2 (if you're using SPF) or part 3 (if you're using native TSO).

Terminology

display station
terminal
controller
emulator program
field
unprotected field
protected field
cursor

program function key
PF key
program access key
PA key
interrupt key
clear key
reset key

Objectives

1. List the components of a typical 3270 system.

2. Find the data-entry, cursor-control, editing, PF, PA, and reset keys on your keyboard, and explain how you'd use each one.

Part 2

How to use SPF

Chapter   2

An introduction to SPF

 As I mentioned in chapter 1, *ISPF* (or just *SPF*) is designed to increase your productivity in an MVS/TSO environment. ISPF, sometimes called *ISPF/PDF* (for *Program Development Facility),* lets you use most of the features of MVS in an interactive, menu-driven fashion, bypassing the cumbersome commands typical of native TSO.

In this chapter, I present an overview of SPF. First, I describe the various functions available under SPF. Then, I explain the basics of using SPF: how to access it, how to use its displays and menus, and so on.

FUNCTIONAL OVERVIEW

As I just mentioned, SPF is menu-driven. That means that most of its functions are controlled by *menus* that present a list of processing options. You simply specify which option you wish to perform.

Figure 2-1 is SPF's *primary option menu*. This menu is displayed when you start SPF. It offers you eleven processing functions to choose from.

42

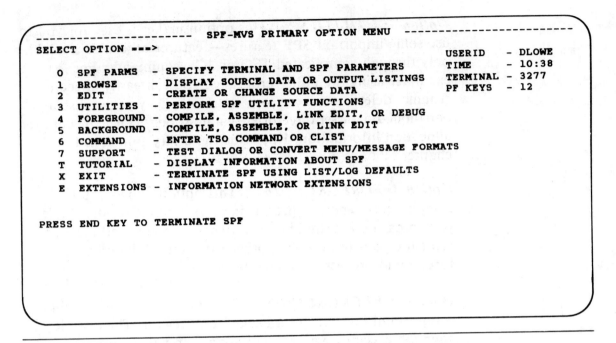

```
--------------------- SPF-MVS PRIMARY OPTION MENU  -----------------------
SELECT OPTION ===>
                                                          USERID   - DLOWE
    0   SPF PARMS  - SPECIFY TERMINAL AND SPF PARAMETERS  TIME     - 10:38
    1   BROWSE     - DISPLAY SOURCE DATA OR OUTPUT LISTINGS TERMINAL - 3277
    2   EDIT       - CREATE OR CHANGE SOURCE DATA          PF KEYS  - 12
    3   UTILITIES  - PERFORM SPF UTILITY FUNCTIONS
    4   FOREGROUND - COMPILE, ASSEMBLE, LINK EDIT, OR DEBUG
    5   BACKGROUND - COMPILE, ASSEMBLE, OR LINK EDIT
    6   COMMAND    - ENTER TSO COMMAND OR CLIST
    7   SUPPORT    - TEST DIALOG OR CONVERT MENU/MESSAGE FORMATS
    T   TUTORIAL   - DISPLAY INFORMATION ABOUT SPF
    X   EXIT       - TERMINATE SPF USING LIST/LOG DEFAULTS
    E   EXTENSIONS - INFORMATION NETWORK EXTENSIONS


PRESS END KEY TO TERMINATE SPF
```

Figure 2-1   The SPF primary option menu

Option 0: SPF PARMS   Various default values are used throughout SPF. For example, when you press PA1, you interrupt whatever function you're currently doing; that's the default value for PA1.

You use option 0 whenever you want to change the SPF defaults. SPF remembers the changes you make, so the next time you access SPF, the changes are still in effect.

Most of the values you can change using this option should be the same throughout an installation. So you won't want to change them on your own. As a result, I don't cover option 0 in this book.

Option 1: BROWSE   This option lets you display the contents of a data set or an output listing—even when the records you want to look at are longer than the line on your screen. Normally, you'll use it to display compiler output. I describe browse in detail in chapter 3.

Option 2: EDIT   This option lets you create or change a data set or library member. It's probably the SPF function you'll use most often. I describe it in chapter 4.

Option 3: UTILITIES   This option makes it easy for you to use some important SPF features—features otherwise available only through complicated TSO or JCL commands. For example, using the utility programs, you can easily allocate, rename, delete, move, or copy data sets. Or you can display partitioned data set directories, catalogs or VTOCs, or data set allocation information. I describe the utility functions in chapter 5.

Option 4: FOREGROUND   This option allows you to compile, link, and test programs in foreground mode. While your program is compiling or linking in foreground mode, you can't use your terminal for other functions. I describe foreground processing in chapter 6.

Option 5: BACKGROUND   This option lets you submit compile-and-link jobs to a background region. Then, while your job executes, you can use your terminal for other functions. However, overall response time for a background compile is often much slower than for a foreground compile. That's because you have to wait for your job to be scheduled.

In chapter 7, I show you how to use option 5. In addition, that chapter describes other SPF facilities for background processing.

Option 6: COMMAND   This option lets you issue a TSO command or CLIST procedure directly, bypassing SPF's menu structure. I describe TSO commands in chapters 8 through 11. CLIST is covered in chapters 12 through 14.

Option 7: SUPPORT   This option lets you test applications created with a component of ISPF called the *dialog manager*. With the dialog manager, you can create simple on-line applications that are similar to the standard facilities of ISPF/PDF. Because the dialog manager is beyond the scope of this book, however, I won't mention it again.

Option T: TUTORIAL   This option displays instructions for using SPF. I'll explain it later in this chapter.

Option X: EXIT   This option terminates SPF using the default processing options for the list and log files. I'll explain list and log files later in this chapter.

Option E: EXTENSIONS   As I've already mentioned, option 7 allows your installation to tailor certain SPF functions to its specific needs or to add new functions altogether. In the primary option menu in figure 2-1, the last selection (option E) invokes a menu of these *extensions* to SPF. Not all installations have this menu selection. So you'll have to find out from your supervisor what SPF extensions are available at your installation—and how you access them.

HOW TO USE SPF

How to access SPF

To gain access to SPF, you must first connect your terminal to the host system (if necessary) and enter a valid TSO LOGON command, as I described in chapter 1. Once TSO displays its READY message, you can invoke SPF by entering this command:

```
ISPF
```

Then, SPF displays its primary option menu, as shown in figure 2-1. (In many installations, a TSO LOGON procedure is created to automatically invoke SPF when you log on. In this case, the READY message never appears and you don't have to enter the ISPF command.)

The format of SPF displays

All SPF displays, or *panels*, have a similar format. In particular, the top two lines of all displays are reserved for system information, the third line is optionally used to display error messages, and the remainder of the screen (including line 3 if no message is displayed) is used to display data. In addition, this graphic:

```
===>
```

is used to indicate fields in which you can enter data (you don't always have to enter data in these fields, though).

The first line of each display contains the display title. The title of the screen in figure 2-1 is this:

```
SPF-MVS PRIMARY OPTION MENU
```

In addition, the righthand side of line 1 is often used to display a short message. For example, during a browse operation, current line and column numbers are displayed in this area. And short error messages are often displayed in this area, too.

You use the second line to enter commands for processing by SPF. For a menu screen, the command area is identified like this:

```
SELECT OPTION ===>
```

For other screens, the command area is identified like this:

```
COMMAND INPUT ===>
```

In either case, you can enter a variety of SPF commands in the command area. If the cursor is positioned somewhere else on the screen, you can easily move it to the command area by pressing the home key.

Some SPF displays don't let you enter a command. In this case, line 2 contains a message like this:

```
ENTER/VERIFY PARAMETERS BELOW:
```

Then, you enter data in the fields in the data area, below line 2.

The third screen line is normally blank, though in browse or edit mode, it does contain data. Whenever a short error message appears in line 1, you can obtain a longer version of it in line 3 by entering HELP in the command area or by pressing PF1/13.

How to use SPF menus

SPF's menus are easy to use. To select a menu option, you simply enter the option's number or letter in the command area. For example, to select the edit option from the primary option menu, you enter 2, like this:

```
SELECT OPTION ===> 2
```

When you press the enter key, SPF displays the first screen of the edit function.

Many of SPF's primary functions lead to additional menus. For example, if you select function 3 (utilities), the next screen displayed is another menu, showing nine additional functions. You can easily bypass the second menu screen by specifying both options at the primary menu, using a period to separate the selections. For example, if you enter this response at the primary menu:

```
SELECT OPTION ===> 3.5
```

the utilities menu is not displayed. Instead, utility option 5 is automatically selected.

How to use the PF and PA keys

Besides entering commands in the command area, you can also control certain SPF functions using the program access (PA) and program function (PF) keys. Figure 2-2 shows the default meanings of the various PA and PF keys. (You can easily change these defaults using the SPF PARMS option.)

As I said in chapter 1, many 3270 terminals require you to use the ALT key and one other key for PF1-12, while PF13-24 require only a single keystroke. As a result, all of the function key assignments for SPF are duplicated. So, you can use PF13 instead of PF1, PF14 instead of PF2, and so on. In this book, I indicate that by specifying function keys like this: PF4/16. That means you can use either PF4 or PF16.

Many of the PF and PA keys described in figure 2-2 are self-explanatory; others will be discussed later in this chapter. Now, I want to explain how two of them—PF3/15 and PF4/16—are used.

PF3/15, the end key, terminates an SPF function. Whenever you have completed processing for an SPF function and wish to return to the previous menu, use PF3/15.

Key	Title	Meaning
PA1	Attention	Interrupt the current operation.
PA2	Reshow	Redisplay the current screen.
PF1/13	Help	Enter the tutorial.
PF3/15	End	Terminate the current operation.
PF4/16	Return	Return to the primary option menu.
PF7/19	Up	Move the screen window up.
PF8/20	Down	Move the screen window down.
PF10/22	Left	Move the screen window left.
PF11/23	Right	Move the screen window right.

Figure 2-2   Commonly used attention and function keys

PF4/16, the return key, is similar in function to PF3/15. The difference is that PF4/16 returns directly to the primary option menu, bypassing any intermediate panels.

You can also use PF4/16 to easily move directly from one option to another. For example, if you're editing a file, you can move directly to the utilities option without displaying the primary option menu. To do this, you code an equals sign followed by the desired option number in the command area, like this:

```
COMMAND INPUT ===> =3
```

Then, when you press PF4/16, SPF goes directly to primary option 3.

The SPF entry panels

Most SPF functions require that you complete at least one *entry panel*. Entry panels generally require you to provide information about data sets and processing options. For example, figure 2-3 shows the entry panel for the edit option. Here, you must enter the data set name for the file to be edited.

```
--------------------------- EDIT - ENTRY PANEL -----------------------------
ENTER/VERIFY PARAMETERS BELOW:

SPF LIBRARY:
   PROJECT ===> DLOWE
   LIBRARY ===> TEST          ===>             ===>             ===>
   TYPE    ===> COBOL
   MEMBER  ===> REORDLST   (BLANK FOR MEMBER SELECTION LIST)

OTHER PARTITIONED OR SEQUENTIAL DATASET:
   DATASET NAME   ===>
   VOLUME SERIAL  ===>              (IF NOT CATALOGED)

DATASET PASSWORD ===>              (IF PASSWORD PROTECTED)

PROFILE NAME     ===>              (BLANK DEFAULTS TO DATASET TYPE)
```

Figure 2-3   The edit entry panel

Data set names   SPF data set names follow basically the same naming conventions as TSO data set names. Each data set name consists of three components: project-id, library-name, and type. Each component of the data set name is eight or fewer alphanumeric characters, starting with a letter. The project-id identifies the project associated with the data set and usually defaults to the user-id from your LOGON command. The library-name can be any name you wish. The type indicates the nature of the data stored in the data set. Although you can code anything in the type field, you should stick to the valid TSO types shown in figure 1-9.

The three components of a data set name are concatenated (strung together) to form the file's MVS data set name. As a result, the data set name for the file specified in figure 2-3 is DLOWE.TEST.COBOL.

If a data set has partitioned organization, you can specify the name of the member to be processed in the field labelled MEMBER. If you omit the member name from the entry panel, SPF displays a list of all the members in the data set, as shown in figure 2-4. You then select the member to be processed by placing an S (for ''select'') next to the member's name.

```
EDIT - DLOWE.TEST.COBOL -----------------------------------------------------
COMMAND INPUT ===>
                                                       SCROLL ===> PAGE
   NAME         VER.MOD   CREATED    LAST MODIFIED   SIZE  INIT  MOD   ID
   INVLST       01.00   84/01/26   84/01/26 14:29    202   202   0   DLOWE
   ORDLST2      01.00   84/01/05   84/01/05 16:44      9     9   0   DLOWE
 S REORDLST     01.00   84/01/26   84/01/26 14:29    202   202   0   DLOWE
   RNDUPDT      01.00   84/01/26   84/01/26 14:29    202   202   0   DLOWE
   SEQUPTD      01.00   84/01/05   84/01/05 16:44      9     9   0   DLOWE
   VSESMNT      01.00   84/01/05   84/01/05 16:44      9     9   0   DLOWE
   VSESMNT2     01.00   84/01/05   84/01/05 16:44      9     9   0   DLOWE
   VSESRUPT     01.00   84/01/05   84/01/05 16:44      9     9   0   DLOWE
   VSESSUPT     01.00   84/01/26   84/01/26 14:29    202   202   0   DLOWE
   VSKSMNT      01.00   84/01/26   84/01/26 14:29    202   202   0   DLOWE
   VSKSRUPT     01.00   84/01/05   84/01/05 16:44      9     9   0   DLOWE
   VSKSSUPT     01.00   84/01/05   84/01/05 16:44      9     9   0   DLOWE
   VSRRMNT      01.00   84/01/26   84/01/26 14:29    202   202   0   DLOWE
   VSRRRUPT     01.00   84/01/05   84/01/05 16:44      9     9   0   DLOWE
   VSRRSUPT     01.00   84/01/26   84/01/26 14:29    202   202   0   DLOWE
   **END**
```

Figure 2-4   An edit member selection list

To process a data set whose name doesn't follow the SPF naming conventions, you must use the OTHER PARTI-TIONED OR SEQUENTIAL DATASET field shown in figure 2-3. If you enter a fully-qualified data set name here, you must enclose it in apostrophes, like this:

```
DATASET NAME ===> 'TESTLIB.COB'
```

In this example, the complete data set name is TESTLIB.COB. If you omit the apostrophes, SPF adds your user-id to the start of the data set name.

If the data set isn't cataloged, you must enter a volume serial number. However, most SPF data sets are cataloged. So you won't use the VOLUME SERIAL field often.

To process a data set that's protected by a standard MVS password, you must enter the correct password in the DATASET PASSWORD field. However, if your installation uses RACF for password protection, you don't have to enter a password for the data set. That's because RACF uses your user-id to determine whether or not you have access to a particular data set.

Job information   Some SPF operations, such as program compilations, execute as batch jobs in a background region. For these functions you must supply an appropriate JOB statement in the entry panel.

I'll say more about background jobs in chapter 7. But in any event, your supervisor can provide appropriate JOB statements when you need them.

User profile   For each SPF user, SPF maintains a *user profile*. The user profile contains default values for many fields of the various entry panels. Whenever you change one of these fields, SPF stores the change in your profile. Then, the next time you recall that panel, the changed value is supplied by default. Because of the user profile, you enter many SPF fields only once. From then on, SPF supplies default values for the fields. (Incidentally, the PROFILE NAME field in figure 2-3 applies only to the edit option; it has nothing to do with your user profile.)

How to use the SPF tutorial (Help)

The SPF *tutorial* provides on-line instructions on how to use SPF. You enter the tutorial in one of two ways. First, you can select option T from the primary option menu to display instructions on how to use the tutorial. Second, you can press the help key (PF1/13) to immediately display the portion of the tutorial that describes the SPF function you're currently performing.

In general, SPF functions are simple and the entry panels are self-explanatory. However, it's easy to forget the formats of SPF commands. So you'll probably find yourself using PF1/13 often when you begin to use SPF.

List and log files

Some SPF operations generate printed output. For example, when you compile a COBOL program, a compiler listing is generated. Printed output like this is collected in a special data set called a *list file*. When you terminate SPF, you specify whether the contents of the listing data set should be printed or scratched (deleted). I'll explain how to terminate SPF—and how to specify whether the listing data set is printed or scratched—in just a moment. Remember, though, that output written to the list file is printed only when you terminate SPF. To obtain output immediately, without terminating SPF, you have to use a utility program.

In addition to compiler listings and other types of listings you request, SPF maintains a record of SPF operations in a special *log file*. To a programmer, the SPF log is of little value. So you normally won't print it unless your installation has a policy that says you should.

How to terminate SPF

The normal way to terminate SPF is to select option X from the primary option menu. This option simply returns to native TSO, using the default values for printing or scratching the log and list files.

If you use the end key (PF3/15), SPF displays the termination panel shown in figure 2-5. Here, you must specify options for the log and list files. For each file, you have four choices: print the file via a background job (J), print the file on a local printer (L), keep the file but don't print it (K), or delete the file without printing it (D).

For the list file, you'll usually specify J or L to print the file. If you specify J, you must complete the job statement information at the bottom of the screen and specify a SYSOUT class. If you specify L, you must provide the system-id for your local printer. You can get the correct values for these fields from your supervisor.

DISCUSSION

I've presented a lot of material in this chapter, so you may well be confused at this point. But don't worry. Because of the interactive nature of SPF, it's easy to learn. When you make a mistake, SPF immediately lets you know. If you need help,

```
 SPECIFY DISPOSITION OF LOG AND LIST DATASETS  ------------------------------------
 ENTER/VERIFY PARAMETERS BELOW:

 LOG OPTIONS FOR THIS SESSION            LIST OPTIONS FOR THIS SESSION
 ----------------------------            ----------------------------
 PROCESS OPTION    ===> J                PROCESS OPTION    ===> J
 SYSOUT CLASS      ===> X                SYSOUT CLASS      ===> X
 LOCAL PRINTER ID ===>                   LOCAL PRINTER ID ===>

 VALID PROCESS OPTIONS:
   J - SUBMIT JOB TO PRINT (AND DELETE)      K - KEEP DATASET (DO NOT PRINT)
   L - ROUTE TO LOCAL PRINTER (AND DELETE)   D - DELETE DATASET (DO NOT PRINT)

 PRESS ENTER TO COMPLETE SPF TERMINATION
 PRESS END KEY TO RETURN TO PRIMARY OPTION MENU

 JOB STATEMENT INFORMATION:  (IF OPTION "J" SELECTED)
   ===> //DLOWEB   JOB (MMA1,DLOWE),'DOUG LOWE'
   ===> //*
   ===> //*
   ===> //*
```

Figure 2-5   The SPF termination panel

you can press PF1/13 to see an explanation of what you are trying to do. And SPF operations that seem complex and confusing at first become second nature with time.

So if you aren't sure you've mastered all the material in this chapter, I suggest you continue with chapter 3. Then, as you use SPF, you can return to this chapter and review the parts you didn't understand.

Terminology

ISPF	extension
SPF	panel
ISPF/PDF	entry panel
Program Development Facility	user profile
menu	tutorial
primary option menu	list file
dialog manager	log file

Objectives

1. Briefly describe the function of each of the SPF primary options:

   a. SPF parms
   b. browse
   c. edit
   d. utilities
   e. foreground
   f. background
   g. command
   h. support
   i. tutorial
   j. exit
   k. extensions

2. Describe the procedures for accessing and terminating SPF.

3. Explain how to move back and forth between SPF menus.

4. Describe these SPF features:

   a. user profile
   b. log file
   c. list file

Chapter 3

How to browse a data set

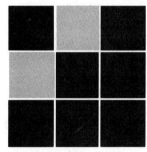

In this chapter, you'll learn how to use SPF's browse option to examine the contents of a data set or member. There are two topics in this chapter. Topic 1 shows you the basics of using browse. When you've completed it, you can move on to chapter 4 if you wish...and you should if you're new to SPF. Topic 2 presents advanced features of browse—features you won't need initially, but which will prove useful as you gain experience with SPF.

TOPIC 1   Basic browse operations

You'll probably use browse most often to examine SYSOUT
data sets—compiler listings, storage dumps, and so on. These
data sets contain 133-byte records—the first byte is a printer-
control character and the remaining 132 bytes contain
alphanumeric data—but browse displays only the 132 bytes of
data. This topic presents the features that enable you to browse
this type of data set.

How to begin a browse session

To access browse, you select option 1 from the primary option
menu. SPF then displays the browse entry panel, shown in
figure 3-1. Here, you enter the data set and member name
for the file you wish to browse. The shaded part of this
example shows I'm going to browse a data set named
DLOWE.REORDLST.LIST. This data set is a compiler listing
I saved from a previous COBOL compilation.

After you enter the data set information, browse displays
the first 22 lines of the source data, as shown in figure 3-2. As
you can see, the righthand side of line 1 shows the current line
number and the columns currently displayed. Here, the current
line is line 0, and columns 1 through 80 are shown. (The line
numbers in the display itself have nothing to do with browse.)

Sometimes, you'll want to identify individual columns
between the left and right margins. To do that, you enter the
word COLS in the command area. Then, browse displays a line
at the top of the data area like the one in figure 3-3. As you
can see, this line makes it easy to figure out the column
locations of the data.

Going back to figure 3-2, notice the TOP OF DATA
indication on line 3. *Top of data* is SPF's term for the first line
of the source file. Likewise, *bottom of data* means the last line
of the source file.

```
----------------------- BROWSE - ENTRY PANEL  -----------------------------
ENTER/VERIFY PARAMETERS BELOW:

SPF LIBRARY:
    PROJECT ===> DLOWE
    LIBRARY ===> REORDLST
    TYPE    ===> LIST
    MEMBER  ===>              (BLANK FOR MEMBER SELECTION LIST)

OTHER PARTITIONED OR SEQUENTIAL DATASET:
    DATASET NAME   ===>
    VOLUME SERIAL ===>        (IF NOT CATALOGED)

DATASET PASSWORD ===>         (IF PASSWORD PROTECTED)
```

Figure 3-1   The browse entry panel

```
 BROWSE - DLOWE.REORDLST.LIST ------------------------- LINE 000000 COL 001 080
 COMMAND INPUT ===>                                         SCROLL ===> HALF
********************************* TOP OF DATA ********************-CAPS ON-**
PP 5740-CB1 RELEASE 2.3  + PTF 8 JAN 28 82          IBM OS/VS COBOL

    1                     15.55.24         JAN 26,1984
        000800 IDENTIFICATION DIVISION.
        000900*
        001000 PROGRAM-ID. REORDLST.
        001100*
        001200 ENVIRONMENT DIVISION.
        001300*
        001400 CONFIGURATION SECTION.
        001500*
        001600 SPECIAL-NAMES.
        001700     C01 IS PAGE-TOP.
        001800*
        001900 INPUT-OUTPUT SECTION.
        002000*
        002100 FILE-CONTROL.
        002200     SELECT BFCRDS ASSIGN TO UT-S-BFCRDS.
        002300     SELECT ORDLST ASSIGN TO UT-S-ORDLST.
        002400*
        002500 DATA DIVISION.
```

Figure 3-2   The browse data display

```
BROWSE - DLOWE.REORDLST.LIST ------------------------- LINE 000030 COL 001 080
COMMAND INPUT ===>                                         SCROLL ===> PAGE
----+----1----+----2----+----3----+----4----+----5----+----6----+----7----+----8
        003400 01  BAL-FWD-CARD.
        003500*
        003600     05  BF-ITEM-NO        PIC 9(5)..
        003700     05  BF-ITEM-DESC      PIC X(20).
        003800     05  FILLER            PIC X(5).
        003900     05  BF-UNIT-PRICE     PIC 999V99.
        004000     05  BF-REORDER-POINT  PIC 9(5).
        004100     05  BF-ON-HAND        PIC 9(5).
        004200     05  BF-ON-ORDER       PIC 9(5).
        004300     05  FILLER            PIC X(30).
        004400*
        004500 FD  ORDLST
        004600     LABEL RECORDS ARE STANDARD
        004700     RECORDING MODE IS F
        004800     RECORD CONTAINS 133 CHARACTERS.
        004900*
        005000 01  PRINT-AREA            PIC X(133).
        005100*
        005200 WORKING-STORAGE SECTION.
        005300*
        005400 01  SWITCHES.
```

Figure 3-3   A browse display with a COLS line

How to scroll through a data set

Browse displays up to 22 lines of 80-character data at a time in an area called the *screen window*. If the file contains more than 22 records or the records are more than 80 bytes long, you must use *scrolling* to move the screen window so you can view all of the data. Scrolling functions let you specify both the direction and the amount of the move.

To specify the scroll direction, you use PF keys. Figure 3-4 shows the default PF key assignments for scrolling. As you can see, PF7/19 moves the screen window up, PF8/20 moves it down, PF10/22 moves it left, and PF11/23 moves it right. As a result, the data *appears* to move on the screen. For example, when you move the screen window down by using PF8/20, the data on the screen appears to move up. Similarly, when you move the screen window right using PF11/23, the screen data appears to move left.

You specify the amount of the scroll by entering a value in the SCROLL field at the righthand side of line 2 in the browse display panel. Figure 3-5 shows the valid scroll amount values. Normally, this value defaults to HALF. That means that the

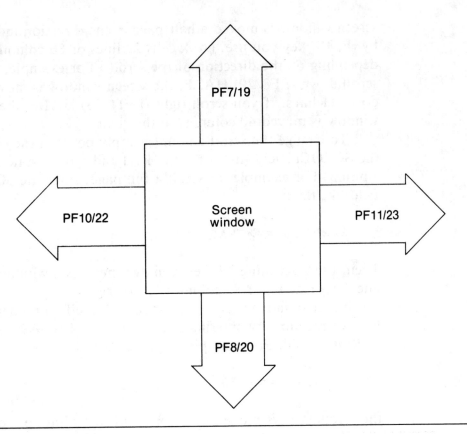

Figure 3-4 PF keys used for scrolling under SPF

Value	Meaning
HALF	Move the screen window half a page (11 lines or 40 columns).
PAGE	Move the screen window one page (22 lines or 80 columns).
n	Move the screen window *n* lines or columns.
MAX	Move the screen window to top, bottom, left, or right margin.
CSR	Move the screen window so data at the current cursor position ends up at the top, bottom, left, or right of the screen.

Figure 3-5 SCROLL values

screen window is moved a half page in the direction indicated by the PF key you use. (A *page* is 22 lines or 80 columns, depending on the direction of the scroll.) For example, if you scroll down (PF8/20) HALF, the screen window is moved down 11 lines. If you scroll right (PF11/23) HALF, the window is moved 40 columns to the right.

To change the scroll amount, simply position the cursor to the SCROLL field (using the tab key) and type in a new scroll amount. For example, to scroll a full page, enter the SCROLL field like this:

```
SCROLL ===> PAGE
```

Then, use a scrolling PF key to move the screen window 22 lines up or down or 80 columns left or right.

You can move the screen window a specific number of lines or columns by entering a number from 1 to 9999 in the SCROLL field. For example, if you enter:

```
SCROLL ===> 50
```

the scrolling keys move the screen window 50 lines or columns.

You can easily move the screen window to the top or bottom of the data or to the left or right margin by entering MAX in the SCROLL field. Then, if you use PF7/19, the screen window is moved to the top of the data (line 0), while PF8/20 moves the window to the bottom of the data. Similarly, PF10/22 returns the screen window to the left margin (column 1), while PF11/23 moves the window to the right margin.

If you enter CSR in the SCROLL field, the amount of the scroll depends on the location of the cursor. If you press PF7/19, the screen window is moved so the current cursor line appears at the top of the screen. If you use PF8/20, the window is moved so the current cursor line appears at the bottom of the screen. PF10/22 moves the window so the current cursor column appears at the left margin of the screen. And PF11/23 moves the window so the current cursor column appears at the right screen margin.

Whenever you change the SCROLL field, the new value you enter remains as the default for subsequent scroll

```
BROWSE - DLOWE.REORDLST.LIST ------------------------- LINE 000011 COL 001 080
COMMAND INPUT ===>                                           SCROLL ===> HALF
       001500*
       001600 SPECIAL-NAMES.
       001700     C01 IS PAGE-TOP.
       001800*
       001900 INPUT-OUTPUT SECTION.
       002000*
       002100 FILE-CONTROL.
       002200     SELECT BFCRDS ASSIGN TO UT-S-BFCRDS.
       002300     SELECT ORDLST ASSIGN TO UT-S-ORDLST.
       002400*
       002500 DATA DIVISION.
       002600*
       002700 FILE SECTION.
       002800*
       002900 FD  BFCRDS
       003000     LABEL RECORDS ARE STANDARD
       003100     RECORDING MODE IS F
       003200     RECORD CONTAINS 80 CHARACTERS.
       003300*
       003400 01  BAL-FWD-CARD.
       003500*
       003600     05  BF-ITEM-NO          PIC 9(5).
```

Figure 3-6 Effect of a half-page scroll down

operations. As a result, if you want to scroll through a listing a page at a time, you need to change the scroll amount to PAGE only once.

If you want to change the scroll amount for a single scroll operation without replacing the default in the SCROLL field, you can enter the scroll amount in the command area instead. The scroll amount in the command area temporarily overrides the scroll amount in the SCROLL area. For example, if you enter:

```
ENTER COMMAND ===> HALF      SCROLL ===> PAGE
```

the scroll moves the window a half page, but PAGE remains as the default scroll amount. So the next time you use one of the scrolling keys, the window will move a full page.

Figure 3-6 shows the effect of a half-page scroll for the browse session started in figures 3-1 and 3-2. Here, I simply typed HALF in the SCROLL field and pressed PF8/20. Now, the current line number is 11. If I pressed PF7/19 at this point, I would return to the display in figure 3-2.

Before the scroll

```
BROWSE - DLOWE.REORDLST.LIST -------------------------- LINE 000209 COL 001 080
COMMAND INPUT ===>                                       SCROLL ===> HALF
   5        REORDLST        15.55.24        JAN 26,1984

*STATISTICS*      SOURCE RECORDS =     202     DATA DIVISION STATEMENTS =      67
*OPTIONS IN EFFECT*      SIZE =  131072  BUF =     16000  LINECNT = 54   SPACE1, FLA
*OPTIONS IN EFFECT*      NODMAP, NOPMAP, NOCLIST, NOSUPMAP,  XREF, NOSXREF,   LO
*OPTIONS IN EFFECT*       TERM,   NUM, NOBATCH, NONAME, COMPILE=01, NOSTATE, NOR
*OPTIONS IN EFFECT*      NOOPTIMIZE, NOSYMDMP, NOTEST,   VERB,   ZWB, SYST, NOEND
*OPTIONS IN EFFECT*      NOLST , NOFDECK,NOCDECK, LCOL2,  L120, NODUMP , NOADV ,
*OPTIONS IN EFFECT*      NOCOUNT, NOVBSUM, NOVBREF, LANGLVL(2)
   6        REORDLST        15.55.24        JAN 26,1984
                                          CROSS-REFERENCE DICTIONARY


DATA NAMES                    DEFN      REFERENCE


BFCRDS                        002200    013000   013500   015000
BAL-FWD-CARD                  003400
BF-ITEM-NO                    003600    016100   016900
BF-ITEM-DESC                  003700    017000
BF-UNIT-PRICE                 003900    017100
BF-REORDER-POINT              004000    014500   017300
```

Figure 3-7 Effect of a half-page scroll right (part 1 of 2)

After the scroll

```
BROWSE - DLOWE.REORDLST.LIST -------------------------- LINE 000209 COL 041 120
COMMAND INPUT ===>                                       SCROLL ===> HALF
   JAN 26,1984

   DATA DIVISION STATEMENTS =      67     PROCEDURE DIVISION STATEMENTS =      45
BUF =     16000  LINECNT = 54  SPACE1, FLAGW, NOSEQ,   SOURCE
NOCLIST, NOSUPMAP,   XREF, NOSXREF,   LOAD, NODECK, APOST, NOTRUNC, NOFLOW
OBATCH, NONAME, COMPILE=01, NOSTATE, NORESIDENT, NODYNAM,   LIB, NOSYNTAX
MDMP, NOTEST,   VERB,   ZWB, SYST, NOENDJOB, NOLVL
NOCDECK, LCOL2, L120, NODUMP , NOADV , NOPRINT,
, NOVBREF, LANGLVL(2)
   JAN 26,1984
  CROSS-REFERENCE DICTIONARY


REFERENCE


013000   013500   015000

016100   016900
017000
017100
014500   017300
```

Figure 3-7 Effect of a half-page scroll right (part 2 of 2)

The LOCATE command

$$\text{LOCATE} \quad \begin{Bmatrix} \text{line-number} \\ \text{label} \end{Bmatrix}$$

Explanation

line-number   A line number relative to the first line of the file (line 0).

label   A previously defined label that refers to a line of the file.

Figure 3-8   The LOCATE command

Figure 3-7 shows the effect of a half-page scroll right using PF11/23. Part 1 shows the display before the scroll; part 2 shows the display after the scroll. Here, you can see that the display has been shifted 40 characters.

Using the scrolling keys is a satisfactory way to view a listing only when the listing is small. Normally, however, a source listing like this contains hundreds or thousands of print lines. Obviously, scrolling a page at a time isn't acceptable for a large file. So, browse provides two commands—LOCATE and FIND—that let you move rapidly through a listing.

The LOCATE command

The LOCATE command lets you move the display to a known point in the source file. Figure 3-8 shows the format of the LOCATE command. Here, you can specify either a line number or a label. I'll get to the label in just a moment. As for the line number, it's simply the relative line number you wish to display (the first line in the file is relative line zero). For example, if you enter this in the command line:

```
LOCATE 1000
```

and press the enter key, the display moves directly to line 1000.

You can easily determine the line number of a line currently displayed by reading the LINE indication at the top of the screen.

You can assign a label to any line in the source file by scrolling to the page that contains the desired line. Then, you enter a period followed by a one- to eight-character label in the command area. For example, in figure 3-9 I assign the label PROC to line 12500 of the source listing. Then, at any time during the browse session I can return directly to this page by entering the command:

```
LOCATE PROC
```

Note that the preceding period is required when you define the label, but not when you refer to it in a LOCATE command. However, if your label begins with a numeral, you must include the period in the LOCATE command to distinguish it from a line number.

Using labels is an efficient way to locate commonly displayed sections of a listing. For example, I sometimes place a label at the beginning of the Working-Storage Section, the Procedure Division, and one or more paragraphs in my COBOL programs. That way, I don't have to remember the line numbers for these lines.

The FIND command

If you don't know the line number of the line you need to display, you can use the FIND command to locate a line that contains a specified string of characters. Figure 3-10 gives the basic format of the FIND command, but there are additional options that I'll cover in topic 2.

In its simplest form, you enter the FIND command like this:

```
FIND PROCEDURE
```

This FIND command locates the next occurrence of the text PROCEDURE—in the case of my COBOL program, probably

```
BROWSE - DLOWE.REORDLST.LIST -----------------------------------------------------
COMMAND INPUT ===> .PROC                                         SCROLL ===> HALF
        012500*
        012600 PROCEDURE DIVISION.
        012700*
        012800 000-PRODUCE-REORDER-LISTING.
        012900*
        013000     OPEN INPUT  BFCRDS
        013100         OUTPUT ORDLST.
        013200     PERFORM 100-PRODUCE-REORDER-LINE
        013300         UNTIL CARD-EOF-SWITCH IS EQUAL TO 'Y'.
        013400     PERFORM 200-PRINT-TOTAL-LINE.
        013500     CLOSE BFCRDS
        013600         ORDLST.
        013700     DISPLAY 'REORDLST  I  1  NORMAL EOJ'.
        013800     STOP RUN.
        013900*
        014000 100-PRODUCE-REORDER-LINE.
        014100*
        014200     PERFORM 110-READ-INVENTORY-RECORD.
        014300     IF CARD-EOF-SWITCH IS NOT EQUAL TO 'Y'
        014400         PERFORM 120-CALCULATE-AVAILABLE-STOCK
        014500         IF AVAILABLE-STOCK IS LESS THAN BF-REORDER-POINT
        014600             PERFORM 130-PRINT-REORDER-LINE.
```

Figure 3-9   Assigning a label that can be used later in a LOCATE command

the start of the Procedure Division. If the search string contains blanks or commas, enclose it in apostrophes, like this:

```
FIND 'PROCEDURE DIVISION'
```

If the search string contains apostrophes, enclose it in quotes, like this:

```
FIND "VALUE 'PROCEDURE'"
```

Here, the FIND command searches for the text, VALUE 'PROCEDURE'. Likewise, if the search string contains quotes, enclosed it in apostrophes, like this:

```
FIND 'VALUE "PROCEDURE"'
```

Here, the FIND command searches for VALUE "PROCEDURE".

One question that often comes up when using the FIND command is how much text should you specify in the search

The FIND command

$$\text{FIND string } \left[\begin{Bmatrix} \underline{\text{NEXT}} \\ \text{PREV} \\ \text{FIRST} \\ \text{LAST} \\ \text{ALL} \end{Bmatrix} \right]$$

Explanation

string	The text string to be found. Must be in apostrophes or quotes if it contains spaces or commas.
NEXT	Start search at current line and locate the next occurrence of the string. (If neither PREV, FIRST, LAST, nor ALL is specified, NEXT is assumed.)
PREV	Start search at current line and locate the previous occurrence of the string (search backwards).
FIRST	Start search at top of data and locate the first occurrence of the string.
LAST	Start search at bottom of data and locate the last occurrence of the string (search backwards).
ALL	Same as FIRST, but also indicate a count of the occurrences of the string in the file.

Figure 3-10   The basic format of the FIND command

string. The answer is a matter of efficiency, so you should understand the efficiency tradeoffs involved. On the one hand, the more characters you specify in the search string, the longer the search takes. On the other hand, the fewer characters you specify, the greater the chance that the FIND command will locate the wrong text.

To illustrate, suppose you are at the start of a COBOL compiler listing and you wish to find the beginning of the Procedure Division. You could enter this FIND command:

```
FIND 'PROCEDURE DIVISION.'
```

but that's probably too many characters in the search string. Or you could enter this FIND command:

```
FIND P
```

but that's probably not enough characters (there are probably many occurrences of the letter P before the Procedure Division header).

The answer, then, is that you should specify only as many characters in the search string as are necessary to distinguish it from other text in the file. But don't be overly concerned about specifying too many characters. Although search time increases slightly for each character in the search string, the unnecessary terminal I/O that results when a FIND locates the wrong text is by far the greater inefficiency.

How to change the search direction   Normally, a FIND command search begins at the current line and continues to the end of the source file. So if the text you're looking for is located *before* the current line, FIND won't locate it. However, you can change the direction of the search by specifying a search order on the FIND command.

If you specify PREV for the search order, the search begins at the current line and continues *backwards* until the text is found or the top of the data is reached. If you specify FIRST, the search starts at the top of the data and stops when it finds the first occurrence of the text or the bottom of the data. If you specify LAST, the search starts at the bottom of the data and works backwards.

If you specify ALL as the search order, the search works like FIRST except that it doesn't stop when it finds the search string. Instead, it continues, locating all occurrences of the string. When the FIND completes, it displays the first occurrence, along with a count indicating how many occurrences of the string it found. Since FIND ALL locates all occurrences of a string in the file, it takes a little longer than FIND FIRST. As a result, you shouldn't use FIND ALL unless you really need to know how many occurrences of a string are in the file.

How to recall a FIND command   If you need to enter the same FIND command more than once in a single browse session, you may find PF5/17 useful. PF5/17 simply repeats the most recent FIND command you issued. So once you've entered a FIND command, you can recall it easily using PF5/17.

How to terminate browse

To terminate a browse operation, you can press the end key (PF3/15). This returns you to the browse entry panel shown in figure 3-1. Then, you can enter another data set to browse or press PF3/15 again to return to the primary option menu. Alternatively, you can press the return key (PF4/16) to return directly to the primary option menu.

Discussion

At the start of this topic, I said you'd use browse most often for SYSOUT data sets like compiler listings, storage dumps, and so on. However, browse is useful for other types of data sets as well. In fact, you can use browse for any sequential or partitioned file—regardless of the file's record length. For example, you can use browse to examine sequential data sets created by a program you're testing. In the next topic, I'll show you some advanced features that not only help you browse SYSOUT data sets, but are useful for examining other types of sequential data sets as well.

Terminology

top of data
bottom of data
screen window
scrolling
page

Objective

Browse a data set using scrolling, LOCATE, and FIND to move the screen window to various parts of the listing.

TOPIC 2   Advanced browse operations

In topic 1 of this chapter, I showed you the basics of using browse. In this topic, you'll learn advanced features of browse, including advanced options of the FIND command, how to display capital and lowercase characters, and how to display hexadecimal data.

If you're a first-time SPF user, you should skip this topic for now. Come back to it when you need to use the advanced browse capabilities it presents.

ADVANCED OPTIONS OF THE FIND COMMAND

Figure 3-11 presents the expanded format of the FIND command. In addition to the search order (NEXT, PREV, etc.), the FIND command lets you specify a *match condition* (CHARS, PREFIX, etc.), column limitations, and advanced options in the search string.

Match conditions

Normally when you specify a string in a FIND command, any combination of characters that match the string satisfies the FIND. For example, if you code this FIND command:

```
FIND ABC
```

any of these strings will match:

```
ABC
ABCDEF
DEFABC
123ABCDEF
```

The FIND command

```
              (NEXT )   (CHARS  )
              |PREV |   |PREFIX |
FIND string [ {FIRST} ] [{SUFFIX }]   [col-1 [col-2]]
              |LAST |   |WORD   )
              (ALL  )
```

Explanation

string	The text string to be found. Must be in apostrophes or quotes if it contains spaces or commas. May also be text string, picture string, hex string, or *, as explained in figure 3-13.
NEXT	Start search at current line and locate the next occurrence of the string. (If neither PREV, FIRST, LAST, nor ALL is specified, NEXT is assumed.)
PREV	Start search at current line and locate the previous occurrence of the string (search backwards).
FIRST	Start search at top of data and locate the first occurrence of the string.
LAST	Start search at bottom of data and locate the last occurrence of the string (search backwards).
ALL	Same as FIRST, but also indicate a count of the occurrences of the string in the file.
CHARS	Any occurrence of the string satisfies the search. (If neither PREFIX, SUFFIX, nor WORD is specified, CHARS is assumed.)
PREFIX	The string must be at the beginning of a word to satisfy the search.
SUFFIX	The string must be at the end of a word to satisfy the search.
WORD	The string must be surrounded by spaces or special characters to satisfy the search.
col-1	Starting column number. If you specify col-1 but **not** col-2 , the string must begin in col-1 to satisfy the search. (Default value is the current left boundary.)
col-2	Ending column number. If specified, the string must start between col-1 and col-2 to satisfy the search. (Default value is the current right boundary.)

Figure 3-11   The complete format of the FIND command

Search options	Examples					
CHARS 'HE'	HE	HEED	SHED	SHE	$HEED	-HE$
PREFIX 'HE'	HE	HEED	SHED	SHE	$HEED	-HE$
SUFFIX 'HE'	HE	HEED	SHED	SHE	$HEED	-HE$
WORD 'HE'	HE	HEED	SHED	SHE	$HEED	-HE$

Figure 3-12   Examples of match conditions

That's because each of these strings contains the characters ABC. You'd also get the same results if you coded the match condition CHARS in the command.

By specifying a match condition other than CHARS, you can indicate that a string matches only if it appears at the beginning of a word (PREFIX), the end of a word (SUFFIX), or as a word itself (WORD). As far as browse is concerned, a *word* is a string of alphanumeric characters with a blank or special character at each end. As a result, ABC is a word in each of these strings:

```
ABC
ABC 123
DEF ABC 123
'ABC'
ABC$
```

In these examples, the special characters are not considered to be part of the word.

Figure 3-12 shows how match conditions affect a search. Here, the shading shows which strings match the search string. Note that a string that makes up a word by itself does *not* satisfy a search for a PREFIX or SUFFIX.

Column limitations

You can easily limit a search to a single column or range of columns by specifying column numbers in the FIND command.

If you specify a single column number, the string must start in that column to satisfy the search. For example, this command:

```
FIND X 72
```

looks for an X in column 72. Similarly,

```
FIND 120-READ 12
```

looks for 120-READ beginning in column 12.

If you specify two column numbers, the string must be located between the columns you specify to qualify. For example,

```
FIND 120-READ 16 72
```

searches for 120-READ between columns 16 and 72.

String formats

The string you specify in a FIND command can have one of several formats, as shown in figure 3-13. You already know about the first two. Now, I'll explain the others.

Text strings   The T format means that it doesn't matter whether the characters in the string are upper or lowercase. So, if you code:

```
FIND T'PERFORM'
```

any of these strings satisfy the search:

```
PERFORM
perform
Perform
pERforM
```

Without the T option, only the first string (PERFORM) would satisfy the search.

String	Meaning
text	String containing no blanks or commas.
'text'	String enclosed in apostrophes—may include blanks or commas.
T'text'	Same as 'text', except upper and lowercase letters are treated the same.
X'hex-digits'	Hexadecimal string.
P'picture'	Picture string (see figure 3-14).
*	Use string from previous FIND.

Figure 3-13   String types

Hexadecimal strings   During a normal browse operation, any non-displayable characters—for example, packed-decimal numbers—are displayed as periods. Using the X string option, however, you can search for the hexadecimal values of such characters. (Later in this topic, I'll show you how to display hexadecimal values.)

To illustrate, suppose you are browsing an inventory master file and you want to locate a record with a unit price of $15.95. Knowing that the unit-price field begins in column 58, and that the PICTURE of the packed-decimal (COMP-3) unit-price field is S9(5)V99, you can code a FIND command like this:

```
FIND X'0001595F' 58
```

Then, a hexadecimal value of 0001595F (decimal value positive 15.95) starting in column 58 satisfies the search.

Picture strings   Picture strings allow you to specify that the character in a specific position of the search string must be a particular type of character, rather than a particular character. For example, you can specify that the first character of a string must be alphanumeric, the second numeric, and the third alphabetic. You do this by coding special characters to represent character types.

Figure 3-14 shows the special characters you can include in a picture string and what they mean. In each case, a single

Character	Meaning
=	Any character
¬	Any non-blank character
.	Any undisplayable character
#	Any numeric character
−	Any non-numeric character (including a blank)
@	Any alphabetic character
<	Any lowercase alphabetic character
>	Any uppercase alphabetic character
$	Any special character

Figure 3-14   Valid picture characters

occurrence of one of these characters corresponds to a single occurrence of any character of the correct type. As a result, if you specify ¬ in the first position of a picture string, the text must contain a non-blank character in its first position to satisfy the search.

Figure 3-15 shows a few examples of picture strings and how they are satisfied. If you'll take a few moments to study this figure, you should have no problem understanding how picture strings work.

Use previous string   You can code an asterisk as a search string, like this:

```
FIND *
```

Then, browse uses the string you specified in the previous FIND command as its search argument. This feature makes it easy to locate every occurrence of a string in a file, since you only need to specify the string once.

Picture string	Examples			
P'==='	ABC-123	PERFORM 120-READ	A BC DE	
P'@@@'	ABC-123	PERFORM 120-READ	A BC DE	
P'###'	ABC-123	PERFORM 120-READ	A BC DE	
P'$'	ABC-123	PERFORM 120-READ	A BC DE	
P'===$###'	ABC-123	PERFORM 120-READ	A BC DE	

Figure 3-15 Examples of picture strings

On the other hand, you can achieve the same effect by pressing PF5/17. That way, you recall the previous FIND command without entering anything in the command area.

Complex FIND commands

Although you don't usually need to, you can combine search direction, match condition, column limitation, and advanced string formats to create complex FIND commands. To illustrate, consider this command:

```
FIND P'##@$' PREV WORD 8
```

Here, the FIND command looks backwards for a word consisting of two numeric characters followed by a single alphabetic character followed by a single special character, starting in column 8. Like I said, though, you probably won't need FIND commands that are this complex very often.

HOW TO DISPLAY LOWERCASE CHARACTERS

Normally, browse converts all characters to uppercase before it displays them. As a result, if your file contains lowercase letters, you won't know it. However, you can disable this conversion by coding a CAPS command, like this:

```
CAPS OFF
```

Then, any lowercase characters are displayed as lowercase letters. To display all characters as uppercase, enter this command:

```
CAPS ON
```

When you enter browse, CAPS ON is the default.

HOW TO DISPLAY HEXADECIMAL CODES

If you're browsing a file that contains undisplayable characters (such as packed-decimal fields), you can display each character as a two-digit hexadecimal code by entering this command:

```
HEX ON
```

Figure 3-16 shows a hexadecimal browse display. As you can see, each row of 80 characters takes three lines in hex mode: one for the normal character display and two for the hexadecimal display.

To determine a character's hexadecimal value, you simply read the two hex digits below the character. As a result, the hexadecimal value of the numeral 0 in column 9 of the first displayed line is F0.

DISCUSSION

Quite frankly, you'll rarely use many of the browse features presented in this topic. However, there are cases where one or more of these features can be a real time-saver. So even though you may not use them often enough to become proficient at them, it's good to know they're available when you need them.

```
 BROWSE - DLOWE.REORDLST.LIST ------------------------ LINE 000103 COL 001 080
 COMMAND INPUT ===>                                          SCROLL ===> PAGE
         010400 01   REORDER-LINE.
44444444FFFFFF4FF44DCDDCCD6DCDC444444444444444444444444444444444444444444444444
00000000010400001009569459039558000000000000000000000000000000000000000000000000
 ------------------------------------------------------------------------------
         010500*
44444444FFFFFF5444444444444444444444444444444444444444444444444444444444444444444
0000000001050000000000000000000000000000000000000000000000000000000000000000000
 ------------------------------------------------------------------------------
         010600     05   RL-CC                      PIC X.
44444444FFFFFF44444FF44DD6CC4444444444444444DCC4E444444444444444444444444444444444
0000000001060000000000500930330000000000000079307B00000000000000000000000000000
 ------------------------------------------------------------------------------
         010700     05   RL-ITEM-NO                 PIC Z(5).
44444444FFFFFF44444FF44DD6CECD6DD4444444444DCC4E4F544444444444144444444444444444444
00000000010700000000005009309354056000000000079309D5DB00000000000000000000000000
 ------------------------------------------------------------------------------
         010800     05   FILLER                     PIC X(5)     VALUE SPACE.
44444444FFFFFF44444FF44CCDDCD4444444444444DCC4E4F54444ECDEC4EDCCC4444444444444444444
00000000010800000000005006933590000000000000079307D5D0000051345027135B0000000000000
 ------------------------------------------------------------------------------
         010900     05   RL-ITEM-DESC               PIC X(20).
```

Figure 3-16   A hexadecimal display

Terminology

match condition
word

Objective

Use advanced FIND options, the CAPS command, and the
HEX command to efficiently browse data sets.

Chapter 4

How to edit a data set

One of the most important tasks of program development is creating and maintaining source programs. To do this under SPF, you use the source file editor, option 2 on the primary option menu. This chapter explains how to use the editor.

There are three topics in this chapter. Topic 1 explains the basics of using the editor: how to specify a source file or member, how to use basic editing commands, and how to save edited data. Topic 2 describes the edit profile and how to change it. (The edit profile controls a variety of editing features, including tabbing, line numbering, and so on.) And topic 3 explains some of the more advanced editing features, such as the CHANGE command.

TOPIC 1   Basic edit operations

Before I show you how to use the SPF editor, let me present a couple of related ideas. First, though you'll use the editor most often for members of partitioned data sets, you can edit sequential files as well. So throughout this chapter, I use the term *source member* to refer to the material that's being edited, whether it's a PDS member or a sequential file.

Second, I want you to understand what's going on during an edit. Once you specify which source member you want to work on, the SPF editor reads the entire member into virtual storage and has you make changes to it there. In other words, the source member still exists in its unedited form on disk. Any changes you make aren't actually applied to it until you terminate edit. At that time, if you say you want to save the edited member, the editor copies its virtual storage version back to disk.

Placing the source member in virtual storage naturally results in improved performance, but it requires a large foreground region and limits the maximum size for source members you can edit. However, this maximum is so large it's not usually a problem.

How to start an edit session

To access SPF's edit function, you select option 2 from the primary option menu. SPF then displays the edit entry panel, shown in figure 4-1. The edit entry panel is similar to the browse entry panel: on it you enter the data set name for the file or member you wish to edit. The shaded portion of figure 4-1 shows I'm preparing to edit a member named REORDLST in a library named DLOWE.TEST.COBOL.

How to concatenate libraries   As you can see in figure 4-1, edit lets you specify up to four entries in the LIBRARY field of the entry panel. It then *concatenates* the libraries; that is, it

```
------------------------------ EDIT - ENTRY PANEL ------------------------------
ENTER/VERIFY PARAMETERS BELOW:

SPF LIBRARY:
    PROJECT  ===> DLOWE
    LIBRARY  ===> TEST       ===>          ===>          ===>
    TYPE     ===> COBOL
    MEMBER   ===> REORDLST   (BLANK FOR MEMBER SELECTION LIST)

OTHER PARTITIONED OR SEQUENTIAL DATASET:
    DATASET NAME   ===>
    VOLUME SERIAL  ===>           (IF NOT CATALOGED)

DATASET PASSWORD ===>            (IF PASSWORD PROTECTED)

PROFILE NAME     ===>            (BLANK DEFAULTS TO DATASET TYPE)
```

Figure 4-1   The edit entry panel

strings them together in a single chain. To locate the member you specify, edit searches the libraries in the order you list them.

For example, suppose you code the data set name entries like this:

```
PROJECT ===> DLOWE
LIBRARY ===> TEST       ===> MASTER
TYPE    ===> COBOL
MEMBER  ===> REORDLST
```

Edit searches DLOWE.TEST.COBOL first to locate the member named REORDLST. If the member isn't found, edit searches DLOWE.MASTER.COBOL next.

Concatenated libraries are used only to retrieve a member. When a member is saved at the end of an edit session, it's always written in the first library you specify on the entry panel. So in the preceding example, REORDLST would be saved in DLOWE.TEST.COBOL, even if it had been retrieved from DLOWE.MASTER.COBOL.

```
 EDIT - DLOWE.TEST.COBOL -------------------------------------------------
 COMMAND INPUT ===>                                    SCROLL ===> PAGE
    NAME           VER.MOD   CREATED     LAST MODIFIED   SIZE  INIT  MOD   ID
    INVLST         01.00    84/01/26   84/01/26 14:29    202   202    0  DLOWE
    ORDLST2        01.00    84/01/05   84/01/05 16:44      9     9    0  DLOWE
 S  REORDLST       01.00    84/01/26   84/01/26 14:29    202   202    0  DLOWE
    RNDUPDT        01.00    84/01/26   84/01/26 14:29    202   202    0  DLOWE
    SEQUPTD        01.00    84/01/05   84/01/05 16:44      9     9    0  DLOWE
    VSESMNT        01.00    84/01/05   84/01/05 16:44      9     9    0  DLOWE
    VSESMNT2       01.00    84/01/05   84/01/05 16:44      9     9    0  DLOWE
    VSESRUPT       01.00    84/01/05   84/01/05 16:44      9     9    0  DLOWE
    VSESSUPT       01.00    84/01/26   84/01/26 14:29    202   202    0  DLOWE
    VSKSMNT        01.00    84/01/26   84/01/26 14:29    202   202    0  DLOWE
    VSKSRUPT       01.00    84/01/05   84/01/05 16:44      9     9    0  DLOWE
    VSKSSUPT       01.00    84/01/05   84/01/05 16:44      9     9    0  DLOWE
    VSRRMNT        01.00    84/01/26   84/01/26 14:29    202   202    0  DLOWE
    VSRRRUPT       01.00    84/01/05   84/01/05 16:44      9     9    0  DLOWE
    VSRRSUPT       01.00    84/01/26   84/01/26 14:29    202   202    0  DLOWE
    **END**
```

Figure 4-2   An edit member selection list

Concatenated libraries are useful because they let you create a hierarchy of libraries. For example, you can create a single master library for a project and multiple test libraries—one for each programmer on the project. Then, you can store completed programs in the master library, using the test libraries for programs still under development. The only restriction here is that all the libraries must have the same project-id and type code.

How to display a member list   If you don't specify a member name on the entry panel and the data set name refers to a partitioned data set, edit displays a *member list*, as shown in figure 4-2. This display lists all of the members from each library specified on the entry panel. If the libraries contain more members than can be shown on a single screen, you can use the standard scrolling keys (PF7/19 and PF8/20) to view the entire list.

To select the member you wish to edit, simply type an S (for "select") next to the member name and press the enter key. In figure 4-2, I've selected the member named REORDLST.

The edit data display

Figure 4-3 shows the edit data display for an existing member. (The edit display for a newly created member is somewhat different. I'll describe it later in this topic.) I've marked it up to show you it consists of three distinct areas.

The top two screen lines are the heading area. In this area, the editor displays informative messages and lets you enter commands.

The first six columns of lines 3-24 are the *line command area*. In this area, the editor displays a line number for each line of the source member. (More about line numbers in just a moment.) Besides displaying line numbers, the line command area serves another function: in it, you can enter line commands that perform certain editing functions, such as deleting or inserting lines. You'll learn how to use the most common line commands later in this topic.

The remaining columns of lines 3-24 are the screen window. Here, data from the source member is displayed. You can change the data in this area simply by typing over it. In addition, you can use your terminal's editing keys (like insert, delete, and erase-EOF) for more complicated editing. As soon as you press the enter key, edit stores any changes you've made in the virtual storage copy of the source member.

Since the screen window here is only 72 characters long, only 72 characters of each source record are displayed. The COLUMNS message in line 1 of figure 4-3 indicates that columns 7 through 78 are currently displayed. You can use the scrolling functions just as you do for browse to move the screen window right or left if you want to display the entire source record. Usually, though, you don't need to see or change data outside the columns that are displayed in the screen window.

Of course, you can also use scrolling functions to move the screen window up or down, just as in browse. And you can use the LOCATE and FIND commands as well. The only restriction is that you can't create labels for the LOCATE command.

Line numbers   During an editing session, the editor assigns *line numbers*, or *sequence numbers*, to each line of your source

Heading area

```
 EDIT - DLOWE.TEST.COBOL(REORDLST) - 01.00 ------------------- COLUMNS 007 078
 COMMAND INPUT ===>                                           SCROLL ===> PAGE
 ****** ************************** TOP OF DATA ***************************
 000100  IDENTIFICATION DIVISION.
 000200 *
 000300  PROGRAM-ID. REORDLST.
 000400 *
 000500  ENVIRONMENT DIVISION.
 000600 *
 000700  CONFIGURATION SECTION.
 000800 *
 000900  SPECIAL-NAMES.
 001000      C01 IS PAGE-TOP.
 001100 *
 001200  INPUT-OUTPUT SECTION.
 001300 *
 001400  FILE-CONTROL.
 001500      SELECT BFCRDS ASSIGN TO UT-S-BFCRDS.
 001600      SELECT ORDLST ASSIGN TO UT-S-ORDLST.
 001700 *
 001800  DATA DIVISION.
 001900 *
 002000  FILE SECTION.
 002100 *
```

Line
command
area

Screen window

Figure 4-3   The edit data display

member, keeping the numbers in sequence as you add and delete lines. As I mentioned a minute ago, these line numbers appear on the edit display to the left of the screen window. In most cases, edit also stores the line numbers in the source records themselves. Depending on the type of data set it is, a source member will have either COBOL format numbering, standard (STD) format numbering, or no numbering at all.

COBOL source files have COBOL format numbers. That means the line numbers are six digits long and are stored in the first six positions of each record. As a result, if you scrolled to column 1 in figure 4-3, you'd see that the first six columns of each record contain a sequence number that matches the line number in the line command area.

Standard format numbers are eight digits long, though edit displays only the last six digits. For fixed-length records, they're stored in the last eight positions of each record. For variable-length records, they're stored in the first eight positions. Standard fixed-length numbering is used for all non-COBOL source files, including assembler, PL/I, CLIST, and CNTL (JCL) files.

Unnumbered data sets, quite naturally, have no line numbers at all. When you edit an unnumbered data set, the editor still creates sequence numbers and displays them in the line command area, but it discards them when you end the edit session. Unnumbered data sets typically contain test data.

In the next section on edit commands, you'll see how the editor keeps the line numbers in sequence as you change a source member. Then, in topic 2, you'll learn how to specify (1) what numbering format a file should have, (2) what numbers the editor should assign to new lines, and (3) when you want the editor to renumber a member.

How to edit a source member

In edit, you use two types of commands. You enter *primary commands* in the command input area. Primary commands generally apply to the entire member. In contrast, *line commands* affect individual lines. You enter line commands in the line command area. That means you have to type over the line numbers that normally appear in that area.

In general, you use line commands more often than primary commands. As a result, I cover the most commonly used line commands and three primary commands in this topic. I describe the less commonly used line commands, as well as most of the primary commands, in topics 2 and 3.

As I've said, you enter line commands by typing over the line numbers in the line command area. Since many line commands contain numbers, it's usually a good idea to erase the line number by pressing the erase-EOF key or typing over it with spaces. If you don't, you can easily do something you don't want to do—like insert 50 lines when you mean to insert just one.

Figure 4-4 summarizes the line commands I cover in this topic. As you can see, line commands let you insert, delete, repeat, copy, or move single lines or blocks of lines.

Inserting lines

I	Insert a single line following this line.
I*n*	Insert *n* lines following this line.

Deleting lines

D	Delete this line.
D*n*	Delete *n* lines starting with this line.
DD	Delete the block of lines beginning with the first DD command and ending with the second DD command.

Repeating lines

R	Repeat this line.
R*n*	Repeat this line *n* times.
RR	Repeat a block of lines.
RR*n*	Repeat a block of lines *n* times.

Copying and moving lines

C	Copy this line.
C*n*	Copy *n* lines starting with this line.
CC	Copy a block of lines.
M	Move this line.
M*n*	Move *n* lines starting with this line.
MM	Move a block of lines.
A	Copy or move lines after this line.
A*n*	Repeat the copy or move *n* times after this line.
B	Copy or move lines before this line.
B*n*	Repeat the copy or move *n* times before this line.

Figure 4-4 Basic line commands

How to insert lines   You use the I line command to insert blank lines into a member. You can code an I by itself to insert one line, or you can code an I followed by a number to insert a block of lines.

Figure 4-5 shows how the INSERT command works. In part 1, I've coded two INSERT commands. The first inserts a single line following line 300; the second inserts four lines following line 800. In other words, the insertion comes immediately after the line on which the INSERT command appears. (I erased the sequence numbers on the lines containing line commands, but you can easily figure them out because the member is numbered in increments of 100.)

86 Chapter 4

I line commands specify the location and number of lines to be inserted

```
EDIT - DLOWE.TEST.COBOL(REORDLST) - 01.00 ------------------ COLUMNS 007 078
COMMAND INPUT ===>                                          SCROLL ===> PAGE
****** *********************** TOP OF DATA ****************************
000100    IDENTIFICATION DIVISION.
000200 *
I         PROGRAM-ID. REORDLST.
000400 *
000500    ENVIRONMENT DIVISION.
000600 *
000700    CONFIGURATION SECTION.
I4        *
000900    SPECIAL-NAMES.
001000        C01 IS PAGE-TOP.
001100 *
001200    INPUT-OUTPUT SECTION.
001300 *
001400    FILE-CONTROL.
001500        SELECT BFCRDS ASSIGN TO UT-S-BFCRDS.
001600        SELECT ORDLST ASSIGN TO UT-S-ORDLST.
001700 *
001800    DATA DIVISION.
001900 *
002000    FILE SECTION.
002100 *
```

Figure 4-5 Inserting lines (part 1 of 4)

When you press the enter key, edit inserts blank lines

```
EDIT - DLOWE.TEST.COBOL(REORDLST) - 01.00 ------------------ COLUMNS 007 078
COMMAND INPUT ===>                                          SCROLL ===> PAGE
****** *********************** TOP OF DATA ****************************
000100    IDENTIFICATION DIVISION.
000200 *
000300    PROGRAM-ID. REORDLST.
''''''
000400 *
000500    ENVIRONMENT DIVISION.
000600 *
000700    CONFIGURATION SECTION.
000800 *
''''''
''''''
''''''
''''''
000900    SPECIAL-NAMES.
001000        C01 IS PAGE-TOP.
001100 *
001200    INPUT-OUTPUT SECTION.
001300 *
001400    FILE-CONTROL.
001500        SELECT BFCRDS ASSIGN TO UT-S-BFCRDS.
001600        SELECT ORDLST ASSIGN TO UT-S-ORDLST.
```

Figure 4-5 Inserting lines (part 2 of 4)

You can enter data into any or all of the blank lines

```
EDIT - DLOWE.TEST.COBOL(REORDLST) - 01.00 ------------------- COLUMNS 007 078
COMMAND INPUT ===>                                            SCROLL ===> PAGE
****** ************************* TOP OF DATA ***************************
000100  IDENTIFICATION DIVISION.
000200 *
000300  PROGRAM-ID. REORDLST.
''''''    AUTHOR.      DOUG LOWE.
000400 *
000500  ENVIRONMENT DIVISION.
000600 *
000700  CONFIGURATION SECTION.
000800 *
''''''    SOURCE-COMPUTER.   IBM-370.
''''''    OBJECT-COMPUTER.   IBM-370.
'''''' *
'''''' 
000900  SPECIAL-NAMES.
001000     C01 IS PAGE-TOP.
001100 *
001200  INPUT-OUTPUT SECTION.
001300 *
001400  FILE-CONTROL.
001500     SELECT BFCRDS ASSIGN TO UT-S-BFCRDS.
001600     SELECT ORDLST ASSIGN TO UT-S-ORDLST.
```

Figure 4-5   Inserting lines (part 3 of 4)

When you press the enter key, edit numbers the new lines and deletes the ones you didn't use

```
EDIT - DLOWE.TEST.COBOL(REORDLST) - 01.00 ------------------- COLUMNS 007 078
COMMAND INPUT ===>                                            SCROLL ===> PAGE
****** ************************* TOP OF DATA ***************************
000100  IDENTIFICATION DIVISION.
000200 *
000300  PROGRAM-ID. REORDLST.
000310  AUTHOR.      DOUG LOWE.
000400 *
000500  ENVIRONMENT DIVISION.
000600 *
000700  CONFIGURATION SECTION.
000800 *
000810  SOURCE-COMPUTER.   IBM-370.
000820  OBJECT-COMPUTER.   IBM-370.
000830 *
000900  SPECIAL-NAMES.
001000     C01 IS PAGE-TOP.
001100 *
001200  INPUT-OUTPUT SECTION.
001300 *
001400  FILE-CONTROL.
001500     SELECT BFCRDS ASSIGN TO UT-S-BFCRDS.
001600     SELECT ORDLST ASSIGN TO UT-S-ORDLST.
001700 *
```

Figure 4-5   Inserting lines (part 4 of 4)

Part 2 of figure 4-5 shows the effect of the two INSERT commands. As you can see, one blank line is inserted following line 300 and four blank lines are inserted following line 800.

Notice that the inserted lines in part 2 of figure 4-5 have apostrophes instead of line numbers. That's because the insertion isn't permanent until you enter data on the inserted line. When you press the enter key, any inserted lines on which you don't enter data are automatically deleted.

To illustrate, part 3 of figure 4-5 shows the data I entered into the inserted lines. As you can see, I didn't enter data into the fourth line inserted after line 800. Part 4 of figure 4-5 shows the screen after I press the enter key. Edit automatically generates line numbers for the data lines I entered and deletes the fourth line following line 800—the line on which I didn't enter data.

How to delete lines   You use the D line command to delete lines from your source member. You can code the DELETE command in one of three ways: (1) code a D to delete a single line; (2) code a D followed by a number to delete more than one line; and (3) code DD on two lines to delete those lines and every line between them.

Figure 4-6 shows how the D command works. In part 1, I've entered two D commands. The first deletes line 310. Then, a D3 command deletes three lines starting with line 810. Part 2 of figure 4-6 shows the display after the deletions. As you can see, lines 310, 810, 820, and 830 have been deleted.

Figure 4-7 shows how to delete a block of lines using the DD command. Here, I'm deleting the same lines I deleted in figure 4-6. Again, I use a D command to delete line 310. This time, though, I use a pair of DD commands rather than a D3 command to delete lines 810, 820, and 830. The effect is the same as in figure 4-6.

The lines indicated by a pair of DD commands do *not* have to be on the same display panel. To delete a block of lines that spans multiple panels, you locate the first line to be deleted and enter a DD command at that line. Then, you scroll to the panel containing the last line to be deleted and enter a DD command at that line. When you enter the second DD command, the indicated lines are deleted. (You can also mark

D line commands tell which lines to delete

```
EDIT - DLOWE.TEST.COBOL(REORDLST) - 01.00 ------------------- COLUMNS 007 078
COMMAND INPUT ===>                                           SCROLL ===> PAGE
****** **************************** TOP OF DATA ******************************
000100  IDENTIFICATION DIVISION.
000200 *
000300  PROGRAM-ID. REORDLST.
D       AUTHOR.       DOUG LOWE.
000400 *
000500  ENVIRONMENT DIVISION.
000600 *
000700  CONFIGURATION SECTION.
000800 *
D3      SOURCE-COMPUTER.   IBM-370.
000820  OBJECT-COMPUTER.   IBM-370.
000830 *
000900  SPECIAL-NAMES.
001000      C01 IS PAGE-TOP.
001100 *
001200  INPUT-OUTPUT SECTION.
001300 *
001400  FILE-CONTROL.
001500      SELECT BFCRDS ASSIGN TO UT-S-BFCRDS.
001600      SELECT ORDLST ASSIGN TO UT-S-ORDLST.
001700 *
```

Figure 4-6   Deleting lines (part 1 of 2)

When you press the enter key, edit deletes the lines

```
EDIT - DLOWE.TEST.COBOL(REORDLST) - 01.00 ------------------- COLUMNS 007 078
COMMAND INPUT ===>                                           SCROLL ===> PAGE
****** **************************** TOP OF DATA ******************************
000100  IDENTIFICATION DIVISION.
000200 *
000300  PROGRAM-ID. REORDLST.
000400 *
000500  ENVIRONMENT DIVISION.
000600 *
000700  CONFIGURATION SECTION.
000800 *
000900  SPECIAL-NAMES.
001000      C01 IS PAGE-TOP.
001100 *
001200  INPUT-OUTPUT SECTION.
001300 *
001400  FILE-CONTROL.
001500      SELECT BFCRDS ASSIGN TO UT-S-BFCRDS.
001600      SELECT ORDLST ASSIGN TO UT-S-ORDLST.
001700 *
001800  DATA DIVISION.
001900 *
002000  FILE SECTION.
002100 *
```

Figure 4-6   Deleting lines (part 2 of 2)

```
EDIT - DLOWE.TEST.COBOL(REORDLST) - 01.00 -------------------- COLUMNS 007 078
COMMAND INPUT ===>                                            SCROLL ===> PAGE
****** ************************** TOP OF DATA ******************************
000100   IDENTIFICATION DIVISION.
000200 *
000300   PROGRAM-ID. REORDLST.
D        AUTHOR.       DOUG LOWE.
000400 *
000500   ENVIRONMENT DIVISION.
000600 *
000700   CONFIGURATION SECTION.
000800 *
DD       SOURCE-COMPUTER.   IBM-370.
000820   OBJECT-COMPUTER.   IBM-370.
DD       *
000900   SPECIAL-NAMES.
001000       C01 IS PAGE-TOP.
001100 *
001200   INPUT-OUTPUT SECTION.
001300 *
001400   FILE-CONTROL.
001500       SELECT BFCRDS ASSIGN TO UT-S-BFCRDS.
001600       SELECT ORDLST ASSIGN TO UT-S-ORDLST.
001700 *
```

Figure 4-7 Deleting a block of lines

the last line, then scroll backwards to mark the first line. But it makes more sense to me to start at the beginning.)

How to repeat lines   The R command lets you repeat a single line or a group of lines one or more times. SPF inserts the repeated lines immediately following the source line. Figure 4-8 shows an example of repeating a single line nine times. In part 1, I've entered the R9 command for line 10200. Part 2 shows the effect of the R command: line 10200 is duplicated in lines 10210 through 10290.

Figure 4-9 shows how to repeat a block of lines. In part 1, the first RR command marks the start of the block. The second RR command indicates the end of the block and the number of times to repeat the block (in this case, three). Part 2 shows the effect of these RR commands—the block of lines is duplicated three times.

Like the DD command, the RR command can repeat a block of lines that spans multiple panels. You simply enter the first RR command to mark the start of the block, then scroll to the panel containing the end of the block and enter the second RR command.

The R line command tells which line to repeat and how many times to repeat it

```
EDIT - DLOWE.TEST.COBOL(REORDLST) - 01.00 -------------------- COLUMNS 007 078
COMMAND INPUT ===>                                             SCROLL ===> PAGE
009800 *
009900  01   HDG-LINE-2.
010000 *
010100       05   HDG2-CC          PIC X.
R9           05   FILLER           PIC X(20)    VALUE '                    '.
010300 *
010400  01   REORDER-LINE.
010500 *
010600       05   RL-CC            PIC X.
010700       05   RL-ITEM-NO       PIC Z(5).
010800       05   FILLER           PIC X(5)      VALUE SPACE.
010900       05   RL-ITEM-DESC     PIC X(20).
011000       05   FILLER           PIC X(5)      VALUE SPACE.
011100       05   RL-UNIT-PRICE    PIC ZZZ.99.
011200       05   FILLER           PIC X(5)      VALUE SPACE.
011300       05   RL-AVAILABLE-STOCK  PIC Z(5).
011400       05   FILLER           PIC X(5)      VALUE SPACE.
011500       05   RL-REORDER-POINT PIC Z(5).
011600       05   FILLER           PIC X(71)     VALUE SPACE.
011700 *
011800  01   TOTAL-LINE.
011900 *
```

Figure 4-8 Repeating lines (part 1 of 2)

When you press the enter key, edit repeats the line 9 times

```
EDIT - DLOWE.TEST.COBOL(REORDLST) - 01.00 -------------------- COLUMNS 007 078
COMMAND INPUT ===>                                             SCROLL ===> PAGE
009800 *
009900  01   HDG-LINE-2.
010000 *
010100       05   HDG2-CC          PIC X.
010200       05   FILLER           PIC X(20)    VALUE '                    '.
010210       05   FILLER           PIC X(20)    VALUE '                    '.
010220       05   FILLER           PIC X(20)    VALUE '                    '.
010230       05   FILLER           PIC X(20)    VALUE '                    '.
010240       05   FILLER           PIC X(20)    VALUE '                    '.
010250       05   FILLER           PIC X(20)    VALUE '                    '.
010260       05   FILLER           PIC X(20)    VALUE '                    '.
010270       05   FILLER           PIC X(20)    VALUE '                    '.
010280       05   FILLER           PIC X(20)    VALUE '                    '.
010290       05   FILLER           PIC X(20)    VALUE '                    '.
010300 *
010400  01   REORDER-LINE.
010500 *
010600       05   RL-CC            PIC X.
010700       05   RL-ITEM-NO       PIC Z(5).
010800       05   FILLER           PIC X(5)      VALUE SPACE.
010900       05   RL-ITEM-DESC     PIC X(20).
011000       05   FILLER           PIC X(5)      VALUE SPACE.
```

Figure 4-8 Repeating lines (part 2 of 2)

RR line commands mark the first and last lines to be repeated

```
EDIT - DLOWE.TEST.COBOL(REORDLST) - 01.00 ------------------- COLUMNS 007 078
COMMAND INPUT ===>                                            SCROLL ===> PAGE
017700 *
017800  140-PRINT-HEADING-LINES.
017900 *
018000        MOVE HDG-LINE-1 TO PRINT-AREA.
018100        PERFORM 160-WRITE-PAGE-TOP-LINE.
RR            MOVE HDG-LINE-2 TO PRINT-AREA.
018300        MOVE 2 TO SPACE-CONTROL.
RR3           PERFORM 150-WRITE-REPORT-LINE.
018500 *
018600  150-WRITE-REPORT-LINE.
018700 *
018800        WRITE PRINT-AREA
018900            AFTER ADVANCING SPACE-CONTROL LINES.
019000        ADD SPACE-CONTROL TO LINE-COUNT.
019100 *
019200  160-WRITE-PAGE-TOP-LINE.
019300 *
019400        WRITE PRINT-AREA
019500            AFTER ADVANCING PAGE-TOP.
019600        MOVE ZERO TO LINE-COUNT.
019700 *
019800  200-PRINT-TOTAL-LINE.
```

Figure 4-9   Repeating a block of lines (part 1 of 2)

When you press the enter key, edit repeats the block of lines 3 times

```
EDIT - DLOWE.TEST.COBOL(REORDLST) - 01.00 ------------------- COLUMNS 007 078
COMMAND INPUT ===>                                            SCROLL ===> PAGE
017700 *
017800  140-PRINT-HEADING-LINES.
017900 *
018000        MOVE HDG-LINE-1 TO PRINT-AREA.
018100        PERFORM 160-WRITE-PAGE-TOP-LINE.
018200        MOVE HDG-LINE-2 TO PRINT-AREA.
018300        MOVE 2 TO SPACE-CONTROL.
018400        PERFORM 150-WRITE-REPORT-LINE.
018410        MOVE HDG-LINE-2 TO PRINT-AREA.
018420        MOVE 2 TO SPACE-CONTROL.
018430        PERFORM 150-WRITE-REPORT-LINE.
018440        MOVE HDG-LINE-2 TO PRINT-AREA.
018450        MOVE 2 TO SPACE-CONTROL.
018460        PERFORM 150-WRITE-REPORT-LINE.
018470        MOVE HDG-LINE-2 TO PRINT-AREA.
018480        MOVE 2 TO SPACE-CONTROL.
018490        PERFORM 150-WRITE-REPORT-LINE.
018500 *
018600  150-WRITE-REPORT-LINE.
018700 *
018800        WRITE PRINT-AREA
018900            AFTER ADVANCING SPACE-CONTROL LINES.
```

Figure 4-9   Repeating a block of lines (part 2 of 2)

How to copy lines   A copy operation is similar to a repeat operation except that besides specifying the line or group of lines to be copied, you also indicate where the lines are copied to (called the *destination*). To mark the lines to copy, you use the C, C*n*, or CC commands. To mark the copy destination, you use an A or a B command. If you specify A, the source lines are placed after the destination line. If you specify B, the source lines are placed before the destination line.

To illustrate, consider figure 4-10. Here, the group of lines from line 2900 to line 3300 is copied after line 4400. Part 1 of figure 4-10 shows the line commands entered for this copy operation; part 2 shows the completion of the copy.

As with the other line commands, you don't have to enter all of the commands necessary for a copy operation on a single panel. In fact, you can mark a block of lines by placing the first CC command on one panel, the second CC command on another panel, and the A or B command on yet another panel.

You can combine a copy and repeat operation into a single operation by specifying a number on the A or B command. For example, had I specified A3 in part 1 of figure 4-10, part 2 would show that the copied lines were repeated three times following line 4400.

How to move lines   A move operation is similar to a copy operation with one exception: when you do a move, the source lines are deleted from their original location after they're moved. The commands you enter for a move are the same as for a copy, except you specify M, M*n*, or MM rather than C, C*n*, or CC.

Figure 4-11 shows a typical move operation. Part 1 shows the line commands used for the move, while part 2 shows the effect of the move. As you can see, the source lines are deleted after they're moved to the destination. This example also shows the effect of using B rather than A to mark the destination.

The RESET command   Many edit commands display informational messages at various screen locations or at various points in your source text. And many commands generate error messages that are displayed in the heading area of the screen. Once you've read these messages, you can

CC line commands tell which block of lines to copy; the A line command marks the destination

```
EDIT - DLOWE.TEST.COBOL(REORDLST) - 01.00 -------------------- COLUMNS 007 078
COMMAND INPUT ===>                                             SCROLL ===> HALF
002800 *
CC       FD  BFCRDS
003000       LABEL RECORDS ARE STANDARD
003100       RECORDING MODE IS F
003200       RECORD CONTAINS 80 CHARACTERS.
CC       *
003400   01  BAL-FWD-CARD.
003500   *
003600       05  BF-ITEM-NO          PIC 9(5).
003700       05  BF-ITEM-DESC        PIC X(20).
003800       05  FILLER              PIC X(5).
003900       05  BF-UNIT-PRICE       PIC 999V99.
004000       05  BF-REORDER-POINT    PIC 9(5).
004100       05  BF-ON-HAND          PIC 9(5).
004200       05  BF-ON-ORDER         PIC 9(5).
004300       05  FILLER              PIC X(30).
A        *
004500   WORKING-STORAGE SECTION.
004600   *
004700   01  SWITCHES.
004800   *
004900       05  CARD-EOF-SWITCH     PIC X        VALUE 'N'.
```

Figure 4-10   Copying lines (part 1 of 2)

When you press the enter key, edit copies the lines

```
EDIT - DLOWE.TEST.COBOL(REORDLST) - 01.00 -------------------- COLUMNS 007 078
COMMAND INPUT ===>                                             SCROLL ===> HALF
002800 *
002900   FD  BFCRDS
003000       LABEL RECORDS ARE STANDARD
003100       RECORDING MODE IS F
003200       RECORD CONTAINS 80 CHARACTERS.
003300   *
003400   01  BAL-FWD-CARD.
003500   *
003600       05  BF-ITEM-NO          PIC 9(5).
003700       05  BF-ITEM-DESC        PIC X(20).
003800       05  FILLER              PIC X(5).
003900       05  BF-UNIT-PRICE       PIC 999V99.
004000       05  BF-REORDER-POINT    PIC 9(5).
004100       05  BF-ON-HAND          PIC 9(5).
004200       05  BF-ON-ORDER         PIC 9(5).
004300       05  FILLER              PIC X(30).
004400   *
004410   FD  BFCRDS
004420       LABEL RECORDS ARE STANDARD
004430       RECORDING MODE IS F
004440       RECORD CONTAINS 80 CHARACTERS.
004450   *
```

Figure 4-10   Copying lines (part 2 of 2)

MM line commands tell which block of lines to move; the B line command marks the destination

```
EDIT - DLOWE.TEST.COBOL(REORDLST) - 01.00 ------------------- COLUMNS 007 078
COMMAND INPUT ===>                                            SCROLL ===> HALF
002800 *
B        FD   BFCRDS
003000        LABEL RECORDS ARE STANDARD
003100        RECORDING MODE IS F
003200        RECORD CONTAINS 80 CHARACTERS.
003300 *
003400  01  BAL-FWD-CARD.
003500 *
003600      05   BF-ITEM-NO           PIC 9(5).
003700      05   BF-ITEM-DESC         PIC X(20).
003800      05   FILLER               PIC X(5).
003900      05   BF-UNIT-PRICE        PIC 999V99.
004000      05   BF-REORDER-POINT     PIC 9(5).
004100      05   BF-ON-HAND           PIC 9(5).
004200      05   BF-ON-ORDER          PIC 9(5).
004300      05   FILLER               PIC X(30).
004400 *
MM       FD   ORDLST
004420        LABEL RECORDS ARE STANDARD
004430        RECORDING MODE IS F
004440        RECORD CONTAINS 132 CHARACTERS.
MM       *
```

Figure 4-11 Moving lines (part 1 of 2)

When you press enter, edit moves the lines

```
EDIT - DLOWE.TEST.COBOL(REORDLST) - 01.00 ------------------- COLUMNS 007 078
COMMAND INPUT ===>                                            SCROLL ===> HALF
002800 *
002810  FD   ORDLST
002820       LABEL RECORDS ARE STANDARD
002830       RECORDING MODE IS F
002840       RECORD CONTAINS 132 CHARACTERS.
002850 *
002900  FD   BFCRDS
003000       LABEL RECORDS ARE STANDARD
003100       RECORDING MODE IS F
003200       RECORD CONTAINS 80 CHARACTERS.
003300 *
003400  01  BAL-FWD-CARD.
003500 *
003600      05   BF-ITEM-NO           PIC 9(5).
003700      05   BF-ITEM-DESC         PIC X(20).
003800      05   FILLER               PIC X(5).
003900      05   BF-UNIT-PRICE        PIC 999V99.
004000      05   BF-REORDER-POINT     PIC 9(5).
004100      05   BF-ON-HAND           PIC 9(5).
004200      05   BF-ON-ORDER          PIC 9(5).
004300      05   FILLER               PIC X(30).
004400 *
```

Figure 4-11 Moving lines (part 2 of 2)

remove them by entering a RESET primary command. Although RESET removes messages that appear within your source text, it doesn't affect the text itself. I'll point out specific times to use RESET throughout the rest of this chapter.

How to create a new member

All the examples in this topic so far have dealt with existing source members. And most of what I've said applies to new members, as well. But there are a few extra points you should be aware of.

To create a new member, you specify a member name that doesn't exist in the library on the edit entry panel in figure 4-1. The library, though, must exist. (You use the data set utility, which I describe in chapter 5, to create a library.)

Once you've filled in the edit entry panel, SPF creates an empty workspace in virtual storage. When you end the edit session, SPF writes the new member onto disk in the library you specified.

Figure 4-12 shows the edit display for a new COBOL member. Here, there are no line numbers or source data. You simply key in the data you want from column 7 on, using the new line key to move from one line to the next. When you've filled up the screen, you can press the enter key. Then, edit will replace the apostrophes in columns 1-6 with appropriate line numbers.

At that point, though, you won't get a new blank screen on which to enter data. Instead, you'll have to use the INSERT command to enter a block of blank lines. Then, you'll go back and enter data on the lines.

I've found the fastest way to create a new member is *not* to press the enter key at the end of the first screenload. Instead, set the SCROLL amount to 20, and in the last line of the screen, enter an I20 command. Then, use PF8/20 to scroll forward 20 lines. The result is a screen much like the one you began with in figure 4-12. The only difference is that the first line doesn't say TOP OF DATA; instead, it's the last line you entered. You then key data into this screen just like you did for the original screen. You can continue using this technique until you've completed your new source member.

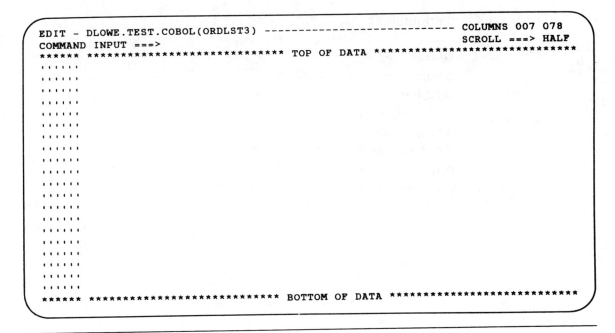

Figure 4-12   The first screen for a new member before any data is entered

How to terminate edit

The usual way to end an edit session is to press the end key
(PF3/15). When you do this, SPF saves your changed member
in the primary library (the first library specified in a chain of
concatenated libraries) and returns to the entry panel. Then,
you can enter another member to edit or press PF3/15 again to
return to the primary option menu. If you aren't going to edit
another member, you can use PF4/16 instead. This key also
saves the changed member, but it returns directly to the
primary option menu.

     If you want to terminate the edit session *without* saving
your changes, you can enter CANCEL in the command input
area and press the enter key. CANCEL returns to the entry
panel without copying the edited member back to the disk.

     A related command, SAVE, saves the member without
terminating edit. When you enter SAVE in the command area,
the virtual storage version of the member is copied to disk and
the edit session continues. In other words, the member you just
saved is still on the screen and you can continue making
changes to it.

Terminology

source member
concatenate
member list
line command area
line number
sequence number
primary command
line command
destination

Objectives

1. Explain how libraries can be concatenated on the edit entry panel.

2. Edit a data set using the insert, delete, repeat, copy, and move line commands.

TOPIC 2   How to control the edit profile

SPF *edit profiles* control editing options such as tab settings, column boundaries, line numbering, and so on. Although SPF provides default profiles for most of your editing needs, you'll use edit more effectively if you know how to tailor its profiles.

This topic is divided into two sections. In the first, I explain the edit profile—what it is, how to display it, and how to switch to a different profile. In the second section, I show you how to change the individual settings of a profile.

THE EDIT PROFILE

For each user, SPF maintains a number of separate edit profiles as members in a library named user-id.SPF.PROFILE. The default edit profiles correspond to data set types and are named accordingly. For example, COBOL is the default profile for data sets whose type is COBOL. If you wish, you can create additional edit profiles with names you make up. So if you have more than one profile requirement for COBOL files, you can create profiles named COB1, COB2, and COB3.

Normally, you don't specify a profile when you edit a data set or member. The profile automatically defaults to the data set's type. So if you edit a COBOL file, you automatically receive the COBOL profile. However, you can specify an alternate edit profile on the edit entry panel, as shown in figure 4-13. Here, I specify an edit profile named COB1. So even though the data set type is COBOL, edit uses the COB1 profile for this editing session.

How to display the edit profile

During an editing session, you can display the edit profile by entering this primary command:

    PROFILE

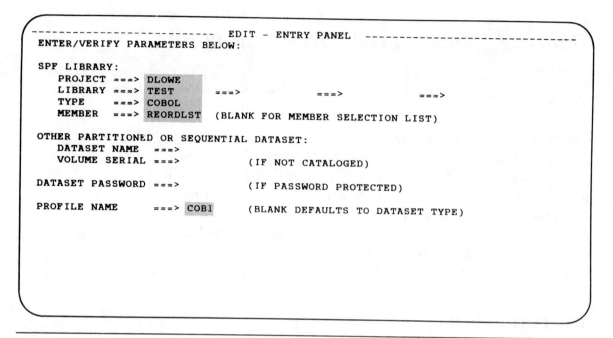

```
-------------------------------- EDIT - ENTRY PANEL  --------------------------------
ENTER/VERIFY PARAMETERS BELOW:

SPF LIBRARY:
   PROJECT ===> DLOWE
   LIBRARY ===> TEST      ===>           ===>          ===>
   TYPE    ===> COBOL
   MEMBER  ===> REORDLST   (BLANK FOR MEMBER SELECTION LIST)

OTHER PARTITIONED OR SEQUENTIAL DATASET:
   DATASET NAME   ===>
   VOLUME SERIAL  ===>           (IF NOT CATALOGED)

DATASET PASSWORD ===>           (IF PASSWORD PROTECTED)

PROFILE NAME     ===> COB1      (BLANK DEFAULTS TO DATASET TYPE)
```

Figure 4-13   Specifying an alternate profile

The profile display looks like the shaded portion of figure 4-14.

The first three lines indicate the profile name (COBOL), the source member's record format and length (FIXED and 80), and the settings of various *edit modes*. Each is either on or off. Thus, in figure 4-14, CAPS mode is on, while HEX mode is off.

Following the three mode lines are lines showing the current settings for TABS, MASK, and BOUNDS. As you'll see later in this topic, TABS controls the location of tab stops, MASK controls the format of lines inserted with an I command, and BOUNDS controls the left and right margins.

The last line is a COLS line, similar to the one in browse, that identifies column positions. If you want to display a COLS line anywhere in your source text during an edit, simply enter COLS in the line command area of any line. Edit will automatically insert a COLS line at that point. To remove a COLS line from the display, delete it using a D line command or enter a RESET command, as described in topic 1.

```
EDIT - DLOWE.TEST.COBOL(REORDLST) - 01.02 ------------------ COLUMNS 007 078
COMMAND INPUT ===>                                          SCROLL ===> HALF
***** ************************** TOP OF DATA ********************************
=PROF> ....COBOL (FIXED - 80)....RECOVERY OFF....NUMBER ON COB.............
=PROF> ....CAPS ON....HEX OFF....NULLS OFF....TABS OFF....................
=PROF> ....AUTONUM OFF....PRINT OFF....STATS ON..........................
=TABS>      *                              *            *
=MASK>      05  FILLER               PIC X(  )    VALUE '
=BNDS> <                                                                 >
=COLS> ---1----+----2----+----3----+----4----+----5----+----6----+----7----+--
000800   IDENTIFICATION DIVISION.
000900 *
001000   PROGRAM-ID. REORDLST.
001100 *
001200   ENVIRONMENT DIVISION.
001300 *
001400   CONFIGURATION SECTION.
001500 *
001600   SPECIAL-NAMES.
001700       C01 IS PAGE-TOP.
001800 *
001900   INPUT-OUTPUT SECTION.
002000 *
002100   FILE-CONTROL.
```

Figure 4-14   An edit profile display

You control the settings for each of the profile options using commands that I describe later in this topic. When you terminate edit, any profile changes you've made are saved as part of the profile.

How to switch to or create a different profile

When you use the PROFILE command, you can specify a profile name that causes edit to switch to a different profile. For example, if you enter this command:

    PROFILE COB3

edit retrieves the profile named COB3. If there is no COB3 profile, edit creates one using the current profile settings. Thus, to create a new profile, you simply change the profile settings individually using the commands I'll describe next, then issue a PROFILE command specifying the new profile name.

HOW TO CHANGE PROFILE SETTINGS

You use a variety of commands to change profile settings. In this section, I first describe profile settings for four important editing functions: tabbing, boundary control, masking, and line numbering. Then, I describe the remaining edit mode settings.

How to use tabs

When you edit a source member, you often need to move the cursor to a particular column to align text. For example, you may want to place all the PIC clauses of a COBOL program in column 36. Normally, you use a cursor key or the space bar to move the cursor to a particular column. If you use edit's tabbing feature, however, you can move the cursor to a particular column location—called a *tab stop*—using a single keystroke.

Edit provides two types of tabs: hardware and logical. When you use *hardware tabs*, you use the 3270's tab key to move the cursor immediately to the next tab stop. When you use *logical tabs*, you enter a special *tab character*—like the #-key or @-key—whenever you want to align text at a tab stop. Then, when you press the enter key, edit replaces the tab characters with the correct number of spaces to align the tabbed text properly.

To illustrate logical tabbing, suppose you have tab stops set at columns 36 and 48. Now, consider figure 4-15. In part 1 of this figure, I've entered text for a record description using the @-key as a tab character. Part 2 of figure 4-15 shows how the text is aligned as a result of logical tabbing.

To implement a hardware tab stop, edit uses a special control character called an *attribute byte*. Attribute bytes control various characteristics of the fields on a 3270 screen, such as whether or not an operator can enter data into the field. Each attribute byte takes up one position on the screen, but it displays as a blank so you can't see it. The only reason you need to be aware of the the presence of attribute bytes when you use hardware tabbing is this: You can't modify the character immediately to the left of a hardware tab stop because that position contains an attribute byte. In other

The @ symbol is the tab key

```
EDIT - DLOWE.TEST.COBOL(REORDLST) - 01.02 ------------------- COLUMNS 007 078
COMMAND INPUT ===>                                            SCROLL ===> HALF
010300 *
010400  01   REORDER-LINE.
010500 *
010600       05   RL-CC@PIC X.
010700       05   RL-ITEM-NO@PIC Z(5).
010800       05   FILLER@PIC X(5)@VALUE SPACE.
010900       05   RL-ITEM-DESC@PIC X(20).
011000       05   FILLER@PIC X(5)@VALUE SPACE.
011100       05   RL-UNIT-PRICE@PIC ZZZ.99.
011200       05   FILLER@PIC X(5)@VALUE SPACE.
011300       05   RL-AVAILABLE-STOCK@PIC Z(5).
011400       05   FILLER@PIC X(5)@VALUE SPACE.
011500       05   RL-REORDER-POINT@PIC Z(5).
011600       05   FILLER@PIC X(71)@VALUE SPACE.
011700 *
011800  01   TOTAL-LINE.
011900 *
012000       05   TL-CC                  PIC X.
012100       05   TL-CARD-COUNT          PIC ZZ,ZZZ.
012200       05   FILLER                 PIC X(24)
012300                                   VALUE ' CARDS IN THE INPUT DECK'.
012400       05   FILLER                 PIC X(102)  VALUE SPACE.
```

Figure 4-15   Logical tabbing (part 1 of 2)

When you press the enter key, edit moves the text to the proper tab stops

```
EDIT - DLOWE.TEST.COBOL(REORDLST) - 01.02 ------------------- COLUMNS 007 078
COMMAND INPUT ===>                                            SCROLL ===> HALF
010300 *
010400  01   REORDER-LINE.
010500 *
010600       05   RL-CC                  PIC X.
010700       05   RL-ITEM-NO             PIC Z(5).
010800       05   FILLER                 PIC X(5)       VALUE SPACE.
010900       05   RL-ITEM-DESC           PIC X(20).
011000       05   FILLER                 PIC X(5)       VALUE SPACE.
011100       05   RL-UNIT-PRICE          PIC ZZZ.99.
011200       05   FILLER                 PIC X(5)       VALUE SPACE.
011300       05   RL-AVAILABLE-STOCK     PIC Z(5).
011400       05   FILLER                 PIC X(5)       VALUE SPACE.
011500       05   RL-REORDER-POINT       PIC Z(5).
011600       05   FILLER                 PIC X(71)      VALUE SPACE.
011700 *
011800  01   TOTAL-LINE.
011900 *
012000       05   TL-CC                  PIC X.
012100       05   TL-CARD-COUNT          PIC ZZ,ZZZ.
012200       05   FILLER                 PIC X(24)
012300                                   VALUE ' CARDS IN THE INPUT DECK'.
012400       05   FILLER                 PIC X(102)  VALUE SPACE.
```

Figure 4-15   Logical tabbing (part 2 of 2)

words, if you define a hardware tab in column 32, you can't change the data in column 31.

When you edit a COBOL source program, you'll probably use hardware tabs most in the Data Division. That's because you want to align PIC clauses and other information in columns, and there's usually no need to enter data in the positions occupied by attribute bytes. In the Procedure Division and other sections of your program where you need to enter data in a more free-form fashion, you'll probably use logical tabbing.

You use two commands to control tabbing. The TABS line command defines the location of each tab stop. The TABS primary command activates hardware or logical tabs. Note that although these two commands have the same name, they have distinct functions. The TABS line command defines the profile TABS line (the fourth line of the profile in figure 4-14), while the TABS primary command changes the setting of the TABS mode in the edit profile (in the second line of the profile in figure 4-14).

How to define tab stops When you enter TABS in the line command area and press enter, SPF responds with a tab line as shown in figure 4-16 (the tab line is shaded). The tab line defines the location of each tab stop. Initially, it's blank. To define a tab stop, you enter an asterisk (*) immediately to the left of the desired tab position. (You place the asterisk to the left of the tab stop because the asterisk defines the location of the attribute byte for hardware tabbing—not the tab stop itself.) For example, the asterisks in columns 11, 35, and 47 of the tab line in figure 4-16 define tab stops in columns 12, 36, and 48.

How to activate TABS mode Once you've defined a tab line, you use a TABS primary command to activate tabbing. Figure 4-17 shows the format of the TABS primary command. As you can see, it has three options. ON/OFF indicates whether you're activating or deactivating TABS mode. If you specify ON, tabbing is activated. If you say OFF, tabbing is turned off and any attribute characters inserted for hardware tabbing are removed. If you don't say ON or OFF, ON is assumed.

```
 EDIT - DLOWE.TEST.COBOL(REORDLST) - 01.02 ------------------- COLUMNS 007 078
 COMMAND INPUT ===>                                            SCROLL ===> HALF
 010300 *
 =COLS> ---1----+----2----+----3----+----4----+----5----+----6----+----7----+---
 010400  01   REORDER-LINE.
 =TABS>          *                          *            *
 010500 *
 010600         05   RL-CC                 PIC X.
 010700         05   RL-ITEM-NO            PIC Z(5).
 010800         05   FILLER               PIC X(5)      VALUE SPACE.
 010900         05   RL-ITEM-DESC         PIC X(20).
 011000         05   FILLER               PIC X(5)      VALUE SPACE.
 011100         05   RL-UNIT-PRICE        PIC ZZZ.99.
 011200         05   FILLER               PIC X(5)      VALUE SPACE.
 011300         05   RL-AVAILABLE-STOCK   PIC Z(5).
 011400         05   FILLER               PIC X(5)      VALUE SPACE.
 011500         05   RL-REORDER-POINT     PIC Z(5).
 011600         05   FILLER               PIC X(71)     VALUE SPACE.
 011700 *
 011800  01   TOTAL-LINE.
 011900 *
 012000         05   TL-CC                PIC X.
 012100         05   TL-CARD-COUNT        PIC ZZ,ZZZ.
 012200         05   FILLER               PIC X(24)
```

Figure 4-16   Defining tab stops

The next option, tab-character, says what character is used for logical tabbing. For example, if you want the pound sign to be the logical tab character, you enter this command:

TABS ON #

Then, you use the pound sign to move from one tab stop to another.

If you omit the tab-character, hardware tabbing is assumed. Then, attribute bytes are inserted before each tab stop and you use the tab key rather than logical tab characters to move from one tab stop to the next.

The ALL option pertains to hardware tabbing only. It says whether or not existing data should be overlaid with attribute bytes. If you omit the ALL option, attribute bytes are not inserted if they overlay non-blank data. If you say ALL, attribute bytes are inserted for every tab stop, even if non-blank data is overlaid. In either case, the attribute bytes appear on the screen only; they're never transferred to the source member.

The TABS command

```
TABS    {ON }  [tab-character] [ALL]
        {OFF}
```

Explanation

ON   Says whether to activate or deactivate TABS mode.
OFF

tab-character   Specifies a character used for logical tabbing. If
                omitted, hardware tabbing is assumed.

ALL   Says to insert attribute bytes for each tab stop, even if
            that causes non-blank data to be overlaid. If you omit
            ALL, only non-blank data is replaced by attribute bytes.

Note: Use this command to change the setting of TABS mode in the edit profile.
Use the TABS **line** command to set tab stops, as shown in figure 4-16.

Figure 4-17   The TABS primary command

For hardware tabbing, you can remove attribute bytes
from a single line by (1) blanking out the line command area
or (2) placing the cursor directly under an attribute byte. In
either case, the attribute bytes in the line are removed when
you press the enter key. They're inserted again the next time
you press the enter key.

Why would you want to temporarily remove attribute
bytes from a single line? One case is when you're entering code
for the Working-Storage Section of a COBOL source program.
Here, you might use hardware tabbing to tab to position 48 for
the VALUE clauses. Sometimes, though, you need to create a
long VALUE clause that starts before column 48 and continues
to the end of the line. To enter that VALUE clause, you first
remove the attribute characters for that one line only.

How to change column boundaries

Left and right margins—or *boundaries*—determine the range of
columns in which you can edit data. Normally, the boundaries
are set based on the type field of the file or library name.

```
EDIT - DLOWE.TEST.COBOL(REORDLST) - 01.02 ----------------- COLUMNS 007 078
COMMAND INPUT ===>                                          SCROLL ===> HALF
010300 *
010400  01   REORDER-LINE.
=BNDS>                           <                              >
010500 *
010600        05   RL-CC                PIC X.
010700        05   RL-ITEM-NO           PIC Z(5).
010800        05   FILLER               PIC X(5)      VALUE SPACE.
010900        05   RL-ITEM-DESC         PIC X(20).
011000        05   FILLER               PIC X(5)      VALUE SPACE.
011100        05   RL-UNIT-PRICE        PIC ZZZ.99.
011200        05   FILLER               PIC X(5)      VALUE SPACE.
011300        05   RL-AVAILABLE-STOCK   PIC Z(5).
011400        05   FILLER               PIC X(5)      VALUE SPACE.
011500        05   RL-REORDER-POINT     PIC Z(5).
011600        05   FILLER               PIC X(71)     VALUE SPACE.
011700 *
011800  01   TOTAL-LINE.
011900 *
012000        05   TL-CC                PIC X.
012100        05   TL-CARD-COUNT        PIC ZZ,ZZZ.
012200        05   FILLER               PIC X(24)
012300                                  VALUE ' CARDS IN THE INPUT DECK'.
```

Figure 4-18   Changing the edit boundaries

For a COBOL file, the left margin is column 7 and the right margin is column 72. Although you can change the data in columns 1-6 and 73-80, the edit commands you'll learn about in topic 3 will only affect the data in columns 7-72.

For an ASM file (assembler source code), the boundaries are set at columns 1 and 71. For other file types, the left margin is column 1 and the right margin is the last position of the record.

To change boundary settings, you use the BOUNDS line command. To illustrate, consider figure 4-18. Here, I entered BOUNDS in the line command area. Edit responded by displaying a bounds line, shaded in figure 4-18. Then, I entered a less-than sign (<) to mark the new left boundary and a greater-than sign (>) to mark the new right boundary. The positions that contain the < and > characters are considered to be within the boundaries.

To restore the boundaries to the default values, you enter a BOUNDS line command and erase the bounds line using the erase-EOF key. The RESET command does not affect boundary settings.

How to use edit masks

An *edit mask* is a pre-defined line that's used as the initial contents of each line you insert using an I line command. Since the edit mask is blank to begin with, any lines you insert with an I command are blank. To change the mask, you enter MASK in the line command area. Edit responds by displaying a mask line, as shown in part 1 of figure 4-19. Then, you enter your edit mask. In this example, I entered a dummy field description as the mask.

Part 1 of figure 4-19 also contains an I line command that inserts 11 lines. Part 2 shows the result of this insertion. As you can see, the mask line is copied into each inserted line. The mask line remains in effect until you change it again, using another MASK command. You can remove the mask line display with a D line command or a RESET primary command. But the mask line is still active even though it's not displayed. The only way to deactivate the mask line is to change it to blanks using another MASK command.

Often, a better way to achieve the effect of an edit mask is to insert one blank line, enter data on it, and repeat the line using an R command. The advantage of this technique is that you don't have to reset the mask line once you're through.

How to control line numbers

To control how edit maintains sequence numbers, you use the four commands shown in figure 4-20. The NUMBER command tells what format line numbers are in. The AUTONUM command says whether or not line numbers are automatically resequenced when you terminate edit. The RENUM command says to resequence the line numbers. And you use the UNNUM command to remove line numbers.

The NUMBER command You use the NUMBER command to control the setting of NUMBER mode. The NUMBER command is coded in one of these three forms:

```
NUMBER ON COBOL

NUMBER ON STD

NUMBER OFF
```

The MASK line command defines the line to be inserted with an I command

```
EDIT - DLOWE.TEST.COBOL(REORDLST) - 01.02 ------------------- COLUMNS 007 078
COMMAND INPUT ===>                                            SCROLL ===> HALF
009000 *
=MASK>        05  FILLER              PIC X( )    VALUE '
009100  01  HDG-LINE-3.
009200 *
I11           05  HDG3-CC             PIC X.
010300 *
010400  01  REORDER-LINE.
010500 *
010600        05  RL-CC               PIC X.
010700        05  RL-ITEM-NO          PIC Z(5).
010800        05  FILLER              PIC X(5)     VALUE SPACE.
010900        05  RL-ITEM-DESC        PIC X(20).
011000        05  FILLER              PIC X(5)     VALUE SPACE.
011100        05  RL-UNIT-PRICE       PIC ZZZ.99.
011200        05  FILLER              PIC X(5)     VALUE SPACE.
011300        05  RL-AVAILABLE-STOCK  PIC Z(5).
011400        05  FILLER              PIC X(5)     VALUE SPACE.
011500        05  RL-REORDER-POINT    PIC Z(5).
011600        05  FILLER              PIC X(71)    VALUE SPACE.
011700 *
011800  01  TOTAL-LINE.
011900 *
```

Figure 4-19 Using an edit mask (part 1 of 2)

When you press the enter key, edit inserts the mask line 11 times

```
EDIT - DLOWE.TEST.COBOL(REORDLST) - 01.02 ------------------- COLUMNS 007 078
COMMAND INPUT ===>                                            SCROLL ===> HALF
009000 *
=MASK>        05  FILLER              PIC X( )    VALUE '
009100  01  HDG-LINE-3.
009200 *
009300        05  HDG3-CC             PIC X.
''''''        05  FILLER              PIC X( )    VALUE '
''''''        05  FILLER              PIC X( )    VALUE '
''''''        05  FILLER              PIC X( )    VALUE '
''''''        05  FILLER              PIC X( )    VALUE '
''''''        05  FILLER              PIC X( )    VALUE '
''''''        05  FILLER              PIC X( )    VALUE '
''''''        05  FILLER              PIC X( )    VALUE '
''''''        05  FILLER              PIC X( )    VALUE '
''''''        05  FILLER              PIC X( )    VALUE '
''''''        05  FILLER              PIC X( )    VALUE '
''''''        05  FILLER              PIC X( )    VALUE '
010300 *
010400  01  REORDER-LINE.
010500 *
010600        05  RL-CC               PIC X.
010700        05  RL-ITEM-NO          PIC Z(5).
010800        05  FILLER              PIC X(5)     VALUE SPACE.
```

Figure 4-19 Using an edit mask (part 2 of 2)

Command			Meaning
NUMBER	{ON OFF}	{STD COBOL}	Defines how line numbers are stored in the member.
AUTONUM	{ON OFF}		Says whether or not line numbers should be resequenced whenever the member is saved.
RENUM	[{STD COBOL}]		Resequence the line numbers. You may specify standard or COBOL numbers if you wish.
UNNUM			Replace line numbers with blanks and turn off NUMBER mode.

Figure 4-20 Primary commands used to control line numbering

If you say NUMBER ON COBOL or NUMBER ON STD, edit checks that the member has valid COBOL or standard line numbers; if the member doesn't, edit resequences the numbers so they're valid. Once NUMBER mode is on, edit automatically maintains line numbers, generating new line numbers for inserted lines and resequencing existing line numbers whenever necessary. As a result, you don't have to renumber the member to insert, move, copy, or repeat lines. If you say NUMBER OFF, edit ignores any line numbers it finds in the file. Instead, it creates its own sequence numbers for temporary use.

When you enter edit using a new profile for the first time, edit scans the source file to determine what types of line numbers are present and sets the NUMBER mode accordingly. So you usually won't use the NUMBER command. The one time you're likely to use the NUMBER command is when you're creating an unnumbered test file. In that case, you'll probably need to issue a NUMBER OFF command.

The AUTONUM command   The AUTONUM command controls the AUTONUM mode, which says whether or not a member should be renumbered automatically each time it's saved. Normally, AUTONUM is off. If you like your members numbered in regular increments, use AUTONUM mode.

The RENUM command   You use the RENUM command to resequence line numbers. RENUM starts with 100 for the first line number and then numbers by 100's. If NUMBER mode is off, RENUM turns it on. You can force COBOL or standard numbers by specifying COBOL or STD on the RENUM command. Since edit automatically resequences line numbers whenever necessary, you won't use the RENUM command often.

The UNNUM command   You use the UNNUM command to remove line numbers from a member. UNNUM replaces any existing line numbers with blanks and turns off NUMBER mode. To restore sequence numbers, use the RENUM command.

Other edit modes

I've already described three edit modes: TABS, NUMBER, and AUTONUM. Figure 4-21 lists all of the edit modes. For each of them (other than TABS and NUMBER), the command you use to turn the option on or off is the mode name followed by the word ON or OFF. So, to activate PRINT mode, you code this command:

```
PRINT ON
```

Now, I'll describe each of the remaining edit modes in detail.

STATS mode   If STATS mode is on, SPF automatically maintains statistics for each member in the library. These statistics are displayed on member selection lists and may be created, reset, or deleted using option 3.5, the reset utility.

Figure 4-22 shows a typical member selection list. Here, you can see the library statistics. The VER.MOD field contains a version and modification level number. Version is initially set to 1 and can be changed only by the reset utility. Each time you edit a member, SPF automatically adds 1 to the modification level number. As a result, a newly created member has a VER.MOD of 1.00, while a member that's been edited four times since its creation has a VER.MOD of 1.04.

The CREATED and LAST MODIFIED fields show the date the member was created and last edited. The SIZE, INIT, and MOD fields show the current number of lines in the member, the number of lines initially in this version, and the number of lines that have been modified since the version was created. Finally, the ID field shows the user-id of the person who edited the member most recently.

Mode	Function
TABS	Controls logical and hardware tabbing.
NUMBER	Controls how line numbers are maintained.
AUTONUM	Controls automatic resequencing.
STATS	Controls automatic maintenance of library statistics.
NULLS	Controls how trailing blanks are handled on the 3270 screen.
PRINT	Controls automatic printing.
RECOVERY	Controls the automatic journal kept for recovery purposes.
HEX	Controls hexadecimal display.
CAPS	Controls automatic conversion of lowercase data to uppercase.

Figure 4-21 Edit modes

For members with standard line numbers, STATS mode affects how the line numbers are maintained. If STATS mode is on, only six digits of each eight-digit line number are used as a sequence number. The last two digits are reserved for the *modification flag*. These digits indicate how many times each line has been modified. If the modification flag is 00, the line hasn't been changed since the member was created. If the modification flag is 02, the line has been modified twice. When STATS mode is off, all eight digits of the line number are used for sequencing. STATS mode doesn't affect line numbering for COBOL members.

NULLS mode   NULLS mode controls how trailing blanks are sent to the screen. If NULLS mode is off (the default), all blanks are sent to the screen. If NULLS mode is on, trailing blanks—the ones that follow the last non-blank character on each line—are sent to the screen as null characters (hex zeros) rather than as blanks.

When NULLS mode is on, response time is better and it's easier to use the insert key. Response time is improved because

```
EDIT - DLOWE.TEST.COBOL ----------------------------------------------------
COMMAND INPUT ===>                                             SCROLL ===> PAGE
   NAME         VER.MOD  CREATED    LAST MODIFIED   SIZE  INIT  MOD   ID
   BFCRDS        01.00  84/01/30  84/01/30 18:12     12    12    0   DLOWE
   INVLST        01.00  84/01/26  84/01/26 14:29    202   202    0   DLOWE
   ORDLST2       01.05  84/01/05  84/01/05 16:44      9     9    0   DLOWE
   PRTFD         01.00  84/01/30  84/01/30 18:16      8     8    0   DLOWE
   REORDLST      01.02  84/01/30  84/01/30 13:58    352   222   12   DLOWE
   RNDUPDT       01.11  84/01/26  84/01/26 14:29    987   902   29   DLOWE
   SEQUPTD       01.06  84/01/05  84/01/05 16:44    549   549    1   DLOWE
   VSESMNT       01.14  84/01/05  84/01/05 16:44    125   229    7   DLOWE
   VSESMNT2      01.00  84/01/05  84/01/05 16:44    194   194    0   DLOWE
   VSESRUPT      01.22  84/01/05  84/01/05 16:44     29    29    2   DLOWE
   VSESSUPT      01.09  84/01/26  84/01/26 14:29    222   204    1   DLOWE
   VSKSMNT       01.02  84/01/26  84/01/26 14:29    202   202    0   DLOWE
   VSKSRUPT      01.17  84/01/05  84/01/05 16:44    439   405   21   DLOWE
   VSKSSUPT      01.13  84/01/05  84/01/05 16:44    385   379   10   DLOWE
   VSRRMNT       01.03  84/01/26  84/01/26 14:29    204   202    5   DLOWE
   VSRRRUPT      01.07  84/01/05  84/01/05 16:44    109    88   14   DLOWE
   VSRRSUPT      01.02  84/01/26  84/01/26 14:29    302   202   12   DLOWE
   **END**
```

Figure 4-22   An edit member selection list

null characters are not actually sent to the terminal. For remote
terminals, the difference in response time can be significant.
But for local terminals, you probably won't notice a difference. As for the insert key, if NULLS mode is off, each line is
filled with blanks. Since all blanks are considered to be data,
you can't use the insert key to insert characters unless you first
erase trailing blanks using the erase-EOF key. When NULLS
mode is on, you don't have to use the erase-EOF key before
you can use the insert key because source lines aren't padded
with blanks.

The disadvantage of NULLS mode is that you have to use
the space bar to move the cursor across the screen when you're
entering new text. If you use a cursor key instead, the entire
line is compressed when you press the enter key. For example,
if you use the cursor key to enter a line like this:

```
05  FILLER    PIC X.
```

it will look like this when you press the enter key:

```
05FILLERPICX.
```

That's because null characters are never transmitted between your terminal and the CPU.

Whether you should specify NULLS ON or OFF depends largely on your personal editing style. If you frequently use the cursor key rather than the space bar to move the cursor across the screen, you should specify NULLS OFF. On the other hand, if you find yourself constantly using the erase-EOF key to delete trailing blanks so you can use the insert key, change NULLS to ON. I think it's best to develop the habit of using the space bar rather than the cursor key. That way, you can set NULLS mode ON and use the insert key easily. But again, it's a matter of personal choice.

PRINT mode   When you terminate edit, a source listing is automatically generated if you made any changes to the member *and* if PRINT mode is on. The source listing is written to the list data set, which isn't printed until you terminate SPF.

For programs in development, you don't want PRINT mode on. Otherwise, each time you edit your program, a source listing is generated. On the other hand, PRINT mode is a good idea for programs in production. That way, each time maintenance is done to the program, it's automatically documented.

RECOVERY mode   If you're worried about system crashes, you can use RECOVERY mode to keep a record of all changes you make during an edit session in a special disk file called the *recovery data set*. The recovery data set is closed only when edit terminates normally. If the system crashes, the recovery data set is left open. When the system comes up and you edit the member again, edit displays a panel that lets you apply the changes stored in the recovery data set. Of course, the price you pay for this extra protection is increased response time.

HEX mode   When HEX mode is on, data is displayed in hexadecimal format. The format, shown in figure 4-23, is the same as the browse hexadecimal display. While in HEX mode, you can change the contents of any byte by changing the character or the two-byte hex code. Thus, you can use HEX mode to create or modify packed-decimal test data. Or, you

```
EDIT - DLOWE.TEST.COBOL(REORDLST) - 01.02 ----------------- COLUMNS 007 078
COMMAND INPUT ===>                                         SCROLL ===> PAGE
008200      05  FILLER              PIC X(4)     VALUE 'ITEM'.
            44444FF44CCDDCD4444444444444444DCC4E4F54444ECDEC47CECD744444444444444444444
            00000050069335900000000000000079307D4D0000513450D9354DB000000000000000000
-----------------------------------------------------------------------------------
008300      05  FILLER              PIC X(12)    VALUE SPACE.
            44444FF44CCDDCD4444444444444444DCC4E4FF5444ECDEC4EDCCC4444444444444444444444
            00000050069335900000000000000079307D12D00051345027135B0000000000000000000
-----------------------------------------------------------------------------------
008400      05  FILLER              PIC X(4)     VALUE 'ITEM'.
            44444FF44CCDDCD4444444444444444DCC4E4F54444ECDEC47CECD744444444444444444444
            00000050069335900000000000000079307D4D0000513450D9354DB000000000000000000
-----------------------------------------------------------------------------------
008500      05  FILLER              PIC X(16)    VALUE SPACE.
            44444FF44CCDDCD4444444444444444DCC4E4FF5444ECDEC4EDCCC4444444444444444444444
            00000050069335900000000000000079307D16D00051345027135B0000000000000000000
-----------------------------------------------------------------------------------
008600      05  FILLER              PIC X(4)     VALUE 'UNIT'.
            44444FF44CCDDCD4444444444444444DCC4E4F54444ECDEC47EDCE744444444444444444444
            00000050069335900000000000000079307D4D0000513450D4593DB000000000000000000
-----------------------------------------------------------------------------------
```

Figure 4-23 An edit hexadecimal display

can create program literals (such as COBOL VALUE clauses) that contain non-displayable data.

CAPS mode   When CAPS mode is on, any lowercase letters you enter are automatically converted to uppercase letters. When CAPS mode is off, no automatic conversion from lower to uppercase occurs. Normally, CAPS mode is on when you're editing COBOL and other types of source files. The only times you would normally deactivate CAPS mode are when you're entering text data like program documentation and when you're creating program literals that require lowercase letters.

DISCUSSION

With the exception of TABS mode, most of the features I presented in this topic are useful only for special applications. As a result, you don't have to study every detail in this topic. Using hardware and logical tabs, however, can be a real time-saver every time. So I suggest you start using the TABS commands right away.

Terminology

edit profile
edit mode
tab stop
hardware tab
logical tab
tab character
attribute byte
boundary
edit mask
modification flag
recovery data set

Objectives

1. Explain the function of the edit profile.

2. Explain the difference between logical tabbing and hardware tabbing.

3. Use the commands described in this topic to modify profile settings for:

   a. tabs
   b. boundaries
   c. masks
   d. line numbers
   e. statistics
   f. null characters
   g. automatic printing
   h. recovery
   i. hexadecimal display
   j. upper and lowercase characters

TOPIC 3   Advanced edit operations

In the first topic of this chapter, I presented the basics of using edit. This topic builds on that base. Here, I present edit commands that let you do more sophisticated editing.

How to exclude lines

You use the group of line commands shown in figure 4-24 to exclude a line or group of lines from the edit display. When you exclude lines, they aren't removed from the source member. They just aren't displayed. Excluded lines are sometimes useful when you have many similar lines of source text—such as a long series of MOVE statements or individual field descriptions within a record description. By excluding these lines, you can display and edit the text that surrounds these lines without unnecessary scrolling.

To illustrate, consider figure 4-25. In part 1 of this figure, I've coded two XX commands to exclude the individual fields of a record description. Part 2 shows the display after the lines have been excluded. As you can see, the entire group of lines is replaced by a single line that indicates how many lines are excluded from the display.

The line that displays in place of excluded lines can be processed by most of the line commands you already know. If you delete it with a D command, all of the excluded lines are deleted. If you copy, move, or repeat it with a C, M, or R command, all of the excluded lines are copied, moved, or repeated.

How to redisplay excluded lines   To redisplay all or a portion of the excluded text, you use an F, L, or S command. The F command redisplays a line or lines starting at the beginning of the excluded lines, while L starts at the end of the excluded lines. For example, if you exclude lines 2010, 2020,

Command	Meaning
X	Exclude this line.
X*n*	Exclude *n* lines.
X X	Exclude this line and all lines between two XX commands.
F	Show the first line of the excluded text.
F*n*	Show the first *n* lines.
L	Show the last line of the excluded text.
L*n*	Show the last *n* lines.
S	Show one line of the excluded text.
S*n*	Show *n* lines.

Figure 4-24   Line commands for excluding and redisplaying source lines

and 2030, then enter F2, lines 2010 and 2020 are redisplayed. On the other hand, if you enter L2, lines 2020 and 2030 are redisplayed.

The S command selects lines to redisplay by checking the indentation level of the text. S always redisplays those lines with the leftmost indentation. Figure 4-26 shows how the S command works. In part 1, five lines of Procedure Division code are excluded from the display. Part 2 shows the S command entered to redisplay a part of the excluded lines. And part 3 shows the redisplayed text. Although an F or L command will leave a single line undisplayed, the S command won't. As a result, an S command sometimes redisplays more lines than you specify. That's the case with line 15400 in figure 4-26.

The S command checks for indentation by scanning the source text from left to right until it finds a non-blank character. In a COBOL program, that means comment lines are usually the first to be redisplayed because the S command finds an asterisk in column 7 first. That's good if the comment lines contain text. But if the comments are blank, it doesn't help much to redisplay them. You probably won't use the selective redisplay capability of the S command often, but when you do, remember that blank comment lines rather than important program lines may be selected for redisplay.

You can also use a RESET command to redisplay excluded lines. Simply enter RESET as described in topic 1.

X X line commands mark the first and last lines to be excluded

```
EDIT - DLOWE.TEST.COBOL(REORDLST) - 01.02 ------------------- COLUMNS 007 078
COMMAND INPUT ===>                                            SCROLL ===> HALF
002800 *
002900  FD   BFCRDS
003000       LABEL RECORDS ARE STANDARD
003100       RECORDING MODE IS F
003200       RECORD CONTAINS 80 CHARACTERS.
003300 *
003400  01   BAL-FWD-CARD.
XX      *
003600       05  BF-ITEM-NO         PIC 9(5).
003700       05  BF-ITEM-DESC       PIC X(20).
003800       05  FILLER             PIC X(5).
003900       05  BF-UNIT-PRICE      PIC 999V99.
004000       05  BF-REORDER-POINT   PIC 9(5).
004100       05  BF-ON-HAND         PIC 9(5).
004200       05  BF-ON-ORDER        PIC 9(5).
XX           05  FILLER             PIC X(30).
005100 *
005110  FD   ORDLST
005120       LABEL RECORDS ARE STANDARD
005130       RECORDING MODE IS F
005140       RECORD CONTAINS 133 CHARACTERS.
005150 *
```

Figure 4-25   Excluding a block of lines (part 1 of 2)

When you press the enter key, edit displays a message instead of the lines

```
EDIT - DLOWE.TEST.COBOL(REORDLST) - 01.02 ------------------- COLUMNS 007 078
COMMAND INPUT ===>                                            SCROLL ===> HALF
002800 *
002900  FD   BFCRDS
003000       LABEL RECORDS ARE STANDARD
003100       RECORDING MODE IS F
003200       RECORD CONTAINS 80 CHARACTERS.
003300 *
003400  01   BAL-FWD-CARD.
- - - - - - - - - - - - - - - - - - - - 9 LINE(S) NOT DISPLAYED
005100 *
005110  FD   ORDLST
005120       LABEL RECORDS ARE STANDARD
005130       RECORDING MODE IS F
005140       RECORD CONTAINS 133 CHARACTERS.
005150 *
005160  01   PRINT-AREA          PIC X(133).
005170 *
005200  WORKING-STORAGE SECTION.
005300 *
005400  01   SWITCHES.
005500 *
005600       05  CARD-EOF-SWITCH    PIC X        VALUE 'N'.
005700 *
```

Figure 4-25   Excluding a block of lines (part 2 of 2)

X X line commands mark the lines to be excluded

```
EDIT - DLOWE.TEST.COBOL(REORDLST) - 01.02 -------------------- COLUMNS 007 078
COMMAND INPUT ===>                                              SCROLL ===> 5
014200          PERFORM 110-READ-INVENTORY-RECORD.
014300       IF CARD-EOF-SWITCH IS NOT EQUAL TO 'Y'
014400          PERFORM 120-CALCULATE-AVAILABLE-STOCK
014500          IF AVAILABLE-STOCK IS LESS THAN BF-REORDER-POINT
014600             PERFORM 130-PRINT-REORDER-LINE.
014700 *
014800  110-READ-INVENTORY-RECORD.
014900 *
XX           READ BFCRDS
015100          AT END
015200             MOVE 'Y' TO CARD-EOF-SWITCH.
015300       IF CARD-EOF-SWITCH IS NOT EQUAL TO 'Y'
XX             ADD 1 TO CARD-COUNT.
015500 *
015600  120-CALCULATE-AVAILABLE-STOCK.
015700 *
015800       ADD BF-ON-HAND BF-ON-ORDER
015900          GIVING AVAILABLE-STOCK
016000          ON SIZE ERROR
016100             DISPLAY 'REORDLST  CALCULATION ERROR FOR ITEM '
016200                'NO. ' BF-ITEM-NO '--CARD IGNORED'
016300             MOVE 99999 TO AVAILABLE-STOCK.
```

Figure 4-26   Redisplaying excluded lines (part 1 of 3)

The S line command tells how many lines to redisplay

```
EDIT - DLOWE.TEST.COBOL(REORDLST) - 01.02 -------------------- COLUMNS 007 078
COMMAND INPUT ===>                                              SCROLL ===> 5
014200          PERFORM 110-READ-INVENTORY-RECORD.
014300       IF CARD-EOF-SWITCH IS NOT EQUAL TO 'Y'
014400          PERFORM 120-CALCULATE-AVAILABLE-STOCK
014500          IF AVAILABLE-STOCK IS LESS THAN BF-REORDER-POINT
014600             PERFORM 130-PRINT-REORDER-LINE.
014700 *
014800  110-READ-INVENTORY-RECORD.
014900 *
S2- - - - - - - - - - - - - - - - - - - - 5 LINE(S) NOT DISPLAYED
015500 *
015600  120-CALCULATE-AVAILABLE-STOCK.
015700 *
015800       ADD BF-ON-HAND BF-ON-ORDER
015900          GIVING AVAILABLE-STOCK
016000          ON SIZE ERROR
016100             DISPLAY 'REORDLST  A  2  CALCULATION ERROR FOR ITEM '
016200                'NO. ' BF-ITEM-NO '--CARD IGNORED'
016300             MOVE 99999 TO AVAILABLE-STOCK.
016400 *
016500  130-PRINT-REORDER-LINE.
016600 *
016700       IF LINE-COUNT IS GREATER THAN LINES-ON-PAGE
```

Figure 4-26   Redisplaying excluded lines (part 2 of 3)

When you press the enter key, edit redisplays the two lines with the leftmost indentation (and the final line, since an S command won't leave just one line excluded)

```
EDIT - DLOWE.TEST.COBOL(REORDLST) - 01.02 ------------------- COLUMNS 007 078
COMMAND INPUT ===>                                            SCROLL ===> 5
014200        PERFORM 110-READ-INVENTORY-RECORD.
014300        IF CARD-EOF-SWITCH IS NOT EQUAL TO 'Y'
014400            PERFORM 120-CALCULATE-AVAILABLE-STOCK
014500            IF AVAILABLE-STOCK IS LESS THAN BF-REORDER-POINT
014600                PERFORM 130-PRINT-REORDER-LINE.
014700 *
014800   110-READ-INVENTORY-RECORD.
014900 *
015000        READ BFCRDS
- - - - - - - - - - - - - - - - - - - - - - - 2 LINE(S) NOT DISPLAYED
015300        IF CARD-EOF-SWITCH IS NOT EQUAL TO 'Y'
015400            ADD 1 TO CARD-COUNT.
015500 *
015600   120-CALCULATE-AVAILABLE-STOCK.
015700 *
015800        ADD BF-ON-HAND BF-ON-ORDER
015900            GIVING AVAILABLE-STOCK
016000            ON SIZE ERROR
016100                DISPLAY 'REORDLST  A  2  CALCULATION ERROR FOR ITEM '
016200                    'NO. ' BF-ITEM-NO '--CARD IGNORED'
016300                MOVE 99999 TO AVAILABLE-STOCK.
016400 *
```

Figure 4-26   Redisplaying excluded lines (part 3 of 3)

The FIND and CHANGE commands

Two editing commands, FIND and CHANGE, have nearly identical formats. Both are shown in figure 4-27. The operation of the FIND command under edit is the same as under browse, with the exception of the X/NX option (I'll explain that option in a few moments). You use the CHANGE command to find a character string and replace it with another string. The only difference in the format of the two commands is that you specify two strings for a CHANGE command, while a FIND command requires only one string. Since you already know how to use FIND, the rest of this section describes CHANGE.

The basic operation of a CHANGE command proceeds in two phases. First, an occurrence of string-1 is located just as if a FIND command were executing. Second, the located text is changed to string-2. For example, this command:

```
CHANGE ABC DEF
```

locates the string ABC and changes it to DEF.

The FIND/CHANGE command

$$\left\{\begin{matrix}\texttt{FIND}\\\texttt{CHANGE}\end{matrix}\right\} \texttt{ string-1 [string-2] } \left[\left\{\begin{matrix}\texttt{NEXT}\\\texttt{PREV}\\\texttt{FIRST}\\\texttt{LAST}\\\texttt{ALL}\end{matrix}\right\}\right] \left[\left\{\begin{matrix}\texttt{CHARS}\\\texttt{PREFIX}\\\texttt{SUFFIX}\\\texttt{WORD}\end{matrix}\right\}\right]$$

$$\left[\left\{\begin{matrix}\texttt{X}\\\texttt{NX}\end{matrix}\right\}\right] \texttt{[col-1 [col-2]]}$$

Explanation

FIND	Look for string-1 in the text.
CHANGE	Look for string-1 in the text and, if found, replace it with string-2.
string-1	The text string to be found. Must be in apostrophes or quotes if it contains spaces or commas. May be a hex string in the form X'hex-digits', a text string in the form T'text-string', or a picture string in the form P'picture-string'.
string-2	The replacement value for string-1. Must be in apostrophes or quotes if it contains spaces or commas. May be a hex value in the form X'hex-digits'. Valid only for CHANGE.
NEXT	Start search at current line and locate the next occurrence of string-1. (If neither PREV, FIRST, LAST, nor ALL is specified, NEXT is assumed.)
PREV	Start search at current line and locate the previous occurrence of string-1 (search backwards).
FIRST	Start search at top of data and locate the first occurrence of string-1.
LAST	Start search at bottom of data and locate the last occurrence of string-1 (search backwards).
ALL	Same as FIRST, but also indicate a count of the occurrences of string-1 in the file.

Figure 4-27   The FIND/CHANGE command (part 1 of 2)

Normally, you don't have to use quotes or apostrophes to enclose strings in a FIND or CHANGE command. However, if a string contains spaces, commas, quotes, or apostrophes, or if the string is the same as a keyword (like ALL), you must enclose it in quotes or apostrophes. If the string contains an

Explanation, continued

CHARS | Any occurence of string-1 satisfies the search. (If neither PREFIX, SUFFIX, nor WORD is specified, CHARS is assumed.)

PREFIX | String-1 must be at the beginning of a word to satisfy the search.

SUFFIX | String-1 must be at the end of a word to satisfy the search.

WORD | String-1 must be surrounded by spaces or special characters to satisfy the search.

X
NX | Controls the search of excluded lines. X says to search only excluded lines; NX says search only lines that are not excluded. (If neither X nor NX is coded, all lines—excluded or not—are searched.)

col-1 | Starting column number. If you specify col-1 but not col-2, string-1 must begin in col-1 to satisfy the search. (Default value is the current left boundary.)

col-2 | Ending column number. If specified, string-1 must start between col-1 and col-2 to satisfy the search. (Default value is the current right boundary.)

Figure 4-27 The FIND/CHANGE command (part 2 of 2)

apostrophe, enclose it in quotes, like this:

```
"VALUE 'TOTAL'"
```

Here, the string is VALUE 'TOTAL'. Likewise, if the string contains quotes, enclose it in apostrophes, like this:

```
'VALUE "TOTAL"'
```

Here, the string is VALUE "TOTAL". If you don't use quotes or apostrophes, the end of the string is marked by a space or comma.

How to change the search direction   You can change the search direction of a CHANGE command by specifying PREV, FIRST, LAST, or ALL. PREV means to search backwards; FIRST means start at the top of the data and search forwards; and LAST means start at the bottom of the data and search backwards. Regardless of the search direction, when the command finds string-1, it changes it to string-2.

The CHANGE command specifies the text change

```
EDIT - DLOWE.TEST.COBOL(REORDLST) - 01.02 -------------------- COLUMNS 007 078
COMMAND INPUT ===> CHANGE BF- INV- ALL                         SCROLL ===> HALF
002700  FILE SECTION.
002800  *
002900  FD  BFCRDS
003000      LABEL RECORDS ARE STANDARD
003100      RECORDING MODE IS F
003200      RECORD CONTAINS 80 CHARACTERS.
003300  *
003400  01  BAL-FWD-CARD.
003500  *
003600      05  BF-ITEM-NO        PIC 9(5).
003700      05  BF-ITEM-DESC      PIC X(20).
003800      05  FILLER            PIC X(5).
003900      05  BF-UNIT-PRICE     PIC 999V99.
004000      05  BF-REORDER-POINT  PIC 9(5).
004100      05  BF-ON-HAND        PIC 9(5).
004200      05  BF-ON-ORDER       PIC 9(5).
004300      05  FILLER            PIC X(30).
005100  *
005110  FD  ORDLST
005120      LABEL RECORDS ARE STANDARD
005130      RECORDING MODE IS F
005140      RECORD CONTAINS 133 CHARACTERS.
```

Figure 4-28   Using the CHANGE command (part 1 of 2)

When you press the enter key, edit changes the text

```
EDIT - DLOWE.TEST.COBOL(REORDLST) - 01.02 ---------------- PREFIX 'BF-' CHANGED
COMMAND INPUT ===>                                         SCROLL ===> HALF
002700  FILE SECTION.
002800  *
002900  FD  BFCRDS
003000      LABEL RECORDS ARE STANDARD
003100      RECORDING MODE IS F
003200      RECORD CONTAINS 80 CHARACTERS.
003300  *
003400  01  BAL-FWD-CARD.
003500  *
==CHG>      05  INV-ITEM-NO        PIC 9(5).
==CHG>      05  INV ITEM-DESC      PIC X(20).
003800      05  FILLER             PIC X(5).
==CHG>      05  INV-UNIT-PRICE     PIC 999V99.
==CHG>      05  INV-REORDER-POINT  PIC 9(5).
==CHG>      05  INV-ON-HAND        PIC 9(5).
==CHG>      05  INV-ON-ORDER       PIC 9(5).
004300      05  FILLER             PIC X(30).
005100  *
005110  FD  ORDLST
005120      LABEL RECORDS ARE STANDARD
005130      RECORDING MODE IS F
005140      RECORD CONTAINS 133 CHARACTERS.
```

Figure 4-28   Using the CHANGE command (part 2 of 2)

String-1	String-2	Text change			
BF-ITEM-NO	BF-ITEM-DESCR	Before:	05	BF-ITEM-NO	PIC X(20).
		After:	05	BF-ITEM-DESCR	PIC X(20).
		Before:	MOVE BF-ITEM-NO TO WS-ITEM.		
		After:	MOVE BF-ITEM-DESCR TO WS-ITEM.		
BF-ITEM-DESCR	BF-ITEM-NO	Before:	05	BF-ITEM-DESCR	PIC X(20).
		After:	05	BF-ITEM-NO	PIC X(20).
		Before:	MOVE BF-ITEM-DESCR TO WS-ITEM.		
		After:	MOVE BF-ITEM-NO TO WS-ITEM.		

Figure 4-29   Changes involving strings of different lengths

If you specify ALL on a CHANGE command, all occurrences of string-1 in the entire source member are changed to string-2. To illustrate, consider figure 4-28. Here, all occurrences of BF- are changed to INV-. Part 1 of figure 4-28 shows the edit display before the CHANGE command executes, while part 2 shows the effect of the CHANGE command. As you can see, six lines have been changed, and each is marked by ==CHG> in the line command area. That makes it easy to verify that your CHANGE command worked as you intended.

As this example shows, the CHANGE command doesn't require that string-1 and string-2 be the same length. If they aren't, CHANGE automatically adjusts the source line so that the change is made correctly. Figure 4-29 shows some more examples of changes involving strings of different lengths. If you'll study this figure for a moment, you'll see that text is shifted left or right to make up for differences in string length. However, this shifting occurs only within the word or words directly affected by the change. Data that isn't directly affected by the change isn't shifted unless necessary. As a result, column alignments are often—but not always—maintained.

How to specify a match condition, column limitations, or a string type   You can specify a match condition for string-1 by saying that string-1 must be a separate word (WORD), the start of a word (PREFIX), or the end of a word (SUFFIX). You can specify column limitations to say what columns are searched for string-1 (the default values are the current column boundaries). You can code either string as a hex value, and string-1 can be coded as a text or picture string. Chapter 3 describes each of these options in detail, so I won't describe them again here.

How to provide for excluded lines   One option that's not available for FIND under browse is X or NX. You use this option when you've excluded lines from the display. If you specify X on a FIND or CHANGE command under edit, only excluded lines are searched. If you say NX, only the lines that are *not* excluded are searched. If you don't say X or NX, all of the source member's lines—excluded or not—are searched by the FIND or CHANGE command.

How to shift source text

You use the group of commands shown in figure 4-30 to shift the contents of a line or group of lines one or more positions to the left or right. A common use for the shift commands is to change the indentation level of a group of source statements. In many cases, it's easier to use the 3270 delete and insert keys to shift data left or right. But when many lines of data are involved, the shift commands can be a real time-saver.

Edit provides two types of shift operations: column and data. A column shift is straightforward: data is simply moved a specified number of columns to the left or right. Data that is shifted beyond the right or left margin is lost, and spaces are inserted where needed.

A data shift is more complex, because SPF tries not to lose meaningful data. For a data shift, non-blank characters are never deleted. Words are not combined. And spaces within apostrophes are not deleted. Often, the effect of a column and data shift is the same. However, in cases where data might be lost, a data shift displays an error message instead of dropping the data. As a result, I recommend you normally use data shifting rather than column shifting.

Data shift command	Column shift command	Meaning
<	(	Shift this line left 2 positions.
<n	(n	Shift this line left n positions.
<<	((	Shift a block of lines left 2 positions.
<<n	((n	Shift a block of lines left n positions.
>	)	Shift this line right 2 positions.
>n	)n	Shift this line right n positions.
>>	))	Shift a block of lines right 2 positions.
>>n	))n	Shift a block of lines right n positions.

Figure 4-30   Line commands for shifting data

You indicate whether you want a column or a data shift by using a greater/less-than sign or a left or right parenthesis. If you use a greater-than (>) or less-than (<) sign, a data shift is performed. Parentheses cause a column shift.

To shift data on a single line, you use a single shift character. To shift data on multiple lines, you use a pair of shift commands, each consisting of two shift characters, just like other group line commands such as DD, CC, and so on. If you specify a number on the shift command, the data is shifted left or right the number of columns you specify. Otherwise, the data is shifted two columns.

To illustrate shifting, consider figure 4-31. Here, I shift a group of lines four characters to the right. In part 1, you can see the original data and the shift commands. In part 2, you can see the effect of the shift. Note that when you're shifting a block of code, you specify the number of columns on only one of the shift commands...it doesn't matter which one.

Another thing to note is that a shift command works only within the column boundaries, as shown in figure 4-32. In part 1, you can see the original text and the BOUNDS and shift commands. Part 2 shows the effect of the shift. Notice that data outside the boundaries isn't shifted.

External data sets

Edit provides several options that involve data sets or members other than the one you're editing. You can copy lines from

The >> line commands mark the first and last lines to be shifted right

```
EDIT - DLOWE.TEST.COBOL(REORDLST) - 01.02 -------------------- COLUMNS 007 078
COMMAND INPUT ===>                                             SCROLL ===> HALF
016900        MOVE BF-ITEM-NO          TO RL-ITEM-NO.
017000        MOVE BF-ITEM-DESC        TO RL-ITEM-DESC.
017100        MOVE BF-UNIT-PRICE       TO RL-UNIT-PRICE.
017200        MOVE AVAILABLE-STOCK     TO RL-AVAILABLE-STOCK.
017300        MOVE BF-REORDER-POINT    TO RL-REORDER-POINT.
017400        MOVE REORDER-LINE        TO PRINT-AREA.
017500        PERFORM 150-WRITE-REPORT-LINE.
017600        MOVE 1 TO SPACE-CONTROL.
017700 *
017800   140-PRINT-HEADING-LINES.
017900 *
>>            MOVE HDG-LINE-1 TO PRINT-AREA.
018100        PERFORM 160-WRITE-PAGE-TOP-LINE.
018200        MOVE HDG-LINE-2 TO PRINT-AREA.
018300        MOVE 2 TO SPACE-CONTROL.
018400        PERFORM 150-WRITE-REPORT-LINE.
018500        MOVE HDG-LINE-3 TO PRINT-AREA.
018600        MOVE 1 TO SPACE-CONTROL.
018700        PERFORM 150-WRITE-REPORT-LINE.
>>4           MOVE 2 TO SPACE-CONTROL.
018900 *
019000   150-WRITE-REPORT-LINE.
```

Figure 4-31   Shifting a block of lines (part 1 of 2)

When you press the enter key, edit shifts the lines 4 positions to the right

```
EDIT - DLOWE.TEST.COBOL(REORDLST) - 01.02 -------------------- COLUMNS 007 078
COMMAND INPUT ===>                                             SCROLL ===> HALF
016900        MOVE BF-ITEM-NO          TO RL-ITEM-NO.
017000        MOVE BF-ITEM-DESC        TO RL-ITEM-DESC.
017100        MOVE BF-UNIT-PRICE       TO RL-UNIT-PRICE.
017200        MOVE AVAILABLE-STOCK     TO RL-AVAILABLE-STOCK.
017300        MOVE BF-REORDER-POINT    TO RL-REORDER-POINT.
017400        MOVE REORDER-LINE        TO PRINT-AREA.
017500        PERFORM 150-WRITE-REPORT-LINE.
017600        MOVE 1 TO SPACE-CONTROL.
017700 *
017800   140-PRINT-HEADING-LINES.
017900 *
018000            MOVE HDG-LINE-1 TO PRINT-AREA.
018100            PERFORM 160-WRITE-PAGE-TOP-LINE.
018200            MOVE HDG-LINE-2 TO PRINT-AREA.
018300            MOVE 2 TO SPACE-CONTROL.
018400            PERFORM 150-WRITE-REPORT-LINE.
018500            MOVE HDG-LINE-3 TO PRINT-AREA.
018600            MOVE 1 TO SPACE-CONTROL.
018700            PERFORM 150-WRITE-REPORT-LINE.
018800            MOVE 2 TO SPACE-CONTROL.
018900 *
019000   150-WRITE-REPORT-LINE.
```

Figure 4-31   Shifting a block of lines (part 2 of 2)

The BNDS line shows the new column boundaries; the)) commands mark the lines to be shifted

```
EDIT - DLOWE.TEST.COBOL(REORDLST) - 01.02 ------------------- COLUMNS 007 078
COMMAND INPUT ===>                                            SCROLL ===> 10
010220        05  FILLER              PIC X(71)    VALUE SPACE.
010300 *
010400  01  REORDER-LINE.
010500 *
=BNDS>                                <                                    >
))            05  RL-CC               PIC X.
010700        05  RL-ITEM-NO          PIC Z(5).
010800        05  FILLER              PIC X(5)     VALUE SPACE.
010900        05  RL-ITEM-DESC        PIC X(20).
011000        05  FILLER              PIC X(5)     VALUE SPACE.
011100        05  RL-UNIT-PRICE       PIC ZZZ.99.
011200        05  FILLER              PIC X(5)     VALUE SPACE.
011300        05  RL-AVAILABLE-STOCK  PIC Z(5).
011400        05  FILLER              PIC X(5)     VALUE SPACE.
011500        05  RL-REORDER-POINT    PIC Z(5).
))4           05  FILLER              PIC X(71)    VALUE SPACE.
011700 *
011800  01  TOTAL-LINE.
011900 *
012000        05  TL-CC               PIC X.
012100        05  TL-CARD-COUNT       PIC ZZ,ZZZ.
012200        05  FILLER              PIC X(24)
```

Figure 4-32   Effect of a shift within boundaries (part 1 of 2)

When you press the enter key, edit shifts only the data within the boundaries

```
EDIT - DLOWE.TEST.COBOL(REORDLST) - 01.02 ------------------- COLUMNS 007 078
COMMAND INPUT ===>                                            SCROLL ===> 10
010220        05  FILLER              PIC X(71)    VALUE SPACE.
010300 *
010400  01  REORDER-LINE.
010500 *
=BNDS>                                <                                    >
010600        05  RL-CC               PIC X.
010700        05  RL-ITEM-NO          PIC Z(5).
010800        05  FILLER              PIC X(5)     VALUE SPACE.
010900        05  RL-ITEM-DESC        PIC X(20).
011000        05  FILLER              PIC X(5)     VALUE SPACE.
011100        05  RL-UNIT-PRICE       PIC ZZZ.99.
011200        05  FILLER              PIC X(5)     VALUE SPACE.
011300        05  RL-AVAILABLE-STOCK  PIC Z(5).
011400        05  FILLER              PIC X(5)     VALUE SPACE.
011500        05  RL-REORDER-POINT    PIC Z(5).
011600        05  FILLER              PIC X(71)    VALUE SPACE.
011700 *
011800  01  TOTAL-LINE.
011900 *
012000        05  TL-CC               PIC X.
012100        05  TL-CARD-COUNT       PIC ZZ,ZZZ.
012200        05  FILLER              PIC X(24)
```

Figure 4-32   Effect of a shift within boundaries (part 2 of 2)

another data set or member into the member you're editing. In SPF terminology, that's called *merging*. Or, you can copy lines from the member you're editing to another data set or member. That's called *segmenting*.

To merge or segment data, you use one of the primary commands summarized in figure 4-33 along with the MOVE/COPY line commands I showed you in topic 1 (C, M, A, and B). Because merge and segment operations are similar to copy and move operations, it's easy to confuse the two. So be sure to remember that the merge and segment commands I present here perform a different function than the MOVE and COPY line commands, even though they're used similarly.

How to merge data   To merge data from a data set or member into the member you're editing, you use a COPY or MOVE primary command (be careful not to confuse these commands with the C and M line commands I described in topic 1). For example, if you enter this command:

```
COPY BFCRDS
```

SPF searches the library you specified on the edit entry panel to locate the member named BFCRDS. Then, it copies that member into the member you're editing. If you enter this command:

```
MOVE BFCRDS
```

the effect is the same except that BFCRDS is deleted from the library after it's included in the member you're editing.

To indicate where the merged data should be placed, you use an A or B line command. These commands have the same meaning as when they're used for a line copy or move operation. Thus, A means place the data after the line containing the A command; B means place the data before the line. Normally, you enter the A or B command on the same panel as you enter the COPY or MOVE primary command. However, you can enter them on different panels if you wish.

Figure 4-34 shows an example of a copy operation. In part 1, you can see the A line command and the COPY primary command. Part 2 shows the result of the merge operation: the

Command	Meaning
COPY [member]	Copy the named member to the position marked by an A or B line command.
MOVE [member]	Copy the named member to the position marked by an A or B line command, then delete the original member.
CREATE [member]	Create a new member using the range of lines marked by C or M commands.
REPLACE [member]	Create a new member or replace an existing member using the range of lines marked by C or M commands.

Note: If member is omitted from any of these commands, a panel is displayed on which you must enter data set and member information.

Figure 4-33   Commands used for merging and segmenting data

text from BFCRDS follows the line that contained the A line command.

Normally, SPF searches the same library for the member you're editing and the member specified on the COPY or MOVE command. However, these members often aren't in the same library. For example, the source member REORDLST might be in a library named DLOWE.TEST.COBOL, while BFCRDS might be in DLOWE.COPY.COBOL.

SPF provides two ways to specify a different library for the COPY/MOVE member. The first is to list a series of concatenated libraries on the edit entry panel. Thus, you can enter these values on the entry panel:

```
PROJECT ===> DLOWE
LIBRARY ===> TEST      ===> COPY      ===>
TYPE    ===> COBOL
```

Then, the libraries DLOWE.TEST.COBOL and DLOWE.COPY.COBOL are searched in order.

Alternatively, you can omit the member name from the COPY or MOVE command. Then, edit responds with a panel like the one in figure 4-35. On it, you supply the data set and member name for the member to be merged. If you're not sure

The COPY command specifies the member to be copied; the A command marks its destination

```
 ┌──────────────────────────────────────────────────────────────────────────
 │ EDIT - DLOWE.TEST.COBOL(REORDLST) - 01.02 -------------------- COLUMNS 007 078
 │ COMMAND INPUT ===> COPY BFCRDS                              SCROLL ===> PAGE
 │ 002900  FD   BFCRDS
 │ 003000       LABEL RECORDS ARE STANDARD
 │ 003100       RECORDING MODE IS F
 │ A            RECORD CONTAINS 80 CHARACTERS.
 │ 005110  FD   ORDLST
 │ 005120       LABEL RECORDS ARE STANDARD
 │ 005130       RECORDING MODE IS F
 │ 005140       RECORD CONTAINS 133 CHARACTERS.
 │ 005150  *
 │ 005160  01   PRINT-AREA              PIC X(133).
 │ 005170  *
 │ 005200  WORKING-STORAGE SECTION.
 │ 005300  *
 │ 005400  01   SWITCHES.
 │ 005500  *
 │ 005600       05   CARD-EOF-SWITCH    PIC X         VALUE 'N'.
 │ 005700  *
 │ 005800  01   WORK-FIELDS.
 │ 005900  *
 │ 006000       05   AVAILABLE-STOCK    PIC S9(5)     COMP-3.
 │ 006100  *
 │ 006200  01   PRINT-FIELDS            COMP          SYNC.
```

Figure 4-34   Merging text (part 1 of 2)

When you press the enter key, edit copies the member BFCRDS into the member REORDLST

```
 ┌──────────────────────────────────────────────────────────────────────────
 │ EDIT - DLOWE.TEST.COBOL(REORDLST) - 01.02 ---------------- MEMBER BFCRDS COPIED
 │ COMMAND INPUT ===>                                      SCROLL ===> PAGE
 │ 002900  FD   BFCRDS
 │ 003000       LABEL RECORDS ARE STANDARD
 │ 003100       RECORDING MODE IS F
 │ 003200       RECORD CONTAINS 80 CHARACTERS.
 │ 003300  *
 │ 003400  01   BAL-FWD-CARD.
 │ 003500  *
 │ 003600       05   BF-ITEM-NO         PIC 9(5).
 │ 003700       05   BF-ITEM-DESC       PIC X(20).
 │ 003800       05   FILLER             PIC X(5).
 │ 003900       05   BF-UNIT-PRICE      PIC 999V99.
 │ 004000       05   BF-REORDER-POINT   PIC 9(5).
 │ 004100       05   BF-ON-HAND         PIC 9(5).
 │ 004200       05   BF-ON-ORDER        PIC 9(5).
 │ 004300       05   FILLER             PIC X(30).
 │ 004400  *
 │ 005110  FD   ORDLST
 │ 005120       LABEL RECORDS ARE STANDARD
 │ 005130       RECORDING MODE IS F
 │ 005140       RECORD CONTAINS 133 CHARACTERS.
 │ 005150  *
 │ 005160  01   PRINT-AREA              PIC X(133).
```

Figure 4-34   Merging text (part 2 of 2)

```
---------------------------------- EDIT - COPY --------------------------------------
 "CURRENT" DATASET: DLOWE.TEST.COBOL(REORDLST)

FROM SPF LIBRARY:
    PROJECT ===> DLOWE
    LIBRARY ===> TEST         ===>              ===>              ===>
    TYPE    ===> COBOL
    MEMBER  ===> BFCRDS

FROM OTHER PARTITIONED OR SEQUENTIAL DATASET:
    DATASET NAME   ===>
    VOLUME SERIAL  ===>            (IF NOT CATALOGED)

DATASET PASSWORD ===>             (IF PASSWORD PROTECTED)

LINE NUMBERS (BLANK FOR ENTIRE MEMBER OR SEQUENTIAL DATASET):
    FIRST LINE    ===>
    LAST LINE     ===>
    NUMBER TYPE   ===>            (STANDARD, COBOL, OR RELATIVE)

PRESS ENTER TO COPY
PRESS END KEY TO CANCEL COPY
```

Figure 4-35   The COPY entry panel

what library contains the member, you can list a series of
libraries for concatenation here, too.

    If you don't want to copy all of a member, you can
specify a range of line numbers. For example, if you enter
these values:

```
    FIRST LINE    ===> 1000
    LAST LINE     ===> 4000
    NUMBER TYPE   ===> COBOL
```

only lines 1000 to 4000 are copied. If the library type is
COBOL, you should say COBOL for NUMBER TYPE.
Otherwise, say STANDARD or RELATIVE. STANDARD
means the source member has non-COBOL numbering;
RELATIVE means the FIRST LINE and LAST LINE are
relative to the beginning of the member and have nothing to do
with line numbers in the member.

How to segment data   Segmenting data is the opposite of
merging data. Instead of copying or moving data from another
member into the member you're editing, data is copied or

moved from the member you're editing to another member. You can delete the text after it's segmented or leave it intact. And you can create a new member or replace an existing one.

You use one of two primary commands to segment data: CREATE or REPLACE. When you use CREATE, data is copied or moved from the member you're editing to a new member. If a member with the same name already exists, an error results. When you use REPLACE, an existing member is replaced. If a member with the same name doesn't exist, a new member is created. To avoid replacing data accidentally, you should use CREATE unless you're sure you want to replace an existing member.

To say what lines are segmented, you use the COPY or MOVE line commands, usually in block form (CC or MM). If you use MM, the lines you specify are deleted from the member you're editing after they're moved to the new member. If you use CC, they're not deleted.

Figure 4-36 shows an example of a create operation. In part 1, I've coded two CC line commands and a CREATE command. Part 2 of figure 4-36 shows the contents of the new member after the CREATE completes.

If you specify a member name on a CREATE command, the new member is always created in the first library you specify on the edit entry panel. To create a member in a different library, omit the member name from the CREATE command. Edit responds with a panel similar to the one in figure 4-35. On it, you specify any library or sequential data set.

Discussion

Although you probably won't use most of the features I've presented in this topic every day, I think you'll find them quite useful on occasion. In particular, the merge and segment functions can save you a lot of time when you reuse portions of an existing library member.

The CREATE command specifies the new member name; the CC commands mark the lines to be copied into the new member

```
EDIT - DLOWE.TEST.COBOL(REORDLST) - 01.02 ------------------- COLUMNS 007 078
COMMAND INPUT ===> CREATE PRTFD                               SCROLL ===> HALF
004000        05   BF-REORDER-POINT      PIC 9(5).
004100        05   BF-ON-HAND            PIC 9(5).
004200        05   BF-ON-ORDER           PIC 9(5).
004300        05   FILLER                PIC X(30).
CC       *
005110   FD  ORDLST
005120        LABEL RECORDS ARE STANDARD
005130        RECORDING MODE IS F
005140        RECORD CONTAINS 133 CHARACTERS.
005150   *
005160   01  PRINT-AREA                  PIC X(133).
CC       *
005200   WORKING-STORAGE SECTION.
005300   *
005400   01  SWITCHES.
005500   *
005600        05   CARD-EOF-SWITCH       PIC X        VALUE 'N'.
005700   *
005800   01  WORK-FIELDS.
005900   *
006000        05   AVAILABLE-STOCK       PIC S9(5)    COMP-3.
006100   *
```

Figure 4-36   Segmenting text (part 1 of 2)

The new member PRTFD

```
EDIT - DLOWE.TEST.COBOL(PRTFD) - 01.00 -------------------- COLUMNS 007 078
COMMAND INPUT ===>                                          SCROLL ===> HALF
****** *************************** TOP OF DATA ******************************
004400   *
005110   FD  ORDLST
005120        LABEL RECORDS ARE STANDARD
005130        RECORDING MODE IS F
005140        RECORD CONTAINS 133 CHARACTERS.
005150   *
005160   01  PRINT-AREA                  PIC X(133).
005170   *
****** *************************** BOTTOM OF DATA ***************************
```

Figure 4-36   Segmenting text (part 2 of 2)

Terminology

merge
segment

Objective

Edit a data set, using the commands described in this topic to do the following:

a. change a text string to a different string of characters.

b. exclude lines.

c. shift data.

d. add data from an existing member to the member you're editing.

e. create a new member or replace an existing one using data from the member you're editing.

Chapter 5

How to perform utility functions

When you select option 3 from the primary option menu, SPF displays the utility selection menu shown in figure 5-1. This chapter shows you how to use most of the utilities available from this menu. It's divided into four topics. Topic 1 shows you how to maintain partitioned data sets using the library utility. Topic 2 shows you how to allocate, rename, delete, catalog, or uncatalog sequential or partitioned data sets using the data set utility. Topic 3 covers the move/copy utility and the hardcopy utility. Together, these utilities let you copy and print data sets. And topic 4 shows you how to list catalog and VTOC entries using the catalog and VTOC utilities.

Three of the utilities available from the menu in figure 5-1 aren't covered in this chapter. Option 5, the reset utility, lets you control the defaults for values like the version number of a member. Since you won't have to do this often...and since it's easy to figure out how to do once you've used some of the other utilities...I don't cover the reset utility in this book. Option 8, the outlist utility, is used when you submit background jobs. I cover it in chapter 7 along with other SPF features used for background processing. Finally, option 9 provides an interface with a word processing system, SCRIPT/VS. I don't cover SCRIPT/VS or option 9 anywhere in this book.

```
------------------------- UTILITY SELECTION MENU -----------------------------
SELECT OPTION ===>

     1  LIBRARY     - LIBRARY UTILITY:
                          PRINT INDEX LISTING OR ENTIRE DATASET
                          PRINT, RENAME, DELETE, OR BROWSE MEMBERS
                          COMPRESS DATASET
     2  DATASET     - DATASET UTILITY:
                          DISPLAY DATASET INFORMATION
                          ALLOCATE, RENAME, OR DELETE ENTIRE DATASET
                          CATALOG OR UNCATALOG DATASET
     3  MOVE/COPY   - MOVE OR COPY MEMBERS OR DATASETS
     4  CATALOG     - CATALOG MANAGEMENT:
                          DISPLAY OR PRINT CATALOG ENTRIES
                          INITIALIZE OR DELETE USER CATALOG ALIAS
     5  RESET       - RESET STATISTICS FOR MEMBERS OF SPF LIBRARY
     6  HARDCOPY    - INITIATE HARDCOPY OUTPUT
     7  VTOC        - DISPLAY OR PRINT VTOC ENTRIES FOR A DASD VOLUME
     8  OUTLIST     - DISPLAY, DELETE, OR PRINT HELD JOB OUTPUT
     9  SCRIPT/VS   - FORMAT, DISPLAY, AND OPTIONALLY PRINT SCRIPT TEXT
```

Figure 5-1   The utility option menu

TOPIC 1   The library utility

The library utility, option 1 on the utility selection menu, lets you perform a variety of operations on partitioned data sets and their members. With the library utility, you can compress a library, print a library index, print a member or an entire library, rename or delete a member, or browse a member.

The library utility has two entry panels. The first, shown in figure 5-2, lets you perform a single operation on an entire library or a specific member. The second panel is a member selection list that lets you perform several operations at once on more than one member.

The library entry panel

On the library entry panel, you enter the name of the partitioned data set you wish to process and a one-character code indicating the function you wish to perform. There are seven function codes you can enter. The codes and their meanings are:

C   Compress the library

X   Print an index listing

L   Print the entire library

P   Print a specific member

R   Rename a member

D   Delete a member

B   Browse a member

For the first three functions, you don't enter a member name because the functions operate on an entire library. The other four functions operate on a specific member, so you must specify a member name.

```
-------------------------------- LIBRARY UTILITY  -------------------------------
SELECT OPTION ===>

   C - COMPRESS DATASET              P - PRINT MEMBER
   X - PRINT INDEX LISTING           R - RENAME MEMBER
   L - PRINT ENTIRE DATASET          D - DELETE MEMBER
   BLANK - DISPLAY MEMBER LIST       B - BROWSE MEMBER

SPF LIBRARY:
   PROJECT ===>
   LIBRARY ===>
   TYPE    ===>
   MEMBER  ===>           (IF OPTION "P", "R", "D", OR "B" SELECTED)
   NEWNAME ===>           (IF OPTION "R" SELECTED)

OTHER PARTITIONED OR SEQUENTIAL DATASET:
   DATASET NAME   ===>
   VOLUME SERIAL  ===>          (IF NOT CATALOGED)

DATASET PASSWORD ===>          (IF PASSWORD PROTECTED)
```

Figure 5-2   The library utility entry panel

Alternatively, you can omit the function code. Then, SPF displays a member selection list. On it, you can specify P, R, D, or B for each member. In a few moments, I'll show you how to print, rename, delete, or browse members using the member selection list. But first, I'll give you examples of compressing a library, printing an index listing, and printing an entire library.

How to compress a library   As you may know, a partitioned data set consists of an *index* (or *directory*) followed by one or more members. Whenever you edit and save a member, the new version of the member is added to the end of the PDS and the index is updated to point to the member's new location. The space occupied by the old version of the member becomes unusable. As a result, a PDS can soon become filled with unusable space. To reclaim this unusable space, you must *compress* the library. It's important that you compress your libraries often. If you don't, they'll quickly use up all of the space allocated to them.

When you compress a PDS, all of its members are moved to the beginning of the PDS (right after the index). Then, the space that was unusable is released so it can be used again. The

```
--------------------------- LIBRARY UTILITY ---------------------------
SELECT OPTION ===> C

   C - COMPRESS DATASET                 P - PRINT MEMBER
   X - PRINT INDEX LISTING              R - RENAME MEMBER
   L - PRINT ENTIRE DATASET             D - DELETE MEMBER
   BLANK - DISPLAY MEMBER LIST          B - BROWSE MEMBER

SPF LIBRARY:
   PROJECT  ===> DLOWE
   LIBRARY  ===> TEST
   TYPE     ===> COBOL
   MEMBER   ===>            (IF OPTION "P", "R", "D", OR "B" SELECTED)
   NEWNAME  ===>            (IF OPTION "R" SELECTED)

OTHER PARTITIONED OR SEQUENTIAL DATASET:
   DATASET NAME   ===>
   VOLUME SERIAL  ===>.          (IF NOT CATALOGED)

DATASET PASSWORD ===>             (IF PASSWORD PROTECTED)
```

Figure 5-3   Compressing a library

library utility invokes a standard OS utility program named
IEBCOPY to compress a library.

Figure 5-3 shows how to compress a PDS using the library
utility. Here, I enter C in the command input area and specify
the library's name. Since a compress operation applies to an
entire library, I don't specify a member name in figure 5-3.
When the library is compressed, SPF displays a message
indicating that the compression was successful.

How to print an index   A PDS index contains the name
and statistics for each member of a partitioned data set. You can
obtain a listing of an index by specifying X in the command
input area of the library utility panel. The listing is added to the
SPF list file and may be routed to a printer when you terminate
SPF.

Figure 5-4 shows the output that results when you print
the index of a source library. At the top of the listing, the
library utility provides general data set information: volume
serial number, device type, space allocation, and so on. For
each member, the listing shows the version and modification
level, the creation date and modification date and time, the

```
PROJECT: DLOWE                                                        DATE: 84/02/21
LIBRARY: TEST                                                         TIME: 13:36
TYPE:    COBOL                                                        PAGE: 001

GENERAL DATA:                      GENERAL DATA:              CURRENT ALLOCATION:      CURRENT UTILIZATION:
  VOLUME SERIAL: MPS600              RECORD FORMAT:    FB        20 TRACKS               13 TRACKS
  DEVICE TYPE:   3350                RECORD LENGTH:    80        2 EXTENTS                2 EXTENTS
  ORGANIZATION:  PO                  BLOCK SIZE:    3,120        20 DIRECTORY BLOCKS      3 DIRECTORY BLOCKS
  CREATION DATE: 84/01/05            1ST EXTENT SIZE:  10                                16 MEMBERS
                                     SECONDARY QUAN:   10
```

MEMBER NAME	VERS.MOD LEVEL	CREATION DATE	DATE AND TIME LAST MODIFIED	CURRENT NO. LINES	INITIAL NO. LINES	MODIFIED NO. LINES	USER ID
BFCRDS	01.00	84/01/30	84/01/30 18:12	12	12	0	DLOWE
INVLST	01.00	84/01/26	84/01/26 14:29	202	202	0	DLOWE
ORDLST2	01.00	84/01/05	84/01/05 15:44	9	9	0	DLOWE
PRTFD	01.00	84/01/30	84/01/30 18:16	8	8	0	DLOWE
REORDLST	01.03	84/01/26	84/02/17 13:09	202	202	0	DLOWE
RNDUPDT	01.00	84/01/26	84/01/26 14:29	202	202	0	DLOWE
SEQUPDT	01.00	84/01/05	84/01/05 16:44	9	9	0	DLOWE
VSEMAINT	01.00	84/01/05	84/01/05 16:44	9	9	0	DLOWE
VSESMNT2	01.00	84/01/05	84/01/05 16:44	9	9	0	DLOWE
VSESRUPT	01.00	84/01/05	84/01/05 16:44	9	9	0	DLOWE
VSKSMNT	01.00	84/01/26	84/01/26 14:29	202	202	0	DLOWE
VSKSRUPT	01.00	84/01/05	84/01/05 16:44	9	9	0	DLOWE
VSKSSUPT	01.00	84/01/05	84/01/05 16:44	9	9	0	DLOWE
VSRRMNT	01.00	84/01/26	84/01/26 14:29	202	202	0	DLOWE
VSRRRUPT	01.00	84/01/05	84/01/05 16:44	9	9	0	DLOWE
VSRRSUPT	01.00	84/01/26	84/01/26 14:29	202	202	0	DLOWE
MAXIMUMS:	01.03	84/01/20	84/02/17 13:09	202	202	0	
TOTALS:				1,304	1,304	0	

END OF MEMBER LIST

Figure 5-4 A library index listing

```
UTILITIES --- DLOWE.TEST.COBOL ------------------------------------------
COMMAND INPUT ===>                                    SCROLL ===> PAGE
   NAME     RENAME  VER.MOD   CREATED    LAST MODIFIED  SIZE  INIT  MOD  ID
   BFCRDS            01.00   84/01/30  84/01/30 18:12   12    12    0  DLOWE
   INVLST            01.00   84/01/26  84/01/26 14:29   202   202   0  DLOWE
   ORDLST2           01.00   84/01/05  84/01/05 16:44   9     9     0  DLOWE
   PRTFD             01.00   84/01/30  84/01/30 18:16   8     8     0  DLOWE
   REORDLST          01.02   84/01/26  84/01/30 13:58   202   202   0  DLOWE
   RNDUPDT           01.00   84/01/26  84/01/26 14:29   202   202   0  DLOWE
   SEQUPTD           01.00   84/01/05  84/01/05 16:44   9     9     0  DLOWE
   VSESMNT           01.00   84/01/05  84/01/05 16:44   9     9     0  DLOWE
   VSESMNT2          01.00   84/01/05  84/01/05 16:44   9     9     0  DLOWE
   VSESRUPT          01.00   84/01/05  84/01/05 16:44   9     9     0  DLOWE
   VSESSUPT          01.00   84/01/26  84/01/26 14:29   202   202   0  DLOWE
   VSKSMNT           01.00   84/01/26  84/01/26 14:29   202   202   0  DLOWE
   VSKSRUPT          01.00   84/01/05  84/01/05 16:44   9     9     0  DLOWE
   VSKSSUPT          01.00   84/01/05  84/01/05 16:44   9     9     0  DLOWE
   VSRRMNT           01.00   84/01/26  84/01/26 14:29   202   202   0  DLOWE
   VSRRRUPT          01.00   84/01/05  84/01/05 16:44   9     9     0  DLOWE
   VSRRSUPT          01.00   84/01/26  84/01/26 14:29   202   202   0  DLOWE
   **END**
```

Figure 5-5   A library utility member list

number of lines currently in the member, the number of lines in the member when it was created, the number of lines modified, and the user-id of the user who created the member.

How to print a library   If you specify L in the command input area of the library utility panel, the entire library is printed. Normally, you want to print only a specific member, so you won't use this function often.

The library member list

As I mentioned earlier, if you leave the command input area blank on the library utility entry panel, SPF displays a member list like the one in figure 5-5. This member list looks much like the member lists for browse and edit, except that it provides space for you to enter a command and, optionally, a new member name for each member. Although you can print, rename, delete, or browse a specific member from the previous entry panel, I think it's easier to do these functions from the member list.

How to print, rename, and delete members   Figure 5-6 gives an example of printing, renaming, and deleting members of a PDS using the member list. In part 1, I specify three functions: P for member REORDLST, R for VSESMNT, and D for VSESSUPT. In addition, I specify a new name for member VSESMNT: VSEMAINT.

Part 2 of figure 5-6 shows the member list after the print, rename, and delete functions have been processed. As you can see, the library utility uses the RENAME column to indicate the status of each member: REORDLST has been printed, VSESMNT has been renamed, and VSESSUPT has been deleted.

How to browse a member   If you specify B next to a member, SPF enters browse mode. You can then examine the member using any of the browse commands I described in chapter 3. When you terminate browse, the library utility panel is redisplayed.

Discussion

When compared with OS utility programs or TSO commands, SPF's library utility makes library maintenance easy. However, there are a few important library maintenance functions that aren't provided by the library utility. In particular, you have to use the allocation option of the data set utility to create a new library or to rename or delete an existing library (I describe the data set utility in topic 2 of this chapter). And to change library statistics, you have to use the reset utility (not covered in this book).

Terminology

index
directory
compress a library

Screen 1: Specify the changes to be made

```
UTILITIES --- DLOWE.TEST.COBOL --------------------------------------------------
COMMAND INPUT ===>                                           SCROLL ===> PAGE
    NAME       RENAME    VER.MOD   CREATED    LAST MODIFIED   SIZE  INIT  MOD   ID
    BFCRDS               01.00    84/01/30   84/01/30 18:12    12    12    0   DLOWE
    INVLST               01.00    84/01/26   84/01/26 14:29   202   202    0   DLOWE
    ORDLST2              01.00    84/01/05   84/01/05 16:44     9     9    0   DLOWE
    PRTFD                01.00    84/01/30   84/01/30 18:16     8     8    0   DLOWE
  P REORDLST             01.02    84/01/26   84/01/30 13:58   202   202    0   DLOWE
    RNDUPDT              01.00    84/01/26   84/01/26 14:29   202   202    0   DLOWE
    SEQUPTD              01.00    84/01/05   84/01/05 16:44     9     9    0   DLOWE
  R VSESMNT   VSEMAINT   01.00    84/01/05   84/01/05 16:44     9     9    0   DLOWE
    VSESMNT2             01.00    84/01/05   84/01/05 16:44     9     9    0   DLOWE
    VSESRUPT             01.00    84/01/05   84/01/05 16:44     9     9    0   DLOWE
  D VSESSUPT             01.00    84/01/26   84/01/26 14:29   202   202    0   DLOWE
    VSKSMNT              01.00    84/01/26   84/01/26 14:29   202   202    0   DLOWE
    VSKSRUPT             01.00    84/01/05   84/01/05 16:44     9     9    0   DLOWE
    VSKSSUPT             01.00    84/01/05   84/01/05 16:44     9     9    0   DLOWE
    VSRRMNT              01.00    84/01/26   84/01/26 14:29   202   202    0   DLOWE
    VSRRRUPT             01.00    84/01/05   84/01/05 16:44     9     9    0   DLOWE
    VSRRSUPT             01.00    84/01/26   84/01/26 14:29   202   202    0   DLOWE
    **END**
```

Figure 5-6   Printing, renaming, and deleting members (part 1 of 2)

Screen 2: The messages show that the changes have been made

```
UTILITIES --- DLOWE.TEST.COBOL --------------------------------------------------
COMMAND INPUT ===>                                           SCROLL ===> PAGE
    NAME       RENAME    VER.MOD   CREATED    LAST MODIFIED   SIZE  INIT  MOD   ID
    BFCRDS               01.00    84/01/30   84/01/30 18:12    12    12    0   DLOWE
    INVLST               01.00    84/01/26   84/01/26 14:29   202   202    0   DLOWE
    ORDLST2              01.00    84/01/05   84/01/05 16:44     9     9    0   DLOWE
    PRTFD                01.00    84/01/30   84/01/30 18:16     8     8    0   DLOWE
    REORDLST  *PRINTED   01.02    84/01/26   84/01/30 13:58   202   202    0   DLOWE
    RNDUPDT              01.00    84/01/26   84/01/26 14:29   202   202    0   DLOWE
    SEQUPTD              01.00    84/01/05   84/01/05 16:44     9     9    0   DLOWE
    VSESMNT   *RENAMED
    VSESMNT2             01.00    84/01/05   84/01/05 16:44     9     9    0   DLOWE
    VSESRUPT             01.00    84/01/05   84/01/05 16:44     9     9    0   DLOWE
    VSESSUPT  *DELETED
    VSKSMNT              01.00    84/01/26   84/01/26 14:29   202   202    0   DLOWE
    VSKSRUPT             01.00    84/01/05   84/01/05 16:44     9     9    0   DLOWE
    VSKSSUPT             01.00    84/01/05   84/01/05 16:44     9     9    0   DLOWE
    VSRRMNT              01.00    84/01/26   84/01/26 14:29   202   202    0   DLOWE
    VSRRRUPT             01.00    84/01/05   84/01/05 16:44     9     9    0   DLOWE
    VSRRSUPT             01.00    84/01/26   84/01/26 14:29   202   202    0   DLOWE
    **END**
```

Figure 5-6   Printing, renaming, and deleting members (part 2 of 2)

Objectives

1. Use the library utility to compress a PDS.

2. Use the library utility to print (1) a PDS index and (2) all the members in a PDS.

3. Use the library utility to print, rename, delete, and browse PDS members.

TOPIC 2   The data set utility

The data set utility lets you perform a variety of functions for non-VSAM data sets. You can allocate, rename, delete, catalog, or uncatalog sequential or partitioned data sets using this utility. Or you can simply display information about a data set. You enter the data set utility by specifying option 2 from the utility selection menu.

When you enter the data set utility, SPF displays the panel shown in figure 5-7. If you enter a data set name here and press the enter key, SPF responds with a panel that shows information about the data set. Alternatively, you can enter a one-character code that indicates a utility function you wish to perform. The valid codes and their meanings are:

A   Allocate a new data set

R   Rename an existing data set

D   Delete an existing data set

C   Catalog an existing data set

U   Uncatalog an existing data set

Now, I'll explain how to perform each of these utility functions.

How to display data set information

As I already said, if you don't enter an option code, SPF displays data set information for the data set you specified on the entry panel. Figure 5-8 shows a typical display of data set information. In addition to general data set information such as record length and block size, this panel shows allocation and current utilization information. I'll explain what this information means next, when I describe the allocate function.

```
-------------------------------- DATASET UTILITY --------------------------------
SELECT OPTION ===>

    A - ALLOCATE NEW DATASET              C - CATALOG DATASET
    R - RENAME ENTIRE DATASET             U - UNCATALOG DATASET
    D - DELETE ENTIRE DATASET
    BLANK - DISPLAY DATASET INFORMATION

SPF LIBRARY:
    PROJECT ===> DLOWE
    LIBRARY ===> TEST
    TYPE    ===> COBOL

OTHER PARTITIONED OR SEQUENTIAL DATASET:
    DATASET NAME  ===>
    VOLUME SERIAL ===>             (IF NOT CATALOGED, REQUIRED FOR OPTION "C")

DATASET PASSWORD ===>             (IF PASSWORD PROTECTED)
```

Figure 5-7   The data set utility entry panel

```
-------------------------------- DATASET INFORMATION --------------------------------
DATASET NAME: DLOWE.TEST.COBOL

GENERAL DATA:                           CURRENT ALLOCATION:
    VOLUME SERIAL:      MPS600              ALLOCATED TRACKS:      20
    DEVICE TYPE:        3350                ALLOCATED EXTENTS:      2
    ORGANIZATION:       PO                  MAXIMUM DIR. BLOCKS:   20
    RECORD FORMAT:      FB
    RECORD LENGTH:      80
    BLOCK SIZE:         3120             CURRENT UTILIZATION:
    1ST EXTENT TRACKS:  10                  USED TRACKS:           13
    SECONDARY TRACKS:   10                  USED EXTENTS:           2
                                            USED DIR. BLOCKS:       3
    CREATION DATE:      84/01/05            NUMBER OF MEMBERS:     16
```

Figure 5-8   A data set information display

How to allocate a sequential data set

Before you can use a data set on an MVS system, you must allocate it. When you allocate a data set, you tell the system the data set's name, its characteristics such as its organization and the length of its records, and how much space it will require. The system then sets aside direct-access space for your file and adds your file's name to its catalog.

To allocate a data set under SPF, you enter the data set name on the data set utility panel and select option A. If a data set already exists with that name, SPF displays an error message. Otherwise, SPF displays the allocate panel, shown in figure 5-9. Here, I'm allocating a sequential data set.

How to specify a volume   If you want to place a data set on a specific volume, you must enter that volume's serial number in the VOLUME SERIAL field. If you leave this field blank, MVS automatically selects a default volume on which the data set is created. Normally, you don't specify the volume serial number.

How to specify space requirements   SPACE UNITS, PRIMARY QUAN, and SECONDARY QUAN work together to specify how much space should be allocated to the data set. The SPACE UNITS field determines the unit of measure for the other two fields. You may allocate space in blocks, tracks, or cylinders of data by specifying BLKS, TRKS, or CYLS.

As a general rule, the primary quantity field (PRIMARY QUAN) should be the amount of space you think the data set will require. In figure 5-9, for example, I think the data set will require five cylinders of disk space.

To allow for errors in estimation or changes in requirements, the secondary quantity field (SECONDARY QUAN) allows for extensions to the primary allocation. Then, if the primary allocation of space isn't large enough for the data set, the secondary allocation is made. If this still isn't enough space, the secondary allocation is repeated until 15 secondary allocations have been made. After that, the only way to allocate more space to the file is to copy or move it to a data set with a larger allocation.

In figure 5-9, I specified five cylinders of primary space and one cylinder of secondary space. As a result, the largest

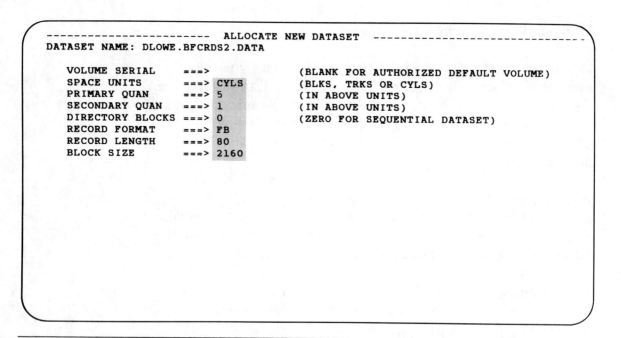

```
----------------------- ALLOCATE NEW DATASET -----------------------------
DATASET NAME: DLOWE.BFCRDS2.DATA

     VOLUME SERIAL      ===>              (BLANK FOR AUTHORIZED DEFAULT VOLUME)
     SPACE UNITS        ===> CYLS         (BLKS, TRKS OR CYLS)
     PRIMARY QUAN       ===> 5            (IN ABOVE UNITS)
     SECONDARY QUAN     ===> 1            (IN ABOVE UNITS)
     DIRECTORY BLOCKS   ===> 0            (ZERO FOR SEQUENTIAL DATASET)
     RECORD FORMAT      ===> FB
     RECORD LENGTH      ===> 80
     BLOCK SIZE         ===> 2160
```

Figure 5-9   Allocating a sequential data set

this file can become is 20 cylinders: five for the primary allocation, and one for each of the 15 secondary allocations. (Incidentally, each allocation—both primary and secondary—is called an *extent*. A data set can have up to 16 extents: one primary and 15 secondary.)

How to specify data set characteristics   The RECORD FORMAT, RECORD LENGTH, and BLOCK SIZE fields let you specify data set characteristics. RECORD FORMAT is normally FB, indicating that the file contains fixed-length, blocked records. It can also be F for fixed-length, unblocked records, or VB or V for variable-length, blocked or unblocked records. RECORD LENGTH, simply enough, specifies the length of each record. BLOCK SIZE should be a multiple of RECORD LENGTH.

How to choose an efficient block size   One of the problems of allocating data sets is deciding what value to use for the block size. For various reasons too complicated to explain here, it generally isn't possible to utilize 100% of the storage space available in each track of direct-access storage. Exactly

3330		3350	
Block size	**Records/track**	**Block size**	**Records/track**
2000	150	2160	216
3120	156	3600	225
6320	158	6160	231

Figure 5-10 Optimum block sizes for 80-byte records on 3330 and 3350 devices

what percentage of direct-access space can be utilized depends on the characteristics of the individual device and the block size of the file. As a result, when you choose the block size for your file, you determine how efficiently that file will utilize direct-access space. Usually, a 95% utilization is considered excellent.

Because each type of direct-access device has different characteristics, a block size that is efficient for one type of device may waste a great deal of space on a different device type. For example, suppose you want to allocate a source library that will contain 10,000 80-byte records. You choose a block size of 3120—that's 39 80-byte records in each block. If the disk device is a 3330, you'll use about 95% of the available space on each track. That's an efficient utilization of disk space. However, the same file on a 3350 device will use only 82% of the available disk space. That's not an efficient utilization of disk space.

Determining the best block size for a file of any given record length on any given device type is a complex task. Fortunately, most data sets you'll allocate under SPF will contain 80-byte records. And although IBM manufactures many different types of disk devices, the 3330 and the 3350 are the most commonly used devices in MVS installations. Selecting the best block size for a file containing 80-byte records on a 3330 or a 3350 is a manageable task. Figure 5-10 lists the block sizes that use disk space most efficiently for files of this type. If you select one of these values, you'll know you're not wasting disk space.

Figure 5-10 also shows the number of records per track for each block size listed. So, if you select a block size of 6160 for a 3350, 231 records are stored in each track. To determine the number of tracks to allocate for a data set, just divide the number of records per track for the block size you select into the number of records in the file and round the result up. For example, a 10,000-record data set with a block size of 6160 on a 3350 requires 44 tracks (10,000 / 231 = 43.29).

How to use default allocation values   Quite frankly, it's difficult at times to remember the correct coding for all of the allocation values for a data set. Fortunately, SPF allows you to model a new data set after an existing one. To do this, simply display the data set information for an existing file. Then, allocate a new data set. SPF remembers the information it displayed for the existing file and supplies it as default values for the new data set.

How to allocate a partitioned data set

Figure 5-11 shows an example of allocating a partitioned data set. The only difference between allocating a sequential and a partitioned data set is the DIRECTORY BLOCKS field. This field indicates how many 256-byte directory blocks should be allocated for the library. If you specify zero for this field, the data set is assumed to be sequential. If you enter a non-zero value, the data set will be partitioned.

The value you enter in the DIRECTORY BLOCKS field depends on the number of members you expect in the library and whether the library contains standard or non-standard members. If the library contains standard SPF source members (members that have SPF statistics), each directory block can accommodate seven member entries. So if you expect 40 members, you should allocate at least six directory blocks.

If the library contains non-standard SPF source members (members that don't have SPF statistics), each directory block can hold up to 21 member entries. Thus, only two directory blocks are required for a 40-member library. (You use the edit profile as described in topic 2 of chapter 4 to control the generation of SPF statistics in source members.)

If you are allocating a *load library* (a load library contains executable programs), allow four members per directory block.

```
---------------------- ALLOCATE NEW DATASET  -------------------------
DATASET NAME: DLOWE.TEST2.COBOL

       VOLUME SERIAL     ===>            (BLANK FOR AUTHORIZED DEFAULT VOLUME)
       SPACE UNITS       ===> TRKS       (BLKS, TRKS OR CYLS)
       PRIMARY QUAN      ===> 10         (IN ABOVE UNITS)
       SECONDARY QUAN    ===> 10         (IN ABOVE UNITS)
       DIRECTORY BLOCKS  ===> 20         (ZERO FOR SEQUENTIAL DATASET)
       RECORD FORMAT     ===> FB
       RECORD LENGTH     ===> 80
       BLOCK SIZE        ===> 3120
```

Figure 5-11   Allocating a partitioned data set

Thus, ten directory blocks are required for a 40-member load
library. Depending on the attributes of each load module, more
than four entries might fit into each block. But four entries per
block is the safest way to compute directory size for a load
library.

How to rename a data set

Figure 5-12 shows how to change the name of a data set. In
part 1, I specify the rename function (R) and the old data set
name. SPF then displays the panel in part 2. When I enter the
new data set name and press the enter key, the data set name is
changed and the catalog is updated.

How to delete a data set

Figure 5-13 shows how to delete a data set. In part 1, I enter
the delete code (D) and the data set name. Then, SPF displays
the confirmation panel shown in part 2. If I press enter at this

Screen 1: **Specify the rename option and the current data set information**

```
---------------------------- DATASET UTILITY -------------- DATASET ALLOCATED
SELECT OPTION ===>  R

   A - ALLOCATE NEW DATASET                 C - CATALOG DATASET
   R - RENAME ENTIRE DATASET                U - UNCATALOG DATASET
   D - DELETE ENTIRE DATASET
   BLANK - DISPLAY DATASET INFORMATION

SPF LIBRARY:
   PROJECT ===> DLOWE
   LIBRARY ===> TEST2
   TYPE    ===> COBOL

OTHER PARTITIONED OR SEQUENTIAL DATASET:
   DATASET NAME  ===>
   VOLUME SERIAL ===>              (IF NOT CATALOGED, REQUIRED FOR OPTION "C")

DATASET PASSWORD ===>             (IF PASSWORD PROTECTED)
```

Figure 5-12   Renaming a data set (part 1 of 2)

Screen 2: **Specify the new data set name**

```
---------------------------- RENAME DATASET ----------------------------------
DATASET NAME: DLOWE.TEST2.COBOL
VOLUME:      MPS600

ENTER NEW NAME BELOW:

SPF LIBRARY:
   PROJECT ===> DLOWE
   LIBRARY ===> TESTGL
   TYPE    ===> COBOL

OTHER PARTITIONED OR SEQUENTIAL DATASET:
   DATASET NAME  ===>

(THE DATASET WILL BE RENAMED AND RECATALOGED)
```

Figure 5-12   Renaming a data set (part 2 of 2)

Screen 1:   Specify the delete option and the data set information

```
------------------------------- DATASET UTILITY ---------------- DATASET RENAMED
 SELECT OPTION ===> D

    A - ALLOCATE NEW DATASET              C - CATALOG DATASET
    R - RENAME ENTIRE DATASET             U - UNCATALOG DATASET
    D - DELETE ENTIRE DATASET
    BLANK - DISPLAY DATASET INFORMATION

 SPF LIBRARY:
    PROJECT ===> DLOWE
    LIBRARY ===> TESTGL
    TYPE    ===> COBOL

 OTHER PARTITIONED OR SEQUENTIAL DATASET:
    DATASET NAME  ===>
    VOLUME SERIAL ===>            (IF NOT CATALOGED, REQUIRED FOR OPTION "C")

 DATASET PASSWORD ===>           (IF PASSWORD PROTECTED)
```

Figure 5-13   Deleting a data set (part 1 of 2)

Screen 2:   Confirm or cancel the delete request

```
------------------------------- CONFIRM DELETE -------------------------------------
 DATASET NAME:  DLOWE.TESTGL.COBOL
 VOLUME:        MPS600
 CREATION DATE: 84/02/09


              PRESS ENTER TO CONFIRM DELETE REQUEST
                 (THE DATASET WILL BE DELETED AND UNCATALOGED)


              PRESS END KEY TO CANCEL DELETE REQUEST
```

Figure 5-13   Deleting a data set (part 2 of 2)

point, the data set is scratched and removed from the catalog.
Or, I can use the end key (PF3/15) to bypass the scratch.

How to catalog or uncatalog a data set

You can change a data set's catalog status by entering C or U
in the command input area. If you enter C, the data set is
added to the catalog. As part of this procedure, you must
specify the volume containing the data set (SPF will prompt
you for it).

If you specify U, the data set is removed from the catalog.
Note that the uncatalog function doesn't scratch the file—it
just removes its entry from the catalog. To refer to a data set
that isn't cataloged, you must specify the serial number for the
volume that contains the file.

Most SPF functions, including browse and edit, assume
that your data sets are cataloged. And the data set utility's
allocate function automatically catalogs new data sets. So you
won't use the catalog and uncatalog functions often.

Discussion

If you've worked before with MVS in batch mode using JCL,
you know that to allocate a data set, you specify a DD
statement for it. Now, I want you to realize that allocating a
data set under SPF is similar to specifying a DD statement that
includes DISP = (NEW,CATLG). In other words, a new data
set is created and cataloged.

If you're familiar with the ALLOCATE command of
native TSO, you should realize that there's a difference
between it and SPF's allocate function. When you issue an
ALLOCATE command under native TSO, you associate a new
or existing data set with a ddname you supply. In contrast,
when you use the SPF allocate function, the data set must be
new and you don't specify a ddname. I'll have more to say
about native TSO's ALLOCATE command in chapter 9. For
now, just think of the SPF allocate function as a subset of the
native TSO ALLOCATE command: the SPF allocate function

lets you create and catalog new data sets, but it doesn't let you associate a data set with a ddname.

If you don't have any JCL or TSO experience, you should realize that for most uses, the data set utility is a substantial improvement over other techniques of allocating data sets. In a background job, you must code complicated JCL parameters on the DD statement to allocate a file. And in native TSO, you have to code equally complicated parameters on the ALLOCATE command.

Still, you can't use the data set utility to allocate all of your data sets. Both the JCL DD statement and the native TSO ALLOCATE command provide options that aren't available under SPF. So if your data set requires one of these options (most don't), you won't be able to use SPF. Also, you can't allocate VSAM files under SPF. Instead, you use AMS commands either in a background job or under native TSO. AMS commands are described in my book, *VSAM: Access Method Services and Application Programming*, available from Mike Murach & Associates, Inc.

Terminology

extent
load library

Objectives

1. Use the data set utility to display data set information.

2. Use the data set utility to allocate, rename, delete, catalog, or uncatalog a data set.

TOPIC 3   The move/copy and hardcopy utilities

In this topic, I cover two SPF utilities that perform related functions. You use the move/copy utility to reproduce a data set, library, or member of a library. You use the hardcopy utility to print a data set or library member.

THE MOVE/COPY UTILITY

The move/copy utility lets you copy or move sequential or partitioned data scts. As part of the copy or move operation, you can print the data set. And for partitioned data sets, you can select specific members to be copied or moved. You invoke the move/copy utility by selecting option 3 from the utilities menu.

Before I describe how you use the move/copy utility, I want to explain the difference between a move and a copy operation. To copy a data set means to reproduce it in another location. After you copy a file, you have two versions of it— the original version and the copied version. To move a data set, however, means to copy the file and scratch the original, so only one version of the file remains.

How to move or copy a sequential data set

To move or copy a sequential data set, you must complete two entry panels, as shown in figure 5-14. When you first select the move/copy utility, the entry panel in part 1 of figure 5-14 is displayed. On this panel, you enter an option code to specify the operation to perform. The four valid option codes and their meanings are:

C   Copy a data set

M   Move a data set

CP   Copy and print the data set

MP   Move and print the data set

Screen 1: Specify the copy option and the "from" data set information

```
--------------------------------- MOVE/COPY UTILITY --------------------------------
SELECT OPTION ===> C

   CP - COPY DATASET OR MEMBER(S) AND PRINT         C - COPY WITHOUT PRINT
   MP - MOVE DATASET OR MEMBER(S) AND PRINT         M - MOVE WITHOUT PRINT

SPECIFY "FROM" DATASET BELOW, THEN PRESS ENTER TO SPECIFY "TO" DATASET

FROM SPF LIBRARY:
    PROJECT ===> DLOWE
    LIBRARY ===> TEST
    TYPE    ===> DATA
    MEMBER  ===>              (BLANK FOR MEMBER LIST, * FOR ALL MEMBERS)

FROM OTHER PARTITIONED OR SEQUENTIAL DATASET:
    DATASET NAME   ===>
    VOLUME SERIAL  ===>           (IF NOT CATALOGED)

DATASET PASSWORD ===>              (IF PASSWORD PROTECTED)
```

Figure 5-14   Copying a data set (part 1 of 2)

Screen 2: Specify the "to" data set information

```
COPY --- FROM DLOWE.TEST.DATA ------------------------------------------------------
SPECIFY "TO" DATASET BELOW

TO SPF LIBRARY:
    PROJECT ===> DLOWE
    LIBRARY ===> TEST1
    TYPE    ===> DATA
    MEMBER  ===>

TO OTHER PARTITIONED OR SEQUENTIAL DATASET:
    DATASET NAME   ===>
    VOLUME SERIAL  ===>           (IF NOT CATALOGED)

DATASET PASSWORD ===>              (IF PASSWORD PROTECTED)


REPLACE LIKE-NAMED MEMBERS        ===> YES (YES OR NO)
"TO" DATASET DISPOSITION (SEQ) ===> OLD (OLD OR MOD)
```

Figure 5-14   Copying a data set (part 2 of 2)

In figure 5-14, I entered C for the option code. As a result, the data set will be copied. For the CP and MP options, the data set is printed as it's copied or moved. The printed output is written to the SPF list data set. You can route it to a printer when you terminate SPF.

Besides the option code, you also enter the data set name information for the input file, called the *from data set*, on the first entry panel. In figure 5-14, the *from* data set is DLOWE.TEST.DATA. For sequential data sets, you should leave the member name blank.

After you've entered the option code and the *from* data set name, SPF displays the second entry panel, shown in part 2 of figure 5-14. On this panel, you enter the data set name for the output file, called the *to data set*. In this example, the *to* data set is DLOWE.TEST1.DATA.

In addition to the *to* data set name, part 2 of figure 5-14 shows two questions you must answer:

```
REPLACE LIKE-NAMED MEMBERS        ===>
"TO" DATASET DISPOSITION (SEQ) ===>
```

The first applies to partitioned data sets only. I'll explain it in a moment. The second applies only to sequential files. It indicates the disposition for the *to* data set—OLD or MOD. If you specify OLD, the copy or move operation erases the previous contents of the *to* data set. MOD causes the copied or moved data to be added at the end of the *to* data set.

For any move or copy operation, both the *from* and *to* data sets must already exist. In other words, move/copy does not allocate a new *to* data set. To create a new copy of a data set, you must first allocate the new data set using the data set utility. Remember, you can easily allocate a new data set using the characteristics of an existing data set by first displaying the existing data set's information.

How to move or copy a partitioned data set

For partitioned data sets, you can move or copy a single member, all members, or selected members of the *from* library.

How to move or copy a single member   Figure 5-15 shows how to use move/copy to move a single member from one library to another. In part 1 of figure 5-15, I specify the option code and the *from* data set and member. Here, I'm going to move (M) a member named REORDLST from a library named DLOWE.TEST.COBOL.

     Part 2 of figure 5-15 shows that the *to* data set is DLOWE.TEST1.COBOL and the member name is the same— REORDLST. (If I wanted to, I could change the member name.) As a result, the member REORDLST is moved from DLOWE.TEST.COBOL to DLOWE.TEST1.COBOL and deleted from DLOWE.TEST.COBOL.

     For any move or copy operation involving libraries, your response to the question:

```
REPLACE LIKE-NAMED MEMBERS          ===>
```

is important. Whether you specify YES or NO here depends on how you want to handle members that exist in both the *from* and *to* libraries. YES means that duplicate members should be deleted from the *to* library before they are copied or moved. NO means that duplicate members should not be copied or moved. So in figure 5-15, REORDLST will be moved to DLOWE.TEST1.COBOL even if that library already has a member with the same name.

How to move or copy an entire library   Figure 5-16 shows how to move or copy all members of a partitioned data set. In part 1, I enter an asterisk (*) as the member name for the *from* library. That means all members are included in the move or copy.

     In part 2 of figure 5-16, I specify NO for REPLACE LIKE-NAMED MEMBERS. So each member of the *from* library is copied to the *to* library unless the *to* library already contains a member with the same name.

How to move or copy selected members   Figure 5-17 shows how to copy or move selected members of a partitioned data set. In part 1, I specify the *from* library but leave the member name blank. Then, in part 2, I specify the *to* library.

Screen 1:   Specify the move option and the "from" data set information

```
------------------------------- MOVE/COPY UTILITY -----------------------------
SELECT OPTION ===> M

    CP - COPY DATASET OR MEMBER(S) AND PRINT      C - COPY WITHOUT PRINT
    MP - MOVE DATASET OR MEMBER(S) AND PRINT      M - MOVE WITHOUT PRINT

SPECIFY "FROM" DATASET BELOW, THEN PRESS ENTER TO SPECIFY "TO" DATASET

FROM SPF LIBRARY:
    PROJECT ===> DLOWE
    LIBRARY ===> TEST
    TYPE    ===> COBOL
    MEMBER  ===> REORDLST  (BLANK FOR MEMBER LIST, * FOR ALL MEMBERS)

FROM OTHER PARTITIONED OR SEQUENTIAL DATASET:
    DATASET NAME  ===>
    VOLUME SERIAL ===>             (IF NOT CATALOGED)

DATASET PASSWORD ===>             (IF PASSWORD PROTECTED)
```

Figure 5-15   Moving a library member (part 1 of 2)

Screen 2:   Specify the "to" data set information

```
MOVE --- FROM DLOWE.TEST.COBOL(REORDLST) --------------------------------------
SPECIFY "TO" DATASET BELOW

TO SPF LIBRARY:
    PROJECT ===> DLOWE
    LIBRARY ===> TEST1
    TYPE    ===> COBOL
    MEMBER  ===> REORDLST   (BLANK UNLESS MEMBER IS TO BE RENAMED)

TO OTHER PARTITIONED OR SEQUENTIAL DATASET:
    DATASET NAME  ===>
    VOLUME SERIAL ===>             (IF NOT CATALOGED)

DATASET PASSWORD ===>             (IF PASSWORD PROTECTED)


REPLACE LIKE-NAMED MEMBERS      ===> YES (YES OR NO)
"TO" DATASET DISPOSITION (SEQ) ===> OLD (OLD OR MOD)
```

Figure 5-15   Moving a library member (part 2 of 2)

Screen 1:   Specify the copy option and the "from" data set information

```
------------------------------ MOVE/COPY UTILITY --------- MEMBER REORDLST MOVED
SELECT OPTION ===> C

    CP - COPY DATASET OR MEMBER(S) AND PRINT          C - COPY WITHOUT PRINT
    MP - MOVE DATASET OR MEMBER(S) AND PRINT          M - MOVE WITHOUT PRINT

SPECIFY "FROM" DATASET BELOW, THEN PRESS ENTER TO SPECIFY "TO" DATASET

FROM SPF LIBRARY:
    PROJECT ===> DLOWE
    LIBRARY ===> TEST
    TYPE    ===> COBOL
    MEMBER  ===> *           (BLANK FOR MEMBER LIST, * FOR ALL MEMBERS)

FROM OTHER PARTITIONED OR SEQUENTIAL DATASET:
    DATASET NAME   ===>
    VOLUME SERIAL  ===>             (IF NOT CATALOGED)

DATASET PASSWORD ===>               (IF PASSWORD PROTECTED)
```

Figure 5-16   Copying an entire library (part 1 of 2)

Screen 2:   Specify the "to" data set information

```
COPY --- FROM DLOWE.TEST.COBOL(*) --------------------------------------------
SPECIFY "TO" DATASET BELOW

TO SPF LIBRARY:
    PROJECT ===> DLOWE
    LIBRARY ===> TEST1
    TYPE    ===> COBOL

TO OTHER PARTITIONED OR SEQUENTIAL DATASET:
    DATASET NAME   ===>
    VOLUME SERIAL  ===>             (IF NOT CATALOGED)

DATASET PASSWORD ===>               (IF PASSWORD PROTECTED)


REPLACE LIKE-NAMED MEMBERS      ===> NO  (YES OR NO)
"TO" DATASET DISPOSITION (SEQ) ===> OLD (OLD OR MOD)
```

Figure 5-16   Copying an entire library (part 2 of 2)

Screen 1: Specify the copy option and the "from" data set information

```
------------------------------- MOVE/COPY UTILITY ------------ 16 MEMBERS COPIED
SELECT OPTION ===> C

    CP - COPY DATASET OR MEMBER(S) AND PRINT        C - COPY WITHOUT PRINT
    MP - MOVE DATASET OR MEMBER(S) AND PRINT        M - MOVE WITHOUT PRINT

SPECIFY "FROM" DATASET BELOW, THEN PRESS ENTER TO SPECIFY "TO" DATASET

FROM SPF LIBRARY:
    PROJECT ===> DLOWE
    LIBRARY ===> TEST
    TYPE    ===> COBOL
    MEMBER  ===>              (BLANK FOR MEMBER LIST, * FOR ALL MEMBERS)

FROM OTHER PARTITIONED OR SEQUENTIAL DATASET:
    DATASET NAME   ===>
    VOLUME SERIAL  ===>            (IF NOT CATALOGED)

DATASET PASSWORD ===>              (IF PASSWORD PROTECTED)
```

Figure 5-17   Copying selected members (part 1 of 4)

Screen 2: Specify the "to" data set information

```
COPY --- FROM DLOWE.TEST.COBOL -------------------------------------------------
SPECIFY "TO" DATASET BELOW

TO SPF LIBRARY:
    PROJECT ===> DLOWE
    LIBRARY ===> TEST1
    TYPE    ===> COBOL

TO OTHER PARTITIONED OR SEQUENTIAL DATASET:
    DATASET NAME   ===>
    VOLUME SERIAL  ===>            (IF NOT CATALOGED)

DATASET PASSWORD ===>              (IF PASSWORD PROTECTED)


REPLACE LIKE-NAMED MEMBERS        ===> YES (YES OR NO)
"TO" DATASET DISPOSITION (SEQ) ===> OLD (OLD OR MOD)
```

Figure 5-17   Copying selected members (part 2 of 4)

Screen 3:   Specify the members to be copied

```
COPY --- FROM DLOWE.TEST.COBOL   TO DLOWE.TEST1.COBOL ------------------------
COMMAND INPUT ===>                                    SCROLL ===> PAGE
    NAME      RENAME    VER.MOD   CREATED    LAST MODIFIED  SIZE  INIT  MOD   ID
    BFCRDS              01.00   84/01/30   84/01/30 18:12    12   12    0  DLOWE
    INVLST              01.00   84/01/26   84/01/26 14:29   202  202    0  DLOWE
    ORDLST2             01.00   84/01/05   84/01/05 16:44     9    9    0  DLOWE
    PRTFD               01.00   84/01/30   84/01/30 18:16     8    8    0  DLOWE
 S  REORDLST            01.03   84/01/26   84/02/17 13:09   202  202    0  DLOWE
    RNDUPDT             01.00   84/01/26   84/01/26 14:29   202  202    0  DLOWE
    SEQUPTD             01.00   84/01/05   84/01/05 16:44     9    9    0  DLOWE
 S  VSEMAINT  VSESMNT   01.00   84/01/05   84/01/05 16:44     9    9    0  DLOWE
    VSESMNT2            01.00   84/01/05   84/01/05 16:44     9    9    0  DLOWE
    VSESRUPT            01.00   84/01/05   84/01/05 16:44     9    9    0  DLOWE
    VSKSMNT             01.00   84/01/26   84/01/26 14:29   202  202    0  DLOWE
    VSKSRUPT            01.00   84/01/05   84/01/05 16:44     9    9    0  DLOWE
 S  VSKSSUPT            01.00   84/01/05   84/01/05 16:44     9    9    0  DLOWE
    VSRRMNT             01.00   84/01/26   84/01/26 14:29   202  202    0  DLOWE
    VSRRRUPT            01.00   84/01/05   84/01/05 16:44     9    9    0  DLOWE
    VSRRSUPT            01.00   84/01/26   84/01/26 14:29   202  202    0  DLOWE
    **END**
```

Figure 5-17   Copying selected members (part 3 of 4)

Screen 4:   The result of the copy

```
COPY --- FROM DLOWE.TEST.COBOL   TO DLOWE.TEST1.COBOL ------------------------
COMMAND INPUT ===>                                    SCROLL ===> PAGE
    NAME      RENAME    VER.MOD   CREATED    LAST MODIFIED  SIZE  INIT  MOD   ID
    BFCRDS              01.00   84/01/30   84/01/30 18:12    12   12    0  DLOWE
    INVLST              01.00   84/01/26   84/01/26 14:29   202  202    0  DLOWE
    ORDLST2             01.00   84/01/05   84/01/05 16:44     9    9    0  DLOWE
    PRTFD               01.00   84/01/30   84/01/30 18:16     8    8    0  DLOWE
    REORDLST  *REPL     01.03   84/01/26   84/02/17 13:09   202  202    0  DLOWE
    RNDUPDT             01.00   84/01/26   84/01/26 14:29   202  202    0  DLOWE
    SEQUPTD             01.00   84/01/05   84/01/05 16:44     9    9    0  DLOWE
    VSEMAINT  *COPIED   01.00   84/01/05   84/01/05 16:44     9    9    0  DLOWE
    VSESMNT2            01.00   84/01/05   84/01/05 16:44     9    9    0  DLOWE
    VSESRUPT            01.00   84/01/05   84/01/05 16:44     9    9    0  DLOWE
    VSKSMNT             01.00   84/01/26   84/01/26 14:29   202  202    0  DLOWE
    VSKSRUPT            01.00   84/01/05   84/01/05 16:44     9    9    0  DLOWE
    VSKSSUPT  *REPL     01.00   84/01/05   84/01/05 16:44     9    9    0  DLOWE
    VSRRMNT             01.00   84/01/26   84/01/26 14:29   202  202    0  DLOWE
    VSRRRUPT            01.00   84/01/05   84/01/05 16:44     9    9    0  DLOWE
    VSRRSUPT            01.00   84/01/26   84/01/26 14:29   202  202    0  DLOWE
    **END**
```

Figure 5-17   Copying selected members (part 4 of 4)

Since I left the member name blank for the *from* library, SPF displays the member selection list shown in part 3 of figure 5-17. Here, you simply enter an S next to each member you want copied. In this example, I copy three members: REORDLST, VSEMAINT, and VSKSSUPT.

The RENAME column of the member list allows you to change the name of a member as it is copied or moved. For example, in part 3 of figure 5-17, I specify that VSEMAINT should be renamed to VSESMNT. Remember that the member name is changed only in the *to* library. The member name in the *from* library is not changed.

Part 4 of figure 5-17 shows the member list after the copy operation has completed. Here, SPF indicates whether or not each member was replaced or added to the *to* library.

THE HARDCOPY UTILITY

You use the hardcopy utility to obtain a printed copy of a data set or library member immediately. Printed output from other sources—such as edit or move/copy—is recorded in SPF's list file, which isn't actually printed until you exit SPF.

The hardcopy utility can produce printed output at a local printer in foreground mode using DSPRINT. Alternatively, you can specify job information for hardcopy to submit a background job to print the data set or member.

You invoke the hardcopy utility by specifying option 6 from the utility menu. Then, SPF displays the hardcopy utility's entry panel, shown in figure 5-18. Here, you specify the hardcopy option (local or background print), the data set information (name, disposition, volume, and password), the print destination (SYSOUT class or local printer-id), and the JOB statement information (for background printing only).

How to print a data set at a local printer

The example in figure 5-18 shows how to print a data set at a local printer. Because I specified L as the hardcopy option, DSPRINT is invoked as a foreground job to print the data set. DSPRINT uses the value in the LOCAL PRINTER ID field to

```
-------------------------------  HARDCOPY UTILITY  ---------------------------------
SELECT OPTION ===> L

     J - GENERATE JCL TO PRINT OR PUNCH DATASET
     L - ROUTE DATASET TO LOCAL PRINTER



DATASET NAME ===> TEST.COBOL(REORDLST)
   DISPOSITION        ===> KEEP            (KEEP OR DELETE)
   VOLUME SERIAL      ===>                 (IF NOT CATALOGED)
   DATASET PASSWORD ===>                   (IF PASSWORD PROTECTED)

   SYSOUT CLASS       ===>                 (IF OPTION "J" SELECTED)
   LOCAL PRINTER ID ===> IBMT2IP1          (IF OPTION "L" SELECTED)

   JOB STATEMENT INFORMATION:  (IF OPTION "J" SELECTED, VERIFY BEFORE PROCEEDING)
     ===> //DLOWEA    JOB (MMA1,DLOWE),'DOUG LOWE'
     ===> //*
     ===> //*
     ===> //*
```

Figure 5-18   Printing a data set at a local printer

route the output to the correct printer. In this example, the
output is routed to a printer named IBMT2IP1. Printer-ids
vary from one installation to the next, so you'll have to ask
your supervisor what printer-id to use.

Unlike other SPF entry panels, the hardcopy panel doesn't
provide project, library, type, and member fields to specify a
data set. Instead, you enter the data set name in the usual TSO
format. In figure 5-18, I entered TEST.COBOL(REORDLST)
as the data set name. Since SPF appends the user-id (project)
to the left of the data set name, the actual MVS data set name
for the file is DLOWE.TEST.COBOL(REORDLST).

If you don't want SPF to append your user-id to a data
set name, simply enclose the name in apostrophes. For
example,

```
DATASET NAME ===> 'SYS2.COMMAND.CLIST($VER)'
```

If you use apostrophes, you must specify the fully qualified
data set name.

The DISPOSITION field lets you say whether a data set
should be kept or deleted after it's been printed. Your response

to this field applies only to sequential data sets—library members are not scratched even if you say DELETE here.

If the data set isn't cataloged, you must enter a volume serial number in the VOLUME SERIAL field. And if the data set is protected by standard MVS security (not RACF), you must supply a password in the PASSWORD field. Normally, you leave these fields blank.

How to print a data set using a background job

To print a data set via a background job, you specify J as the hardcopy option. Then, hardcopy generates the JCL necessary to print the data set using the JOB statement provided in the JOB STATEMENT INFORMATION field and the output class indicated in the SYSOUT CLASS field. If you're not familiar with JCL, find out from your supervisor what values to code in these fields.

Each time you complete the hardcopy entry panel, hardcopy generates a job step that invokes a system utility named IEBGENER to print the specified data set. As a result, you can print three data sets with a single job simply by completing the entry panel three times. The job isn't actually submitted for JES background processing until you return to the utilities menu by pressing PF3/15.

To illustrate, consider figure 5-19. In part 1, I specify the hardcopy option (J), the data set and member, the disposition (KEEP), the SYSOUT class (X), and the JOB statement information. Part 2 shows the next panel SPF displays. It indicates that JCL has been generated. Here, you have three options: (1) enter J and another data set name to generate more JCL; (2) enter CANCEL to return to the utilities menu without submitting the job; or (3) press the end key (PF3/15) to submit the job. Part 3 shows the panel SPF displays when you submit the job for background processing. Here, you can see that the job named DLOWEA has been submitted. The MVS job number for this job is JOB00504. When you press the enter key, SPF returns to the utilities menu.

Screen 1:   Specify the option, data set, and job information

```
------------------------------- HARDCOPY UTILITY  ---------------------------------
SELECT OPTION ===> J

   J - GENERATE JCL TO PRINT OR PUNCH DATASET
   L - ROUTE DATASET TO LOCAL PRINTER



DATASET NAME ===> TEST.COBOL(REORDLST)
   DISPOSITION        ===> KEEP           (KEEP OR DELETE)
   VOLUME SERIAL    ===>                  (IF NOT CATALOGED)
   DATASET PASSWORD ===>                  (IF PASSWORD PROTECTED)

SYSOUT CLASS      ===> X                  (IF OPTION "J" SELECTED)
LOCAL PRINTER ID ===>                     (IF OPTION "L" SELECTED)

JOB STATEMENT INFORMATION:   (IF OPTION "J" SELECTED, VERIFY BEFORE PROCEEDING)
   ===> //DLOWEA    JOB (MMA1,DLOWE),'DOUG LOWE'
   ===> //*
   ===> //*
   ===> //*
```

Figure 5-19   Printing a data set via a background job (part 1 of 3)

Screen 2:   The JCL has been generated; press the end key to submit the job

```
------------------------------ HARDCOPY UTILITY  ------------------ JCL GENERATED
SELECT OPTION ===> J

   J - GENERATE MORE JCL TO PRINT OR PUNCH DATASET
   CANCEL - EXIT WITHOUT SUBMITTING JOB

PRESS END KEY TO SUBMIT JOB

DATASET NAME ===> TEST.COBOL(REORDLST)
   DISPOSITION        ===> KEEP           (KEEP OR DELETE)
   VOLUME SERIAL    ===>                  (IF NOT CATALOGED)
   DATASET PASSWORD ===>                  (IF PASSWORD PROTECTED)

SYSOUT CLASS      ===> X

JOB STATEMENT INFORMATION:
        //DLOWEA    JOB (MMA1,DLOWE),'DOUG LOWE'
        //*
        //*
        //*
```

Figure 5-19   Printing a data set via a background job (part 2 of 3)

Screen 3: **The job has been submitted for background processing**

```
------------------------------ HARDCOPY UTILITY ------------------ JCL GENERATED
SELECT OPTION ===> J

   J - GENERATE MORE JCL TO PRINT OR PUNCH DATASET
   CANCEL - EXIT WITHOUT SUBMITTING JOB

PRESS END KEY TO SUBMIT JOB

DATASET NAME ===> TEST.COBOL(REORDLST)
   DISPOSITION        ===> KEEP            (KEEP OR DELETE)
   VOLUME SERIAL      ===>                 (IF NOT CATALOGED)
   DATASET PASSWORD ===>                   (IF PASSWORD PROTECTED)

SYSOUT CLASS       ===> X

JOB STATEMENT INFORMATION:
     //DLOWEA    JOB (MMA1,DLOWE),'DOUG LOWE'
     //*
     //*
     //*
JOB DLOWEA(JOB00504) SUBMITTED
***
```

Figure 5-19 Printing a data set via a background job (part 3 of 3)

Terminology

from data set
to data set

Objectives

1. Distinguish between a copy and a move operation.

2. Use the copy/move utility to reproduce a data set, either with or without printing it.

3. Use the hardcopy utility to print a data set.

TOPIC 4   The catalog and VTOC utilities

In this topic, I cover two related SPF utilities: the catalog utility and the VTOC utility. You use the catalog utility to list the catalog entries for your data sets. And you use the VTOC utility to list the data sets on a particular direct-access volume.

THE CATALOG UTILITY

You invoke the catalog utility by selecting option 4 from the utility option menu. The catalog utility itself has four options. You use two of them to obtain catalog listings. You use the other two to define or delete a user catalog alias.

How to list catalog entries

Figure 5-20 shows the catalog management panel SPF displays when you select option 4 from the utilities option menu. Here, you enter an option code (P to print the catalog listing or a space to display it at your terminal), a project name (usually, your user-id), and one or more parameters. In figure 5-20, I leave the option blank so the catalog list will be displayed at my terminal. I specify my user-id (DLOWE) as the project name, and I leave the parameter field at its default setting: NAME. (I'll explain other options for the parameter field in a moment.)

Figure 5-21 shows the output that results from figure 5-20. If the output contains more lines than will fit on a single display panel, you can use scrolling commands to see all of it. Part 1 of figure 5-21 shows the first page of the catalog listing; part 2 shows the last page. For each data set cataloged under the project name you specify, two lines are shown. The first line lists the entry type (NONVSAM for standard sequential and partitioned data sets) and the data set name; the second line lists the name of the user catalog that contains the entry

```
------------------------------- CATALOG MANAGEMENT -------------------------------
SELECT OPTION ===>

   I - INITIALIZE (DEFINE) USER CATALOG ALIAS
   D - DELETE USER CATALOG ALIAS
   P - PRINT CATALOG ENTRIES
   BLANK - DISPLAY CATALOG ENTRIES

PROJECT NAME ===> DLOWE

AMS LIST CATALOG PARAMETER:    (IF OPTION "P" OR "BLANK" SELECTED)
          ===> NAME

CATALOG NAME:  (IF OPTION "I" SELECTED)
          ===>
```

Figure 5-20   The catalog management utility entry panel

(more about user catalogs in a minute). For example, in part 1 of figure 5-21, the first entry shown is for a non-VSAM data set named DLOWE.BFCRDS.DATA, cataloged in a user catalog named VCAT.MPS600.

At the end of the catalog listing are summary lines that show the total number of entries displayed. These totals are shown in part 2 of figure 5-21. Here, you can see that 25 entries were displayed, all of them for non-VSAM files.

On an MVS system, all files...both VSAM and non-VSAM...are cataloged in VSAM catalogs. As a result, SPF's catalog utility invokes the VSAM utility program, IDCAMS, to produce catalog listings.

That's where the AMS LIST CATALOG PARAMETER field in figure 5-20 comes in. The contents of this field are included as a parameter on the LISTCAT command that IDCAMS uses to produce the catalog listing. In addition, the value you specify in the PROJECT NAME field is included in the LISTCAT command as a LEVEL parameter. So, the values I specify in figure 5-20 cause the following LISTCAT command to be processed by IDCAMS:

```
LISTCAT LEVEL('DLOWE') NAME
```

```
 CATALOG LISTING FOR DLOWE ---------------------------- LINE 000000 COL 001 080
 COMMAND INPUT ===>                                        SCROLL ===> MAX
********************************* TOP OF DATA ********************-CAPS ON-**
 IDCAMS   SYSTEM SERVICES                                     TIME: 14:57:45

  LISTCAT LEVEL(DLOWE) -
  NAME
NONVSAM ------- DLOWE.BFCRDS.DATA
      IN-CAT --- VCAT.MPS600
NONVSAM ------- DLOWE.COBOL.SYM
      IN-CAT --- VCAT.MPS600
NONVSAM ------- DLOWE.HOLD.CLIST
      IN-CAT --- VCAT.MPS600
NONVSAM ------- DLOWE.ISPPARM
      IN-CAT --- VCAT.MPS600
NONVSAM ------- DLOWE.JCL.CNTL
      IN-CAT --- VCAT.MPS600
NONVSAM ------- DLOWE.LIST.LIST
      IN-CAT --- VCAT.MPS600
NONVSAM ------- DLOWE.NEW.LIST
      IN-CAT --- VCAT.MPS600
NONVSAM ------- DLOWE.NEW.TESTLIST
      IN-CAT --- VCAT.MPS600
NONVSAM ------- DLOWE.NEWLINK.LINKLIST
```

Figure 5-21   The first page of a catalog listing (part 1 of 2)

```
 CATALOG LISTING FOR DLOWE ---------------------------- LINE 000053 COL 001 080
 COMMAND INPUT ===>                                        SCROLL ===> HALF
      IN-CAT --- VCAT.MPS600
NONVSAM ------- DLOWE.TEST1.COBOL
      IN-CAT --- VCAT.MPS600
 IDCAMS   SYSTEM SERVICES                                     TIME: 14:57:45
          THE NUMBER OF ENTRIES PROCESSED WAS:
                   AIX ----------------0
                   ALIAS --------------0
                   CLUSTER ------------0
                   DATA ---------------0
                   GDG ----------------0
                   INDEX --------------0
                   NONVSAM -----------25
                   PAGESPACE ----------0
                   PATH ---------------0
                   SPACE --------------0
                   USERCATALOG --------0
                   TOTAL -------------25
          THE NUMBER OF PROTECTED ENTRIES SUPPRESSED WAS 0
 IDC0001I FUNCTION COMPLETED, HIGHEST CONDITION CODE WAS 0

 IDC0002I IDCAMS PROCESSING COMPLETE. MAXIMUM CONDITION CODE WAS 0
******************************* BOTTOM OF DATA ******************-CAPS ON-**
```

Figure 5-21   The last page of a catalog listing (part 2 of 2)

Parameter	Meaning
NAME	List the data set name and entry type for each catalog entry.
HISTORY	List the data set name, entry type, owner-id, creation date, and expiration date for each catalog entry.
VOLUME	List HISTORY information plus the vol-ser and device type allocated to each catalog entry.
ALL	List all catalog fields for each catalog entry.

Figure 5-22   LISTCAT parameters

If you're not familiar with IDCAMS, all this may not make much sense to you. But don't worry about it. The only reason I bring it up is that you can specify any valid LISTCAT parameter in the parameter field. The most useful group of LISTCAT parameters are the ones that control the amount of information that appears on the listing. Figure 5-22 summarizes those parameters. And figure 5-23 shows a sample of the output each produces. So you can use these parameters even if you're not familiar with IDCAMS and the LISTCAT command. The other LISTCAT parameters you can use are documented in the IBM manual, *OS/VS2 Access Method Services*.

Although it isn't apparent on the catalog management entry panel, you can specify all or part of a fully qualified data set name in the PROJECT NAME field. Normally, you just specify the high-level qualifier. However, suppose you code the PROJECT NAME field like this:

```
PROJECT NAME ===> DLOWE.TEST
```

Then, only those data sets whose names begin with DLOWE.TEST are listed in the catalog listing.

If you specify P as the catalog management option, the catalog listing is written to the SPF list data set rather than displayed at the terminal. When you terminate SPF, you can print the list data set at a local printer or via a background job.

NAME output

```
NONVSAM ------- DLOWE.TEST.COBOL
     IN-CAT --- VCAT.MPS600
```

HISTORY output

```
NONVSAM ------- DLOWE.TEST.COBOL
     IN-CAT --- VCAT.MPS600
     HISTORY
          OWNER-IDENT-------(NULL)      CREATION----------84.030
          RELEASE           2           EXPIRATION--------00.000
```

VOLUME output

```
NONVSAM ------- DLOWE.TEST.COBOL
     IN-CAT --- VCAT.MPS600
     HISTORY
          OWNER-IDENT-------(NULL)      CREATION----------84.030
          RELEASE           2           EXPIRATION--------00.000
     VOLUMES
          VOLSER-----------MPS600       DEVTYPE------X'3050200B'
```

ALL output

```
NONVSAM ------- DLOWE.TEST.COBOL
     IN-CAT --- VCAT.MPS600
     HISTORY
          OWNER-IDENT-------(NULL)      CREATION----------84.030
          RELEASE           2           EXPIRATION--------00.000
     VOLUMES
          VOLSER-----------MPS600       DEVTYPE------X'3050200B'    FSEQN-----------------0
     ASSOCIATIONS--------(NULL)
```

Figure 5-23   LISTCAT output obtained with various parameters

How to initialize or delete a user catalog alias

Before you can understand what the I and D options do, you must understand how user catalogs work. A *user catalog* is a catalog that contains entries for users' data sets. In contrast, a *master catalog* contains entries only for system data sets and user catalogs. Within an MVS system, there can be many user catalogs but only one master catalog. If user data sets were

cataloged in the master catalog, the master catalog would
contains thousands of entries. So, all of your SPF data sets are
cataloged in a user catalog.

How does SPF determine which user catalog to use for
your data sets? It follows a simple MVS cataloging convention:
the high-level qualifier of the data set name indicates which
user catalog to use. In SPF terms, that means the project-id
points to the user catalog. So, for a data set named
DLOWE.TEST.COBOL, DLOWE indicates the user catalog
that contains the catalog entry.

Because of an MVS limitation, each direct-access volume
is associated with only one user catalog; you can't have two or
more user catalogs for data sets on a single volume. In other
words, every cataloged data set on a particular direct-access
volume must be cataloged in the same user catalog. This
limitation creates a problem: if SPF used the project-id as the
user catalog name, the data sets for only one project could be
stored on a single direct-access volume. Since most projects
won't fill up a whole volume, that would result in a lot of
wasted disk space.

To avoid this problem, most installations create a separate
user catalog for each volume. For example, notice the catalog
name in figure 5-21: VCAT.MPS600. That's the name of the
user catalog for the volume named MPS600. All of the data
sets on that volume, regardless of their project names, are
cataloged in VCAT.MPS600.

To maintain the MVS convention of using the high-level
qualifier to indicate the user catalog name, a catalog alias is
used. Quite simply, a *catalog alias* is an alternate name for a
user catalog. For example, suppose I establish DLOWE as an
alias for VCAT.MPS600. Then, whenever I use DLOWE as the
high-level qualifier in a data set name (or as the PROJECT ID
field in an SPF entry panel), MVS uses VCAT.MPS600 for the
user catalog instead. To store the data sets for more than one
project on a single direct-access volume, you simply create
several catalog alias names that refer to the same user catalog.

That's what you use the I and D options for: to initialize
or delete a user catalog alias. In effect, these options let you
create and delete project names. To create a new project name,
specify the I option, the project name, and the name of the
user catalog associated with the project. If the project doesn't

already exist, SPF creates a user catalog alias so that any data sets you allocate using the new project name are cataloged in the user catalog you specify.

To delete a project name, you should first delete all of the data sets associated with the project. Then, specify option D and the project name. SPF will remove the user catalog alias, so the project name can't be used.

THE VTOC UTILITY

You use the VTOC utility to display or print VTOC entries. A *VTOC*, which stands for *Volume Table of Contents*, is a directory of all data sets stored on a volume. Every direct-access volume has a VTOC, and all of the data sets on the volume are recorded in the VTOC—even if the data sets aren't cataloged in a user catalog. Besides each data set's name, the VTOC records the physical characteristics (block size, organization, and so on) and disk location for each file on the volume.

Figure 5-24 shows the VTOC utility's entry panel. As you can see, the VTOC utility provides two options. If you specify option P, the VTOC listing is written to the list data set. If you leave the option field blank, the VTOC listing is displayed at your terminal. In addition, you must enter the volume name for the volume whose VTOC you want to list. And, optionally, you can enter a project name to limit the number of data sets listed. Since a single direct-access volume often contains hundreds—sometimes thousands—of data sets, I recommend you specify a project name. Otherwise, you'll get pages of output.

Figure 5-24 requests a terminal display of data sets for project DLOWE on a disk volume named MPS600. The resulting output is shown in figure 5-25. Besides the volume information in the heading, this listing shows the data set organization (PS for sequential files, PO for partitioned data sets), the number of tracks allocated, the percentage of tracks actually in use, and the number of extents for each data set on the volume. If this listing is too long to fit on one screen (as is usually the case), you can use normal scrolling functions to view the entire listing.

```
-------------------------------- VTOC UTILITY -----------------------------------
SELECT OPTION ===>

   P - PRINT VTOC ENTRIES
   BLANK - DISPLAY VTOC ENTRIES

ENTER PARAMETERS BELOW:

   VOLUME   ===> MPS600
   PROJECT  ===> DLOWE      (BLANK FOR ENTIRE VOLUME)
```

Figure 5-24   The VTOC utility entry panel

```
VTOC LISTING FOR VOLUME MPS600 ------------------------ LINE 000000 COL 001 080
COMMAND INPUT ===>                                      SCROLL ===> PAGE
********************************* TOP OF DATA *********************-CAPS ON-**
   VOLUME: MPS600
   UNIT:   3350

   VOLUME DATA:            VTOC DATA:              FREE SPACE:  TRACKS CYLINDERS
      TRACKS:    16800        TRACKS:      52         SIZE:      3949    118
      %USED:       76 %       %USED:       16 %       LARGEST:   1170     39
      DATA SETS:   351     FREE DSCBS:  2066
      TRKS/CYL:     30                            FREE EXTENTS:    46

   DATA SET NAME                         DSORG   TRACKS    %USED   XTENTS
   ------------------------------------------------------------------------------
   DLOWE.BFCRDS.DATA                      PS      1 TRKS   100 %    1 X
   DLOWE.COBOL.SYM                        PS     10 TRKS     0 %    1 X
   DLOWE.HOLD.CLIST                       PO     11 TRKS     9 %    1 X
   DLOWE.ISPPARM                          PO      1 TRKS   100 %    1 X
   DLOWE.JCL.CNTL                         PO     10 TRKS    10 %    1 X
   DLOWE.LIST.LIST                        PS      1 TRKS   100 %    1 X
   DLOWE.NEW.LIST                         PS      8 TRKS    62 %    2 X
   DLOWE.NEW.TESTLIST                     PS      2 TRKS     0 %    1 X
   DLOWE.NEWLINK.LINKLIST                 PS      1 TRKS   100 %    1 X
   DLOWE.ORDLST.OUTLIST                   PS      1 TRKS   100 %    1 X
```

Figure 5-25   A VTOC listing

DISCUSSION

If you're like me, you'll use the catalog and VTOC utilities often. It seems I'm constantly forgetting data set names... particularly for those data sets I don't often use. If I know which volume the data set is on, I prefer to use the VTOC utility because its output is so much easier to read. However, if I don't know the vol-ser, I use the catalog utility so that all my cataloged data sets are listed.

It's a good idea to run the catalog or VTOC utility periodically to see if you can scratch any unnecessary data sets. And if you use the VTOC utility for this purpose, you'll also be able to monitor your critical source libraries so you'll know when to compress them or when to allocate more space to them.

Terminology

user catalog
master catalog
catalog alias
VTOC
Volume Table of Contents

Objectives

1. Use the catalog utility to (1) display catalog entries, (2) initialize a user catalog alias, and (3) delete a user catalog alias.

2. Use the VTOC utility to list VTOC entries.

Chapter 6

How to compile, link-edit, and test a program in foreground mode

As a programmer, you'll probably use SPF most for program development. You've already learned how to perform many basic program development tasks under SPF: browsing, editing, allocating data sets, and so on. This chapter, though, explains the critical program development tasks of compiling, link-editing, and testing programs.

There are several methods you can use to compile, link-edit, and test programs under SPF. This chapter explains the method for which SPF is designed: compiling, link-editing, and testing programs in foreground mode using familiar SPF selection and entry panels. After I've explained this method, I'll briefly describe the others.

FOREGROUND PROGRAM DEVELOPMENT

When you select option 4 from the primary option menu, SPF displays a selection panel similar to figure 6-1. Here, you can compile or assemble a program using one of the system compilers or the assembler, link-edit a program using the standard linkage editor, or interactively debug a COBOL or FORTRAN program. Because all of these features except the system assembler and linkage editor require licensed program products, your shop may

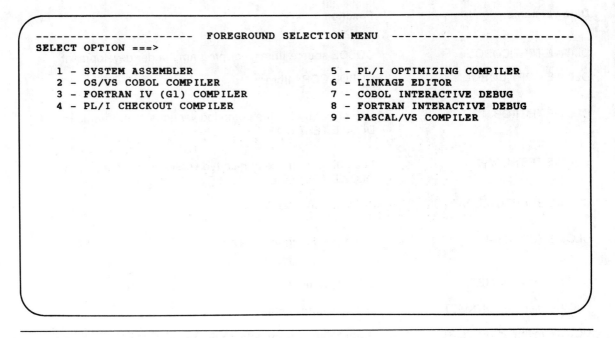

```
------------------------ FOREGROUND SELECTION MENU -------------------------
SELECT OPTION ===>

       1 - SYSTEM ASSEMBLER           5 - PL/I OPTIMIZING COMPILER
       2 - OS/VS COBOL COMPILER       6 - LINKAGE EDITOR
       3 - FORTRAN IV (G1) COMPILER   7 - COBOL INTERACTIVE DEBUG
       4 - PL/I CHECKOUT COMPILER     8 - FORTRAN INTERACTIVE DEBUG
                                      9 - PASCAL/VS COMPILER
```

Figure 6-1　The foreground selection menu

not have all of them. Or, your shop may have added additional compilers, such as VS BASIC or the CICS command-level translator. Your shop may or may not have modified the foreground selection menu to reflect the products it has installed.

In this chapter, I'll describe how you use each of the three main types of options—assemble/compile, link-edit, and interactive debug—in a COBOL environment. With few exceptions, program development for other programming languages, like PL/I or assembler, is the same.

Libraries and output listings

Before I go on, I want to point out that foreground program development uses a variety of libraries and data sets. Figure 6-2 lists the data set names I created for this book. Although the naming conventions at your shop may be different and although you may not be working in COBOL, these names should serve as examples of the types of data sets you need.

Usually, you'll have at least two COBOL libraries: a test library that contains versions of programs under development

Data set name	Function
DLOWE.TEST.COBOL	COBOL source library for programs under development
DLOWE.COPY.COBOL	COBOL COPY library
DLOWE.TEST.OBJ	Object library for the compiled versions of programs in DLOWE.TEST.COBOL
DLOWE.TEST.LOAD	Load library for the link-edited versions of programs in DLOWE.TEST.OBJ
DLOWE.SUBPROG.LOAD	Subprogram load library
DLOWE.TEST.SYM	Symbolic debugging library
DLOWE.member.LIST	COBOL compiler listing
DLOWE.member.LINKLIST	Linkage-editor listing
DLOWE.member.TESTLIST	Output listing from debugging session

Figure 6-2   Data sets used for program development (COBOL)

and a COPY library that contains members included via COPY statements. (You maintain the members in these libraries using the editor as described in chapter 4.) Normally, you'll concatenate these libraries on the edit and compile entry panels so that they'll be searched in this order: first the test library, then the COPY library.

For a one-programmer project, a single test library is sufficient. For a multi-programmer project, however, you'll probably have one test library for each programmer. And for a large project, you may have an additional COBOL library: a master source library that contains only final versions of programs.

All of the foreground compilers place the compiled version of the program, called an *object module*, in an OBJ library with the same name as the source library. Thus, if the source library is DLOWE.TEST.COBOL, the *object library* will be DLOWE.TEST.OBJ. The member name for the source and object program is the same.

The linkage editor places its output, called a *load module*, in a *load library*, again with the same name. So, in the above example, the load library is DLOWE.TEST.LOAD. In addition, any called subprograms must be kept in a load library. Generally, the subprogram library follows SPF naming conventions, so DLOWE.SUBPROG.LOAD is a valid name. However, system subprogram libraries, like the ones that contain compiler subroutines, follow the MVS conventions for naming system data sets. For example, SYS1.COBLIB is the name of the COBOL compiler subroutine library.

The interactive debugging options let you monitor a program as it runs, allowing you to look at the values of various fields to make sure the program's executing properly. To debug a COBOL program using the interactive debugger, you must use a *symbolic debugging file*. This partitioned data set, whose type qualifier is SYM, is automatically allocated by the foreground compiler. It's used by the interactive COBOL debugger to obtain symbolic information—such as data names and statement numbers—when you debug your program.

Output listings generated by the foreground compilers are placed in a sequential data set (not a library) whose type is LIST. For example, DLOWE.REORDLST.LIST is a valid name for a compiler listing. For a linkage-editor listing, the type qualifier is LINKLIST. Thus, a valid name for a link listing is DLOWE.REORDLST.LINKLIST. And for the output from the interactive debugger, the type is TESTLIST. So DLOWE.REORDLST.TESTLIST is a valid name for a debugging listing.

Now, I'll show you how these files are used as you develop a program in foreground mode.

How to compile a program

To compile a program, you select one of the compilers— options 1 through 5, or option 9, in figure 6-1. To compile a COBOL program, you select option 2: the OS/VS COBOL compiler. Figure 6-3 shows the panel SPF displays when you select the COBOL compiler. On it, you provide the library and member name for the source program you wish to compile. In this example, I compile the member REORDLST in the library DLOWE.TEST.COBOL.

Any additional compiler input—such as a COPY library— should be specified as additional libraries on the entry panel.

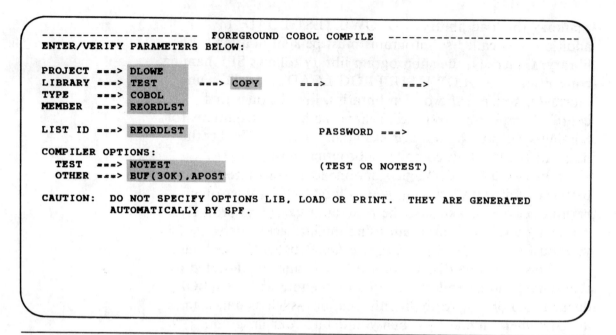

```
----------------------- FOREGROUND COBOL COMPILE -----------------------------
ENTER/VERIFY PARAMETERS BELOW:

PROJECT ===> DLOWE
LIBRARY ===> TEST        ===> COPY        ===>            ===>
TYPE    ===> COBOL
MEMBER  ===> REORDLST

LIST ID ===> REORDLST                     PASSWORD ===>

COMPILER OPTIONS:
  TEST  ===> NOTEST                       (TEST OR NOTEST)
  OTHER ===> BUF(30K),APOST

CAUTION:  DO NOT SPECIFY OPTIONS LIB, LOAD OR PRINT.  THEY ARE GENERATED
          AUTOMATICALLY BY SPF.
```

Figure 6-3 The foreground COBOL compile entry panel

For example, COPY is specified as an additional input library in figure 6-3. As a result, DLOWE.COPY.COBOL will be used as a COPY library for this compile.

Actually, all of the libraries listed on the entry panel are searched when you use a COPY statement. So, the data set DLOWE.TEST.COBOL is used as a COPY library too. For example, suppose REORDLST contains this COPY statement:

```
COPY BFREC.
```

Since DLOWE.TEST.COBOL is the first library specified on the entry panel, it's the first library searched for the BFREC member. If the COPY member isn't found there, the next library—in this case, DLOWE.COPY.COBOL—is searched.

If you want to change the search order for COPY libraries, you can specify the COPY library first, followed by your source library. But that changes the search order for the source member as well. In other words, the COPY library will be searched before the TEST library to find REORDLST.

The LIST ID field in figure 6-3 requests a name for the data set that contains the compiler listing. The full data set name follows this pattern:

```
project-id.list-id.LIST
```

Normally, you use the source member name as the list-id. So, in figure 6-3, the list data set is named DLOWE.REORDLST.LIST.

Compiler options   The *compiler options* control optional features of the COBOL compiler. The COBOL entry panel provides two lines for compiler options. The first indicates whether you intend to use the COBOL debugger. If you do, you must specify TEST. Otherwise, say NOTEST.

If you say TEST here, the COBOL compiler generates a symbolic debugging file for use by the debugger. This file is a member of a partitioned data set whose name is the same as the first source library you specify in the entry panel, except its type is SYM. The member name is the same as the source member name. Thus, if I had specified TEST in figure 6-3, the name of the symbolic debugging file would have been DLOWE.TEST.SYM(REORDLST).

The OTHER option line lets you specify other compiler options. In some installations, you must specify a few specific compiler options for the compiler to work properly. For example, at my installation I must specify two options: BUF and APOST. The BUF option in figure 6-3 specifies a buffer size of 30K bytes. The APOST option says that apostrophes (') rather than quotes (") are used to mark non-numeric literals. The particular options you must code here may vary for your installation.

Figure 6-4 lists some of the COBOL compiler options you're likely to use. Most of them control optional compiler output generated in the compiler listing, such as a Data Division map and a cross-reference listing. The underlined values are IBM standard defaults, though the defaults at your installation may be different. At any rate, you'll have to find out from your supervisor which options you must code.

Figure 6-4 also explains three compiler options automatically generated by SPF: LIB, LOAD, and PRINT. Since SPF generates these options, you should *not* include them on the entry panel.

Parameter	Meaning
<u>SOURCE</u> NOSOURCE	Print the source listing.
DMAP <u>NODMAP</u>	Print a Data Division map.
PMAP <u>NOPMAP</u>	Print a Procedure Division map.
CLIST <u>NOCLIST</u>	Print a condensed Procedure Division map—can't be used with PMAP.
<u>VERB</u> NOVERB	Print procedure names and verb names on the Procedure Division map; meaningful only when you specify PMAP or CLIST.
XREF <u>NOXREF</u>	Print a cross-reference listing.
<u>APOST</u> QUOTE	Indicates whether apostrophes (') or quotes (") are used to mark non-numeric literals.
BUF(*n*)	Specifies how much buffer space to allow. You can specify *n* as an integer or use K to represent units of 1024 bytes. Thus, BUF(2048) and BUF(2K) have the same meaning.

Options supplied by SPF

LIB	Supplies a list of partitioned data sets used to process COPY statements.
LOAD	Supplies the name of the object library.
PRINT	Supplies the name of the print file.

Figure 6-4   Common COBOL compiler options

Compiler output   Once you complete the entry panel and press the enter key, your terminal temporarily enters native TSO mode. As a result, information is sent to your terminal line by line. When the screen is filled, TSO displays ✱✱✱ on line 24. Then, when you press the enter key, the screen is cleared and the line-by-line display resumes at line 1.

During the course of compilation, the compiler displays progress messages. These are shown in figure 6-5. The first progress message indicates that the COBOL prompter has been invoked (the COBOL prompter is the TSO program that

```
-------------------------- FOREGROUND COBOL COMPILE --------------------------
ENTER/VERIFY PARAMETERS BELOW:

PROJECT ===> DLOWE
LIBRARY ===> TEST         ===>            ===>            ===>
TYPE    ===> COBOL
MEMBER  ===> REORDLST

LIST ID ===> REORDLST                     PASSWORD ===>

COMPILER OPTIONS:
  TEST  ===> NOTEST                       (TEST OR NOTEST)
  OTHER ===> BUF(30K),APOST

CAUTION:  DO NOT SPECIFY OPTIONS LIB, LOAD OR PRINT.  THEY ARE GENERATED
          AUTOMATICALLY BY SPF.

TSO COBOL PROMPTER PP 5734-CP1 RELEASE 1.4

REL2.3 OS/VS COBOL IN PROGRESS
***
```

Figure 6-5   A successful foreground COBOL compilation

invokes the COBOL compiler for foreground processing). The
second message indicates that OS/VS COBOL is in progress.
Figure 6-5 is how your screen will appear when the compile is
finished and the program contains no errors. When you press
the enter key, SPF returns to the COBOL entry panel.

Figure 6-6 shows how your terminal appears when compilation errors are detected. Because the compiler output is too
long to fit on one screen, figure 6-6 consists of three parts. The
diagnostic messages in figure 6-6 begin in the middle of part 2
and continue to the end of part 3.

If your installation has installed the TSO session manager,
you can enter it from a compiler's entry screen by pressing a
scrolling PF key (such as PF8/20) rather than the enter key.
Then, the compiler output is displayed under the session
manager (described in detail in chapter 8). You'll be able to
scroll forward or backward through the output, making it
easier to examine the diagnostic messages in detail. Otherwise,
as I mentioned earlier, native TSO will display the listing line
by line, clearing the screen after it's full when you press the
enter key. At that point, you can't go back to what's been
previously displayed.

The entry screen with the beginning of the compiler output

```
----------------------- FOREGROUND COBOL COMPILE  -----------------------
ENTER/VERIFY PARAMETERS BELOW:


PROJECT ===> DLOWE
LIBRARY ===> TEST        ===>COPY      ===>            ===>
TYPE    ===> COBOL
MEMBER  ===> REORDLST

LIST ID ===> REORDLST                    PASSWORD ===>

COMPILER OPTIONS:
  TEST  ===> NOTEST                      (TEST OR NOTEST)
  OTHER ===> BUF(30K),L132,APOST

CAUTION:  DO NOT SPECIFY OPTIONS LIB, LOAD OR PRINT.  THEY ARE GENERATED
          AUTOMATICALLY BY SPF.

TSO COBOL PROMPTER PP 5734-CP1 RELEASE 1.4

REL2.3 OS/VS COBOL IN PROGRESS
*STATISTICS*     SOURCE RECORDS =   202      DATA DIVISION STATEMENTS =    66
 PROCEDURE DIVISION STATEMENTS =    44
*OPTIONS IN EFFECT*     SIZE = 131072  BUF =   30720  LINECNT = 54  SPACE1, FL
***
```

Figure 6-6 A foreground COBOL compilation with diagnostics (part 1 of 3)

The second screenload of compiler output with the beginning of the diagnostic messages

```
 AGW, NOSEQ,    SOURCE
  *OPTIONS IN EFFECT*        NODMAP, NOPMAP, NOCLIST, NOSUPMAP, NOXREF, NOSXREF,   L
OAD, NODECK, APOST, NOTRUNC, NOFLOW
  *OPTIONS IN EFFECT*        TERM,   NUM, NOBATCH, NONAME, COMPILE=01, NOSTATE, NO
RESIDENT, NODYNAM,   LIB, NOSYNTAX
  *OPTIONS IN EFFECT*      NOOPTIMIZE, NOSYMDMP, NOTEST,    VERB,   ZWB, SYST, NOEN
DJOB, NOLVL
  *OPTIONS IN EFFECT*      NOLST , NOFDECK,NOCDECK, LCOL2,  L120, NODUMP , NOADV ,
 NOPRINT,
  *OPTIONS IN EFFECT*      NOCOUNT, NOVBSUM, NOVBREF, LANGLVL(2)
  019 COMPILATION ERRORS.HIGHEST SEVERITY  E
  CARD    ERROR MESSAGE


  2200    IKF2146I-C     RECORD SIZE IN RECORD-CONTAINS CLAUSE DISAGREES WITH COM
PUTED RECORD SIZE. 00084
                        ASSUMED.
  3800    IKF1043I-W     END OF SENTENCE SHOULD PRECEDE 05 . ASSUMED PRESENT.
  6400    IKF1001I-E     NUMERIC LITERAL NOT RECOGNIZED AS LEVEL NUMBER BECAUSE L
INE-COUNTER ILLEGAL AS
                        USED. SKIPPING TO NEXT LEVEL, SECTION OR DIVISION.
  6600    IKF2142I-E     ALPHABETIC OR ALPHANUMERIC ITEM HAS ILLEGAL USAGE. PICTU
RE CHANGED TO 9.
  9100    IKF1087I-W     ' ASTERISK ' SHOULD NOT BEGIN A-MARGIN.
  ***
```

Figure 6-6 A foreground COBOL compilation with diagnostics (part 2 of 3)

The last screenload of compiler output

```
    9100    IKF1004I-E      INVALID WORD ASTERISK . SKIPPING TO NEXT RECOGNIZABLE WO
RD.
   10800    IKF1004I-E      INVALID WORD VALUE . SKIPPING TO NEXT RECOGNIZABLE WORD.
   12400    IKF2039I-C      PICTURE CONFIGURATION ILLEGAL. PICTURE CHANGED TO 9 UNLE
SS USAGE IS 'DISPLAY-ST',
                            THEN L(6)BDZ9BDZ9.
   12400    IKF2129I-C      VALUE CLAUSE LITERAL DOES NOT CONFORM TO PICTURE. CHANGE
D TO ZERO.
   14200    IKF1087I-W      ' PERFORM ' SHOULD NOT BEGIN A-MARGIN.
   14500    IKF3001I-E      DO NOT DEFINED. DELETING TILL LEGAL ELEMENT FOUND.
   14500    IKF4032I-C      NO ACTION INDICATED IF PRECEDING CONDITION IS TRUE. NEXT
SENTENCE ASSUMED.
   16700    IKF3001I-E      LINE-COUNT NOT DEFINED. TEST DISCARDED.
   17000    IKF3001I-E      BF-ITEM-DESC NOT DEFINED. DISCARDED.
   18000    IKF3001I-E      PRINT NOT DEFINED. DISCARDED.
   18000    IKF4052I-E      AREA     MAY NOT BE TARGET FIELD FOR DNM=2-265   (GRF) IN
MOVE STATEMENT, AND IS
                            DISCARDED.
   19400    IKF3001I-E      LINE-COUNT NOT DEFINED. SUBSTITUTING TALLY .
   20000    IKF3001I-E      LINE-COUNT NOT DEFINED. DISCARDED.
   20400    IKF3001I-E      WS-CARD-COUNT NOT DEFINED. DISCARDED.

   ***
```

Figure 6-6   A foreground COBOL compilation with diagnostics (part 3 of 3)

Normally, you'll make a note of the errors displayed when you compile a program. If, however, the errors are extensive, you'll want to print the compiler output. The easiest way to do this is to use the hardcopy utility (option 3.6), described in chapter 5. The compiler output written to the list data set contains a complete source listing, diagnostics, and other output depending on what compiler options you specify.

You can also browse the compiler listing if you wish. In fact, all of the browse examples in chapter 3 were taken from a browse session using the compiler listing from the COBOL compile generated by figure 6-3.

How to link-edit a program

Before you can execute a compiled program, you must *link-edit* it. When you link-edit a program, the program's combined with any subprograms you invoke with CALL statements along with any compiler subroutines to form a load module that's ready to be executed by MVS.

To invoke the *linkage editor*, select option 6 from the foreground menu. SPF then displays the panel shown in figure 6-7. On it, you enter the library and member name of the object module created by the compiler. In this example, I link-edit REORDLST in DLOWE.TEST.OBJ. The link-edited load module is placed in DLOWE.TEST.LOAD using the same member name.

If you need to include a subprogram library for the linkage editor, specify it as an additional library on the entry panel. The linkage editor will search up to four libraries you specify on the entry panel to resolve subprogram calls. The libraries are searched in the order you list them, so if the same subprogram name occurs in more than one library, be sure to list the correct library first.

The LIST ID field works much like it does for a compiler. The full data set name for the list file follows this pattern:

```
project-id.list-id.LINKLIST
```

So in figure 6-7, the list file is DLOWE.REORDLST.LINKLIST.

I suggest you leave the linkage-editor options at your installation's default. As for the compiler subroutine libraries, they may vary from one installation to the next. In general, COBOL programs require one subroutine library, named SYS1.COBLIB. You must specify compiler subroutine libraries in apostrophes, since they don't follow standard SPF naming conventions.

How to debug a COBOL program

Option 7 from the foreground menu provides access to the interactive COBOL debugger. As I said earlier, the debugger lets you monitor the execution of a program, displaying the contents of variables at will. I'm not going to describe the details of using the debugger here; instead, I describe them in chapter 10. Once you enter the interactive debugger from SPF, you use it just as I describe in chapter 10.

Figure 6-8 shows the debug entry panel displayed when you select option 7. Here, you specify the project-id and library name for the load library (debug assumes LOAD for

```
--------------------------- FOREGROUND LINKAGE EDIT ---------------------------
ENTER/VERIFY PARAMETERS BELOW:

PROJECT ===> DLOWE
LIBRARY ===> TEST        ===>            ===>            ===>
TYPE    ===> OBJ
MEMBER  ===> REORDLST

LIST ID ===> REORDLST                      PASSWORD ===>

LINKAGE EDITOR OPTIONS:
        ===> LET,LIST,MAP

CAUTION:  DO NOT SPECIFY OPTIONS LIB, LOAD OR PRINT.  THEY ARE GENERATED
          AUTOMATICALLY BY SPF.

COMPILER SUBROUTINE LIBRARIES:              (IN APOSTROPHES)
        ===> 'SYS1.COBLIB'
        ===>
```

Figure 6-7   The foreground linkage-edit entry panel

the type). Then, you specify up to four program names for the programs and subprograms you wish to debug. Each must have a corresponding member in the SYM library. Next, you specify the name of the load library member you wish to execute. Normally, the first PROG ID field and the LOAD MEMBER field are the same. They don't have to be, though.

It's easy to become confused about the PROG ID and LOAD MEMBER fields, so let me explain them more carefully. The PROG ID fields identify up to four program modules to debug. These names correspond to the names you specify in the PROGRAM-ID paragraphs of the COBOL source programs. As a result, if you're debugging a program named PROG1 that calls a COBOL subprogram named SUBPROG1 and you want to debug *both* the main program and the subprogram, you'll specify two PROG IDs: PROG1 and SUBPROG1. As I mentioned a moment ago, for each PROG ID, there must be a corresponding member in the SYM library. Thus, in this example, there must be members named PROG1 and SUBPROG1 in the SYM library.

Most of the time, though, the subprograms your main program uses will already be tested and debugged. If that's the

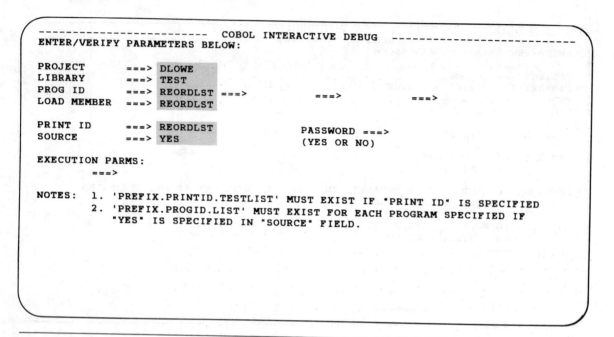

```
------------------------- COBOL INTERACTIVE DEBUG -------------------------
ENTER/VERIFY PARAMETERS BELOW:

PROJECT      ===> DLOWE
LIBRARY      ===> TEST
PROG ID      ===> REORDLST ===>          ===>           ===>
LOAD MEMBER  ===> REORDLST

PRINT ID     ===> REORDLST            PASSWORD ===>
SOURCE       ===> YES                 (YES OR NO)

EXECUTION PARMS:
       ===>

NOTES:   1. 'PREFIX.PRINTID.TESTLIST' MUST EXIST IF "PRINT ID" IS SPECIFIED
         2. 'PREFIX.PROGID.LIST' MUST EXIST FOR EACH PROGRAM SPECIFIED IF
            "YES" IS SPECIFIED IN "SOURCE" FIELD.
```

Figure 6-8   The COBOL interactive debug entry panel

case, you'll specify just the main program name in the PROG ID field. In other words, you don't have to name all the subprograms your main program uses...just the ones you actually want to debug. Likewise, if you're writing a new subprogram and you want to test and debug it, you can specify just the subprogram name in the PROG ID field; you don't have to specify the name of the main program.

As for the LOAD MEMBER field, it specifies the member name of a load module in the load library. That member is the one that's loaded and executed first during a debugging session. Again, in our example, suppose that PROG1 and SUBPROG1 were link-edited together to form a load module named LOAD1. Then, you would specify LOAD1 as the LOAD MEMBER. Typically, however, the member name for the load module is the same as the program name for the main program it contains. So the LOAD MEMBER field will usually be the same as one of the PROG ID fields.

If you want to route debugging output to a print file, you must specify a print-id. The print file name will be created following this pattern:

```
project-id.print-id.TESTLIST
```

You must allocate the print file using the data set utility (option 3.2.) before you run the debugger.

If you wish to examine the source listing during the debug session, enter YES in the SOURCE field. If you do, the compiler list file (.LIST) must exist for each PROG ID you specify.

DISCUSSION

In this chapter, I've presented the techniques used to develop programs in foreground mode using SPF. There are, however, other program development techniques commonly used under TSO. Besides using the foreground option, you can invoke the foreground compilers and debuggers directly by using TSO commands. Furthermore, you can place the commands in a CLIST to make them easier to use. Under SPF, you can invoke these commands or CLISTs using option 6 from the primary option menu. I cover the TSO commands for foreground program development in chapter 10 and CLISTs in chapters 12-14.

Another alternative for program development is background processing. I'll explain how you can use SPF features for background program development in chapter 7. And in chapter 11, I'll explain the native TSO features that support background processing.

Terminology

object module	symbolic debugging file
object library	compiler option
load module	link-edit
load library	linkage editor

Objective

Use the SPF foreground option to compile, link-edit, and test a program.

Chapter 7

How to process background jobs

As you know, an MVS system with TSO has two types of regions in which jobs execute: foreground and background. Foreground regions execute TSO jobs. As a result, when you use TSO (or SPF), a job is executed in a foreground region on your behalf. Background regions are used for non-time-sharing jobs. In other words, background regions are generally used for batch jobs, while foreground regions are used where user interaction is required.

A TSO user in a foreground region often needs to initiate processing in a background region. For example, suppose you're developing a program that will be processed in a background region once it's in production. You can use the foreground processing features of TSO and SPF to edit, compile, and link-edit the program. You may even use the interactive COBOL debugger for the initial program testing. But eventually you'll have to process the program in a background region to make sure it's thoroughly tested. And, depending on factors unique to your installation, you may find it better to compile and link-edit programs in a background region.

THE LIFE CYCLE OF A JOB

Figure 7-1 describes the life cycle of a typical background job under MVS. To begin, the job is submitted for execution by a system operator, by a TSO user, or by a job executing in another region. Once a job is submitted for execution, it's placed in a job queue, where it waits until a region is available to execute it. How long it waits in the job queue depends on a number of factors, including its storage and I/O device requirements and the job class assigned to it when it was submitted.

Every job submitted for execution under MVS must have a *job name*. This name, one to eight characters in length, is specified in the JCL for the job. When you refer to a job you've submitted, you usually use its job name. However, MVS does not require that job names be unique. As a result, it's perfectly acceptable to submit two jobs with the same job name. MVS assigns a unique *job-id* to each job as it's submitted. So if you submit more than one job with the same job name, you must use the job-id rather than the job name to identify each job.

When a region becomes available for your job, JES2/JES3 starts a reader/initiator task to begin your job. As your job executes, MVS generates informational messages that are collected in the job output and stored in a SYSOUT queue. In addition, programs executed by the job's steps can generate output that's written to a SYSOUT queue. Data in a SYSOUT queue is held there until it's printed at a local or remote printer, copied to a data set, or deleted.

Each data set written to a SYSOUT queue is assigned a one-character *SYSOUT class* that determines how the output is printed. Each SYSOUT class is normally associated with a printer or a group of printers. Typically, SYSOUT class A is used for the installation's main printer or printers. Other SYSOUT classes may be assigned to specific printers or other devices.

If a SYSOUT class isn't associated with a printer or other device, it's called a *reserved class*. Any output written to a

1. The job is submitted for execution by a system operator, a TSO user, or another background job.

2. The job waits in a job queue.

3. The job is selected for execution by the job scheduler.

4. The job executes.

5. The job output is collected and held in a SYSOUT queue.

6. The job output is routed to its final destination and removed from the SYSOUT queue.

Figure 7-1   The life cycle of a background job

reserved class is held in the SYSOUT queue until an operator (1) directs it to a specific printer, (2) directs it to another SYSOUT class, or (3) deletes it. At my installation, class X is defined as a reserved class.

When you submit a background job from TSO, you usually want to direct the output to a reserved class. Then, you can examine the output at your terminal and determine if you should print it or delete it.

As an SPF user, you need to know how to do three things before you can effectively manage background jobs. First, you need to know how to submit a job for background processing. Second, you need to know how to monitor the status of a job you've submitted to see if it's waiting for execution, executing, or waiting for its output to be printed. And third, you need to know how to retrieve the output for a job that's completed.

HOW TO SUBMIT A BACKGROUND JOB

SPF provides two basic methods for submitting jobs for background processing. The first is the background option, option 5 on the primary option menu. This option is designed specifically for submitting jobs that compile and link-edit programs. The background option automatically generates the JCL necessary to process your job, so you don't have to create any JCL yourself. The second method is the SUBMIT

```
 --------------------------  BACKGROUND SELECTION MENU  --------------------------
 SELECT OPTION ===>

     1 - SYSTEM ASSEMBLER              4 - PL/I CHECKOUT COMPILER
     2 - OS/VS COBOL COMPILER          5 - PL/I OPTIMIZING COMPILER
     3 - FORTRAN IV (G1) COMPILER      6 - LINKAGE EDITOR
                                       9 - PASCAL/VS COMPILER




 JOB STATEMENT INFORMATION:  (VERIFY BEFORE PROCEEDING)
     ===> //DLOWEE    JOB (MMA1,DLOWE),'DOUG LOWE'
     ===> //*
     ===> //*
     ===> //*
```

Figure 7-2   The background selection menu

command of the edit function. When you use the SUBMIT
command, you must create the job's JCL statements yourself.

How to submit a job using the background option

When you select the background option by entering option 5
from the primary option menu, SPF displays a selection menu
like the one shown in figure 7-2. Here, you can select one of
six compilers (assembler, COBOL, FORTRAN, PASCAL, and
two versions of PL/I) or the linkage editor. This menu is
similar to the foreground processing menu described in chapter
6. The main difference is that the background option generates
JCL statements that are submitted to a background region for
later processing, while the foreground option invokes the compilers, linkage editor, or interactive debugger for immediate
processing in a foreground region. In addition, you must
supply JOB statement information on the background option
menu. I'll explain how you code this information in a moment.

When you select one of the background options, a second
panel is displayed. On it, you enter data set information,

compiler options, and so on. Once you've completed this panel, SPF generates the JCL necessary to process the function you selected. Then, it returns to the background menu, where you can select another background option. The JCL for the second and subsequent background options you select is added to the end of the JCL already generated. As a result, you can create a job with more than one step by selecting more than one background option. The job isn't submitted for processing until you return to the primary option menu by pressing PF3/15.

To illustrate, consider figure 7-3. Here, I generate a job to compile and link-edit a COBOL program. In part 1, I select option 2—the OS/VS COBOL compiler. SPF then displays the background COBOL entry panel, shown in part 2. (Note that it's similar to the entry panel for a foreground COBOL compile as described in chapter 6.) Here, I supply the library and member names for the program I wish to compile. In this case, the library is DLOWE.TEST.COBOL and the member is REORDLST. In addition, I specify a SYSOUT class (X) and appropriate compiler options.

All of the background options require that you enter either a LIST ID or a SYSOUT CLASS to determine how printed output should be handled. If you specify a SYSOUT CLASS, the output will be routed to the appropriate class by JES2/JES3. If, however, you specify a LIST ID, the output will be added to a list data set whose name follows this format:

```
project-id.list-id.LIST
```

Thus, if I specify REORDLST as the LIST ID, the output is stored in a data set named DLOWE.REORDLST.LIST. In this case, the output is not directed to a JES2/JES3 output queue.

Whether you should use a LIST ID or a SYSOUT CLASS depends on factors unique to your installation. In either case, you can examine the output at your terminal or route it to a local or remote printer. If you specify a LIST ID, you use the browse option to examine the output and you use the hardcopy utility to print it. If you specify a SYSOUT CLASS, you use the outlist utility for these functions. (I'll describe the outlist utility later in this chapter.)

Once you complete the COBOL entry panel, SPF returns to the background menu, as shown in part 3 of figure 7-3.

Screen 1:   Specify the processor option for the compile

```
---------------------- BACKGROUND SELECTION MENU ----------------------
SELECT OPTION ===> 2

    1 - SYSTEM ASSEMBLER              4 - PL/I CHECKOUT COMPILER
    2 - OS/VS COBOL COMPILER          5 - PL/I OPTIMIZING COMPILER
    3 - FORTRAN IV (G1) COMPILER      6 - LINKAGE EDITOR
                                      9 - PASCAL/VS COMPILER




JOB STATEMENT INFORMATION:  (VERIFY BEFORE PROCEEDING)
   ===> //DLOWEE    JOB (MMA1,DLOWE),'DOUG LOWE'
   ===> //*
   ===> //*
   ===> //*
```

Figure 7-3   Generating a background compile-and-link job (part 1 of 5)

Screen 2:   Enter the information needed for the compile

```
---------------------- BACKGROUND COBOL COMPILE ----------------------
ENTER/VERIFY PARAMETERS BELOW:

PROJECT ===> DLOWE
LIBRARY ===> TEST      ===>          ===>          ===>
TYPE    ===> COBOL
MEMBER  ===> REORDLST

LIST ID ===>                      (BLANK FOR HARDCOPY LISTING)
SYSOUT CLASS ===> X               (IF HARDCOPY REQUESTED)

COMPILER OPTIONS:
  TEST  ===> NOTEST               (TEST OR NOTEST)
  OTHER ===> SOURCE,XREF,CLIST,DMAP
```

Figure 7-3   Generating a background compile-and-link job (part 2 of 5)

Screen 3:   Specify the processor option for the link

```
------------------------ BACKGROUND SELECTION MENU ------------- JCL GENERATED
SELECT OPTION ===> 6

    1 - SYSTEM ASSEMBLER              4 - PL/I CHECKOUT COMPILER
    2 - OS/VS COBOL COMPILER          5 - PL/I OPTIMIZING COMPILER
    3 - FORTRAN IV (G1) COMPILER      6 - LINKAGE EDITOR
                                      9 - PASCAL/VS COMPILER

ENTER OPTION TO CONTINUE GENERATING JCL
ENTER CANCEL ON OPTION LINE TO EXIT WITHOUT SUBMITTING JOB
PRESS END KEY TO SUBMIT JOB

JOB STATEMENT INFORMATION:
        //DLOWEE   JOB (MMA1,DLOWE),'DOUG LOWE'
        //*
        //*
        //*
```

Figure 7-3   Generating a background compile-and-link job (part 3 of 5)

Screen 4:   Enter the information needed for the link

```
------------------------- BACKGROUND LINKAGE EDIT ---------------------------
ENTER/VERIFY PARAMETERS BELOW:

PROJECT ===> DLOWE
LIBRARY ===> TEST      ===>          ===>          ===>
TYPE    ===> OBJ
MEMBER  ===> REORDLST

LIST ID ===>                    (BLANK FOR HARDCOPY LISTING)
SYSOUT CLASS ===> X             (IF HARDCOPY REQUESTED)

LINKAGE EDITOR OPTIONS:
   TERM  ===>                   (TERM OR BLANK)
   OTHER ===> LET,LIST,MAP

COMPILER SUBROUTINE LIBRARIES:   (IN APOSTROPHES)
      ===> 'SYS1.COBLIB'
      ===>
```

Figure 7-3   Generating a background compile-and-link job (part 4 of 5)

Screen 5:   The job has been submitted

```
-------------------------- BACKGROUND SELECTION MENU ------------- JCL GENERATED
SELECT OPTION ===>

    1 - SYSTEM ASSEMBLER              4 - PL/I CHECKOUT COMPILER
    2 - OS/VS COBOL COMPILER          5 - PL/I OPTIMIZING COMPILER
    3 - FORTRAN IV (G1) COMPILER      6 - LINKAGE EDITOR
                                      9 - PASCAL/VS COMPILER


ENTER OPTION TO CONTINUE GENERATING JCL
ENTER CANCEL ON OPTION LINE TO EXIT WITHOUT SUBMITTING JOB
PRESS END KEY TO SUBMIT JOB

JOB STATEMENT INFORMATION:
      //DLOWEE    JOB (MMA1,DLOWE),'DOUG LOWE'
      //*
      //*
      //*

JOB DLOWEE(JOB03136) SUBMITTED
***
```

Figure 7-3   Generating a background compile-and-link job (part 5 of 5)

There are a couple of points to note here. First, notice the message at the upper righthand corner of the screen: JCL GENERATED. That means the JCL necessary to process the COBOL compiler has been generated. Any background options selected now are added to the end of the JCL stream, creating additional job steps.

Second, notice the three options explained in the center of the screen. Here, you can enter another option to generate more JCL, enter the word CANCEL to return to the primary option menu without submitting the JCL generated, or press the end key (PF3/15) to submit the JCL generated. In part 3 of figure 7-3, I select option 6 to generate the JCL to link-edit my program.

Part 4 of figure 7-3 shows the linkage-editor entry panel. Like the compile panel, it's similar to the entry panel for a foreground link-edit job. Here, I supply the data set information (DLOWE.TEST.OBJ is the library name, REORDLST is the member name), a SYSOUT CLASS (X), appropriate link-edit options, and the name of the system library that contains the required compiler subroutines. After I complete this entry panel and press enter, the display will be just like part 3 of figure 7-3.

To submit the job for background processing, you simply press PF3/15. Then, SPF issues a TSO SUBMIT command to submit the job for processing in a background region (I cover the SUBMIT command in chapter 11). The SUBMIT command generates a message, shown in part 5 of figure 7-3, to verify that the job has been submitted. Then, when you press the enter key, SPF returns to the primary option menu.

How to supply job information   To submit a job for background processing using the background option, you must supply information SPF uses to create a JOB statement. The background option menu provides four lines for this purpose. Here, SPF automatically displays the job information you used for your last job. If that information's acceptable, you can reuse it as is. For example, for the job in figure 7-3, I was satisfied with the JOB statement shown in part 1, so I didn't change it at all. On the other hand, you can change or add any information you need to reflect your JOB statement requirements.

The only new value SPF provides each time in these lines is a default job name. This name consists of your user-id followed by a single character. Initially, this character is the letter A. Thus, for my user-id, the initial job name is DLOWEA. Each time you submit a job, SPF increments this character. So, the second job I submit has DLOWEB for its job name, followed by DLOWEC, and so on. Once the job name reaches DLOWEX, it cycles back to DLOWEA. If you wish, you can change the job name to any name you wish (within the limits of your installation).

Figure 7-4 shows four examples of coding JOB statement information. In example 1, I've coded the minimum JOB statement information. I've supplied an account number (MMA1), a user-id, and a programmer name (my name in apostrophes).

Example 2 is a little more complex. Here, I've supplied some additional JOB statement parameters. The CLASS parameter says that my job should execute in class N. And the MSGLEVEL parameter tells what messages I want displayed in the job output.

Example 1

```
JOB STATEMENT INFORMATION:   (VERIFY BEFORE PROCEEDING)
  ===> //DLOWEE    JOB (MMA1,DLOWE),'DOUG LOWE'
  ===> //*
  ===> //*
  ===> //*
```

Example 2

```
JOB STATEMENT INFORMATION:   (VERIFY BEFORE PROCEEDING)
  ===> //DLOWEE    JOB (MMA1,DLOWE),'DOUG LOWE',
  ===> //            CLASS=N,
  ===> //            MSGLEVEL=(0,0)
  ===> //*
```

Example 3

```
JOB STATEMENT INFORMATION:   (VERIFY BEFORE PROCEEDING)
  ===> //DLOWEE    JOB (MMA1,DLOWE),'DOUG LOWE'
  ===> //JOBLIB    DD  DSN=DLOWE.PROGLIB,DISP=SHR
  ===> //*
  ===> //*
```

Example 4

```
JOB STATEMENT INFORMATION:   (VERIFY BEFORE PROCEEDING)
  ===> /*PRIORITY 4
  ===> //DLOWEE    JOB (MMA1,DLOWE),'DOUG LOWE'
  ===> /*ROUTE PRINT RMT193
  ===> //*
```

Figure 7-4   Examples of JOB statement information

Example 3 shows how to specify a JOBLIB for your job.
Here, the JOB statement is followed by a JOBLIB DD statement that identifies DLOWE.PROGLIB as the JOBLIB—the
program library that MVS will search to find the programs
executed during the job. For background jobs created by the
background option, you won't normally specify a JOBLIB.
That's because the assembler, compilers, and linkage editor are
usually stored in the system program library (SYS1.LINKLIB),
which is one of the libraries that MVS always searches.

Example 4 shows how you can specify JES2 or JES3 control statements along with the JOB statement. Here, the /*PRIORITY statement says to assign job dispatching priority 4 to my job. And the /*ROUTE statement says that all the printed output generated by the job should be routed to a remote printer named RMT193.

My purpose here is not to teach you JCL or JES statements. Instead, I just want to show how you can use the JOB statement field to supply various JCL parameters. If you don't understand the MSGLEVEL parameter or the /*PRIORITY statement, don't worry about it. Just remember that you can code more than a simple JOB statement in the JOB statement field.

JCL generated by the background option   Figure 7-5 shows the actual job stream that was generated by the background options selected in figure 7-3. If you're not familiar with JCL, you can skip this figure—it's not crucial to your understanding of background processing.

Notice that for each background option selected, two job steps are generated. The first invokes a program named ISPSCAN. This program searches the libraries supplied in the entry panel for the specified member. If it finds the member, it copies it to a temporary data set named &TEMP1. The second step invokes the appropriate processing program (a compiler, assembler, or linkage editor) to process &TEMP1.

How to submit a job using the SUBMIT command of edit

The background option I just described is useful, but it has one major drawback: it lets you generate JCL only for the specific processing options it allows. If you want to invoke any other processing program—such as the CICS command-level translator—you can't do it using the background option. Instead, you must create the JCL yourself.

The SUBMIT command of edit (option 2 from the primary option menu) makes it easy to create JCL streams and submit them for processing. First, you use the editing features you already know to create the JCL statements you need. Normally, this JCL is saved as a member of a JCL library

```
1      //DLOWEE   JOB (MMA1,DLOWE),'DOUG LOWE',
       // USER=DLOWE,GROUP=MMA1,PASSWORD=
       ***
       ***
       ***
2      //SCAN     EXEC  PGM=ISPSCAN,PARM='REORDLST',COND=(12,LE)
       ***------------------------------------------------------------
       ***   COBOL COMPILE ---- TO DLOWE.TEST.OBJ(REORDLST)
       ***------------------------------------------------------------
       ***
       *** INSERT A STEPLIB DD HERE IF ISPSCAN IS NOT IN YOUR SYSTEM LIBRARY
       ***
3      //IN       DD    DSN=DLOWE.TEST.COBOL,DISP=SHR
4      //OUT      DD    UNIT=SYSDA,DISP=(NEW,PASS),SPACE=(CYL,(2,2)),
       //               DSN=&TEMP1
       ***------------------------------------------------------------
5      //COBOL    EXEC  PGM=IKFCBL00,REGION=192K,COND=(12,LE),
       // PARM=(NOTEST,
       //      'SOURCE,XREF,CLIST,DMAP')
6      //SYSPRINT DD    SYSOUT=(X)
7      //SYSIN    DD    DSN=&TEMP1,DISP=(OLD,DELETE)
8      //SYSPUNCH DD    DUMMY
9      //SYSUT1   DD    UNIT=SYSDA,SPACE=(CYL,(2,2))
10     //SYSUT2   DD    UNIT=SYSDA,SPACE=(CYL,(2,2))
11     //SYSUT3   DD    UNIT=SYSDA,SPACE=(CYL,(2,2))
12     //SYSUT4   DD    UNIT=SYSDA,SPACE=(CYL,(2,2))
13     //SYSLIB   DD    DSN=DLOWE.TEST.COBOL,DISP=SHR
14     //SYSLIN   DD    DSN=DLOWE.TEST.OBJ(REORDLST),DISP=OLD
       ***------------------------------------------------------------
15     //SCAN     EXEC  PGM=ISPSCAN,PARM='REORDLST',COND=(12,LE)
       ***------------------------------------------------------------
       ***   LINKAGE EDIT ----- TO DLOWE.TEST.LOAD(REORDLST)
       ***------------------------------------------------------------
       ***
       *** INSERT A STEPLIB DD HERE IF ISPSCAN IS NOT IN YOUR SYSTEM LIBRARY
       ***
16     //IN       DD DSN=DLOWE.TEST.OBJ,DISP=SHR
17     //OUT      DD UNIT=SYSDA,DISP=(NEW,PASS),SPACE=(CYL,(2,2)),
       //            DSN=&TEMP1
       ***------------------------------------------------------------
18     //LINK     EXEC PGM=IEWL,REGION=192K,COND=(12,LE),
       // PARM=(,
       //      'LET,LIST,MAP')
19     //SYSPRINT DD  SYSOUT=(X)
20     //SYSLIN   DD  DSN=&TEMP1,DISP=(OLD,DELETE)
21     //OBJECT   DD  DSN=DLOWE.TEST.OBJ,DISP=SHR
22     //SYSLIB   DD  DSN=DLOWE.TEST.LOAD,DISP=SHR
23     //SYSLMOD  DD  DSN=DLOWE.TEST.LOAD(REORDLST),
       //             DISP=SHR,DCB=(BLKSIZE=3072)
24     //SYSUT1   DD  UNIT=SYSDA,DISP=NEW,SPACE=(CYL,(2,2))
```

Figure 7-5   The JCL generated for a compile-and-link job

(JCL libraries have CNTL as their type qualifier). Then you enter SUBMIT as a primary command, and the JCL in the member you're editing is submitted for processing as a background job.

To illustrate, consider figure 7-6. Here, I'm editing a member named COBOL in DLOWE.TEST.CNTL. This member contains the JCL statements necessary to compile and execute REORDLST in DLOWE.TEST.COBOL. In part 1 of figure 7-6, you can see how I entered a SUBMIT primary command. Part 2 shows how TSO responded with a one-line message saying the job was submitted. You must press the enter key here to return to edit mode.

Frankly, I prefer the SUBMIT command of edit over the background option. That's because once I've created the JCL to compile and link-edit a program, all I have to do is submit it. In contrast, if you use the background option, you have to go through the COBOL and link-edit panels each time you want to submit the job.

Other methods of submitting background jobs

Besides the background option and the SUBMIT command of edit, SPF provides several additional methods of submitting background jobs. Throughout SPF, you'll find options for routing printed output to a local printer or for submitting a job to print the output. These options generate their own JCL, though you must supply JOB statement information. You've seen several examples so far in this book. For instance, in chapter 5, you saw how to use the hardcopy utility to submit background print jobs. And in chapter 2, you saw how to print the log and list files using a background job.

Another alternative is to select the TSO command option (option 6 from the primary option menu) and enter a TSO SUBMIT command. If you've created a JCL library and wish to submit one of its members without altering the JCL, this is the easiest method to use. I explain the SUBMIT command in chapter 11.

THE OUTLIST UTILITY

Once you've submitted a job for background processing, you can use the outlist utility to monitor its progress or display its output. You invoke the outlist utility by selecting option 8

Enter the SUBMIT command during the edit of a JCL file

```
EDIT - DLOWE.TEST.CNTL(COBOL) -------------------------------- COLUMNS 001 072
COMMAND INPUT ===> SUBMIT                                      SCROLL ===> 20
****** ***************************** TOP OF DATA *****************************
000100 //MMA1X      JOB   (MMA1,DLOWE),'DOUG LOWE'
000200 //           EXEC  COBUCG
000300 //COB.SYSIN DD     DSN=DLOWE.TEST.COBOL(REORDLST),DISP=SHR
000400 //GO.SYSOUT DD     SYSOUT=A
000500 //BFCRDS     DD     DSN=DLOWE.TEST.DATA(BFCRDS),DISP=SHR
000600 //ORDLST     DD     SYSOUT=A
000700 //SYSUDUMP   DD     SYSOUT=A
****** *************************** BOTTOM OF DATA ***************************
```

Figure 7-6   Using the SUBMIT command of edit (part 1 of 2)

The JCL you're editing is submitted as a job

```
EDIT - DLOWE.TEST.CNTL(COBOL) -------------------------------- COLUMNS 001 072
COMMAND INPUT ===> SUBMIT                                      SCROLL ===> 20
****** ***************************** TOP OF DATA *****************************
000100 //MMA1X      JOB   (MMA1,DLOWE),'DOUG LOWE'
000200 //           EXEC  COBUCG
000300 //COB.SYSIN DD     DSN=DLOWE.TEST.COBOL(REORDLST),DISP=SHR
000400 //GO.SYSOUT DD     SYSOUT=A
000500 //BFCRDS     DD     DSN=DLOWE.TEST.DATA(BFCRDS),DISP=SHR
000600 //ORDLST     DD     SYSOUT=A
000700 //SYSUDUMP   DD     SYSOUT=A
****** *************************** BOTTOM OF DATA ***************************
JOB MMA1X(JOB03133) SUBMITTED
***
```

Figure 7-6   Using the SUBMIT command of edit (part 2 of 2)

```
-------------------------------- OUTLIST UTILITY --------------------------------
SELECT OPTION ===>

    L - LIST JOB NAMES/ID'S VIA THE TSO STATUS COMMAND
    D - DELETE JOB OUTPUT FROM SYSOUT HOLD QUEUE
    P - PRINT JOB OUTPUT AND DELETE FROM SYSOUT HOLD QUEUE
    R - REQUEUE JOB OUTPUT TO A NEW OUTPUT CLASS
    BLANK - DISPLAY JOB OUTPUT

FOR JOB TO BE SELECTED:
    JOBNAME ===>
    CLASS   ===>
    JOBID   ===>

FOR JOB TO BE REQUEUED:
    NEW OUTPUT CLASS ===>

FOR JOB TO BE PRINTED:                      (A FOR ANSI    )
    PRINTER CARRIAGE CONTROL ===>           (M FOR MACHINE )
                                            (BLANK FOR NONE)
```

Figure 7-7   The outlist utility entry panel

from the utilities menu. Then, SPF displays the outlist entry panel, shown in figure 7-7.

The outlist utility provides five options. You invoke four of them using a one-letter option code, as follows:

L   List the names and job-ids of active background jobs

D   Delete job output

P   Print job output

R   Requeue job output to a different output class

The fifth option is to display job output at your terminal. You select it by leaving the option field blank.

How to list job names

Option L issues a TSO STATUS command to display the status of jobs you've submitted for background processing (I describe the STATUS command in chapter 11). Figure 7-8 shows an example of listing job names. Here, I specify L in the

```
----------------------------- OUTLIST UTILITY  ---------------------------------
SELECT OPTION ===> L

    L - LIST JOB NAMES/ID'S VIA THE TSO STATUS COMMAND
    D - DELETE JOB OUTPUT FROM SYSOUT HOLD QUEUE
    P - PRINT JOB OUTPUT AND DELETE FROM SYSOUT HOLD QUEUE
    R - REQUEUE JOB OUTPUT TO A NEW OUTPUT CLASS
    BLANK - DISPLAY JOB OUTPUT

FOR JOB TO BE SELECTED:
    JOBNAME ===>
    CLASS   ===>
    JOBID   ===>

FOR JOB TO BE REQUEUED:
    NEW OUTPUT CLASS ===>

FOR JOB TO BE PRINTED:                     (A FOR ANSI    )
    PRINTER CARRIAGE CONTROL ===>          (M FOR MACHINE )
                                           (BLANK FOR NONE)

JOB DLOWEE(JOB03136) ON OUTPUT QUEUE
***
```

Figure 7-8 Listing job names

option field. SPF in turn issues a STATUS command, which displays a line near the bottom of the screen indicating that I've submitted one job for background processing, DLOWEE, and that it's finished processing and is waiting in an output queue. If I had submitted more than one job, additional lines would be displayed.

How to display or print job output

Once a background job has completed processing and is waiting in an output queue, you can use the outlist utility to display or print its output. On the outlist entry panel, you must specify the job name and, if you've submitted more than one job with the same name, the job-id. (You can tell the job-id by listing the job name. In figure 7-8, the job-id for the job named DLOWEE is JOB03136.) If you wish, you can also specify a job class to further identify the job. I usually leave the CLASS field blank, though.

If you leave the option field blank, SPF retrieves the job output and displays it at your terminal. Figure 7-9 shows the

```
 OUTLIST LISTING FOR DLOWEE ---------------------------- LINE 000000 COL 001 080
 COMMAND INPUT ===>                                         SCROLL ===> HALF
 ******************************** TOP OF DATA *********************-CAPS ON-**
 1                       J E S 2   J O B   L O G  --  S Y S T E M   M V S E  --  N O D
 -
 13.31.29 JOB 3136   ICH70001I DLOWE     LAST ACCESS AT 13:29:04 ON MONDAY, MARCH
 13.31.29 JOB 3136   $HASP373 DLOWEE     STARTED - INIT 1 - CLASS A - SYS MVSE
 13.31.29 JOB 3136   IEF403I DLOWEE - STARTED - TIME=13.31.29
 13.31.32 JOB 3136                                              --TIMINGS (MINS.)--
 13.31.32 JOB 3136   JOBNAME   STEPNAME PROCSTEP    RC    EXCP    CPU    SRB   CLOCK
 13.31.32 JOB 3136   DLOWEE    SCAN                 00      49    .00    .00     .0
 13.32.00 JOB 3136   DLOWEE    COBOL                12     565    .01    .00     .4
 13.32.01 JOB 3136   DLOWEE    SCAN              FLUSH       0    .00    .00     .0
 13.32.01 JOB 3136   DLOWEE    LINK              FLUSH       0    .00    .00     .0
 13.32.01 JOB 3136   IEF404I DLOWEE - ENDED - TIME=13.32.01
 13.32.01 JOB 3136   DLOWEE    ENDED.  NAME-DOUG LOWE            TOTAL CPU TIME=
 13.32.01 JOB 3136   $HASP395 DLOWEE     ENDED
     1      //DLOWEE   JOB (MMA1,DLOWE),'DOUG LOWE',
            // USER=DLOWE,GROUP=MMA1,PASSWORD=
            ***
            ***
            ***
     2      //SCAN    EXEC  PGM=ISPSCAN,PARM='REORDLST',COND=(12,LE)
            ***-------------------------------------------------------------------
```

Figure 7-9   Displaying job output

first panel of a typical job display. Here, you can see the
system messages indicating the completion status of each step
in the job. You use standard browse commands to display the
entire job output.

If you specify P as the option, the panel in figure 7-10 is
displayed. Here, you specify how you want to print the job
output—at a local printer (specify option L and a local printer-
id) or as a background job (specify option J, a SYSOUT class,
and the JOB statement information). In figure 7-10, I say that
the printed output should be routed to a local printer named
IBMT2IP1.

Another way to print held job output is to change its
SYSOUT class from a reserved class to a class assigned to an
appropriate printer. For example, suppose class X is defined as
a reserved print class in your installation, while class M is
assigned to a printer in your group or department. To direct
output held in class X to your printer, all you need to do is
change its output class from X to M.

```
---------------------- OUTLIST UTILITY PRINT OPTIONS  ----------------------
SELECT OPTION ===> L

    J - SUBMIT JOB TO PRINT
    L - ROUTE TO LOCAL PRINTER
    BLANK AND END KEY DELETES FROM SYSOUT HOLD QUEUE WITHOUT PRINTING

SYSOUT CLASS      ===>                    (IF OPTION "J" SELECTED)
LOCAL PRINTER ID ===> IBMT2IP1            (IF OPTION "L" SELECTED)

JOB STATEMENT INFORMATION:  (IF OPTION "J" SELECTED)
    ===> //DLOWEF   JOB (MMA1,DLOWE),'DOUG LOWE'
    ===> //*
    ===> //*
    ===> //*
```

Figure 7-10   Printing job output

That's where the requeue option comes in. If you specify
option R, a job name, and a new output class on the outlist
entry panel, the held output for the specified job is assigned to
the output class you specify.

In any event, the exact procedures for printing job output
vary from one installation to the next. So you'll have to find
out from your supervisor what the correct procedures are and
when you should use each one.

How to delete job output

Besides displaying job names or displaying, printing, or
requeuing job output, the outlist utility lets you delete job
output. That means the job is removed from the output queue
but isn't printed or displayed. Note that if you print job output
using option P or requeue it using option R, the output is
automatically deleted after it's printed. But if you display it

rather than print it, it stays in the queue. So remember to delete your jobs after you've displayed them.

DISCUSSION

Besides the SPF elements I presented in this chapter, there are native TSO commands that you can use for background processing as well. I cover them in chapter 11. Quite frankly, many programmers prefer to use the native TSO commands. That's because SPF's background capabilities are limited, so you have to use other facilities—like the edit function and the outlist utility—to do many of the tasks related to background processing.

Whether you use the foreground or the background facility to compile and link-edit programs depends mostly on your personal preference and your shop's standards. Response time is generally better when you use the foreground option. But when you use a background job, you can code your own JCL to invoke programs other than the standard language processors and linkage editor. And as an added bonus, you can use your terminal for other functions while your job is executing in a background region.

Terminology

job name
job-id
SYSOUT class
reserved class

Objectives

1. Use the SPF background option to create and submit a background job that compiles and link-edits a program.

2. Use the SUBMIT command of edit to submit a background job.

3. Use the outlist utility to (1) monitor job status and (2) display or print job output.

Part 3

How to use
TSO commands

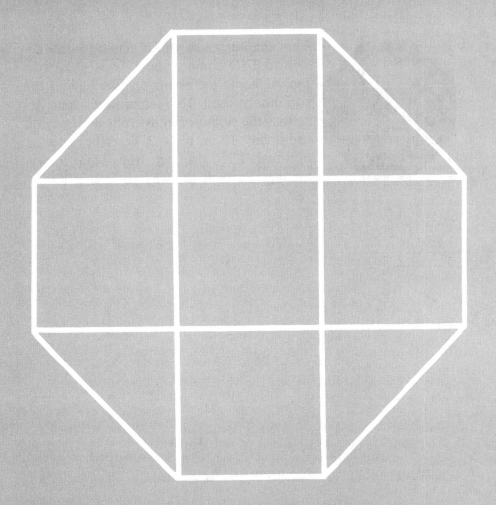

Chapter 8

An introduction to TSO commands

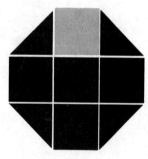

This chapter gives you a general introduction to TSO commands. It consists of two topics. Topic 1 presents an overview of the commonly used TSO commands and describes the rules you must follow when you use them. Then, topic 2 describes how an optional TSO product, the TSO session manager, affects the way you use TSO.

TOPIC 1   Basic TSO commands and coding rules

Figure 8-1 lists the TSO commands I cover in detail in this book. Although TSO provides many others, these are the ones you'll probably use most often. And once you've mastered these commands, you'll have no trouble learning how to use the others from the IBM manuals. So in this topic, I briefly describe these commands along with coding rules and other considerations for using them.

TSO COMMANDS: AN OVERVIEW

I've divided the commands in figure 8-1 into five categories: session management, basic data set management, data set allocation, foreground program development, and background job. This isn't how the commands are classified in the IBM manual (they're described in alphabetical order with no classification at all). But I think this classification makes sense.

Session management commands

Session management commands are designed to help you control your TSO session. Obviously, this group includes the LOGON and LOGOFF commands, which let you start and end a session. I also include the HELP command in this category, because it provides information on how to use other TSO commands. I described the LOGON and LOGOFF commands in chapter 1. And I'll describe the HELP command later in this topic.

Basic data set management commands

Basic data set management commands perform routine functions like copying or renaming files. The first four

Command	Function

Session management commands

LOGON	Start a terminal session.
LOGOFF	End a terminal session.
HELP	Display explanatory information.

Basic data set management commands

LISTCAT	List catalog entries.
LISTDS	List data set information.
RENAME	Change the name of a data set.
DELETE	Scratch a data set.
COPY	Reproduce a data set or member.
LIST	Display the contents of a data set or member.
DSPRINT	Print the contents of a data set or member.
EDIT	Modify the contents of a data set or member.

Data set allocation commands

ALLOCATE	Allocate a data set.
FREE	Free an allocated data set.
LISTALC	List data sets currently allocated.

Foreground program development commands

ASM	Assemble a program.
COBOL	Compile a COBOL program.
FORT	Compile a FORTRAN program.
PLI	Compile a PL/I program.
PLIC	Compile a PL/I program using the checkout compiler.
VSAPL	Invoke the VS APL processor.
VSBASIC	Invoke the VS BASIC processor.
LINK	Link-edit a compiled program.
CALL	Execute a link-edited program.
LOADGO	Link-edit and execute a compiled program.
TESTCOB	Test a COBOL program.

Background job commands

SUBMIT	Submit a job for background processing.
STATUS	Display the current status of submitted jobs.
OUTPUT	Obtain output from background jobs.
CANCEL	Cancel a submitted job.

Figure 8-1   The TSO commands covered in this book (not including CLIST commands)

commands in this category don't need much extra comment here. The LISTCAT command lists cataloged data sets; the LISTDS command lists information for specific data sets; the RENAME command changes the name of a data set; and the DELETE command scratches a data set.

The next two commands both provide essential functions —the COPY command reproduces a data set, while the LIST command displays the contents of a data set at your terminal. However, they're *not* a part of standard TSO. Instead, they're licensed separately from IBM as part of the *TSO Data Utilities* package. As a result, you'll have to check whether they're available at your installation or whether you'll be using other commands for these functions. (Incidentally, the Data Utilities package provides two other commands—FORMAT and MERGE—that I don't cover in this book. If you need to use them, they're documented in the IBM manual *OS/VS2 TSO Data Utilities: COPY, FORMAT, LIST, MERGE User's Guide and Reference*—order number GC28-6765.)

The next command, DSPRINT, prints a data set at an on-line printer. But like COPY and LIST, DSPRINT is a separately licensed product. So, though most TSO installations use DSPRINT, you'll have to check whether it's available to you.

The last command listed in this group, EDIT, is TSO's general-purpose editor. In most installations, though, EDIT is *not* used as a general-purpose editor. That's because there are a variety of other editors available—including SPF's editor—that provide substantially better features. However, EDIT is sometimes helpful when you're using a CLIST.

I'll describe all the basic data set management commands in detail in topic 1 of the next chapter.

Data set allocation commands

Data set allocation commands let you allocate and deallocate data sets. If you're familiar with OS JCL, you'll soon realize that the ALLOCATE command provides nearly the same functions as the DD statement. You use it to create new data sets or to define existing data sets for programs you run under TSO. The FREE command deallocates a data set previously allocated with an ALLOCATE command. And the LISTALC command lists the names of all data sets currently allocated to you.

Quite frankly, it's difficult to understand the concept of data set allocation if you haven't had much MVS or TSO experience. So if you're confused about the allocation commands right now, don't worry. Everything will make sense when I describe the commands in topic 2 of chapter 9.

Foreground program development commands

Foreground program development commands help you compile and test programs. Most of the commands listed in figure 8-1 in this category compile source programs using various compilers. The LINK command link-edits a compiled program to produce a load module which you can execute using the CALL command. The LOADGO command does essentially the same thing as the LINK and CALL commands but doesn't create a permanent load module. And the TESTCOB command helps you debug COBOL programs. I cover these commands in chapter 10.

Background job commands

Background job commands let you manage batch jobs in a background region. You use the SUBMIT command to initiate a background job. Then, you use the STATUS command to monitor the job's progress. When the job has completed, you use the OUTPUT command to retrieve its output. And you can use the CANCEL command to remove the job from the system. I cover background job commands in chapter 11.

TSO commands compared with SPF options

If you're familiar with SPF, you've probably been comparing the TSO commands with their equivalent SPF options. Figure 8-2 lists the equivalent SPF options for the TSO commands I cover in this book. Here, you can see that the main area of variation is in the allocation commands. The term *allocate* has

TSO command	SPF option
Session management	
LOGON	None
LOGOFF	X followed by LOGOFF
HELP	T (tutorial) or help key
Basic data set management	
LISTCAT	3.4 (list catalog utility)
LISTDS	3.2 (data set utility)
RENAME	3.2 (data set utility)
DELETE	3.2 (data set utility)
COPY	3.3 (move/copy utility)
LIST	1 (browse)
DSPRINT	3.6 (hardcopy utility)
EDIT	2 (edit)
Data set allocation	
ALLOCATE	3.2 (data set utility—not exactly the same function)
FREE	None
LISTALC	None
Foreground program development	
ASM	4.1 (foreground assembler)
COBOL	4.2 (foreground COBOL)
FORT	4.3 (foreground FORTRAN)
PLI	4.5 (foreground PL/I)
PLIC	4.4 (foreground PL/I—checkout compiler)
VSAPL	None
VSBASIC	None
LINK	4.6 (foreground link-edit)
CALL	None
LOADGO	None
TESTCOB	4.7 (COBOL interactive debugger)
Background jobs	
SUBMIT	5 (background processing)
	SUBMIT command of 2 (edit)
STATUS	3.8 (outlist utility)
OUTPUT	3.8 (outlist utility)
CANCEL	3.8 (outlist utility)

Figure 8-2   A comparison of TSO commands and SPF options

a slightly different meaning under TSO than it does under SPF. That's why there aren't equivalent SPF options for the FREE and LISTALC commands. But though it provides for fewer functions, the SPF allocate option is considerably easier to use than the ALLOCATE command.

I also want to stress that the SPF browse and edit options are a dramatic improvement over the TSO LIST and EDIT commands. And SPF provides many library management features that aren't available under standard TSO. Many shops, however, have added extensions to TSO to provide these functions. And many have added a full-screen editor to supplement or replace the EDIT command.

HOW TO USE TSO COMMANDS

Before you can learn the specifics of how to use individual TSO commands, you need to learn the syntax rules that apply to all TSO commands. In addition, you need to know how TSO responds to your commands with mode messages, prompts, and error messages. And finally, you need to know about two systems that affect how you enter TSO commands: SPF and the TSO session manager.

TSO command syntax

When you code a TSO command, you must follow a few rules. To begin with, all TSO commands follow this pattern:

```
command-name operands
```

The *command-name* field identifies the TSO function you wish to invoke. The *operands* (sometimes called *parameters*) provide information specific to each command.

You code TSO command operands in free form (that is, without worrying about which column they start in), separating them with commas or spaces. Some of the operands are *positional operands*. The location of a positional operand within a command is significant to its meaning. For example, consider this TSO command:

```
COPY TEST.COBOL TEST1.COBOL
```

The first operand (TEST.COBOL) names the input file for the COPY command. The second operand (TEST1.COBOL) names the output file. You can see how the positions of these operands determine their meanings.

Other operands are *keyword operands*. Keyword operands don't depend on their position within a command for their meaning. Instead, TSO recognizes keyword operands wherever they appear within a command. To illustrate, consider this command:

```
FREE ALL HOLD
```

Here, TSO recognizes two keywords: ALL and HOLD (FREE is the command name). The presence of these keywords affects how the command is processed; if you omit either one, the command is processed differently. But the order in which the keywords are specified makes no difference. So this command:

```
FREE HOLD ALL
```

has the same meaning.

Many keyword operands require that you supply a value within parentheses, like this:

```
DDNAME(OUTDD)
```

Here, TSO recognizes the keyword DDNAME and associates the value OUTDD with it. Some keyword operands require two or more values within the parentheses, separated by commas or spaces, as in this example:

```
SPACE(100 50)
```

Within the keyword operand, the *suboperands* are positional.

Abbreviation   As you gain experience with TSO, you'll find that many of the command and keyword combinations you use frequently require more keystrokes than seem necessary. Fortunately, TSO lets you abbreviate commands and keywords liberally.

To begin with, many TSO command names have an abbreviated form. For example, you can specify DEL as the command name for the DELETE command. Figure 8-3 gives the abbreviated form for each of the commands I cover in this book.

As for keyword operands, TSO lets you abbreviate them by specifying only as many characters as are necessary to distinguish the keyword from other keywords within the same command. For example, all of these are valid abbreviations for the LISTALC command's STATUS operand:

STATUS

STATU

STAT

STA

ST

But S isn't acceptable because it could be confused with the SYSNAMES operand.

Because the minimum abbreviations for keyword operands depend on the other operands available for the same command, they're often difficult to remember. As a result, I suggest you avoid using excessive abbreviation until you become proficient with the TSO commands.

How to continue a TSO command on another line   If a command requires so many operands that you can't code it in the 80 columns of a single terminal line, you must continue it to the next line. Unfortunately, the procedure for doing this depends on a number of factors, including which telecommunications access method (TCAM or VTAM) is used at your installation and what optional features your 3270 terminal is configured with. So you may have to experiment a bit to determine exactly how to enter multi-line commands.

In some cases, you can enter multi-line commands by pressing the new line key at the end of each line. That moves the cursor to the next line, where you can continue the command. It may also generate a field mark character, which displays as a semicolon on your terminal. In other cases, you may have to enter a continuation character—either a plus sign

Full command name	Abbreviation
LOGON	
LOGOFF	
HELP	H
LISTCAT	LISTC
LISTDS	LISTD
RENAME	REN
DELETE	DEL
COPY	
LIST	
DSPRINT	DSP
EDIT	E
ALLOCATE	ALLOC
FREE	
LISTALC	LISTA
ASM	
COBOL	
FORT	
PLI	
PLIC	
VSAPL	
VSBASIC	
LINK	
CALL	
LOADGO	LOAD
TESTCOB	
SUBMIT	SUB
STATUS	ST
OUTPUT	OUT
CANCEL	

Figure 8-3   Abbreviations for TSO commands

(+) or a hyphen (−)—at the end of each continued line, like this:

```
ALLOCATE DSNAME(TEST.COBOL) DDNAME(SYSUT2) +
NEW CATALOG SPACE(100 10) CYLINDERS DIR(10)
```

Here, the plus sign means the command continues on the next line.

How to specify data set names   Most TSO commands require that you supply one or more data set names as positional or keyword operands. I described how you specify data set names under TSO in chapter 1. Now, I just want to review two important points.

First, TSO supplies your user-id for you, so you don't have to include it in your data set names. As a result, if your user-id is DLOWE and you enter TEST.COBOL as a data set name, TSO looks for a data set named DLOWE.TEST.COBOL. Throughout the rest of this book, I'll assume the user-id is DLOWE.

Second, if you do *not* want TSO to automatically include your user-id in a data set name, you must enclose the data set name in apostrophes, like this:

```
'SYS1.CLIST'
```

Here, the fully qualified data set name is SYS1.CLIST; TSO doesn't add your user-id to the name.

The HELP command   If you forget the syntax of a command, you can use the HELP command to refresh your memory. If you enter the word HELP by itself, TSO displays a summary of all its available commands. If you enter HELP followed by a command name, TSO provides an explanation of that command, including the command's syntax and an explanation of each of its operands.

System responses

During a TSO session, TSO displays short messages at your terminal. These messages fall into four categories: mode messages, prompts, informational messages, and broadcast messages.

Mode messages   The *mode messages* tell you that TSO is ready to accept a command. The most common mode message is this:

```
READY
```

When you see this at your terminal, it means TSO is waiting for you to enter a command. Other mode messages appear when you enter a command that has its own set of sub-commands, such as OUTPUT or TESTCOB. For example, if you see this mode message,

```
OUTPUT
```

it means TSO is waiting for you to enter an OUTPUT subcommand. I'll describe OUTPUT and TESTCOB subcommands later in this book.

Prompts   If you enter a command that has an error in it, or if you omit a required operand, TSO responds with a *prompt* that describes the problem and asks you to reenter the operand. For example, the LIST command requires a data set name. Suppose you enter the command without a data set name, like this:

```
LIST
```

Then, TSO responds with a message asking you to enter a data set name. Prompts are easy to identify because they always end with a question mark.

Informational messages   Many of TSO's messages simply provide information about the progress of a command's execution. These *informational messages* may or may not be of importance to you. Usually, they indicate that all is well. Sometimes, however, an informational message indicates a problem that requires your attention.

Broadcast messages   *Broadcast messages* are created by a system operator or another TSO user. In general, you'll receive a set of broadcast messages when you log on. These messages may inform you of important events like scheduled inter-ruptions in your system's availability. So it's a good idea to check them briefly.

Related systems

Before I show you how to use specific TSO commands, you need to know how two related products affect the way you use TSO. They are SPF and the TSO session manager.

How to invoke TSO commands from SPF   When you use SPF, you invoke most of the commonly used TSO functions via menu selections. As a result, you don't use TSO commands on a day-by-day basis. But you will want to use them in certain situations.

You can invoke any TSO command from SPF by selecting option 6 from the primary option menu. SPF then displays the command entry panel shown in figure 8-4. Here, your terminal is in native TSO mode and you can enter any TSO command you wish. You return to SPF by pressing PF3/15.

When should you use TSO commands from option 6 rather than normal SPF options? The answer is largely a matter of experience. Certain functions can't be done from SPF, so you'll have to use native TSO commands. But as you gain experience, you'll find that some functions—for example, foreground program development—can be done under SPF but are easier to do under native TSO.

The TSO session manager   As I mentioned in chapter 1, the TSO session manager is designed to make it easier to use the full-screen capabilities of the 3270. Although the session manager doesn't fundamentally change the line-by-line nature of TSO, it does provide some substantial benefits. I show you how to use the session manager in the next topic. If your installation uses the session manager, you should read that topic. Otherwise, feel free to move directly to chapter 9.

Terminology

command name	suboperand
operand	mode message
parameter	prompt
positional operand	informational message
keyword operand	broadcast message

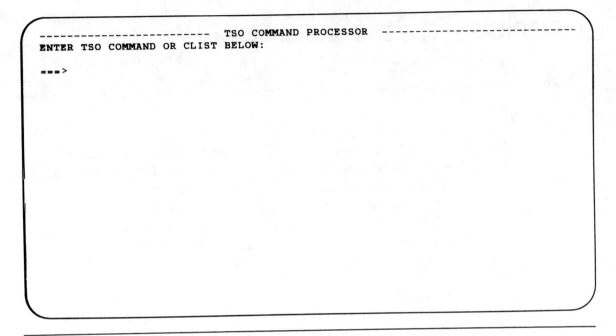

```
------------------------------ TSO COMMAND PROCESSOR  ------------------------------
ENTER TSO COMMAND OR CLIST BELOW:

===>
```

Figure 8-4   SPF's TSO command processor panel

Objectives

1. Briefly describe five categories of TSO commands.

2. Describe the rules for creating TSO commands.

3. Describe these types of TSO system responses:

   a. mode messages
   b. prompts
   c. informational messages
   d. broadcast messages

4. Describe how you invoke a TSO command from SPF.

TOPIC 2   The TSO session manager

As I said in topic 1, the *TSO session manager* acts as an
interface between 3270-type terminals and TSO. In essence, the
session manager converts the line-by-line operations of native
TSO into full-screen operations that take advantage of the
3270's capabilities. As a result, the session manager makes it
much easier to use the facilities of TSO.

Streams and windows

To act as an interface between native TSO and the user, the
session manager uses special data sets called *streams*. Quite
simply, each record in a stream represents one line sent to or
received from a terminal. As a session manager user, you
communicate with streams: you can look at information in
them or add information to them. The session manager, in
turn, communicates with TSO via the streams: it presents
commands one line at a time from a stream and stores TSO's
output in a stream.

To illustrate, figure 8-5 shows how two of the session
manager's streams work together (though there are many other
streams, these are the only two I'll describe in this chapter).
One stream, called the *TSOIN stream*, receives commands you
enter at your terminal and in turn passes them on to TSO. The
other, called the *TSOOUT stream*, receives TSO's output and
passes it on to your terminal. In addition, each time you enter
a command into the TSOIN stream, it's copied directly to the
TSOOUT stream. As a result, the TSOOUT stream contains
TSO output intermixed with your commands. In short, the
TSOOUT stream is an exact image of the terminal screen for a
non-session manager TSO session.

So far, this is probably very confusing. What puts it all
together is the idea of windows. Under the session manager, a
window is a part of your terminal's screen that's linked to one

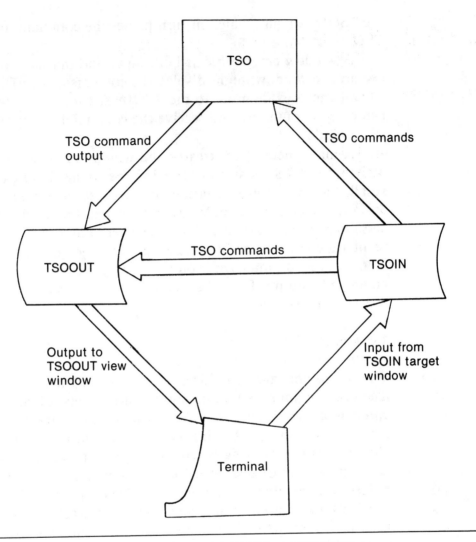

Figure 8-5 How the session manager uses the TSOIN and TSOOUT streams

of the session manager's streams. For example, one part of your terminal screen is used as a window that views the TSOOUT stream. That way, whenever TSO adds information to the TSOOUT stream, you can see it in the screen window that views that stream.

Similarly, some portions of your terminal's screen are used as windows that provide input to a stream. For example, one window might be linked to the TSOIN stream. When you enter a TSO command in that window, the command is passed on to the TSOIN stream, which in turn passes the command on to TSO.

A window can double as both input and output. For example, a window might display the contents of the TSOOUT stream and provide input to the TSOIN stream. That way, you can enter a command and receive the command's output in the same window.

A major benefit of streams and windows is that all of the activity for a TSO session is saved in the streams and can be recalled at any time. In contrast, data is lost once it's removed from the screen when you're working under TSO without the session manager. Under native TSO, then, you often have to reenter a command because its output is no longer displayed. With the session manager, you can simply recall the command's output from the stream in which it was saved.

Commands and PF keys

The session manager provides a command language of its own. The most commonly used commands are the scrolling commands, which let you move a window from one part of a stream to another. That's how you recall data from a stream. I'll describe the scrolling commands later in this topic.

Another set of session manager commands lets you redefine the windows and streams you're using. You don't normally use these commands, however—at least, not at first. Instead, you use the arrangement of streams and windows supplied by IBM, called the *default format*.

Session manager commands can be associated with PF keys so that by pressing a single PF key, you can invoke a complete session manager command. That makes it easy to use common session manager commands. Figure 8-6 shows the default PF key assignments. These are the assignments that are in effect when you first enter the session manager. Although you can change these assignments, you usually don't need to, and I don't show you how to do so in this book. But I do explain the PF key functions that are shaded in figure 8-6 in this topic. The others, though sometimes useful, represent functions that are beyond the scope of this book.

Key	Function
PF1	Print screen snapshots.
PF2	Change scroll amount.
PF3	Enter command.
PF4	Take screen snapshot.
PF5	Find text.
PF6	Switch between TSOIN and TSOOUT.
PF7	Scroll up.
PF8	Scroll down.
PF9	Scroll up max.
PF10	Scroll left.
PF11	Scroll right.
PF12	Scroll down max.

Figure 8-6   PF key functions under the session manager

The default screen format

Figure 8-7 shows a typical session manager display. Although it's not apparent, this display actually consists of ten windows. Of the ten, six display headings. So only four of the windows are important to you. Those four windows are shown in figure 8-8.

The *MAIN window* takes up most of the display screen—19 full lines. It displays the contents of the TSOOUT stream. When you use one of the scrolling commands I'll describe in a moment, it's the MAIN window that is scrolled. (You can scroll other windows, but you usually don't.)

The *CURRENT window* is smaller than the MAIN window—it's only two lines of 62 characters each. It displays the last two lines of the TSOOUT stream. So when you scroll the TSOOUT stream in the MAIN window, the most recent

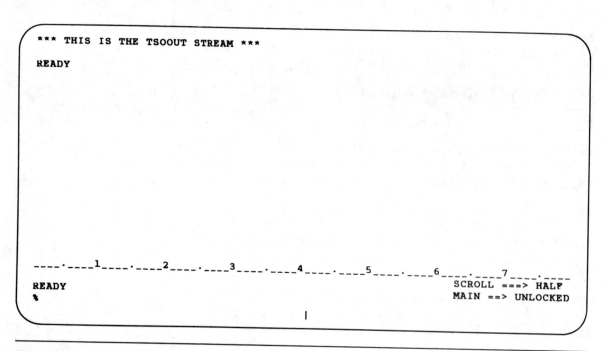

Figure 8-7   The TSO session manager screen

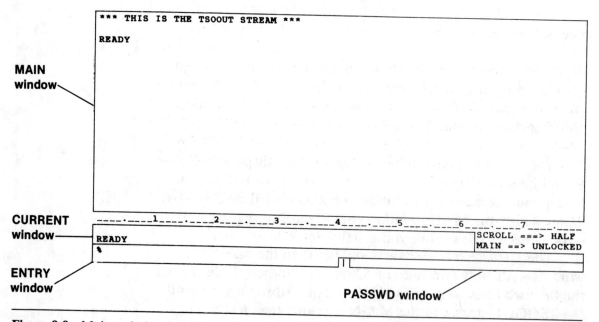

Figure 8-8   Major windows on the session manager screen

information in the TSOOUT stream will still be shown in the CURRENT window.

The *ENTRY window* is tied to the TSOIN stream. It's here that you normally enter your TSO commands. The percent sign (%) identifies the start of the ENTRY window. Normally, you enter the first letter of your TSO command directly over the percent sign. It's there to help you invoke a CLIST using a technique called implicit execution. I don't explain CLISTs or implicit execution until chapter 12, so ignore the percent sign for now.

You use the last window in figure 8-8, the *PASSWD window*, only when TSO prompts you for a password. This window is tied to the TSOIN stream just like the ENTRY window, but data isn't displayed as it's entered. In other words, no characters appear on the screen when you enter a password; the cursor simply moves across the window as though you were entering spaces.

Besides the ENTRY and PASSWD windows, the MAIN and CURRENT windows are also tied to the TSOIN stream for input. So although those windows normally display data from the TSOOUT stream, any data you enter in them will be sent to the TSOIN stream and processed by TSO as a command.

One common use of the MAIN window as input is when you're entering several commands that vary only slightly. In this case, you enter the first command in the ENTRY window. After the command is processed, it's displayed in the MAIN window along with the command's output. To enter the second command, you just move the cursor to the command in the MAIN window, make any changes necessary by typing over the command and using the insert and delete keys, and press the enter key. The command will be sent to the TSOIN stream and processed again by TSO.

In fact, any line you change in the MAIN or CURRENT window is sent to the TSOIN stream. So if you modify four lines in the MAIN window, four lines are sent to TSOIN.

To illustrate how you use the default screen windows to enter TSO commands, consider figure 8-9. In part 1, I enter a simple TSO command—LISTCAT—in the ENTRY window. Notice how I typed directly over the percent sign that's normally displayed at the start of the ENTRY window. Part 2

Enter the command

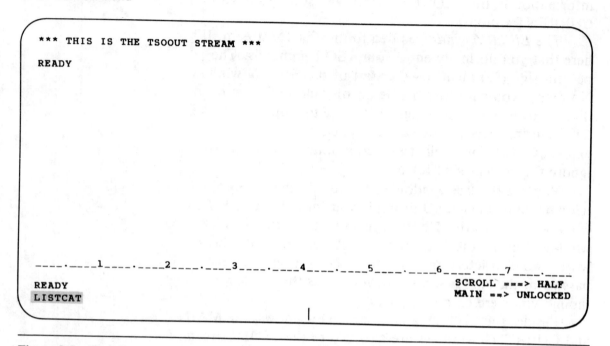

```
*** THIS IS THE TSOOUT STREAM ***
READY




                                                          .






----.----1----.----2----.----3----.----4----.----5----.----6----.----7----.----
READY                                               SCROLL ===> HALF
LISTCAT                                             MAIN ==> UNLOCKED

                             |
```

Figure 8-9   Entering a TSO command under the session manager (part 1 of 2)

The resulting output

```
READY
LISTCAT
IN CATALOG:VCAT.MPS600
DLOWE.BFCRDS.DATA
DLOWE.ISPPARM
DLOWE.REORDLST.LINKLIST
DLOWE.REORDLST.LIST
DLOWE.SPFEDITA.BACKUP
DLOWE.TEST.CLIST
DLOWE.TEST.CNTL
DLOWE.TEST.COBOL
DLOWE.TEST.LIST
DLOWE.TEST.LOAD
DLOWE.TEST.OBJ
DLOWE.TEST.SYM
DLOWE.TEST1.COBOL
READY


----.----1----.----2----.----3----.----4----.----5----.----6----.----7----.----
DLOWE.TEST1.COBOL
READY                                               SCROLL ===> HALF
%                                                   MAIN ==> UNLOCKED

                             |
```

Figure 8-9   Entering a TSO command under the session manager (part 2 of 2)

of this figure shows how the screen appears after TSO processes the LISTCAT command. The output from the command is displayed in the MAIN window. And the last two lines displayed in the MAIN window are also displayed in the CURRENT window. The percent sign is restored to the ENTRY window, so I can enter another TSO command there.

How to scroll through a data set

Under the default screen format, the MAIN window displays 19 lines of 79 columns each. During a TSO session, the TSOOUT stream collects more than 19 lines after you enter just one or two commands. So the MAIN window generally displays just a portion of the TSOOUT stream's records. In addition, the records in the TSOOUT stream may be longer than 79 characters. To display TSOOUT records other than the ones currently shown, or to show data beyond the first 79 columns of each record, you use *scrolling*.

To use scrolling, you have to specify both the direction and the amount of the scroll. To specify the scrolling direction, you use PF keys. Figure 8-10 shows the default PF key assignments for scrolling. As you can see, PF7 moves the window up to display previous TSOOUT entries, while PF8 moves the window down. PF11 moves the window to the right to display data past the first 79 characters, while PF10 moves the window to the left.

Note that the PF keys move the window, not the data in the stream. As a result, the data *appears* to move on the screen, but in the opposite direction that the PF key would indicate. For example, if you move the window down by using PF8, the data on the screen appears to move up. Similarly, when you move the window right using PF11, the data appears to move to the left.

The amount of the scroll is indicated by the screen field at the righthand side of line 21, labelled:

```
SCROLL ===>
```

The value in this field tells you how far the scroll function moves the window.

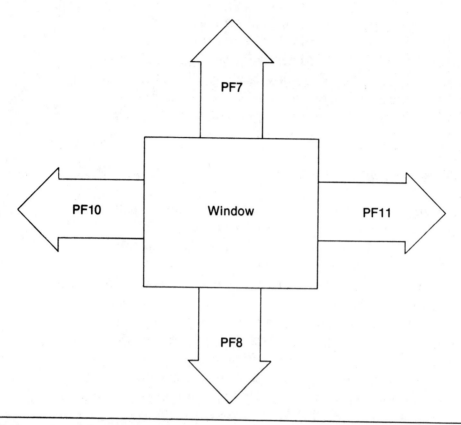

Figure 8-10   PF keys used for scrolling under the session manager

Figure 8-11 shows the valid scroll amount values. Normally, the scroll amount defaults to HALF. That means that the window is moved a half page in the direction indicated by the PF key you use. (A *page* is determined by the size of the window being scrolled—for the MAIN window, it's 19 lines or 80 columns, depending on the direction of the scroll.) For example, if you scroll half a page down (PF8), the window is moved down 9 lines. If you scroll half a page right (PF11), the window is moved 40 columns to the right.

To change the scroll amount, you enter the new scroll value in the ENTRY window (type directly over the percent sign) and press PF2. That changes the value in the SCROLL field, so future scroll keys move the data according to the new scroll value.

You can scroll a specific number of lines or columns by entering a number in the scroll field. For example, if you enter

Value	Meaning
HALF	Move the screen window half a page.
PAGE	Move the screen window a full page.
n	Move the screen window *n* lines or columns.
MAX	Move the screen window to the top, bottom, left, or right margin.

Note: Scroll amounts are set by entering the correct value in the ENTRY window and pressing PF2.

Figure 8-11   SCROLL values

50 in the ENTRY window and press PF2, the scrolling keys move the window 50 lines or columns.

You can easily move the window to the top or bottom of a stream or to the left or right margin by entering MAX as the scroll amount. Then, if you use PF7, the window is moved to the oldest entry in the stream, while PF8 moves the window to the most recent entry in the stream. Similarly, PF10 returns the window to the left margin (column 1) while PF11 moves the window to the right margin. Alternatively, you can use PF9 or PF12 to move the window to the top or bottom of the stream *without* changing the scroll value to MAX. PF9 moves the window to the oldest data in the stream, while PF12 moves the window to the newest data.

Figure 8-12 shows the effect of a half-page scroll during a TSO session. To set up this display, I entered an OUTPUT command that caused many pages of output to be written to the TSOOUT stream. Then, I used scrolling commands to move backwards in the stream to the point shown in part 1 of figure 8-12. Notice that the SCROLL field indicates that the scroll value is HALF. When I press PF8, the display changes as shown in part 2. As you can see, the display has moved up 9 lines. If I pressed PF7 at this point, I would return to the display in part 1.

Figure 8-13 shows the effect of a half-page scroll right using PF11. Part 1 shows the display before the scroll; part 2 shows the display after the scroll. Here, you can see that the display has been shifted 40 characters.

Before the scroll

```
PP 5740-CB1 RELEASE 2.3  + PTF 8 JAN 28 82              IBM OS/VS COBOL

    1                        11.47.50        APR 23,1984
00001     000800 IDENTIFICATION DIVISION.
00002     000900*
00003     001000 PROGRAM-ID. REORDLST.
00004     001100*
00005     001200 ENVIRONMENT DIVISION.
00006     001300*
00007     001400 CONFIGURATION SECTION.
00008     001500*
00009     001600 SPECIAL-NAMES.
00010     001700      C01 IS PAGE-TOP.
00011     001800*
00012     001900 INPUT-OUTPUT SECTION.
00013     002000*
00014     002100 FILE-CONTROL.
00015     002200      SELECT BFCRDS ASSIGN TO UT-S-BFCRDS.
00016     002300      SELECT ORDLST ASSIGN TO UT-S-ORDLST.
----.----1----.----2----.----3----.----4----.----5----.----6----.----7----.----
                                                     SCROLL ===> HALF
READY                                                MAIN ==>   LOCKED
%
```

Figure 8-12   Effect of a half-page scroll down (part 1 of 2)

After the scroll

```
00007     001400 CONFIGURATION SECTION.
00008     001500*
00009     001600 SPECIAL-NAMES.
00010     001700      C01 IS PAGE-TOP.
00011     001800*
00012     001900 INPUT-OUTPUT SECTION.
00013     002000*
00014     002100 FILE-CONTROL.
00015     002200      SELECT BFCRDS ASSIGN TO UT-S-BFCRDS.
00016     002300      SELECT ORDLST ASSIGN TO UT-S-ORDLST.
00017     002400*
00018     002500 DATA DIVISION.
00019     002600*
00020     002700 FILE SECTION.
00021     002800*
00022     002900 FD   BFCRDS
00023     003000      LABEL RECORDS ARE STANDARD
00024     003100      RECORDING MODE IS F
00025     003200      RECORD CONTAINS 80 CHARACTERS.
----.----1----.----2----.----3----.----4----.----5----.----6----.----7----.----
                                                     SCROLL ===> HALF
READY                                                MAIN ==>   LOCKED
%
```

Figure 8-12   Effect of a half-page scroll down (part 2 of 2)

Before the scroll

```
   10        REORDLST          11.47.50        APR 23,1984
 *STATISTICS*     SOURCE RECORDS =    202     DATA DIVISION STATEMENTS =     67
 *OPTIONS IN EFFECT*        SIZE =  131072  BUF =    12288  LINECNT = 57   SPACE1, FL
 *OPTIONS IN EFFECT*        DMAP, NOPMAP,   CLIST, NOSUPMAP,   XREF, NOSXREF,    L
 *OPTIONS IN EFFECT*      NOTERM, NONUM, NOBATCH, NONAME, COMPILE=01, NOSTATE, NO
 *OPTIONS IN EFFECT*      NOOPTIMIZE, NOSYMDMP, NOTEST,   VERB,    ZWB, SYST, NOEN
 *OPTIONS IN EFFECT*      NOLST , NOFDECK,NOCDECK, LCOL2,  L120,    DUMP ,   ADV ,
 *OPTIONS IN EFFECT*      NOCOUNT, NOVBSUM, NOVBREF, LANGLVL(2)
   11        REORDLST          11.47.50        APR 23,1984
                                               CROSS-REFERENCE DICTIONARY


 DATA NAMES                          DEFN     REFERENCE


 BFCRDS                             000015   000125   000130   000145
 BAL-FWD-CARD                       000027
 BF-ITEM-NO                         000029
 BF-ITEM-DESC                       000030   000165
 ____.____1____.____2____.____3____.____4____.____5____.____6____.____7____.____
                                                        SCROLL ===> HALF
 READY                                                  MAIN ==>   LOCKED
 %
```

Figure 8-13   Effect of a half-page scroll right (part 1 of 2)

After the scroll

```
    APR 23,1984
     DATA DIVISION STATEMENTS =     67     PROCEDURE DIVISION STATEMENTS =     45
 BUF =   12288  LINECNT = 57  SPACE1, FLAGW,   SEQ,   SOURCE
   CLIST, NOSUPMAP,   XREF, NOSXREF,    LOAD, NODECK, QUOTE, NOTRUNC, NOFLOW
 OBATCH, NONAME, COMPILE=01, NOSTATE, NORESIDENT, NODYNAM, NOLIB, NOSYNTAX
 MDMP, NOTEST,    VERB,    ZWB, SYST, NOENDJOB, NOLVL
 NOCDECK, LCOL2,  L120,    DUMP ,   ADV , NOPRINT,
   NOVBREF, LANGLVL(2)
    APR 23,1984
    CROSS-REFERENCE DICTIONARY


 REFERENCE


 000125   000130   000145


 000165
 ____.____5____.____6____.____7____.____8____.____9____.____10___.____11___.____
                                                        SCROLL ===> HALF
 READY                                                  MAIN ==>   LOCKED
 %
```

Figure 8-13   Effect of a half-page scroll right (part 2 of 2)

Locked and unlocked windows   Before I go on, let me explain the difference between an unlocked window and a locked window. When a window is *unlocked*, it's scrolled automatically by the session manager so that the most current data in the stream is always displayed. When you enter the session manager, both the MAIN and the ENTRY windows are unlocked. So as you enter TSO commands, both windows are automatically scrolled so the most recent entries in the TSOOUT stream are displayed. Once you use a scrolling key, however, the MAIN window is *locked*. That means it's *not* automatically scrolled as entries are added to the TSOOUT stream. Instead, the window moves only in response to your scrolling commands.

Now that you know about locked and unlocked windows, you'll understand why the default screen format provides two windows to view the TSOOUT stream: MAIN and CURRENT. Since the MAIN window can become locked when you enter a scrolling command, the CURRENT window remains unlocked throughout your TSO session. Thus, the CURRENT window *always* displays the two most current lines from the TSOOUT stream, even when the MAIN window is locked.

The status of the MAIN window is shown beneath the scroll amount field. In figure 8-9, the MAIN window is unlocked because no scrolling keys have been used. But in figure 8-12, the MAIN window is locked. To unlock the MAIN window once it's locked, use PF12 to move the window to the end of the stream. The status of the MAIN window will return to UNLOCKED.

How to find text

Sometimes, you need to scroll the MAIN window repeatedly to display a certain portion of the TSOOUT stream. For example, in figure 8-12, I had to scroll through several hundred lines of text before I came to the start of my compiler listing. If the part of the TSOOUT stream you're looking for contains a unique series of characters, you can use a find operation to scroll directly to it. A find operation searches backwards through the TSOOUT stream. So if the text you're looking for is past your current location in the stream, you should first use PF12 to scroll to the end of the stream.

To start a find operation, you enter the text string you're looking for in the ENTRY window. Then, you press PF5. The session manager then scrolls the window backwards until it finds the specified text. If the text string contains any spaces, commas, or parentheses, you must enclose it in apostrophes, like this:

```
'PIC (X)'
```

And if the text contains apostrophes, double them, like this:

```
'VALUE ''SALES REPORT''.'
```

Here, the text string for the find is VALUE 'SALES REPORT'.

Discussion

I've presented only a small subset of the session manager's capabilities in this topic. The IBM manual (*Session Manager User's Guide and Reference*, SC28-0912) describes more than 20 session manager commands. Some of these allow you to change PF key assignments. So if you use a certain command repeatedly, you can assign it to a PF key and press only the one key whenever you want to enter that command. Many of the other session manager commands let you change the default screen format. For example, you can divide the screen in half, into two large windows, and scroll through each one separately.

At this point, I just want you to realize that the session manager is both powerful and flexible. The default key assignments and screen format I've presented in this topic are adequate for most applications. But as you gain experience with the session manager, you may want to experiment with its capabilities.

Terminology

TSO session manager
stream
TSOIN stream
TSOOUT stream
window
default format
MAIN window
CURRENT window
ENTRY window
PASSWD window
scrolling
page
unlocked window
locked window

Objectives

1. Describe how the session manager uses streams and windows as an interface between a user and TSO.

2. Describe the function of these windows:

    a. MAIN
    b. CURRENT
    c. ENTRY
    d. PASSWD

3. Under the session manager, (1) scroll through a data set and (2) use a find operation to locate specific text.

Chapter 9

Data set management and allocation commands

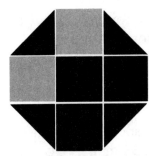

In this chapter, I present the TSO commands you use to manage data sets. This chapter consists of two topics. Topic 1 describes the basic data set management commands. These commands let you list catalog and data set information, rename or delete data sets or members, and copy, change, or list data sets or members. Topic 2 describes the TSO commands you use to allocate data sets. These commands let you create new data sets or prepare a data set to be processed by a foreground program.

TOPIC 1 Data set management commands

In this topic, I describe eight basic data set management commands: LISTCAT, LISTDS, RENAME, DELETE, COPY, LIST, EDIT, and DSPRINT. These commands let you perform basic data set management functions like listing catalog entries, listing data set information, changing data set names, scratching data sets, reproducing data sets, and displaying, changing, or printing the contents of a data set.

How to list catalog entries

Figure 9-1 gives the format of the LISTCAT command, which lets you list entries in an MVS catalog. If you omit all the operands, LISTCAT displays the name of each data set cataloged under your user-id. The LISTCAT operands let you control the number of entries displayed or the amount of information displayed for each entry.

If you want to list catalog entries for a specific data set or group of data sets, you can code an ENTRIES or LEVEL operand. Both have similar functions but different coding requirements. For the ENTRIES operand, you supply one or more data set names. TSO supplies your user-id as the high-level qualifier for each data set name you supply, unless you enclose the name in apostrophes.

Within a data set name specified in an ENTRY operand, you can replace one of the qualifiers with an asterisk. Then, the name is a *generic data set name*. That means the name may refer to more than one data set. For example, suppose you code the ENTRIES operand like this:

```
ENTRIES(TEST.*)
```

Here, any data set name with your user-id as its first qualifier, TEST as its second qualifier, and *any* value as its third qualifier is listed.

The LISTCAT command

```
LISTCAT  [{ENTRIES(data-set-names)}]
         [{LEVEL(level)          }]

         [{NAME   }]
         [{HISTORY}]
         [{VOLUME }]
         [{ALL    }]
```

Explanation

ENTRIES   Specifies the data set names to be listed. If more than one name is specified, they must be separated by commas or spaces. You can use an asterisk (*) for one of the levels in a data set name; in that case, more than one data set may be listed.

LEVEL   Specifies one or more levels of qualification for the data sets to be listed. For example, if you specify LEVEL(DLOWE.TEST), any data set starting with DLOWE.TEST is listed.

NAME   Specifies what information to list for each catalog entry. NAME says to list the data
HISTORY   set name and entry type. HISTORY says to list the data set name, entry type, owner-
VOLUME   id, creation date, and expiration date. VOLUME says to list HISTORY information
ALL   plus the vol-ser and device type. And ALL says to list all catalog fields. (NAME is the default.)

Figure 9-1   The LISTCAT command

You can specify more than one data set name in an ENTRIES operand, like this:

```
ENTRIES(TEST.COBOL TEST.OBJ)
```

Here, the catalog entries for two data sets are listed.

The LEVEL operand is similar to the ENTRIES operand, with two significant differences. First, the LEVEL operand does *not* add your user-id as the high-level qualifier of a data set. Second, you specify one or more levels of qualification in a LEVEL operand, rather than a complete data set name. For example, if you code this LEVEL operand,

```
LEVEL(DLOWE.TEST)
```

any data set starting with DLOWE.TEST will be listed, whether the data set name has two, three, or more levels in its

Catalog data set name	ENTRIES(TEST.*)	ENTRIES(*.COBOL)	LEVEL(DLOWE.TEST)	LEVEL(DLOWE)
DLOWE.TEST.COBOL	X	X	X	X
DLOWE.TEST.OBJ	X		X	X
DLOWE.TEST.LOAD	X		X	X
DLOWE.TEST.BF.DATA			X	X
DLOWE.COPY.COBOL		X		X

Figure 9-2 Effect of various ENTRIES and LEVEL parameters in the LISTCAT command (shows which data sets will be listed)

name. In contrast, if you specify a two-level data set name in an ENTRIES operand, only data sets with names of two levels are listed, even if one of the levels is an asterisk.

To illustrate the differences between the ENTRIES and LEVEL operands, figure 9-2 shows which of five data set names are listed for each of four ENTRIES and LEVEL operands. The first ENTRIES operand lists the three data sets whose names consist of three levels, the second of which is TEST. The second ENTRIES operand lists the two data sets whose names consist of three levels, the third of which is COBOL. The first LEVEL operand lists the data sets whose names have DLOWE and TEST as their first and second qualifiers, regardless of how many levels of qualification the name contains.

The last LEVEL operand is a special case. Here, I code my user-id as the LEVEL. As a result, all of my data sets are listed. You never have to code a LEVEL operand like this, however. That's because if you don't code a LEVEL operand or an ENTRIES operand, TSO supplies your user-id as the default LEVEL.

I usually use the LEVEL operand rather than ENTRIES. Because LEVEL doesn't require that you specify all levels of qualification in a data set name, it's more useful when you're trying to remember a data set name you've forgotten. I use the ENTRIES operand when I want to list catalog information for a specific data set.

The other operands for the LISTCAT command control how much information is displayed for each catalog entry. If

Example 1

```
LISTCAT
```

Example 2

```
LISTCAT ENTRIES(TEST.COBOL TEST.OBJ TEST.LOAD) ALL
```

Example 3

```
LISTCAT ENTRIES(TEST.*) ALL
```

Example 4

```
LISTCAT LEVEL(DLOWE.TEST) ALL
```

Figure 9-3   Examples of the LISTCAT command

you don't include any of these operands—or if you say NAME
—only the data set name and its type are listed. If you specify
HISTORY, TSO lists the data set's name and type along with
its owner-id, creation date, and expiration date. If you specify
VOLUME, TSO lists the HISTORY information plus the
volume serial number and device type of the volume on which
the data set resides. And if you specify ALL, all of the catalog
information for the data set is listed.

LISTCAT examples   Figure 9-3 shows four examples of the
LISTCAT command. In example 1, I code just LISTCAT.
Figure 9-4 shows output that's typical of a LISTCAT command with no operands specified. Here, all of my data sets are
listed.

Example 2 shows a LISTCAT command that says to
list all available catalog information for three data sets:
TEST.COBOL, TEST.OBJ, and TEST.LOAD. In example 3, I
say to list all catalog information for all data sets whose names
consist of three levels, the second of which is TEST. And in
example 4, I say to list all catalog information for all data sets
whose names begin with DLOWE.TEST.

```
READY
LISTCAT
 IN CATALOG:VCAT.MPS600
 DLOWE.BFCRDS.DATA
 DLOWE.ISPPARM
 DLOWE.REORDLST.LINKLIST
 DLOWE.REORDLST.LIST
 DLOWE.SPFEDITA.BACKUP
 DLOWE.TEST.CLIST
 DLOWE.TEST.CNTL
 DLOWE.TEST.COBOL
 DLOWE.TEST.LOAD
 DLOWE.TEST.OBJ
 DLOWE.TEST.SYM
 DLOWE.TEST1.COBOL
 READY
```

Figure 9-4   Typical LISTCAT command output

The LISTDS command

```
LISTDS   (data-set-names)

         [MEMBERS]

         [HISTORY]

         [STATUS]

         [LEVEL]
```

Explanation

data-set-names   A list of data set names to be listed. If only one data set is specified, the parentheses aren't needed. You can replace one or more levels of qualification with an asterisk (*). In that case, more than one data set may be listed.

MEMBERS   List the member names for a partitioned data set.

HISTORY   List the creation and expiration dates and the owner-id.

STATUS   List the ddname associated with the data set as well as the data set's disposition (KEEP, DELETE, CATLG, or UNCATLG).

LEVEL   If you specify LEVEL, the data set list specifies high-level qualifiers rather than fully-qualified data set names. Thus, any data sets whose high-level qualifiers match those specified in the data-set-names area are listed.

Figure 9-5   The LISTDS command

Example 1

```
LISTDS TEST.COBOL
```

Example 2

```
LISTDS (TEST.COBOL TEST.OBJ TEST.LOAD)
```

Example 3

```
LISTDS TEST.*
```

Example 4

```
LISTDS TEST LEVEL
```

Example 5

```
LISTDS TEST MEMBERS HISTORY STATUS LEVEL
```

Figure 9-6   Examples of the LISTDS command

How to list data set information

Figure 9-5 shows the format of the LISTDS command, used to
list information about one or more data sets. As you can see,
you can code several operands on the LISTDS command.
Figure 9-6 gives examples of how each operand is used.

Example 1 in figure 9-6 shows the simplest form of
the LISTDS command. As a result of this command, TSO
displays the record format, logical record size, block size,
data set organization, and volume serial number for
DLOWE.TEST.COBOL.

Example 2 shows a more complex LISTDS command.
Here, information for three data sets is listed:
DLOWE.TEST.COBOL, DLOWE.TEST.OBJ, and
DLOWE.TEST.LOAD. Notice that if you specify more
than one data set, you must enclose the list of data sets in
parentheses.

Example 3 shows how you can use an asterisk in a data set name. Here, I want to list all data sets whose names consist of three qualifiers, the second of which is TEST (the first corresponds to my user-id).

Example 4 shows how to achieve a similar result using the LEVEL operand. Here, I want to list data set information for all data sets whose names begin with DLOWE.TEST, regardless of how many qualifiers are in the name. For the LISTDS command, the LEVEL operand has the same effect as it does for the LISTCAT command, although its syntax is different.

Example 5 shows how to code the other LISTDS operands. MEMBERS means that the names of each member of a partitioned data set should be listed. HISTORY means that the file's creation date, expiration date, and owner identification should be listed. And STATUS means that the data set's allocation information should be listed (I'll explain data set allocation in topic 2 of this chapter).

Figure 9-7 shows the output generated by three LISTDS commands. The first shows the standard LISTDS information. The second shows a list of member names, while the third shows STATUS and HISTORY information.

How to rename a data set

You use the RENAME command to change the name of a data set or a member of a partitioned data set. As you can see in figure 9-8, the format of the RENAME command is simple. You specify two data set names: the name of the data set whose name you wish to change and the new name for the data set. If you specify an existing data set name as the new name, you'll get an error message and the data set name won't change.

Example 1 in figure 9-9 shows a basic RENAME command. Here, a data set named DLOWE.TEST.COBOL is renamed to DLOWE.ARTEST.COBOL.

Example 2 in figure 9-9 shows how you can use generic data set names in a RENAME command. Here, only the second-level qualifier of each affected data set is changed. For

Example 1

```
LISTDS TEST.COBOL
 DLOWE.TEST.COBOL
 --RECFM-LRECL-BLKSIZE-DSORG
   FB    80    3120    PO
 --VOLUMES--
   MPS600
```

Example 2

```
LISTDS TEST.COBOL MEMBERS
 DLOWE.TEST.COBOL
 --RECFM-LRECL-BLKSIZE-DSORG
   FB    80    3120    PO
 --VOLUMES--
   MPS600
 --MEMBERS--
   ORDLST2
   REORDLST
```

Example 3

```
LISTDS TEST.COBOL STATUS HISTORY
 DLOWE.TEST.COBOL
 --RECFM-LRECL-BLKSIZE-DSORG-CREATED---EXPIRES---SECURITY--DDNAME---DISP
   FB    80    3120    PO    01/05/84    * *      RACF     SYS00015 KEEP
 --VOLUMES--
   MPS600
```

Figure 9-7   Typical LISTDS command output

example, suppose you have these three data sets:

> DLOWE.TEST.COBOL
>
> DLOWE.TEST.OBJ
>
> DLOWE.TEST.LOAD

Here, the data sets are renamed to:

> DLOWE.ARTEST.COBOL
>
> DLOWE.ARTEST.OBJ
>
> DLOWE.ARTEST.LOAD

The RENAME command

```
RENAME   old-name    new-name

         [ALIAS]
```

Explanation

old-name   The name of an existing data set or member of a partitioned data set. You can replace one or more levels of qualification with an asterisk (*).

new-name   The new name of the data set or PDS member. You can replace one or more levels of qualification with an asterisk (*). When you rename a member, you can specify just the new member name in parentheses, omitting the PDS name.

ALIAS   Valid only when you rename a member of a PDS; specifies that the new name is an alias of the old member

Figure 9-8   The RENAME command

Whenever you use generic data set names in a RENAME command, the asterisks must be in the same position for both data set names.

To change the name of a partitioned data set member, you specify the complete PDS and member name for the first operand. For the second operand, however, you can omit the name of the PDS itself and supply just the new member name in parentheses. Example 3 in figure 9-9 shows how to do this. Here, a member named REORDLST is renamed to ORDLST2.

The ALIAS operand is valid only when you rename a PDS member. It says that instead of changing the name of the member, you want to create a second name, called an *alias*, for the same member. Thus, after the command in example 4 of figure 9-9 executes, you can refer to the member as REORDLST or ORDLST2.

Under normal circumstances, there's no reason to create a member alias. But there are special circumstances where it's desirable to have a member alias. For example, suppose you've created a command procedure (CLIST) that compiles a COBOL program. The member name for the procedure is COMPILE, but you want to let users abbreviate the command as COMP. So, you leave the member in the CLIST library

Example 1

```
RENAME TEST.COBOL ARTEST.COBOL
```

Example 2

```
RENAME TEST.* ARTEST.*
```

Example 3

```
RENAME TEST.COBOL(REORDLST) (ORDLST2)
```

Example 4

```
RENAME TEST.COBOL(REORDLST) (ORDLST2) ALIAS
```

Figure 9-9 Examples of the RENAME command

under its original name: COMPILE. Then, you create a member name alias: COMP. Now, whether you specify COMPILE or COMP, the same CLIST is invoked.

How to scratch a data set

Figure 9-10 gives the format of the DELETE command, used to scratch data sets. And figure 9-11 gives four examples that show how to use the DELETE command. In the first example, I delete a single data set. Example 2 shows how to specify a list of data sets to be deleted. And example 3 shows how to specify a generic data set name. Here, any data sets that conform to the generic data set name are deleted.

The PURGE operand, used in example 4 in figure 9-11, says to bypass expiration date checking. Normally, TSO won't let you delete a data set unless its expiration date has passed. (A data set's *expiration date* says when the data set is no longer needed.) When you specify PURGE on a DELETE command, the data set is scratched even if its expiration date hasn't passed. Of course, you should be careful about how you use the PURGE operand. Otherwise, you'll inadvertently scratch important data sets.

The DELETE command

```
DELETE    (data-set-names)

          [PURGE]
```

Explanation

data-set-names   Specifies a list of data set names to be scratched. If you specify only one data set name, you can omit the parentheses. One level of qualification (not the highest) can be an asterisk; in that case, more than one data set may be scratched.

PURGE   Scratch the data set even if its expiration date has **not** passed.

Figure 9-10   The DELETE command

Example 1

```
DELETE TEST.COBOL
```

Example 2

```
DELETE (TEST.COBOL TEST.OBJ TEST.LOAD)
```

Example 3

```
DELETE TEST.*
```

Example 4

```
DELETE TEST.* PURGE
```

Figure 9-11   Examples of the DELETE command

The COPY command

```
COPY  old-data-set-name    new-data-set-name
```

Explanation

old-data-set-name   Specifies the name of an existing data set or PDS member.

new-data-set-name   Specifies the name of the new data set or PDS member to which the old
                         data set is copied. It should **not** exist.

Figure 9-12   The COPY command

How to copy a data set

The operation of the COPY command is simple. You specify
two data set names, as shown in the format in figure 9-12, and
the first data set is copied to the second data set. As a result,
the second data set should *not* exist before you issue the COPY
command.
    To illustrate, consider this COPY command:

```
COPY TEST.COBOL ARTEST.COBOL
```

Here, a data set named DLOWE.TEST.COBOL is copied to
DLOWE.ARTEST.COBOL.
    If the copy operation involves partitioned data sets, the
second data set can be an existing library. In that case,
members are copied one by one from the first data set to the
second. If there are members that exist in both libraries, they
too are copied, so the original versions in the second library
are lost.
    The COPY command is part of a separate package of
TSO commands, so it's not available at all TSO installations.
But since copying a data set is a basic data set management
function, most installations that don't have the command
package have created their own equivalent of the COPY
command. Simply be aware that if your installation doesn't
have the command package, the format in figure 9-12 may not
apply to your version of COPY.

The LIST command

```
LIST    data-set-name
```

Explanation

data-set-name   The name of the data set or PDS member to be listed.

Figure 9-13   The LIST command

How to list a data set

Like the COPY command, the LIST command is part of the TSO command package, so it may not be available at your installation. Instead, your installation may have created its own version of the LIST command. Or it may employ some other technique for listing data sets.

In any event, figure 9-13 gives the basic format of the LIST command. Here, you supply a data set name. Then, the LIST command displays the contents of the data set at your terminal. For example, if you enter this command:

```
LIST TEST.COBOL(REORDLST)
```

the member named REORDLST in TEST.COBOL is listed at your terminal.

How to edit a data set

As you know, the EDIT command used to be the main text editor under TSO. Since the introduction of the 3270, however, most installations have replaced EDIT with SPF or extended it to provide similar capabilities. Still, there are occasions when you'll want to use EDIT for simple editing functions. That's why I present it here.

Figure 9-14 gives the format of the EDIT command. The only required operands are library name, member name, and type. EDIT combines the type with the library and member names and the current user-id to form the complete data set

The EDIT command

```
EDIT   library(member)   type   [{OLD}]
                                 [{NEW}]
```

Explanation

library(member)   The library and member to be edited.

type   The type qualifier to be added to the user-id, library, and member to form
                  the complete data set name.

OLD   If you say OLD, EDIT assumes you're editing an existing member and
NEW   enters edit mode. If you say NEW, EDIT assumes you're editing a new
                  member and enters input mode. If you omit this operand, EDIT assumes
                  OLD for existing members and NEW for new members.

Figure 9-14   The EDIT command

name. To illustrate, suppose you enter this EDIT command:

```
EDIT TEST(REORDLST) COBOL
```

Here, the complete data set name (assuming DLOWE is the user-id) is DLOWE.TEST.COBOL(REORDLST).

The OLD and NEW operands say whether you're editing an existing data set (OLD) or creating a new one (NEW). You don't need to specify either of these operands because EDIT assumes OLD for existing members and NEW for non-existant members. It's common practice to include one of these operands, however. That way, you'll get an error message if you attempt to create a member that already exists.

Besides saying whether you're editing a new or old member, the NEW and OLD operands control what mode EDIT initially enters. For a new member, EDIT enters *input mode*. In input mode, you can enter data directly into your member. For an old member, EDIT enters *edit mode*. In edit mode, you can enter a variety of EDIT subcommands that let you manipulate the data in your member.

Input mode   As I just said, input mode lets you enter data directly into your member. You just key in the data one line at

```
EDIT TEST(REORDLST) COBOL NEW
 INPUT
00010   IDENTIFICATION DIVISION.
00020 *
00030   PROGRAM-ID.  REORDLST.
00040 *
00050   ENVIRONMENT DIVISION.
00060 *
00070   INPUT-OUTPUT SECTION.
00080
EDIT
```

Figure 9-15   Using EDIT in input mode

a time, pressing the enter key after each line. EDIT automatically adds each line to the end of your member. When you've
finished adding lines, you enter a null line by pressing the enter
key without keying in any data first. Then, EDIT enters edit
mode and doesn't add the null line to your member.

Most of the members you'll edit will contain line numbers
that identify each line of text. In input mode, EDIT automatically supplies those line numbers, starting with 10 and
counting up in increments of 10 (10, 20, 30, and so on.) As a
result, you don't have to worry about line numbers in input
mode.

Figure 9-15 shows a brief editing session using input mode.
Here, I enter an EDIT command to edit a member named
REORDLST in TEST.COBOL. Since the member is new,
EDIT enters input mode, displaying these prompts:

```
INPUT
00010
```

The first prompt tells you EDIT is in input mode. The second
is the line number for the first line of text in the member.

The REORDLST member before editing

```
00010   IDENTIFICATION DIVISION.
00020 *
00030   PROGRAM-ID.   REORD.
00040 *
00050 *
00060        MOVE BF-ITEM-DESC TO RL-ITEM-DESC.
00070   INPUT-OUTPUT SECTION.
```

The editing session

```
EDIT TEST(REORDLST) COBOL OLD
  EDIT
00030   PROGRAM-ID.   REORDLST.
00045   ENVIRONMENT DIVISION.
00060
```

The REORDLST member after editing

```
00010   IDENTIFICATION DIVISION.
00020 *
00030   PROGRAM-ID.  REORDLST.
00040 *
00045   ENVIRONMENT DIVISION.
00050 *
00070   INPUT-OUTPUT SECTION.
```

Figure 9-16   Using the insert/replace/delete function

In this example, I enter seven lines of text (lines 10 through 70). Then I enter a null line on line 80. As a result, EDIT does *not* add line 80 to the member but instead enters edit mode, as indicated by the EDIT message.

Edit mode   In edit mode, EDIT doesn't prompt you for input. Instead, it lets you enter code so you can make changes to your member.

To insert or replace a single line in a member, you simply enter a line number followed by text. If the line already exists in the member, it's replaced. Otherwise, it's inserted. To delete a single line, you enter just the line number with no text.

To illustrate, look at figure 9-16. The top part of the figure shows a portion of a member that contains several errors. The middle part of the figure shows an editing session in which I replace line 30, insert line 45, and delete line 60. The bottom part of the figure shows the member after the editing session.

While this technique is fine for changing a line or two at a time, you'll want to use the EDIT subcommands for more extensive editing. There are 33 EDIT subcommands in all, but in this book, I cover only the ones shown in figure 9-17. Once you learn these subcommands, you'll be able to handle most of your editing requirements. And you'll have no trouble learning the more advanced editing subcommands from the IBM manual.

Most of the EDIT subcommands require that you identify the line or lines the subcommand affects. Normally, you just supply one or more line numbers. That's called *line-number editing*.

Another technique, called *context editing*, uses a pointer called the *current line pointer* to indicate the line being processed. You indicate the current line pointer in an EDIT subcommand by coding an asterisk rather than a line number. For example, this subcommand:

```
DELETE 1000
```

says to delete line 1000. But this subcommand:

```
DELETE *
```

says to delete the line indicated by the current line pointer.

EDIT provides a series of subcommands to move the current line pointer up or down within the member. But since you'll do most of your editing using line-number editing, I don't cover those subcommands in this book. The only reason I even mention context editing here is because you can't use line-number editing for data sets that don't have line numbers—such as data sets containing test data.

How to insert more than one line   To add more than a few lines at a time to your member, you should use the INPUT subcommand. When you issue an INPUT subcommand, EDIT returns to input mode. But instead of adding lines to the end of your member, it adds lines following the line you specify in

Subcommand	**Function**
`INPUT  line-number  [increment]`	Enters input mode so you can insert one or more lines following line-number. When increment is coded, it becomes the increment value for the new line numbers.
`DELETE  start-line  [end-line]`	Deletes the range of lines specified.
`CHANGE  start-line   [end-line]` `        old-string   new-string   [ALL]`	Changes old-string to new-string within the specified range of lines. ALL says to change all occurrences of old-string; otherwise, only the first occurence is changed.
`LIST  [start-line]  [end-line]`	Lists the specified range of lines.
`RENUM  [new-first-line]  [increment]`	Resequences line numbers. The new line numbers start with new-first-line and are incremented according to the increment value. The default for either operand is 10.
`END  {SAVE / NOSAVE}`	Ends the editing session. SAVE says to rewrite the member with the changes made during the editing session; NOSAVE means the changes aren't kept.

Note: To edit the line indicated by the current line pointer, code an asterisk (*) instead of a line number in the EDIT subcommands.

Figure 9-17 Some EDIT subcommands

the subcommand. For example, if you enter this subcommand:

    INPUT 4000

lines are inserted following line 4000.

When you use the INPUT subcommand, you have to make sure there are enough unused line numbers to accommodate the lines you're adding. Otherwise, an error message will be displayed and EDIT will return to edit mode when you run out of line numbers—although the lines already added will remain in the member.

You can provide enough line numbers in one of two ways. First, before you issue the INPUT subcommand, you can renumber your member using a large increment—like 100. I describe the subcommand necessary to do this later on. Second, you can specify a small increment—like one or two—on the INPUT subcommand itself. For example, this subcommand:

```
INPUT 2210 1
```

adds lines following line 2210, numbering the new lines in increments of one. As a result, the first new line will be 2211.

How to delete more than one line   To delete more than one line from your member, you use the DELETE subcommand. On it, you specify two line numbers, like this:

```
DELETE 100 500
```

Here, all lines between (and including) lines 100 and 500 are deleted.

As you can see from the format in figure 9-17, you can also use the DELETE subcommand to delete a single line by omitting the end-line operand. But as I said earlier, it's easier to use the delete function as shown in figure 9-16 for a single line deletion.

How to change text   You use the CHANGE subcommand to change text within your member. On it, you specify one or two line numbers. If you specify just one, the change affects only the one line; if you specify two, the change affects each line between and including the two lines specified.

Following the line numbers, you specify two text strings: first, the existing text string; then, the string to which the first string should be changed. The strings don't have to be the same length; EDIT makes any adjustments necessary.

There are two ways you can code the text strings in a CHANGE subcommand. First, you can enclose both of them in apostrophes, like this:

```
CHANGE 30 'POR' 'PRO'
```

Here, the string POR is changed to PRO in line 30.

The second way is to use a *delimiter*. The delimiter can be any character you choose—as long as it doesn't occur in either of the text strings. You must code it three times: before the first string, between the two strings, and after the second string. To illustrate, consider this CHANGE subcommand:

```
CHANGE 30 /POR/PRO/
```

Here again, POR is changed to PRO in line 30. The delimiter is a slash.

There's one restriction on the use of delimiters. If the first character of either string is an asterisk, you *cannot* use a slash as the delimiter. That's because the combination of a slash and an asterisk marks the beginning of a comment, so TSO doesn't correctly interpret the change. (You'll learn how to code comments in chapter 13.)

If you want to change *every* occurrence of a string in the line or lines you specify, you must code ALL on the CHANGE subcommand. Otherwise, only the first occurrence of the string is changed. For example, to change this line:

```
50   ADD BF-ON-HAND BF-ON-ORDER
```

to this:

```
50   ADD INV-ON-HAND INV-ON-ORDER
```

you have to code this:

```
CHANGE 50 /BF-/INV-/ ALL
```

Without ALL, the result will be:

```
50   ADD INV-ON-HAND BF-ON-ORDER
```

How to list lines   The LIST subcommand lets you list lines from your member. If you enter LIST without any operands, the entire member is listed. If you code one line number, that line is listed. And if you code two line numbers, a range of lines is listed.

If your installation doesn't have the LIST command, you can use the LIST subcommand of EDIT to list your data sets. It's a little awkward, but it works.

How to renumber a member   Sometimes, when you've made many changes to a member, you'll find that the line numbers seem almost random. In some places, you'll have large gaps, while in other places, you'll have lines numbered in small increments. In a case like this, you can use the RENUM command to resequence your line numbers in fixed increments.

If you enter RENUM with no operands, your member is renumbered starting with 10 using an increment of 10. You can change that, however, by specifying a starting line number and an increment on your RENUM command. For example, if you code:

```
RENUM 1000 100
```

your member is renumbered starting with 1000 and using an increment of 100. As a result, your lines are numbered 1000, 1100, 1200, and so on.

How to end an editing session   You use the END subcommand to end an editing session. If you code:

```
END SAVE
```

any changes you made during the editing session are incorporated into your member. If you code:

```
END NOSAVE
```

your changes are lost. Normally, you'll say END SAVE.

How to print a data set

As I mentioned in chapter 1, DSPRINT is a TSO facility that lets you print data sets at a printer without having to wait while the data set prints. Although DSPRINT is optional, it's available at most TSO installations. So I'll describe it in some detail here.

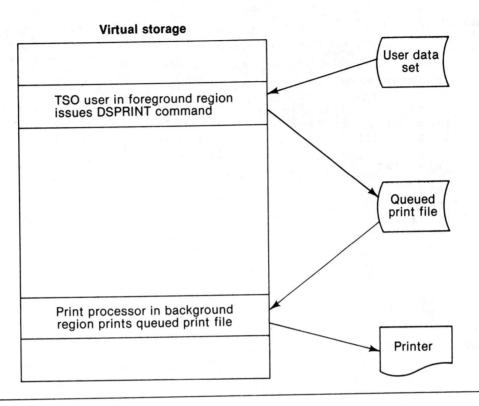

Figure 9-18   How DSPRINT works

Figure 9-18 shows how DSPRINT works. To invoke a DSPRINT print operation, a TSO user running in a fore-ground region issues a DSPRINT command. The DSPRINT command copies a data set specified by the user to a *print file*. Then, a *background print processor* running in a background region copies the print file to the printer. If more than one print file is queued for a single printer, the background print processor handles the files in turn. As a result, two or more TSO users can start a DSPRINT print operation on the same printer without worrying about the listings being overlapped.

Figure 9-19 gives the format of the DSPRINT command. Though it has several operands, only the first two are required. They tell DSPRINT the name of the data set you wish to print and the name of the printer on which you wish the data set printed. Since printer names vary from one installation to the next, you'll have to find out from your supervisor what printer name to use.

The DSPRINT command

```
DSPRINT   data-set-name

          printer-name

   [ {NUM(location,length)  } ]
   [ {SNUM(location,length) } ]
   [ {NONUM                  } ]

   [LINES(start[:end])]

   [ {SINGLE} ]
   [ {DOUBLE} ]
   [ {CCHAR } ]

   [ {FOLD     } ]
   [ {TRUNCATE } ]

   [ {EJECT   } ]
   [ {NOEJECT } ]
```

Figure 9-19   The DSPRINT command (part 1 of 2)

How to handle line numbers   The NUM, SNUM, and NONUM operands tell DSPRINT how to handle line numbers in the data set. In general, COBOL source files have a line number in the first six positions of each record; non-COBOL source files—like assembler, PL/I, CLIST, and CNTL (JCL) files—have a line number in the last eight positions of each record; and data files have no line numbers at all.

If you say NUM, DSPRINT looks for line numbers in the position you specify. For example:

```
NUM(73,8)
```

means the line numbers start in position 73 and are 8 bytes long. The line numbers are printed in the first columns of each print line even if they're located in the middle or at the end of the records in the data set.

In the case of COBOL files, where the line numbers are located at the start of the file, you don't need to specify NUM unless you're going to use the LINES operand, which I'll describe in a moment. Since DSPRINT prints each record as it

Explanation

data-set-name	The name of the data set or member to be printed.
printer-name	The installation-defined name associated with the printer on which you wish to print the data set.
NUM SNUM NONUM	Defines how line numbers are to be printed. NUM says that line numbers are contained in the position indicated by location and length and should be printed at the start of each print line. SNUM means that the line numbers are contained in the specified position, but should not be printed. NONUM means that no special line-number processing is to be done; if line numbers are present, they are printed just as if they were data. (NONUM is the default.)
LINES	Specifies the starting and ending line numbers for the records to be printed. If you omit LINES, all of the records in the data set are printed. If you omit the ending line number, the end of the file is assumed. You must specify NUM or SNUM if you specify LINES.
SINGLE DOUBLE CCHAR	Specifies how the printed lines are to be spaced. SINGLE means to single-space the listing. DOUBLE means to double-space the listing. And CCHAR means to use the control characters in the file to determine spacing. CCHAR is meaningful only if the file contains printer control characters. (SINGLE is the default.)
FOLD TRUNCATE	Says what to do with records that are too long to be printed on a single line. FOLD says to continue the record on the next print line; TRUNCATE says to ignore the remainder of the record. (FOLD is the default.)
EJECT NOEJECT	Says whether to force a new page after the header block is printed. (NOEJECT is the default.)

Figure 9-19 The DSPRINT command (part 2 of 2)

appears in the file, the line numbers will be printed at the start of each line anyway.

The SNUM operand tells DSPRINT that the data set contains line numbers in the position you specify, but that you don't want the line numbers printed. And the NONUM operand tells DSPRINT to do no special line number processing. If your data set contains line numbers and you specify NONUM, the line numbers are printed along with the rest of the data in the records.

How to control the amount of output The LINES operand tells DSPRINT that you don't want to print all of the data set.

Instead, you want to print a subset of the file identified by the line numbers you provide in the LINES operand. If you provide just one line number, the listing begins at the number you specify and continues to the end of the file. For example, if you say LINES(1000), the listing starts at line 1000. If you specify two numbers separated by a colon, the listing starts at the first line number and ends at the second. Thus, to print lines 1000 through 2000, you would say LINES(1000:2000). Since the LINES operand depends on line numbers in the data set, you must include a NUM or SNUM operand to tell DSPRINT where the line numbers are located.

How to format the output   The SINGLE, DOUBLE, and CCHAR operands tell DSPRINT how to space the output listing. If you say SINGLE, or don't specify any of the three, the listing is single-spaced. If you say DOUBLE, the listing is double-spaced. If the data set contains printer control characters, you should say CCHAR. Then, DSPRINT will use the control characters in the data set to space the listing.

The FOLD and TRUNCATE operands tell TSO what to do if the data set's records are longer than the printer's line length. If you say FOLD, or don't specify anything, the record is continued on the next print line. If you say TRUNCATE, the part of the record that can't be printed on one line isn't printed at all.

At the start of each printed data set, DSPRINT prints a short heading that identifies the data set and the user who requested the print operation. The EJECT and NOEJECT operands tell DSPRINT whether the header should be on a separate page or at the top of the first page of output. If you say EJECT, the header appears on a separate page before the first page of output. If you say NOEJECT, or don't say anything, the header and the first page of data are printed on the same page.

DSPRINT has additional operands that let you change the top and bottom margin size, print only certain columns of the input records, or change the printer line width. Since these functions aren't commonly needed, I don't cover them here.

DSPRINT examples   Figure 9-20 gives four examples of the DSPRINT command to print a member named REORDLST in

Example 1

```
DSPRINT TEST.COBOL(REORDLST) IBMT2IP1
```

Example 2

```
DSPRINT TEST.COBOL(REORDLST) IBMT2IP1 NUM(1,6) EJECT
```

Example 3

```
DSPRINT TEST.COBOL(REORDLST) IBMT2IP1 NUM(1,6) LINES(2100:4000)
```

Example 4

```
DSPRINT TEST.COBOL(REORDLST) IBMT2IP1 NONUM EJECT DOUBLE
```

Figure 9-20   Examples of the DSPRINT command

a partitioned data set named DLOWE.TEST.COBOL. In example 1, I supply just the data set and member name and the printer name. That causes DSPRINT to print the member using its default format. In example 2, I tell DSPRINT that the line numbers are 6 bytes long and start in column 1. I also say to print the header on a separate page. In example 3, I supply the NUM operand and tell DSPRINT to print only lines 2100 through 4000. And in example 4, I tell DSPRINT to ignore line numbers, print the heading on a separate page, and double-space the listing.

Discussion

In this topic, I've presented a set of TSO commands you'll probably use daily as you manipulate data sets. Unfortunately, it's impossible to present all of the commands you'll use frequently because each installation adds its own commands or tailors the existing commands to suit its own needs. For example, your installation may have added commands to compress a library or list data set space allocation information. So you'll have to find out from your supervisor what additional TSO commands are available to you.

Terminology

generic data set name
alias
expiration date
input mode
edit mode
line-number editing
context editing
current line pointer
delimiter
print file
background print processor

Objective

Use the following commands for data set management:

a. LISTCAT

b. LISTDS

c. RENAME

d. DELETE

e. COPY

f. LIST

g. EDIT

h. DSPRINT

TOPIC 2   Data set allocation commands

In chapter 1 of this book, I described an MVS feature called dynamic allocation that lets a program reserve a data control block (DCB) for a file without specifying file information in the JCL. Instead, the program itself supplies the DCB information before it opens the file. The program can reuse a DCB by closing the file, changing the DCB information, and opening another file using the same DCB. As a result, a single DCB can serve many files.

While it's not common to write application programs that use dynamic allocation, TSO itself uses dynamic allocation for many of the data sets you access during a TSO session. For example, if you issue a COPY command to copy one data set to another, TSO dynamically *allocates* the two data sets. It releases, or *deallocates*, them when the copy operation is complete.

TSO provides several commands that let you use dynamic allocation directly. In this topic, I cover three of them: ALLOCATE, FREE, and LISTALC. The ALLOCATE command lets you allocate a data set. The FREE command lets you deallocate a data set. And the LISTALC command lets you display a list of all data sets currently allocated to your TSO session.

THE ALLOCATE COMMAND

As you know, a data set is identified by a data set name. When a program refers to a data set, however, it uses a symbolic name called a *ddname*. One of the main functions of the ALLOCATE command is to associate a particular data set name with a ddname. Then, a program can refer to the data set by its ddname.

In some cases, you use an ALLOCATE command to prepare a data set for processing by a program that you'll run in foreground mode. For example, you may want to run the

IEBCOPY utility program to compress a partitioned data set. Or you may want to run an application program you've written in COBOL or some other language. Before you run the program, you must issue a series of ALLOCATE commands to associate the data sets used by the program with the specific ddnames required by that program (in the case of IEBCOPY, for example, the ddnames are SYSPRINT, SYSIN, SYSUT3, and SYSUT4).

Sometimes, though, you don't intend to invoke a foreground program to process a data set. Instead, you want to create a new data set. In this case, you again use the ALLOCATE command, but you don't have to specify a ddname at all. TSO assigns a system-generated ddname to the data set, and you don't need to know what it is.

When used to relate an existing data set to a specific ddname, the ALLOCATE command has a relatively simple format. So I'll explain that usage first. Then, I'll show you how to use the ALLOCATE command to create a new data set. After that, I'll describe three alternate forms of the ALLOCATE command.

How to associate an existing data set with a ddname

Figure 9-21 shows the basic format for the ALLOCATE command when used to associate an existing data set with a ddname. The DSNAME operand gives the data set's name. As usual, TSO adds your user-id to the beginning of the data set name unless you enclose it in apostrophes. If the data set is cataloged, the DSNAME operand completely identifies the file. But if it's not cataloged, you'll have to supply the UNIT and VOLUME operands as well. I'll describe those operands in a moment.

The DDNAME operand supplies the ddname for the data set. For a system utility program, you can find out what ddnames are required by reading appropriate system documentation. For a COBOL application program, the ddname is the name you supply in the ASSIGN clause of the file's SELECT statement. For example, suppose your COBOL program contains this statement:

```
SELECT BAL-FWD-CARDS ASSIGN TO UT-S-BFCRDS
```

The ALLOCATE command

```
ALLOCATE        {DSNAME(data-set-name) }
                {DATASET(data-set-name)}

                {DDNAME(ddname)}
                {FILE(ddname)  }

                {OLD}
                {SHR}
                {MOD}

                {KEEP     }
                {DELETE   }
                {UNCATALOG}

                UNIT(device)

                VOLUME(volume-serial-number)
```

Explanation

DSNAME DATASET	The data set name for the data set to be allocated.
DDNAME FILE	The ddname to be associated with the data set.
OLD SHR MOD	The status of the data set. OLD means you want exclusive control of the data set. SHR means you want shared access to the data set. And MOD means you want to extend a data set. (OLD is the default.)
KEEP DELETE UNCATALOG	The disposition of the data set. KEEP means you want to keep the data set as it is. DELETE means you want to delete the data set. UNCATALOG means you want to keep the data set but remove it from the catalog. The disposition is not processed until the data set is deallocated when you issue a FREE command or log off. (KEEP is the default.)
UNIT	The device or device type for the file. Not required for a cataloged data set.
VOLUME	The volume serial number for the volume that contains the file. Not required for a cataloged data set.

Figure 9-21   The ALLOCATE command for existing data sets

In this case, you must use an ALLOCATE command to allocate a data set for the ddname BFCRDS.

If you wish, you can say FILE instead of DDNAME and DATASET instead of DSNAME. The alternate terms have the same meaning. As a result, these two ALLOCATE commands have identical meanings:

```
ALLOCATE DSNAME(BFCRDS.DATA) DDNAME(BFCRDS)
ALLOCATE DATASET(BFCRDS.DATA) FILE(BFCRDS)
```

I prefer to use DDNAME and DSNAME because those terms correspond to the equivalent parameters used on a standard batch JCL DD statement.

Status values   OLD, SHR, or MOD define the file's *status*. If you say OLD, you're telling TSO that you want exclusive control over an existing data set. If another foreground or background program tries to access the same file, it will have to wait until you're finished.

When you code SHR, you're telling TSO that you don't want exclusive control over the file (SHR means share, so more than one program or user can access the file at the same time). You should code SHR when you access a file of general interest—such as a program library—unless you're updating that file.

When you code MOD, you're telling TSO that you want to *extend* an existing file. That means that when your program performs output operations on the file, the new records are added at the end of any existing records.

Disposition values   KEEP, DELETE, and UNCATALOG specify the file's *disposition*. These operands tell TSO what to do with the file when you're finished processing it (that is, when you issue a FREE command, which I'll describe later in this topic, or when you log off). KEEP means, naturally, to keep the file. If the file is cataloged, it remains cataloged. KEEP is the default if you don't specify a disposition.

DELETE tells TSO to remove all references to the file and make it unavailable for future access. This includes removing the catalog entry if the file was cataloged. Any request to retrieve a file that's been deleted causes an error.

UNCATALOG tells TSO that the file was previously cataloged and now its entry should be removed from the catalog. But the file itself is not deleted. As a result, any future ALLOCATE commands for the file will have to include UNIT and VOLUME operands to completely identify the file.

The location of the file   If you're accessing a file that isn't cataloged, you have to tell TSO where the file resides. You use two ALLOCATE operands to do this. You use the UNIT operand to tell TSO what type of device the file resides on. And you use the VOLUME operand to tell TSO the specific serial number of the volume that contains the file.

For the UNIT operand, you can specify a specific device type—such as 3330 or 3350. So if you code UNIT(3350), the data set must reside on a a 3350-type disk. Typically, though, you'll specify a *group name* that includes all devices of a particular kind. Each installation defines its own group names, so you'll have to check with your supervisor to find out what group names you can use. Usually, names like TAPE, DISKA, or SYSDA are used to indicate the groups of associated devices. So if you code UNIT(SYSDA), the file can reside on any disk device belonging to the SYSDA category.

The VOLUME operand gives the volume serial number of the specific volume containing the file. For example, if you code VOLUME(TSO0001), TSO looks on the volume named TSO0001 to locate the file. If that volume isn't mounted on the system when you issue the ALLOCATE command, the system instructs an operator to mount it.

Examples of allocating existing data sets   Figure 9-22 gives three examples of ALLOCATE commands for existing data sets. In example 1, a data set named DLOWE.TEST.COBOL (TSO adds my user-id to the data set name) is associated with a ddname of SYSUT1. Then, any program that accesses a data set using that ddname will process DLOWE.TEST.COBOL.

Example 2 shows a data set named DLOWE.TEST.DATA associated with a ddname of BFCRDS. Here, the status is MOD. So any new records added to this data set will be placed at the end of the file.

Example 3 shows how to allocate an uncataloged data set. Here, a file named AR.DAILY.TRANS on a TAPE volume labelled MMA010 is associated with a ddname of ARTRANS.

Example 1

```
ALLOCATE DSNAME(TEST.COBOL) DDNAME(SYSUT1)
```

Example 2

```
ALLOCATE DSNAME(TEST.DATA) DDNAME(BFCRDS) MOD
```

Example 3

```
ALLOCATE DSNAME('AR.DAILY.TRANS') DDNAME(ARTRANS) +
UNIT(TAPE) VOLUME(MMA010)
```

Figure 9-22 Examples of ALLOCATE commands for existing data sets

Since most—if not all—of the direct-access data sets you'll process will be cataloged, you'll use this form of the ALLOCATE command mostly for tape data sets.

How to create a new data set

Figure 9-23 gives an expanded format for the ALLOCATE command that lets you create new data sets. Some of the operands in figure 9-23 (DSNAME, DDNAME, UNIT, and VOLUME) you already know. The other operands supply information required to create a data set: how much space to allocate to the file, when the file can be deleted, and the specific characteristics of the file.

One important point before I go on: the DDNAME operand in figure 9-23 is optional. If you're going to process the data set using a foreground program, you should specify a ddname in the DDNAME operand. But if you're just creating an empty file that you're not going to process with a foreground program, you can omit the DDNAME operand. TSO will assign a ddname for you, but you don't have to know what it is.

Disposition values You already know how to code disposition values when you allocate an existing data set. When you allocate a new data set, you must supply a disposition value to tell MVS whether or not the data set is permanent.

If you say CATALOG, or let the disposition default to CATALOG by coding nothing, MVS creates a catalog entry so you can retrieve the data set later without specifying unit and volume information. If you say KEEP, MVS retains the data set but doesn't create a catalog entry for it. And if you say DELETE, MVS removes the data set when you free it.

How to allocate space to a file   When you create a data set, you must tell TSO how much space to allocate to the file. To do this, you tell TSO three things: (1) how many units of space to allocate, (2) how big each unit is, and (3) how much space to allocate to the directory (required for partitioned data sets only).

You use the SPACE operand to specify how many units of space to allocate to a file. You specify space in both primary and secondary allocations. The *primary allocation* is the amount of space that should be initially allocated to the file. It's the first number you code in a SPACE operand, and it should represent the total amount of space you expect the file will require.

The *secondary allocation* provides for additional space beyond the primary allocation. When a file grows beyond the amount of space the primary allocation provided, the secondary allocation is made. If that still isn't enough space, the secondary allocation is made again. Up to 15 secondary allocations can be made before the file runs out of space.

To illustrate, suppose you code this SPACE operand:

```
SPACE(10 5)
```

Here, 10 units are allocated initially. The secondary allocation is 5 units. So, this file can grow to a maximum of 85 units (10 units of primary allocation plus 15 secondary allocations of 5 units each).

The next set of operands, TRACKS and CYLINDERS, says how large each unit of allocated space is. If you say TRACKS, space is allocated in terms of direct-access tracks. If you say CYLINDERS, whole cylinders of space are allocated. If you omit both TRACKS and CYLINDERS, space is allocated using the block size you specify in the BLKSIZE operand, which I'll discuss later.

The ALLOCATE command

```
ALLOCATE      DSNAME(data-set-name)

              DDNAME(ddname)

             ⎧KEEP    ⎫
             ⎨CATALOG ⎬
             ⎩DELETE  ⎭

              UNIT(device)

              VOLUME(volume-serial-number)

              SPACE(primary secondary)

             ⎧TRACKS   ⎫
             ⎨CYLINDERS⎬
             ⎩         ⎭

              DIR(directory-space)

             ⎧EXPDT(expiration-date) ⎫
             ⎨RETPD(retention-period)⎬
             ⎩                       ⎭

              DSORG(organization)

              RECFM(record-format)

              LRECL(record-length)

              BLKSIZE(block-size)

              LIKE(model-data-set-name)
```

Explanation

DSNAME	Specifies the name of the data set to be created.
DDNAME	The ddname associated with the file. If omitted, TSO generates a default ddname.
KEEP CATALOG DELETE	The disposition of the data set. KEEP means you want to retain the data set. CATALOG means you want to retain the data set and create a catalog entry for it. And DELETE means you want to delete the data set when you're through with it. (CATALOG is the default.)

Figure 9-23   The ALLOCATE command for new data sets (part 1 of 2)

Explanation   (continued)

UNIT
Identifies the device type. May be a specific device (like 3350) or a device class (like SYSDA). If omitted, MVS chooses a device based on your profile—normally SYSDA.

VOLUME
Specifies the volume serial number of the volume that will contain the file. If omitted, your default volume is used.

SPACE
Says how much space should be allocated to the data set. Space is in units of tracks, cylinders, or blocks, depending on how you code other options in the ALLOCATE command. Primary allocation is allocated initially. When additional space is needed, extents are allocated using the secondary allocation.

TRACKS
CYLINDERS
Defines the unit of measure for SPACE. If you say TRACKS, space is allocated in tracks. If you say CYLINDERS, space is allocated in cylinders. If you omit both TRACKS and CYLINDERS, space is allocated in blocks, defined by the BLKSIZE operand.

DIR
Says how many 256-byte directory blocks should be allocated for a partitioned data set.

EXPDT
Defines the date after which the file can be deleted. The date is specified in the form yyddd, where yy is the year and ddd is the day within the year. So 85001 is January 1, 1985.

RETPD
An alternative to EXPDT, RETPD defines the expiration date as a retention period. After the specified number of days have elapsed, the file can be scratched.

DSORG
Specifies the data set's organization: PS for sequential files, PO for partitioned data sets.

RECFM
Defines the record format. Specify RECFM(F) for fixed-length, unblocked records. Use RECFM(F,B) for fixed-length, blocked records.

LRECL
Defines the file's record length in bytes.

BLKSIZE
Defines the file's block size in bytes.

LIKE
Specifies a data set name from which other ALLOCATE operands are derived. All of the operands listed here (other than DSNAME) can be derived from a model data set.

Figure 9-23   The ALLOCATE command for new data sets (part 2 of 2)

Note that whether you code TRACKS or CYLINDERS or default to the block size has a dramatic effect on how much space is allocated to your file. For example, if you say:

```
SPACE(10 10) TRACKS
```

10 tracks are assigned to your file. But if you say

```
SPACE(10 10) CYLINDERS
```

10 cylinders are assigned. On a 3350, that's 30 times as much space.

You use the last space allocation operand, DIR, when you create a partitioned data set. It says how many directory blocks to allocate for the file. Each directory block is 256 bytes long and normally can hold entries for 21 members. So if you expect that the library will contain a maximum of 200 members, you should allocate 10 directory blocks. If the library will contain load modules, each directory holds only 4 member entries. So for a 200-member load library, you should allocate 50 directory blocks.

How to specify an expiration date   A file's *expiration date* says when the file is no longer needed and can be deleted. In the first topic of this chapter, you saw how the DELETE command checks the expiration date before it deletes a file, and you saw how you can override the expiration date check to delete the file even if the expiration date hasn't arrived. In addition, some installations automatically delete all data sets whose expiration dates have passed. In such an installation, you can expect that any data set you create today will be gone tomorrow, unless you explicitly assign an expiration date.

You use one of two ALLOCATE operands to assign an expiration date. The EXPDT operand assigns a specific date as the expiration date. You specify this date in the form *yyddd*, where *yy* is the year and *ddd* is the day within the year. So 85001 is January 1, 1985, and 85365 is December 31, 1985.

Quite frankly, I have trouble remembering the relative day within the year for a date like July 23 (especially if it's a leap year). I find it's usually easier to use the RETPD operand. This operand assigns a *retention period* to the file. So if you specify RETPD(30), the file's expiration date will be 30 days from today.

How to describe a file's characteristics   When you create a new data set, you must define the file's characteristics. Specifically, you must define: the file's organization (usually, sequential or partitioned); the format of the file's records (variable or fixed, blocked or unblocked); the length of the file's records; and the length of each block of records.

You use the DSORG operand to define the file's organization. If you specify DSORG(PS), the file is sequential. If you specify DSORG(PO), the file is a partitioned data set.

The RECFM operand identifies the format of the file's records. Although there are many possible combinations of record format characteristics you can code, you'll usually code the RECFM operand like this:

```
RECFM(F,B)
```

Here, the records are fixed-length and blocked. Other common record formats are: RECFM(F) for fixed-length, unblocked records; RECFM(V,B) for variable-length, blocked records; and RECFM(V) for variable-length, unblocked records.

The LRECL operand defines the logical record length for the file. For 80-byte records such as COBOL source records, specify LRECL(80). For variable-length records, specify the longest possible record length plus four bytes for a system record-count field.

The BLKSIZE operand defines the size of each block of records. In topic 2 of chapter 5, I described some factors that affect an efficient choice for block size. The value you code for this operand also affects the space allocation for the file if you don't specify TRACKS or CYLINDERS.

How to model a data set after an existing file   You can simplify the coding required for an ALLOCATE command by using the LIKE operand to model a new data set after an existing one. When you specify the name of an existing file in a LIKE operand, you can omit any of the other operands except DSNAME. Then, MVS will obtain the values for those operands from the data set label of the LIKE file. If you want to change one or more of those values, you simply code the appropriate operands and MVS will use the values you specify.

Using a model data set can be a real time-saver, particularly if you don't remember the optimum block size for a particular blocking factor and device type. Be careful, though, about modeling a small data set after a very large one. If you don't override the space allocation values, you'll allocate too much space to your file.

Examples of allocating new data sets   Figure 9-24 gives four examples of ALLOCATE commands for creating data sets. In example 1, I create a sequential data set (DSORG(PS)) named DLOWE.BFCRDS.DATA. The file will be assigned 10 tracks of primary space, with a secondary allocation of 5 tracks. The file consists of fixed-length, blocked records. The record length is 80 bytes, and the block size is 3200 bytes.

The ALLOCATE command in example 2 creates the same data set as the ALLOCATE command in example 1, except that in example 2, I associate a ddname (BFCRDS) with the newly-created data set. Then, I can run a foreground program to load records into the file. The ALLOCATE command in example 1 assigns a system-generated ddname to the new file.

In example 3, I create a partitioned data set (DSORG(PO)) named DLOWE.TEST.COBOL. This file has 100 tracks of primary space and a secondary allocation of 50 tracks. I allocate 10 directory blocks, so the library will hold a maximum of 210 source members. The 80-byte records are fixed-length and blocked (6160 bytes per block), and the file will be kept for 60 days.

In example 4, I create a new data set, modeling it after an existing data set named SAMP.TEST.COBOL. All of the data set characteristics and space allocation operands will be obtained from the data set label for the model file. The new file will be placed on a direct-access device (SYSDA), on a volume named TVOL36.

Other ALLOCATE command formats

Besides the formats presented in figures 9-21 and 9-23, you can code the ALLOCATE command using one of several other

Example 1

```
ALLOCATE DSNAME(BFCRDS.DATA) SPACE(10 5) TRACKS DSORG(PS) +
RECFM(F,B) LRECL(80) BLKSIZE(3200)
```

Example 2

```
ALLOCATE DSNAME(BFCRDS.DATA) DDNAME(BFCRDS) SPACE(10 5) +
TRACKS DSORG(PS) RECFM(F,B) LRECL(80) BLKSIZE(3200)
```

Example 3

```
ALLOCATE DSNAME(TEST.COBOL) SPACE(100 50) TRACKS DIR(10) +
DSORG(PO) RECFM(F,B) LRECL(80) BLKSIZE(6160) RETPD(60)
```

Example 4

```
ALLOCATE DSNAME(TEST.COBOL) LIKE('SAMP.TEST.COBOL') +
UNIT(SYSDA) VOLUME(TVOL36)
```

Figure 9-24   Examples of ALLOCATE commands for new data sets

formats. Figure 9-25 shows three commonly used ALLOCATE command formats. You use these formats when your foreground program has special processing requirements.

Format 1 in figure 9-25 is used when you want to receive input from or direct output to your terminal. The asterisk in the DSNAME operand simply says that your terminal is to be used as the data set. This form of the ALLOCATE command is particularly useful when you're testing programs. For input files, you can supply test data interactively. And for output files, you can view program results immediately.

You use format 2 in figure 9-25 to simulate the presence of a file without actually processing the file. To do this, you code DUMMY instead of a DSNAME operand. Whenever your program tries to read a record from a DUMMY file, an end-of-file indication is passed to your program. And when your program tries to write a record to a DUMMY file, no data is transferred. This form of the ALLOCATE command is also useful when testing a program. (Incidentally, you can

Format 1

```
ALLOCATE      DSNAME(*)

              DDNAME(ddname)
```

Format 2

```
ALLOCATE      DUMMY

              DDNAME(ddname)
```

Format 3

```
ALLOCATE      DDNAME(ddname)

              SYSOUT(class)

              [{HOLD  }]
              [{NOHOLD}]

              [DEST(station-id)]
```

Explanation

DSNAME	An asterisk as the data set name means your terminal is used as a data set for input or output.
DUMMY	A data set is to be simulated. No actual I/O is done.
DDNAME	The ddname for the data set.
SYSOUT	Directs output to JES2/JES3 using the specified SYSOUT class. Output is not actually released for processing by JES2/JES3 until you deallocate the data set by issuing a FREE command or by logging off.
HOLD NOHOLD	HOLD means the data set is held in the SYSOUT queue until released by an operator or TSO user. NOHOLD means the output is **not** held but is released for processing. This parameter overrides the default specified for the SYSOUT class.
DEST	Specifies the installation-defined station-id for a remote site to which the output is routed.

Figure 9-25   Alternate formats for the ALLOCATE command

Example 1

```
ALLOCATE DSNAME(*) DDNAME(REORDLST)
```

Example 2

```
ALLOCATE DUMMY DDNAME(BFCRDS)
```

Example 3

```
ALLOCATE DDNAME(ORDLST) SYSOUT(X)
```

Example 4

```
ALLOCATE DDNAME(ORDLST) SYSOUT(A) DEST(RMT200)
```

Figure 9-26   Examples of alternate ALLOCATE commands

achieve exactly the same effect by coding a data set name of
NULLFILE in the DSNAME operand.)

You use format 3 in figure 9-25 to direct program output
to a SYSOUT queue. Here, you specify the ddname for the file
and a SYSOUT class. The output from your program is
directed to a SYSOUT queue for processing by JES2/JES3
according to the SYSOUT class. Normally, you can specify
SYSOUT(A) to direct the output to a system printer. But if
you direct the output to a held SYSOUT class, or if you code
HOLD on the ALLOCATE command, the output will be
retained in the output queue. You can retrieve it later using the
OUTPUT command, which I'll describe in chapter 11. Or, you
can route it to a different output class by using the FREE
command, which I'll explain later in this topic.

If you want to route SYSOUT data to a remote printer
(such as a 2780/3780 station), you can code the DEST
operand. Here, you enter the installation-defined station-id for
the remote printer you want to use. Then, when that station
signs on to the system, the output will be delivered to it.

Examples of other ALLOCATE formats   Figure 9-26 gives
four examples of ALLOCATE commands following the
formats presented in figure 9-25. In example 1, I assign my

terminal as the file for ddname REORDLST. In example 2, I assign ddname BFCRDS to a DUMMY file. Example 3 routes output directed to ddname ORDLST to SYSOUT class X. And example 4 routes output directed to ddname ORDLST to a remote site named RMT200, using SYSOUT class A.

OTHER DATA SET ALLOCATION COMMANDS

Besides the ALLOCATE command, TSO provides several other commands you can use to manage data set allocation. Now, I'll describe two of them: FREE and LISTALC. The others aren't used often, so I don't cover them in this book.

The FREE command

You use the FREE command to deallocate data sets you allocated with an ALLOCATE command. Why would you want to deallocate a data set? Mainly because the disposition you specified on the ALLOCATE command—CATALOG, KEEP, DELETE, or UNCATALOG—isn't actually processed until you deallocate the data set. Similarly, SYSOUT data isn't actually released to JES2/JES3 until you deallocate it. Normally, all of your data sets are implicitly deallocated when you end your terminal session by entering a LOGOFF command. The FREE command lets you deallocate your data sets without logging off.

Figure 9-27 gives the format of the FREE command. Its operands fall into three categories: (1) those used to identify which data sets to deallocate; (2) those used to change the final disposition of a data set; and (3) those used to change the routing for a SYSOUT data set.

How to identify which data sets to free   You code ALL, DSNAME, or DDNAME to identify which data sets you want to deallocate. If you say ALL, then all of the data sets currently allocated to you are freed. If you want to deallocate specific data sets, you use DSNAME or DDNAME. The DSNAME operand lets you list one or more data sets by name. The DDNAME operand lets you list one or more ddnames.

The FREE command

FREE $\begin{Bmatrix} \text{ALL} \\ \text{DSNAME(data-set-names)} \\ \text{DDNAME(ddnames)} \end{Bmatrix}$

$\begin{bmatrix} \begin{Bmatrix} \text{KEEP} \\ \text{CATALOG} \\ \text{UNCATALOG} \\ \text{DELETE} \end{Bmatrix} \end{bmatrix}$

$\begin{bmatrix} \text{SYSOUT(class)} \end{bmatrix}$

$\begin{bmatrix} \begin{Bmatrix} \text{HOLD} \\ \text{NOHOLD} \end{Bmatrix} \end{bmatrix}$

$\begin{bmatrix} \text{DEST(station-id)} \end{bmatrix}$

Explanation

ALL DSNAME DDNAME	Identifies the data sets to be freed. ALL means to free all allocated data sets. DSNAME means to free the named data sets. DDNAME means to free the data sets allocated under the specified ddnames.
KEEP CATALOG UNCATALOG DELETE	Overrides the disposition specified when you allocated the data set. KEEP means to retain the data set. CATALOG means to retain the data set and create a catalog entry for it. UNCATALOG means to retain the data set but remove it from the catalog. And DELETE means to delete the data set.
SYSOUT	Reroutes SYSOUT output to the specified class.
HOLD NOHOLD	Overrides the HOLD/NOHOLD operand you specified when you allocated the data set. HOLD means to keep the data set in the SYSOUT queue until released by an operator or TSO user. NOHOLD means to release the data set from the queue.
DEST	Routes the output to the specified remote station.

Figure 9-27   The FREE command

Either way, the effect is the same: the data sets you specify are deallocated.

How to change the disposition of a data set   When you free a data set, the disposition assigned to it when it was allocated is processed. You can change that disposition, however, by specifying KEEP, DELETE, CATALOG, or UNCATALOG on the FREE command. These operands have the same meanings as they do for the ALLOCATE command. When used here, they override the corresponding operands entered on the ALLOCATE commands for the files being freed.

How to change SYSOUT routing   You can also change the final routing of a SYSOUT data set by specifying SYSOUT, HOLD/NOHOLD, or DEST on a FREE command. Again, these operands mean the same thing here as they do in an ALLOCATE command. Bear in mind, though, that you can't specify any of these operands unless the file was assigned to SYSOUT when it was allocated.

Examples of FREE commands   Figure 9-28 gives five examples of the FREE command. In example 1, I free all data sets previously allocated. Example 2 frees three specific data sets by name: DLOWE.TEST.COBOL, DLOWE.TEST.OBJ, and DLOWE.TEST.LOAD. Example 3 frees one data set identified by the ddname BFCRDS. Example 4 frees the same data set as example 3, but changes its final disposition to DELETE. As a result, this data set is deleted even if its ALLOCATE command said to keep or catalog it.

Example 5 in figure 9-28 frees a SYSOUT data set and changes its output routing. Here, the SYSOUT class is changed to A and DEST is specified so the output is routed to a remote site named RMT200. Any corresponding operands on the original ALLOCATE command for this data set are overridden.

The LISTALC command

Figure 9-29 shows the format of the LISTALC command. This command displays the name and other information for each data set currently allocated to you. If you enter LISTALC with no operands, only the names of the data sets are listed. If you code one or more of the four operands, additional information is listed.

If you say STATUS, TSO lists the ddname and disposition for each data set currently allocated. If you say HISTORY, TSO lists the file's creation and expiration dates and owner-id

Example 1

```
FREE ALL
```

Example 2

```
FREE DSNAME(TEST.COBOL TEST.OBJ TEST.LOAD)
```

Example 3

```
FREE DDNAME(BFCRDS)
```

Example 4

```
FREE DDNAME(BFCRDS) DELETE
```

Example 5

```
FREE DDNAME(ORDLST) SYSOUT(A) DEST(RMT200)
```

Figure 9-28   Examples of the FREE command

as well. MEMBERS causes the member names for each allocated partitioned data set to be listed. Finally, SYSNAMES
lists the names of system-generated files like SYSOUT data
sets.

Figure 9-30 shows an example of LISTALC output. Most
of the data sets listed here are allocated automatically when
you log on. Some of them are defined by DD statements in the
JCL procedure executed to start your terminal session. Others
are allocated by ALLOCATE commands in a CLIST that's
automatically executed when you log on.

DISCUSSION

In this topic, I've presented just a small subset of the
ALLOCATE command's operands. IBM's TSO manual
describes many more that let you define additional options for
disk and tape data sets. Still, the ALLOCATE operands I
presented here should be all you'll need to allocate most types

The LISTALC command

```
LISTALC [STATUS]

        [HISTORY]

        [MEMBERS]

        [SYSNAMES]
```

Explanation

STATUS   List the ddname and disposition for each allocated data set.

HISTORY   List the creation date, expiration date, and owner-id for each allocated data set.

MEMBERS   List the member names for each allocated partitioned data set.

SYSNAMES   List complete names of data sets whose names were generated by the system (such as SYSOUT data sets).

Figure 9-29   The LISTALC command

```
READY
LISTALC
 SYS2.TSO.LOGON
 TERMFILE
 TERMFILE
 TERMFILE
 TERMFILE
 TERMFILE
 SYS1.PLICLNK
 VCAT.MPS600
 SYS2.COMMAND.CLIST
 SYS2.ISP.BASE.ISPPLIB
 SYS1.ISPPLIB
 SYS2.ISP.BASE.ISPMLIB
 SYS1.ISPMLIB
 SYS2.ISP.BASE.ISPSLIB
 SYS1.ISPSLIB
 DLOWE.ISPPARM
 DLOWE.TEST.COBOL(REORDLST )
 JES2.TSU09603.SO0106
 DLOWE.BFCRDS.DATA
 READY
```

Figure 9-30   Typical LISTALC command output

of data sets. And if you master the material in this topic,
you'll have no trouble understanding the TSO manual when
you need to use additional operands.

One important point worth remembering here is that you
use the ALLOCATE command to define non-VSAM data sets
only. To create a VSAM data set, you use IDCAMS' DEFINE
command. Since VSAM file creation is beyond the scope of
this book, I don't cover the DEFINE command here. Instead,
I suggest you get a copy of my book, *VSAM: Access Method
Services and Application Programming,* available from Mike
Murach & Associates, Inc.

Terminology

allocate
deallocate
ddname
status
extend a file
disposition
group name
primary allocation
secondary allocation
expiration date
retention period

Objective

Use the ALLOCATE, FREE, and LISTALC commands to
manage data set allocation.

Chapter 10

Foreground program development commands

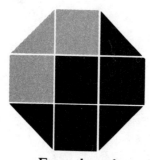

In this chapter, I present the TSO commands you use to perform the critical program development tasks of compiling, link-editing, and testing programs. This chapter consists of two topics. In topic 1, I present the TSO commands you use to compile, link-edit, and run a program. Then, in topic 2, I describe the interactive COBOL debugger.

Even though topic 2 is specific to COBOL, you may want to read it if you're developing assembler or FORTRAN programs. It will give you some idea of how to use the interactive debuggers for those languages (the assembler debugger is TEST; the FORTRAN debugger is TESTFORT). On the other hand, if you're using PLIC or VSBASIC, you can run your programs interactively without a special debugging program. So you can skip topic 2.

TOPIC 1 How to compile, link-edit, and execute a program

TSO provides commands that let you invoke most of the standard language translators, including the COBOL, FORTRAN, and PL/I compilers, the assembler, and the VS BASIC and APL processors. In addition, a TSO command lets you invoke the linkage editor to prepare your compiled programs for execution. Since most program development is done using the COBOL language, this topic describes in detail how to compile and link-edit COBOL programs. The commands for compiling programs written in other languages are similar.

Libraries and output listings

Before I go on, I want to point out that you use a variety of libraries and data sets when you develop a COBOL program using TSO commands. Figure 10-1 lists the data set names I created for this book. Although the naming conventions at your shop may be different and you may not be working in COBOL, these names should serve as examples of the types of data sets you need.

Usually, you'll have at least two COBOL libraries: a test library that contains versions of programs under development and a COPY library that contains members included via COPY statements. You maintain the members in these libraries using an editor like SPF's edit option.

For a one-programmer project, a single test library is sufficient. For a multi-programmer project, however, you'll probably have one test library for each programmer. And for a large project, you may have an additional COBOL library: a master source library that contains only final versions of programs.

All of the foreground compilers place the compiled version of the program, called an *object module*, in an OBJ library with the same name as the source library. Thus, if the source

Data set name	Function
DLOWE.TEST.COBOL	COBOL source library for programs under development
DLOWE.COPY.COBOL	COBOL COPY library
DLOWE.TEST.OBJ	Object library for the compiled versions of programs in DLOWE.TEST.COBOL
DLOWE.TEST.LOAD	Load library for the link-edited versions of programs in DLOWE.TEST.OBJ
DLOWE.SUBPROG.LOAD	Subprogram load library
DLOWE.TEST.SYM	Symbolic debugging library
DLOWE.member.LIST	COBOL compiler listing
DLOWE.member.LINKLIST	Linkage-editor listing
DLOWE.member.LOADLIST	Loader listing
DLOWE.member.TESTLIST	Output listing from debugging session

Figure 10-1   Data sets used for program development (COBOL)

library is DLOWE.TEST.COBOL, the *object library* will be DLOWE.TEST.OBJ. The member name for the source and object program is the same.

The linkage editor places its output, called a *load module*, in a LOAD library, again with the same name. So, in the above example, the *load library* is DLOWE.TEST.LOAD. In addition, any called subprograms must be kept in a load library. Generally, the subprogram library follows TSO naming conventions. So DLOWE.SUBPROG.LOAD is a valid subprogram library name. But system subprogram libraries, like the ones that contain compiler subroutines, follow MVS conventions for naming system data sets. For example, SYS1.COBLIB is the name of the COBOL compiler subroutine library.

To debug a COBOL program using the interactive debugger, you must use a *symbolic debugging file*. This partitioned data set, whose type qualifier is SYM, is automatically allocated by the foreground compiler if it doesn't already exist. It's used by the interactive COBOL debugger to obtain symbolic information—such as data names and statement numbers—when you debug your program.

Output listings generated by foreground compilers are placed in a sequential data set (*not* a library) whose type is LIST. For example, DLOWE.REORDLST.LIST is a valid name for a compiler listing. For a linkage-editor listing, the type qualifier is LINKLIST. Thus, a valid name for a link listing is DLOWE.REORDLST.LINKLIST. And for the output from the interactive debugger, the type is TESTLIST. So DLOWE.REORDLST.TESTLIST is a valid name for a debugging listing.

Now, I'll show you how you use these files as you compile and link-edit a COBOL program.

The COBOL command

Figure 10-2 gives the format of the COBOL command. The COBOL command invokes the *COBOL prompter*, which prepares certain required data sets and invokes the standard COBOL compiler for foreground processing. As you can see, the COBOL command has a number of operands. The only required operand is the data set name that supplies the source program as input to the compiler.

The LOAD operand tells COBOL where to put the object program. If you omit the LOAD operand, COBOL creates the object program as a member in a library whose name is the same as the input library's, but whose type qualifier is OBJ. So you won't normally code the LOAD operand. If you don't want COBOL to create an object module, say NOLOAD. (Incidentally, don't be confused by the LOAD operand: the compiler output is an object module, not a load module.)

The PRINT operand says whether or not you want to generate a compiler listing. If you omit PRINT, the COBOL prompter creates a data set name using the input member name with a type qualifier of LIST. If you want to change that data set name, specify a PRINT operand. If you want the compiler output to go to your terminal, code an asterisk (*) as the print file name. And if you want to suppress compiler output, say NOPRINT.

The COBOL command

```
COBOL       data-set-name

            [{LOAD(object-module-name)}]
            [{NOLOAD                  }]

            [{PRINT(print-file-name)}]
            [{PRINT(*)              }]
            [{NOPRINT               }]

            [{LIB(library-names)}]
            [{NOLIB             }]

            [options]
```

Explanation

data-set-name	The COBOL source program. Usually a member of a partitioned data set.
LOAD	Specifies an alternate location for the object program.
NOLOAD	Specifies that no object program should be created.
PRINT	Specifies an alternate location for the print file. An asterisk (*) directs print output to the terminal.
NOPRINT	Specifies that no print file should be created.
LIB	Provides a list of libraries which are searched for COPY members. The libraries are searched in the order in which you list them.
NOLIB	Says that the source program contains no COPY statements. (NOLIB is the default.)
options	One or more of the compiler options listed in figure 10-3.

Figure 10-2 The COBOL command

If you use a COPY statement in your COBOL program, you should define the library containing the COPY member with a LIB operand. In the LIB operand, you can specify more than one library. In that case, the libraries are searched in the order in which you list them to locate the member being copied.

In addition to the operands listed in figure 10-2, you can supply one or more *compiler options* that control other aspects

Option	Meaning
SOURCE NOSOURCE	Print the source listing.
DMAP NODMAP	Print a Data Division map.
PMAP NOPMAP	Print a complete Procedure Division map.
CLIST NOCLIST	Print a condensed Procedure Division map. Can't be used with PMAP.
VERB NOVERB	Print procedure names and verb names on the Procedure Division map; meaningful only when you code CLIST or PMAP.
XREF NOXREF	Print a cross-reference listing.
SXREF NOSXREF	Print a cross-reference listing sorted into alphabetical order.
APOST QUOTE	Indicates whether apostrophes (') or quotes (") are used to mark non-numeric literals.
BUF(n)	Specifies how much buffer space to allow. You can specify n as an integer or use K to represent units of 1024 bytes. Thus, BUF(2048) and BUF(2K) are the same.
TERM NOTERM	Display status information and error messages at the TSO terminal.
TEST NOTEST	Create a symbolic debugging file so the program can be tested using the interactive COBOL debugger.

Figure 10-3   Common COBOL compiler options

of the compiler's operation. Figure 10-3 lists some of the more commonly used compiler options. I've indicated the IBM-supplied default settings for these options by underlining the default values. But your installation may have changed those defaults, so you need to check with your supervisor about which options you should use.

At any rate, the options you choose that deal with compiler output—like SOURCE, DMAP, and so on—affect the PRINT operand on the COBOL command. If none of

Example 1

```
COBOL TEST.COBOL(REORDLST)
```

Example 2

```
COBOL TEST.COBOL(REORDLST) LIB(COPY.COBOL) TEST
```

Example 3

```
COBOL TEST.COBOL(REORDLST) DMAP CLIST XREF
```

Figure 10-4 Examples of the COBOL command

those options are active, no print file will be created even if you specify PRINT. Also, note that you use another compiler option—TERM—to say whether status information and error messages are sent to the terminal. TERM works independently of PRINT.

COBOL examples   Figure 10-4 shows three examples of the COBOL command. Example 1 shows the simplest form of the COBOL command. Here, I specify just a data set name. All of the other operands assume their default settings. In example 2, I specify a LIB operand and the TEST option. In this case, any COPY statements in the COBOL program will retrieve members from COPY.COBOL, the copy library I've specified. And since I've said TEST, I'll be able to test the program later using the interactive COBOL debugger.

Example 3 shows how to code options that create additional compiler output. Here, the compiler listing will include a Data Division map (DMAP), a condensed Procedure Division listing (CLIST), and a cross-reference listing of data names (XREF), in addition to the source listing.

The LINK command

Before you can execute a compiled program, you must *link-edit* it. When you link-edit a program, the program's combined with any subprograms you invoke using CALL statements and

The LINK command

```
LINK      data-set-name

          [LOAD(load-module-name)]

          ⎡⎧PRINT(print-file-name)⎫⎤
          ⎢⎨PRINT(*)              ⎬⎥
          ⎣⎩NOPRINT               ⎭⎦

          [LIB(library-names)]

          COBLIB
```

Explanation

data-set-name	The program to be link-edited.
LOAD	Specifies an alternate location for the load module.
PRINT	Specifies an alternate location for the print file. An asterisk (*) directs print output to the terminal.
NOPRINT	Specifies that no print file should be created.
LIB	Supplies one or more subprogram libraries used to retrieve called subprograms. The libraries are searched in the order in which you list them.
COBLIB	Specifies that the COBOL subroutine library (SYS1.COBLIB) should be used to retrieve compiler subroutines.

Figure 10-5   The LINK command

with any compiler subroutines to form a load module that's
ready to be executed by MVS.

You use the LINK command to invoke the linkage editor
from TSO. Figure 10-5 gives the format of the LINK command. Here, the data set name specifies the input to the
linkage editor—usually an object module previously created by
a language translator. The LOAD operand tells the linkage
editor where to put the link-edited load module. Usually, you'll
omit this operand so the load module will be placed in the
proper load library.

The PRINT operand tells how to handle the link listing.
If you omit this operand, the link listing is written to a

Example 1

```
LINK TEST.OBJ(REORDLST) COBLIB
```

Example 2

```
LINK TEST.OBJ(REORDLST) LIB(SUBPROG.LOAD) COBLIB
```

Figure 10-6   Examples of the LINK command

LINKLIST data set. If you code a print file name, the link listing is written to the file you specify. If you code PRINT(*), the link listing is sent directly to your terminal. And if you say NOPRINT, the link listing is suppressed.

If your program invokes subprograms via a CALL statement or its equivalent, you'll have to supply the name of the load library that contains the subprograms with a LIB operand. If you specify more than one library in a LIB operand, they're searched in the order in which you list them. The last operand—COBLIB—says that the program also invokes subprograms contained in a system subroutine library (SYS1.COBLIB). You must code COBLIB when you link-edit a COBOL program.

LINK examples   Figure 10-6 gives two examples of the LINK command. In example 1, I link-edit a program named REORDLST that's in a library named TEST.OBJ. In example 2, I link-edit the same program but include SUBPROG.LOAD as a subprogram library. Any user subprograms called by REORDLST must be contained in SUBPROG.LOAD.

The CALL command

Once you've link-edited your program, you can execute it in foreground mode by issuing a CALL command (the format is shown in figure 10-7). Before you issue a CALL command, however, you must issue an ALLOCATE command for each data set processed by your program.

For example, suppose you want to run a program named REORDLST in a load library named DLOWE.TEST.LOAD.

The CALL command

```
CALL      data-set-name

          ['parameter-string']
```

Explanation

data-set-name   The name of the load module to be executed. You can omit the type qualifier since LOAD is assumed.

'parameter-string'   A parameter string that's passed to the program.

Figure 10-7   The CALL command

The program requires two data sets, BFCRDS and ORDLST. To invoke this program, you could enter these three TSO commands:

```
ALLOCATE DSNAME(BFCRDS.DATA) DDNAME(BFCRDS)
ALLOCATE DSNAME(*) DDNAME(ORDLST)
CALL TEST(REORDLST)
```

The CALL command assumes LOAD is the qualifier for the load library. And since I allocated the output file (ORDLST) to the terminal, the program's output is displayed.

If your program requires run-time parameters, you supply them in apostrophes following the name of the load module. For example, suppose you code a CALL command like this:

```
CALL TEST(REORDLST) 'JANUARY'
```

Here, the word JANUARY is passed to REORDLST as a parameter. Since most COBOL programs don't use parameters, you won't specify a parameter string often.

The LOADGO command

The LOADGO command, whose format is shown in figure 10-8, combines the functions of the LINK and CALL commands. The input to the LOADGO command is an object

The LOADGO command

```
LOADGO    data-set-name

          ['parameter-string']

         (PRINT(print-file-name))
        [{PRINT(*)                }]
         (NOPRINT                 )

          [LIB(library-names)]

           COBLIB
```

Explanation

data-set-name	The name of the object program to be link-edited.
'parameter-string'	A parameter string that's passed to your program.
PRINT	Specifies an alternate location for the print file. An asterisk (*) directs print output to the terminal.
NOPRINT	Says that no print file should be created.
LIB	Supplies one or more subprogram libraries used to retrieve called subprograms. The libraries are searched in the order in which you list them.
COBLIB	Says to include SYS1.COBLIB as a subroutine library.

Figure 10-8   The LOADGO command

module created by a compiler. LOADGO link-edits the object module and loads and executes the result. The main difference between the LOADGO command and the LINK and CALL commands is that the LOADGO command does *not* create a permanent load module in a load library. Although the LOADGO command link-edits the object program before executing it, it doesn't use the system linkage editor to do this. Instead, it uses another system program called the *loader* to link-edit, load, and execute the program.

The PRINT operand in figure 10-8 tells what to do with the loader's listing. If you omit this operand, the loader listing is written to a LOADLIST file. Otherwise, the listing is written to the file you specify. If you specify an asterisk (*), the listing is sent to your terminal. And if you say NOPRINT, the loader listing is suppressed.

The LIB operand defines the subprogram libraries used to locate subprograms that are linked together before your program is executed. And COBLIB tells LOADGO to use the standard COBOL subroutine library (SYS1.COBLIB) in addition to the libraries you specify in the LIB operand.

To illustrate the LOADGO command, suppose you issue this command:

```
LOADGO TEST.OBJ(REORDLST) LIB(SUBPROG.LOAD) COBLIB
```

Here, member REORDLST in TEST.OBJ is link-edited using SUBPROG.LOAD for called subprograms and SYS1.COBLIB for compiler subroutines. If the link-edit is successful, the program is loaded into storage and executed. For your program to execute properly, of course, you must issue the appropriate ALLOCATE commands for the data sets your program processes.

In some cases, the LOADGO command may save you some time because you don't have to link-edit and execute your program separately. In general, though, I recommend you use the LINK and CALL commands rather than the LOADGO command for two reasons. First, it's more efficient to create a load module with the LINK command if you're going to execute your program more than once between compilations. And second, your program has to be processed by the LINK command if you want to debug it using the interactive COBOL debugger.

Other programming languages

Besides COBOL, TSO provides commands to compile programs written in other languages. Figure 10-9 summarizes those commands. I won't describe them in detail here. Instead, I refer you to the appropriate IBM manual for detailed information. And for an overview on how to use one of these commands, just enter HELP followed by the command name. In any event, once you compile your program, you still use the LINK and CALL commands (or the LOADGO command) to link-edit and execute it.

Command	Function
ASM	Assemble a program.
FORT	Compile a FORTRAN program using the G compiler.
PLI	Compile a PL/I program using the optimizing compiler.
PLIC	Invoke the PL/I checkout compiler.
VSAPL	Invoke the VS APL processor.
VSBASIC	Invoke the VS BASIC processor.

Figure 10-9   TSO commands for other language processors

Discussion

Because compiling and link-editing a program usually involves entering a COBOL command with one or more operands and a LINK command with operands, I recommend you create a simple command procedure (CLIST) that contains the required entries. Then, you can compile and link-edit a program by entering one simple command. I'll show you how to create and use CLISTs in chapter 12.

Terminology

object module
object library
load module
load library
symbolic debugging file
COBOL prompter
compiler option
link-edit
loader

Objective

Use the COBOL, LINK, and CALL commands to compile, link-edit, and execute a COBOL program.

TOPIC 2   The interactive COBOL debugger

In a traditional batch-oriented system, the most common way to test and debug a program is to submit the program for processing in a background region. Then, when the program completes, you inspect its output to determine if it executed properly. If the output's in error—or if the program ends abnormally and produces a storage dump—you review the program listing in a desperate attempt to locate the bug. For the most part, there are few effective tools to help you locate a bug in this manner.

Under TSO, however, you can use the *interactive COBOL debugger* to help you test and debug programs interactively. Basically, the interactive COBOL debugger lets you monitor the execution of your program at your terminal. You can control how statements in your program are executed. You can examine the contents of data fields and change them if you wish. You can trace the flow of paragraphs or sections in your program. And unlike storage-dump debugging, the interactive COBOL debugger is symbolic. That means you use actual COBOL data names and statement numbers rather than hexadecimal addresses.

In this topic, I describe how to use the interactive COBOL debugger. First, I describe how to invoke the debugger using the TESTCOB command. Then, I describe how to use the basic tools of the debugger: how to monitor your program's execution, how to monitor its data, how to list segments of the source program, and how to use some of the advanced features of debug, such as subcommand lists and techniques for debugging subprograms.

Before I go on, I want to point out that I am *not* trying to teach you how to debug COBOL programs in this topic. So I'm not going to explain the likely causes of various abend codes. Instead, I want to teach you how to use the TESTCOB command so you'll be able to debug your programs more easily.

HOW TO INVOKE THE DEBUGGER

Before you can use the debugger, you must issue two ALLOCATE commands. One of them must assign a ddname to the symbolic debugging file produced when you compiled the program (remember, you must specify the TEST compiler option on the COBOL command to produce a debug file). The other ALLOCATE command assigns a ddname to the load library that contains the link-edited version of your program.

Once you've allocated these two files, you can issue a TESTCOB command to invoke the debugger. Figure 10-10 gives the format of the TESTCOB command. On it, you must specify (1) the program-id for the program you're debugging, (2) the ddname you previously allocated to the symbolic debugging file, (3) the load member name for the program you're debugging, and (4) the ddname you previously allocated to the load library containing the program.

To illustrate, consider figure 10-11. Here, I issue two ALLOCATE commands. The first one associates the ddname LOADLIB with a data set named DLOWE.TEST.LOAD. That data set contains the load member for the program I'm going to debug. The second ALLOCATE command associates the ddname SYMDD with the symbolic debug file produced by the COBOL compiler—DLOWE.TEST.SYM(REORDLST). Notice here that I specify only the library name for the load library. In contrast, I specify both the library *and* the member names for the symbolic debug file.

After I issue the ALLOCATE commands, I issue a TESTCOB command that says REORDLST is the program name (taken from the PROGRAM-ID paragraph in the COBOL source program), SYMDD is the debug file, REORDLST is the load member name, and LOADLIB is the load library.

If you think this format for the TESTCOB command seems complicated and confusing, you're right. Unfortunately, there's nothing you can do about it (except possibly code a CLIST to simplify the required entries). So don't let the complicated format bother you.

If you want to keep output from your TESTCOB session so you can print or display it later, you must specify a PRINT

The TESTCOB command

```
TESTCOB  (program-id:ddname1)
          LOAD(member:ddname2)
         [PRINT(ddname3)]
         [PARM('parameter-string')]
```

Explanation

program-id	The name from the PROGRAM-ID paragraph of the program to be debugged.
ddname1	The ddname allocated to the symbolic debug file.
LOAD	Says that member identifies the name of the load member for the file and ddname2 is the ddname allocated to the load library that contains the member.
PRINT	Routes output from the debug session to the device or file allocated to ddname3.
PARM	Specifies a parameter string that's passed to the program.

Figure 10-10   The TESTCOB command

```
 READY
ALLOCATE DSNAME(TEST.LOAD) DDNAME(LOADLIB)
 READY
ALLOCATE DSNAME(TEST.SYM(REORDLST)) DDNAME(SYMDD)
 READY
TESTCOB (REORDLST:SYMDD) LOAD(REORDLST:LOADLIB)
 TESTCOB
```

Figure 10-11   Invoking the interactive COBOL debugger

operand on the TESTCOB command. That also requires that you issue another ALLOCATE command to assign a ddname to the print file. For example, you might issue this command:

```
ALLOCATE DSNAME(REORDLST.TESTLIST) DDNAME(LISTDD)
```

Then, you would specify PRINT(LISTDD) on the TESTCOB command.

If your program requires execution-time parameters, you specify them in the PARM operand. You code this field much as you do for an EXEC statement in standard batch JCL. For example, suppose you code this PARM operand:

```
PARM('JANUARY')
```

Then, the word JANUARY is passed to your program as a parameter. Since most COBOL programs don't use execution-time parameters, you won't use the PARM operand often.

After you've entered your TESTCOB command, the interactive debugger displays this mode message:

```
TESTCOB
```

That means it's waiting for you to enter a subcommand to direct your debugging session. Now, I'll describe how you can use these subcommands to monitor your program's execution, its data, and so on.

HOW TO MONITOR YOUR PROGRAM'S EXECUTION

TESTCOB lets you monitor your program's execution in two ways. First, you can establish *breakpoints* at one or more statements in your program. Then, whenever those statements are about to be executed, your program is interrupted and TESTCOB displays a message telling which statement is about to execute. At that point, you can resume your program's execution or enter a subcommand to display the contents of a field, set another breakpoint, or do some other TESTCOB processing.

The second way to monitor program execution is to use a *trace*. A trace displays information about your program's execution without actually interrupting the program.

Statement references Before I go on, I want you to understand how TESTCOB refers to individual statements in your program. TESTCOB follows this format when it refers to a particular Procedure Division statement:

```
program-id.statement-number.verb-number
```

Program-id identifies the program that contains the statement. Normally, this will be the name of the program you're executing. However, if your program calls subprograms, program-id will name the subprogram if that's where the interrupt occurs.

Statement-number identifies the number of the Procedure Division statement that was about to execute when the interrupt occurred. This number corresponds to the number you code in columns 1-6 of the source program—it's *not* the compiler-generated line number that appears in the source listing.

Verb-number is only significant when you code more than one COBOL verb on a single line. It indicates which verb was about to execute when the interrupt occurred: if it's one, the first verb on the line was about to execute; if it's two, the second verb was about to execute; and so on. It's a good practice to limit yourself to one COBOL verb on each line of your Procedure Division. If you do that, the verb number will always be one.

To illustrate TESTCOB's statement-referral notation, consider this message:

```
REORDLST.002100.1
```

This refers to the first verb on line 2100 in the program named REORDLST.

Now that you know how TESTCOB refers to Procedure Division statements, I'll show you how to use TESTCOB subcommands to start or resume a program's execution, to use breakpoints, and to establish a program trace.

How to start or resume your program's execution

TESTCOB doesn't automatically begin executing your program. Instead, after you enter the TESTCOB command, it displays a TESTCOB mode message and waits for you to enter a subcommand. Here, you can set a breakpoint, establish a trace, or just start your program executing.

TESTCOB provides two subcommands for starting your program's execution. The most commonly used is GO. If you simply enter the word GO, your program begins executing and continues until a breakpoint occurs, an abend occurs, or your program executes a STOP RUN statement. Then, the TESTCOB mode message is displayed again and you can enter another subcommand.

The RUN subcommand is like the GO subcommand except that it ignores any breakpoints you've established. So the RUN subcommand causes your program to execute to its completion —either an abend or a STOP RUN.

As I've already mentioned, you use the RUN or GO subcommand to start your program executing when you first enter TESTCOB. In addition, you use the RUN or GO subcommand to resume your program's execution after it's been interrupted by a breakpoint or an abend. But once your program ends by executing a STOP RUN, you can't resume it with a RUN or GO subcommand.

If you specify a statement number on a RUN or GO subcommand, program execution starts at the specified statement. For example, if you enter this subcommand:

```
GO REORDLST.005000.1
```

execution begins at the first verb in line 5000 in REORDLST. You can achieve the same result like this:

```
GO 5000
```

Here, the first verb in line 5000 is assumed because you omitted the verb number. And, assuming that REORDLST is the program that's been executing, you can omit the program-id.

Coding a statement number on a RUN or GO subcommand is the same as issuing a GO TO statement in the COBOL program itself. You'll use this feature most when you're testing a single section of code repeatedly, perhaps changing the value of a data field between each execution.

How to use breakpoints

One of the most powerful features of the interactive debugger is the ability to use breakpoints. Basically, a breakpoint is a specific point in your program where you want to temporarily interrupt program execution. Then, you can use other TESTCOB subcommands to inspect data fields, display the status of files, or perform other debugging functions.

TESTCOB provides three types of breakpoints. A *NEXT breakpoint* lets you execute your program one statement at a time by setting a breakpoint at the next statement that's executed. An *unconditional breakpoint* sets a breakpoint at a specific statement number you supply; your program is interrupted whenever that statement is about to execute. And a *conditional breakpoint* interrupts your program whenever a condition you specify occurs—for example, whenever a particular field's value changes.

How to use a NEXT breakpoint   A NEXT subcommand establishes a breakpoint at the next statement that's executed. To set a NEXT breakpoint, you just enter the NEXT subcommand with no operands, like this:

    NEXT

Then, when you enter a GO subcommand, only one statement of your program is executed, after which the breakpoint is taken.

There are two situations in which a NEXT breakpoint is particularly useful. The first is when your program reaches a decision point—such as an IF statement—and you want to see which statement of your program is executed next. By setting a NEXT breakpoint, you cause your program to be interrupted after the next statement executes, even though you don't know in advance what that statement is.

The second situation where a NEXT breakpoint is helpful is when you first enter TESTCOB. Before you start your program with a GO subcommand, you *cannot* use certain TESTCOB subcommands, including the ones you use to examine and change your program's data. That's because TESTCOB doesn't actually load your program into storage until you issue a GO or RUN subcommand. But if you enter a NEXT subcommand followed by a GO subcommand, TESTCOB loads your program and interrupts it *before* the first statement executes. Then, you can enter any TESTCOB subcommand you wish.

How to use an unconditional breakpoint   An unconditional breakpoint causes your program to be interrupted whenever a particular statement is about to be executed. To use unconditional breakpoints, you need to know about two TESTCOB subcommands, the AT and OFF subcommands. Figure 10-12 gives the formats of these commands.

You use the AT subcommand to establish one or more breakpoints in your program. Basically, you provide one or more statement numbers in the AT subcommand. Then, whenever one of those statements is about to be executed, TESTCOB interrupts your program's execution and lets you enter one or more subcommands. When you enter a GO or RUN subcommand, your program continues until the next breakpoint.

To set one breakpoint, you simply say AT followed by the statement number for the breakpoint you wish to set. For example, if you enter this subcommand:

```
AT 2100
```

a breakpoint is established at statement 2100.

To specify more than one statement number in an AT subcommand, separate them with commas and enclose the entire list in parentheses. For example, this subcommand:

```
AT (2100,2500,3000)
```

sets three breakpoints, at lines 2100, 2500, and 3000.

The AT subcommand

```
AT  statement-list
    [(subcommand-list)]
```

The OFF subcommand

```
OFF [statement-list]
```

Explanation

statement-list One or more statement numbers specified as: (1) a single number; (2) several numbers separated by commas and enclosed in parentheses; or (3) a range of numbers separated by a colon. If no statements are specified in an OFF subcommand, all unconditional breakpoints are deleted.

subcommand-list A series of TESTCOB subcommands, separated by semicolons, that is automatically executed when the specified breakpoint occurs.

Figure 10-12 Subcommands used for unconditional breakpoints

You can also specify a range of statement numbers in an AT subcommand, like this:

```
AT 2100:5000
```

Here, a breakpoint is established at every statement between (and including) lines 2100 and 5000. This form of the AT subcommand is useful when you want to "single-step" a segment of your program to locate an elusive program bug.

On an AT subcommand, you can specify a list of TESTCOB subcommands to be executed automatically when the breakpoint occurs. I'll describe how—and why—you'll use this feature in a few moments.

You use the OFF subcommand to remove one or more breakpoints you've previously set using the AT subcommand. In an OFF subcommand, you specify statement numbers just as in an AT subcommand. You can specify a single statement number, like this:

```
OFF 2100
```

Here, the breakpoint at line 2100 is removed. To specify more than one statement number, separate them by commas and enclose the entire list in parentheses, like this:

```
OFF (2100,2500,3000)
```

Here, the three breakpoints at lines 2100, 2500, and 3000 are removed. You can specify a range of statements, like this:

```
OFF 2100:5000
```

Here, all of the breakpoints between (and including) lines 2100 and 5000 are removed. And finally, you can specify an OFF subcommand with no operands. In that case, all of your unconditional breakpoints are deleted.

How to use a conditional breakpoint   A conditional breakpoint interrupts your program based on the contents of a particular data field. As a result, conditional breakpoints let you monitor the contents of specific data fields to see when they are changed or when they attain a particular value.

You use two subcommands for conditional breakpoints. The WHEN subcommand establishes a conditional breakpoint. And the OFFWN subcommand removes one or more conditional breakpoints. These subcommands are shown in figure 10-13.

For the WHEN subcommand, you must specify a one- to four-character identifier. You use this identifier later to remove the breakpoint. And TESTCOB displays this identifier whenever your program is interrupted as a result of the breakpoint. The identifier must be unique during a TESTCOB session.

After the identifier, you specify either a single data name or an expression. If you specify just a data name, that field is evaluated each time a program statement is executed. Whenever the field's value changes, your program is interrupted. For example, suppose you enter this WHEN subcommand:

```
WHEN ITNO BF-ITEM-NO
```

The WHEN subcommand

```
WHEN    identifier

        {data-name    }
        {(expression)}
```

The OFFWN subcommand

```
OFFWN    [identifier]
```

Explanation

identifier	A one- to four-character string that uniquely identifies a conditional breakpoint. For an OFFWN subcommand, you can specify more than one identifier by separating them with commas and enclosing the list in parentheses. If no identifiers are specified in an OFFWN command, all conditional breakpoints are deleted.
data-name	If you specify a data name rather than an expression, the breakpoint is taken whenever the contents of that data name change.
expression	A relational condition in this form: data-name operator value where operator is a relational operator selected from the list in figure 10-14 and value is another data name or a literal value.

Figure 10-13   Subcommands used for conditional breakpoints

Here, your program is interrupted whenever the value of BF-ITEM-NO changes. ITNO is the identifier associated with this conditional breakpoint.

You can test a field for a specific value by coding an expression that compares the field with another field or a literal. To do this, you use one of the operators shown in figure 10-14. For example, suppose you code this WHEN subcommand:

```
WHEN HIT (AVAILABLE-STOCK LT BF-REORDER-POINT)
```

Operator	Meaning
EQ =	Equal to
GT >	Greater than
LT <	Less than
NE ¬=	Not equal to
GE >=	Greater than or equal to
LE <=	Less than or equal to

Figure 10-14 Relational operators for conditions

Here, your program will be interrupted whenever the value of
AVAILABLE-STOCK is less than the value of BF-REORDER-
POINT. Notice here that the entire expression must be
enclosed in parentheses. Even so, complex or compound
conditions are not allowed.

To remove one or more conditional breakpoints, you
specify one or more identifiers from WHEN subcommands in
an OFFWN subcommand. For example, if you enter this
OFFWN subcommand:

```
OFFWN ITNO
```

the ITNO conditional breakpoint is removed. To specify more
than one conditional breakpoint, enclose the list in parentheses,
like this:

```
OFFWN (ITNO,HIT)
```

Here, two conditional breakpoints are removed. Finally, if you
enter the OFFWN subcommand without any identifiers, all the
conditional breakpoints you've set are removed.

The LISTBRKS subcommand   The LISTBRKS subcommand displays all of your active breakpoints, including NEXT breakpoints, unconditional breakpoints, and conditional breakpoints. In addition, the LISTBRKS subcommand tells you if a program trace is in effect. I'll describe the program trace feature next. Since LISTBRKS has no operands, you enter just the word LISTBRKS.

How to trace program flow

Figure 10-15 gives the format of the TRACE subcommand. You use the TRACE subcommand to initiate or terminate a program trace. A program trace helps you track your program's execution by displaying information about the program as it executes. The output generated by a TRACE subcommand is similar to the output generated by COBOL's TRACE statement. If you specify PRINT, the output's routed to the print file specified on the TESTCOB command.

   The ENTRY operand starts a trace of programs and subprograms. Each time a program transfers control to another program via a CALL statement, the new program's name (taken from the PROGRAM-ID paragraph) is displayed. When control returns to the calling program, the calling program's name is displayed. This type of trace helps you check that your subprograms are being invoked in the correct sequence.

   The PARA and NAME operands both start a trace of the execution of your program's paragraphs and sections. If you say PARA, the statement number of each paragraph or section is displayed whenever that paragraph or section is about to be executed. If you say NAME, the actual paragraph or section name is displayed rather than the statement number. Since the output created by NAME is much easier to follow than that created by PARA, I recommend you use NAME.

   If you enter a TRACE subcommand with no operands, PARA is assumed. So you'll normally enter the TRACE subcommand like this:

```
TRACE NAME
```

Then, actual paragraph and section names rather than statement numbers are displayed.

The TRACE subcommand

```
TRACE    [ {ENTRY}
           {PARA }
           {NAME }
           {OFF  } ]

         [PRINT]
```

Explanation

ENTRY   List each program's program-id as it is entered via a CALL or EXIT PROGRAM
             statement.

PARA   List the statement number corresponding to each paragraph or section as it is
             entered. (PARA is the default.)

NAME   List the actual paragraph or section name as the paragraph or section is entered.

OFF   Deactivate any previous TRACE subcommand.

PRINT   Direct the output to the file specified on the PRINT operand of the TESTCOB
             command.

Figure 10-15   The TRACE subcommand

To stop a program trace, you enter the TRACE subcommand with the OFF operand, like this:

```
TRACE OFF
```

Then, the trace ends.

Figure 10-16 shows output typical of that generated by the TRACE subcommand. As you can see, a list of paragraph and section names makes it easy to follow the execution of a program. (Incidentally, figure 10-16 also shows the TESTCOB display that results from a program abend. In this example, the program abended at line 13700 with an abend code of 0C4.)

HOW TO MONITOR YOUR PROGRAM'S DATA

Besides monitoring your program's statements as they execute, TESTCOB lets you monitor your program's data. You use the

```
TRACE NAME
 TESTCOB
GO
 TRACING REORDLST
 014000 100-PRODUCE-REORDER-LINE
 014800 110-READ-INVENTORY-RECORD
 015600 120-CALCULATE-AVAILABLE-STOCK
 014000 100-PRODUCE-REORDER-LINE
 014800 110-READ-INVENTORY-RECORD
 015600 120-CALCULATE-AVAILABLE-STOCK
 016500 130-PRINT-REORDER-LINE
 017800 140-PRINT-HEADING-LINES
 019600 160-WRITE-PAGE-TOP-LINE
 019000 150-WRITE-REPORT-LINE
 019000 150-WRITE-REPORT-LINE
 019000 150-WRITE-REPORT-LINE
 014000 100-PRODUCE-REORDER-LINE
 014800 110-READ-INVENTORY-RECORD
 020200 200-PRINT-TOTAL-LINE
 019000 150-WRITE-REPORT-LINE
 PROGRAM UNDER TESTCOB ENDED ABNORMALLY, SYSTEM CODE OC4
 LAST PSW BEFORE ABEND FF8500049000004C
 REORDLST.013700.1
```

Figure 10-16   Typical TRACE subcommand output

LIST subcommand to display the contents of one or more data
fields. You use the SET subcommand to change the contents of
data fields. And because COBOL data names can be cumber-
some to type repeatedly, the EQUATE and DROP subcommands let you substitute a short name for a longer one.
Finally, the LISTFILE subcommand lets you display the status
of a file.

How to list data fields

Figure 10-17 shows the format of the LIST subcommand, used
to display the contents of one or more data fields. In a LIST
subcommand, you specify one or more *identifiers*. Each
identifier can be a data name, an index name, or one of the
COBOL special registers like DATE or TALLY. If you specify
PRINT on the LIST subcommand, output is routed to the
print file specified on the TESTCOB command.

You specify the identifiers much like you specify statement
numbers in an AT subcommand. You can specify just one
identifier, like this:

```
LIST BF-ITEM-NUMBER
```

The LIST subcommand

```
LIST {identifier-list}
     {ALL          }

     [PRINT]
```

Explanation

identifier-list   One or more identifiers specified as: (1) a single data name; (2) several data names separated by commas and enclosed in parentheses; or (3) a range of data names separated by a colon. An identifier can be a COBOL data name, an index name, or a COBOL special register.

ALL   List all of the program's data names, index names, special registers, and the TGT.

PRINT   Direct the output to the file specified on the PRINT operand of the TESTCOB command.

Figure 10-17   The LIST subcommand

Here, the value of the field named BF-ITEM-NUMBER is displayed. Or, you can specify several identifiers separated by commas and enclosed in parentheses, like this:

```
LIST (BF-ITEM-NUMBER,BF-ON-HAND,BF-ON-ORDER)
```

Here, the contents of three fields is listed. Finally, you can specify a range of identifiers, like this:

```
LIST BF-ITEM-NUMBER:BF-ON-ORDER
```

Here, the value of each data field coded in the record description between—and including—BF-ITEM-NUMBER and BF-ON-ORDER is listed.

If you specify ALL on a LIST subcommand, all of your program's data is displayed. That includes all index names, data names, and special registers. It also includes the contents of a special table called the *task global table*, or *TGT*. The TGT contains many fields used to control the proper execution

of your program, most of which are of little concern to you.
You probably won't use the ALL operand often. That's
because it can result in a large quantity of output. It's usually
better to specify the field or fields you want to display.

What the LIST output looks like   The LIST output is
formatted according to how the field is defined in the COBOL
program. Alphanumeric items are displayed in standard
character format if possible; if they contain unprintable
characters, they're displayed in hexadecimal. Numeric items,
whether they're zoned decimal or packed decimal, are
displayed as decimal values. If you specify a group item, the
elementary items that make up the group are displayed on
separate lines. If the field is subscripted, each occurrence is
displayed on a separate line, preceded by its subscript value.
And if you specify an index name, the occurrence number
corresponding to the index name's value is displayed.

Each item displayed by the LIST subcommand is labeled
by the field's location in storage, its statement number, level
number, name, and type code. The type code says how the
field is defined in the COBOL program—whether it's alphanumeric, packed decimal, or some other data type. Figure
10-18 shows the type codes along with their meanings.

LIST displays each item's level number as a *normalized
level number*. That means that level numbers are numbered
sequentially from one, even though you might number by two's
or five's in your source program. For example, if you code
three levels numbered 01, 05, and 10, the corresponding
normalized level numbers are 01, 02, and 03.

Figure 10-19 shows output typical of the LIST subcommand. Here, I enter this subcommand:

```
LIST BAL-FWD-CARD
```

Since BAL-FWD-CARD is a group item, its subordinate fields
are listed individually. The level numbers are normalized (my
program contains 05 levels, not 02 levels), and the content of
each field is formatted according to the field's PICTURE.

Type code	Meaning
A	Alphabetic
AN	Alphanumeric
ANE	Alphanumeric edited
NE	Numeric edited
ND	Numeric display (external decimal)
ND-OT	Numeric display, overpunch sign trailing
ND-OL	Numeric display, overpunch sign leading
ND-ST	Numeric display, separate sign trailing
ND-SL	Numeric display, separate sign leading
NP	Numeric packed decimal (COMP-3)
NP-S	Numeric packed decimal, signed
NB	Numeric binary (COMP)
NB-S	Numeric binary, signed
F	Floating point (COMP-1 or COMP-2)
FD	Floating point display
*	Subscripted item

Figure 10-18   LIST type codes

```
LIST BAL-FWD-CARD
           003400   01 BAL-FWD-CARD
  11B818   003600   02 BF-ITEM-NO          ND      00101
  11B81D   003700   02 BF-ITEM-DESC        AN      GENERATOR
  11B831   003800   02 FILLER              AN
  11B836   003900   02 BF-UNIT-PRICE       ND      100.00
  11B83B   004000   02 BF-REORDER-POINT    ND      00100
  11B840   004100   02 BF-ON-HAND          ND      00070
  11B845   004200   02 BF-ON-ORDER         ND      00050
  11B84A   004300   02 FILLER              AN
     00000200
TESTCOB
```

Figure 10-19   Typical LIST subcommand output

The SET subcommand

```
SET identifier-1 = {identifier-2}
                   {literal     }
```

Explanation

identifier-1   The data name or index name whose value is to be changed.

identifier-2   The data name or index name whose value is moved to identifier-1.

literal   A literal value that's moved to identifier-1.

Note: The move operation follows the standard COBOL MOVE rules.

Figure 10-20   The SET subcommand

How to change a data field

Figure 10-20 shows the format of the SET subcommand, used to change the contents of a data field. The operation of the SET command is simple: the contents of identifier-1 is replaced by the contents of identifier-2 or the literal. For example, consider this SET subcommand:

```
SET BF-ITEM-NO = 100
```

Here, the value of BF-ITEM-NO is changed to 100.

    If the lengths or types of the sending and receiving fields differ, the SET subcommand follows the rules for a standard COBOL MOVE statement. Thus, values are truncated or padded with spaces as necessary, and data is converted from one form to another, just as when you code a MOVE statement in your COBOL program. And, of course, certain combinations of sending and receiving fields aren't valid. For example, you can't move an alphanumeric value to a numeric packed-decimal field.

    Because the rules for certain types of moves are obscure, it's a good idea to check the results of your SET subcommand by following it with a LIST subcommand. That way, you'll know if your SET subcommand worked as you intended.

The EQUATE subcommand

```
EQUATE   symbol   data-name
```

The DROP subcommand

```
DROP [symbol]
```

Explanation

symbol   A character string that follows the rules for forming a COBOL data name. Usually shorter than the actual data name it will stand for. For a DROP subcommand, you can specify more than one symbol by separating them with commas and enclosing the entire list in parentheses. If no symbols are specified in a DROP subcommand, all symbols are deleted.

data-name   The data name which the specified symbol represents. Can also be an index name or a special register like TALLY.

Figure 10-21   The EQUATE and DROP subcommands

How to shorten data names

In your COBOL programs, I strongly recommend that you use data names that are meaningful. For example, a data name like AVAILABLE-STOCK is much more meaningful than X or AVSTK. Since one of the primary goals of program development is to create programs that are easy to read and maintain, I can't stress this point too much.

Still, longer data names can be an irritation during a TESTCOB session. Fortunately, TESTCOB provides two subcommands that let you substitute a shorter name for a longer one. These two subcommands, EQUATE and DROP, are shown in figure 10-21.

The EQUATE subcommand lets you assign a *symbol* to a data name or index name. For example, consider this EQUATE subcommand:

```
EQUATE ITEM BF-ITEM-NO
```

The LISTFILE subcommand

```
LISTFILE   file-name

           [PRINT]
```

Explanation

file-name	The name of the file whose status is to be listed.
PRINT	Direct the output to the file specified on the PRINT operand of the TESTCOB command.

Figure 10-22 The LISTFILE subcommand

Once you've entered this command, you can use the symbol ITEM instead of the data name BF-ITEM-NO throughout your TESTCOB session.

The DROP subcommand lets you remove a previously defined symbol. So if you enter:

```
DROP ITEM
```

you can no longer use ITEM to refer to BF-ITEM-NO. You can specify several symbols in a single DROP subcommand, like this:

```
DROP (ITEM,COST,DESCR)
```

Here, three symbols are deleted. If you enter DROP with no symbols, all of your symbols are deleted.

How to display the status of a file

The LISTFILE subcommand, whose format is given in figure 10-22, displays the status of a data set at your terminal. On the LISTFILE subcommand, you specify a file name that's defined in your program by an FD statement. If you include the PRINT operand, the output is written to the print data set you specified when you issued the TESTCOB command.

```
LISTFILE BFCRDS
 FD BFCRDS
 DSORG PS
 DSNAME DLOWE.BFCRDS.DATA
 OPEN INPUT , LRECL 00080, BLKSIZE 00080, RECFM F
 TESTCOB
```

Figure 10-23   Typical LISTFILE subcommand output

Figure 10-23 gives output that's typical of the LISTFILE subcommand. Here, I enter a LISTFILE subcommand like this:

```
LISTFILE BFCRDS
```

In response, TESTCOB displays significant information about the file, including the file's organization (PS means sequential), data set name (DLOWE.BFCRDS.DATA), open mode (input), record length (80), block size (80), and recording mode (fixed). As you debug your program, this information can help you determine the cause of file-related problems.

HOW TO USE A SUBCOMMAND LIST IN AN UNCONDITIONAL BREAKPOINT

Now that you know how to use a variety of TESTCOB subcommands, you're ready to see how an advanced feature of the AT subcommand lets you execute several subcommands automatically whenever a breakpoint occurs. To use this feature, you just specify a list of subcommands on an AT subcommand. Each subcommand in the list is separated by semicolons, and the entire list is enclosed in parentheses. The subcommands in the list are executed before control returns to your terminal. And if the list contains a GO subcommand, control doesn't return to your terminal at all; instead, your program automatically resumes execution.

To illustrate, suppose you want to list the contents of a field named AVAILABLE-STOCK each time statement 3200 is executed. But you don't want to type LIST and GO subcommands repeatedly. You can enter this subcommand:

```
AT 3200 (LIST AVAILABLE-STOCK;GO)
```

Here, a breakpoint is established at statement 3200. Then, whenever the breakpoint is taken, the LIST and GO sub-commands are automatically executed. The effect of this breakpoint is that the value of AVAILABLE-STOCK is listed each time statement 3200 is executed.

The IF subcommand

Although there are many possible uses for coding a subcommand list, the most common is to list the contents of one or more data fields and resume program execution. In some cases, however, you want to resume program execution only under certain conditions. For example, you may want to list the contents of a field and resume program execution if that field is less than another field. The IF subcommand, whose format is shown in figure 10-24, lets you do just that. You can enter an IF subcommand by itself, if you wish. But its normal use is in a subcommand list.

You specify an expression in an IF subcommand just as you do in a WHEN subcommand, so I won't restate the rules here. After the expression, you say either HALT or GO to tell TESTCOB what to do if the expression is true. If you say HALT, TESTCOB stops your program's execution and returns control to your terminal if the expression is true. If you say GO, TESTCOB resumes your program's execution if the expression is true. In either case, control returns to the next subcommand in the list if the expression is false.

To illustrate, consider this AT subcommand:

```
AT 3200 (IF (AVAIL LT REORDER) HALT;GO)
```

Here, the IF subcommand is executed each time the breakpoint at line 3200 is taken. AVAIL is compared with REORDER. If the expression is true—that is, if AVAIL is less than REORDER—the program is halted and control returns to the terminal. Otherwise, the next subcommand in the list is executed. In this case, the next subcommand is GO, so the program continues.

Suppose you entered this AT subcommand:

```
AT 3200 (IF (AVAIL GE REORDER) GO)
```

The IF subcommand

```
IF (expression) {GO  }
                {HALT}
```

Explanation

expression   A relational condition formed following the rules for an expression in a WHEN subcommand.

GO   Says that program execution should be immediately resumed if the expression is true.

HALT   Says that control should return to the user immediately if the expression is true.

Figure 10-24   The IF subcommand

Here, program execution continues if AVAIL is greater than or equal to REORDER. Otherwise, control is returned to the terminal, since there are no more subcommands in the list to be executed. If you compare this subcommand list with the previous one, you'll see that they both have the same effect: the program continues executing until AVAIL is less than REORDER.

HOW TO DISPLAY SOURCE STATEMENTS

Figure 10-25 gives the format of the SOURCE subcommand, which you can use to display one or more lines of your source program at your terminal. On the SOURCE subcommand, you supply a single line number or a range of line numbers separated by a colon. You must also supply a ddname that's allocated to the compiler's print data set. So if you intend to use the SOURCE subcommand, you should issue an ALLOCATE command before you invoke TESTCOB so the source listing will be available.

Quite frankly, the SOURCE subcommand isn't very useful. In my opinion, it's far better to have a printed version of the compiler listing available as you debug your program. That way, you won't erase important debugging information (like LIST output) to display source lines. And you'll be able

The SOURCE subcommand

```
SOURCE     {line-1          }     ddname
           {line-1:line-2   }
```

Explanation

line-1   The starting line number. If line-2 isn't specified, only line-1 is listed.

line-2   The ending line number when a range of lines is to be listed.

ddname   The ddname allocated to the file that contains the source listing.

Figure 10-25   The SOURCE subcommand

to mark corrections directly on the source listing. In short, you probably won't use the SOURCE subcommand much unless your installation has a policy that restricts printouts of compiler listings or the turnaround time for hardcopy output is excessive.

HOW TO DEBUG A SUBPROGRAM

Up to now, I've assumed you're debugging a program that doesn't call subprograms. If your program does call one or more subprograms, you use some of the TESTCOB features a little differently.

To begin with, you must specify each program and subprogram you want to debug on the TESTCOB command, along with a ddname allocated to the SYM file for each program or subprogram. For example, suppose you're debugging a program named REORDLST that calls two subprograms: CONVDAT and PUTERR. Figure 10-26 shows the commands necessary to allocate the data sets and invoke TESTCOB. As you can see, you specify a list of program-ids and ddnames for the programs you're debugging. But you still specify a single load module, since the main program and the subprograms are link-edited together to create the load module.

As your program executes and interrupts occur, the statement numbers TESTCOB displays reflect which program

```
  READY
ALLOCATE DSNAME(TEST.LOAD) DDNAME(LOADLIB)
  READY
ALLOCATE DSNAME(TEST.SYM(REORDLST)) DDNAME(SYMDD1)
  READY
ALLOCATE DSNAME(TEST.SYM(CONVDAT)) DDNAME(SYMDD2)
  READY
ALLOCATE DSNAME(TEST.SYM(PUTERR)) DDNAME(SYMDD3)
  READY
TESTCOB (REORDLST:SYMDD1,CONVDAT:SYMDD2,PUTERR:SYMDD3) LOAD(REORDLST:LOADLIB)
  TESTCOB
```

Figure 10-26 Invoking TESTCOB to debug a main program and two subprograms

or subprogram is currently executing. For example, if TESTCOB displays this statement number:

```
PUTERR.1500.1
```

you know that the subprogram named PUTERR is executing.

To debug a program that's not currently executing, you have to specify the program name on the TESTCOB subcommands. For example, suppose that you need to debug the PUTERR subprogram and that line 5300 in REORDLST is the CALL statement that invokes PUTERR. Assuming that REORDLST is currently executing, you first set a breakpoint at line 5300 like this:

```
AT 5300
```

Then, your program is interrupted just before line 5300 executes. Now, you want to set a range of breakpoints in PUTERR so you can single-step through the subprogram from lines 1000 to 3000. If you entered this subcommand:

```
AT 1000:3000
```

the breakpoints would be set for lines 1000 through 3000 of REORDLST, since that's the program currently executing. So you have to enter the AT subcommand like this:

```
AT PUTERR.1000:PUTERR.3000
```

Then, the breakpoints are established for lines 1000 through 3000 of PUTERR.

You can also refer to data names in this fashion. For example, if you enter this command:

```
LIST AVAILABLE-STOCK
```

AVAILABLE-STOCK in the current program is listed. But if you enter

```
LIST PUTERR.AVAILABLE-STOCK
```

AVAILABLE-STOCK in the subprogram named PUTERR is listed.

Finally, remember that you can use the ENTRY operand of the TRACE subcommand to trace subprogram execution. As a result, you can make sure the correct subprograms are executing at the right times.

HOW TO TERMINATE TESTCOB

There are two ways to exit TESTCOB. Normally, you issue an END subcommand, like this:

```
END
```

Then, control returns to TSO and the READY message is displayed.

The other way to end TESTCOB is to enter a DUMP subcommand, like this:

```
DUMP
```

Then, control returns to TSO and a storage dump is generated. To use the DUMP subcommand, you must issue an ALLOCATE command for ddname SYSUDUMP or SYSABEND before you start your TESTCOB session. Normally, you'll use SYSUDUMP, and allocate it to a SYSOUT class, like this:

```
ALLOCATE DDNAME(SYSUDUMP) SYSOUT(A)
```

If you use SYSABEND, the dump will be much larger, containing a lot of information you don't need. In any event, you should use the DUMP subcommand only as a last resort when you can't isolate a program bug using the interactive debugger.

DISCUSSION

As a testing and debugging tool, the interactive COBOL debugger is vastly superior to the storage-dump approach. So if you're still debugging your programs in batch mode using storage dumps, I suggest you start using the interactive COBOL debugger right now, if it's available. Having read the introduction this topic presents, you'll be able to learn how to use TESTCOB quickly.

Terminology

interactive COBOL debugger	unconditional breakpoint
breakpoint	conditional breakpoint
trace	identifier
program-id	task global table
statement-number	TGT
verb-number	normalized level number
NEXT breakpoint	symbol

Objectives

1. Invoke TESTCOB to debug a COBOL program. The program may or may not use called subprograms.

2. Describe how to use the following TESTCOB features:
   a. NEXT breakpoint
   b. unconditional breakpoint
   c. conditional breakpoint
   d. program trace

3. Use TESTCOB subcommands to examine and change the contents of data fields as your program executes.

Chapter 11

Background job commands

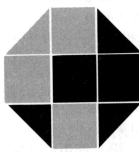

As you know, an MVS system with TSO has two types of regions in which jobs execute: foreground and background regions. Foreground regions execute TSO jobs. As a result, when you use TSO, a job is executed in a foreground region on your behalf. Background regions are used for non-time-sharing jobs. In other words, background regions are generally used for batch jobs, while foreground regions are used when user interaction is required.

A TSO user in a foreground region often needs to initiate processing in a background region. For example, suppose you're developing a program that will be processed in a background region once it's in production. You can use the foreground processing features of TSO to compile and link-edit the program. You may even use the interactive COBOL debugger for the initial program testing. But eventually you'll have to process the program in a background region to make sure it's thoroughly tested. And, depending on factors unique to your installation, you may find it better to compile and link-edit your programs in a background region.

1. The job is submitted for execution by a system operator, a TSO user, or another background job.

2. The job waits in a job queue.

3. The job is selected for execution by the job scheduler.

4. The job executes.

5. The job output is collected and held in a SYSOUT queue.

6. The job output is routed to its final destination and removed from the SYSOUT queue.

Figure 11-1 · The life cycle of a background job

The life cycle of a job

Figure 11-1 describes the life cycle of a typical background job under MVS. First, the job is submitted for execution by a system operator, a TSO user, or a job executing in another region. Once a job is submitted for execution, it's placed in a job queue, where it waits until a region is available to execute it. How long it waits in the job queue depends on a number of factors, including its storage and I/O device requirements and the job class assigned to it when it was submitted.

Every job submitted for execution under MVS must have a *job name*. This name, one to eight characters in length, is specified in the JCL for the job. Under TSO, a job name must be your user-id followed by a single character. Thus, DLOWEA is a valid job name for user DLOWE.

When you refer to a job you've submitted, you usually use its job name. However, MVS does not require that job names be unique. As a result, it's perfectly acceptable to submit two jobs with the same job name. MVS assigns a unique *job-id* to each job as it's submitted. So if you submit more than one job with the same job name, you must use the job-id rather than the job name to identify each job.

When a region becomes available for your job, JES2/JES3 starts a reader/initiator task to begin your job. As your job executes, MVS generates informational messages that are collected in the job output and stored in a SYSOUT queue. In addition, programs executed by the job's steps can generate output that's written to a SYSOUT queue. Data in a SYSOUT queue is held there until it's printed at a local or remote printer, copied to a data set, or deleted.

Each data set written to a SYSOUT queue is assigned a one-character *SYSOUT class* that determines how the output is printed. Each SYSOUT class is normally associated with a printer or a group of printers. Typically, SYSOUT class A is used for the installation's main printer or printers. Other SYSOUT classes may be assigned to specific printers or other devices.

If a SYSOUT class isn't associated with a printer or other device, it's called a *reserved class*. Any output written to a reserved class is held in the SYSOUT queue until an operator (1) directs it to a specific printer, (2) directs it to another SYSOUT class, or (3) deletes it. At my installation, class X is defined as a reserved class.

When you submit a background job from TSO, you usually want to direct the output to a reserved class. Then, you can examine the output at your terminal to determine if you should print it or delete it.

As a TSO user, you need to know how to do four things before you can effectively manage background jobs. First, you need to know how to use the SUBMIT command to submit a job for background processing. Second, you need to know how to use the CANCEL command to delete a job you've submitted. Third, you need to know how to use the STATUS command to monitor the status of a job you've submitted so you can see if it's waiting for execution, executing, or waiting for its output to be printed. And fourth, you need to know how to use the OUTPUT command to retrieve the output for a job that's completed.

The SUBMIT command

Figure 11-2 shows the format of the SUBMIT command. The operation of the SUBMIT command is simple: the data set or member you specify is submitted as a background job. SUBMIT assumes that the type qualifier for each data set is CNTL. So if you issue this SUBMIT command:

```
SUBMIT JOB1
```

The SUBMIT command

```
SUBMIT   data-set-name

         [JOBCHAR(character)]
```

Explanation

data-set-name   The name of the data set or member to be submitted for background processing. If you specify more than one data set or member, separate the names with commas and enclose the entire list in parentheses.

character   A single letter or digit that's appended to your user-id to form a job name if the job stream doesn't contain a JOB statement.

Figure 11-2   The SUBMIT command

the data in DLOWE.JOB1.CNTL is submitted as a background job (assuming DLOWE is the user-id). If you want to specify a fully-qualified data set name, enclose it in apostrophes.

The data set or member you specify must contain valid job-control statements in order for the job to execute properly. However, if the data set doesn't contain a JOB statement, TSO will generate one for you using your user-id and account information. You'll be prompted for the single character to be added to your user-id for the job name. Or, you can supply the job character on the SUBMIT command by specifying the JOBCHAR parameter, like this:

```
SUBMIT JOB1 JOBCHAR(A)
```

If you wish, you can code more than one job in a single data set or member. To do this, code all of the JCL and data for the first job. Then, code the JOB statement and additional JCL and data for the second job. For example, if a data set or member contains three JOB statements, three separate jobs are submitted when you specify the data set or member in a SUBMIT command.

You can also specify more than one data set or member in a SUBMIT command by separating the names with commas and enclosing the entire list in parentheses. In that case, the data sets or members are treated as if they were a continuous stream of JCL and data to be submitted. One or more jobs will actually be submitted, depending on how many JOB statements are in the input stream.

To illustrate, suppose you create two data sets. The first, DLOWE.JCL.CNTL, contains JCL statements to execute a program. The second, DLOWE.DATA.CNTL, contains data that's processed by the program. To submit this job for background processing, you issue this SUBMIT command:

```
SUBMIT (JCL,DATA)
```

Then, the two data sets are processed in sequence to create a single job.

The CANCEL command

You use the CANCEL command to remove from the job queue a job you've previously submitted using the SUBMIT command. Figure 11-3 gives the format of the CANCEL command. As you can see, you must specify a job name. And if more than one job is currently using the same job name, you must specify a job-id to uniquely identify the job you wish to cancel. (You can find out what the job-id is by entering a STATUS command, which I'll describe next.)

If you specify PURGE on a CANCEL command, the job is deleted. If the job hasn't executed yet, it's removed from the job queue. If it's currently executing, it's terminated. In any event, all of the job's output is deleted from the SYSOUT queue.

If you specify NOPURGE, or if you default to NOPURGE by not specifying PURGE or NOPURGE, the job is terminated if it's executing. Its output, however, is not deleted. So you can examine it using an OUTPUT command (as I'll describe in a minute) or delete it using a CANCEL command with the PURGE operand.

The CANCEL command

```
CANCEL  {job-name            }
        {job-name(job-id)}

       [{PURGE  }]
        {NOPURGE}
```

Explanation

job-name	Specifies one or more jobs to be cancelled. If you specify more than one job, you must separate the job names with commas and enclose the entire list in parentheses. If more than one job exists with the same name, you must specify the job-id in parentheses.
PURGE NOPURGE	PURGE means to remove the job's output from the SYSOUT queue. NOPURGE means that the job should be cancelled if it's executing, but the output should **not** be removed from the job queue. (NOPURGE is the default.)

Figure 11-3   The CANCEL command

To illustrate the CANCEL command, suppose you enter:

```
CANCEL DLOWEA(JOB0403) .PURGE
```

Here, JOB0403 is the job-id for the job I want to cancel; the job name is DLOWEA. Since I specify PURGE, any job output will be deleted.

The STATUS command

A submitted job has one of three possible status conditions: (1) waiting for execution, (2) executing, or (3) waiting for output. The STATUS command, shown in figure 11-4, tells you the current status for one or more of your jobs. It identifies the jobs by listing both their job names and their job-ids.

If you enter just the word STATUS with no operands, TSO displays the status of each job you've submitted. You can limit the output to one or more jobs by specifying one or more job names with or without job-ids. Then, TSO displays the status of the jobs you've specified. To specify more than one

The STATUS command

```
STATUS  [{job-name           }]
         {job-name(job-id)   }
```

Explanation

job-name   The name of the job whose status is listed. If you specify more than one job, you
                    must separate the job names with commas and enclose the entire list in
                    parentheses. If there's more than one job with the same name, you must supply
                    the job-id in parentheses. If you don't specify a job name, all of your jobs are
                    listed.

Figure 11-4   The STATUS command

job, separate the job names with commas and enclose the list
in parentheses, like this:

```
STATUS (DLOWEA,DLOWEB)
```

Here, TSO lists the status of two jobs.

The OUTPUT command

You use the OUTPUT command to process job output. With
the OUTPUT command, you can display the output at your
terminal, delete it, or route it to another SYSOUT class or a
remote printer.

Figure 11-5 gives a simplified format for the OUTPUT
command. There are other operands besides the ones shown
here. I've chosen to present just the ones that are most useful
for program development under TSO. Rather than discuss each
OUTPUT operand separately, I'll describe them in context
with the examples presented in figure 11-6.

In example 1 of figure 11-6, I direct the output from a job
named DLOWEA to my terminal. Once the output starts displaying at my terminal, I can interrupt it using PA1. Then, I
can enter one of several subcommands, which I'll describe in a
moment.

The OUTPUT command

```
OUTPUT    {job-name           }
          {job-name(job-id)   }

          [NEWCLASS(class-name)]

          [DEST(station-id)]

          [{HOLD    }]
          [{NOHOLD  }]

          [CLASS(class-names)]

          [DELETE]

          [PAUSE]
```

Explanation

job-name   The name of the job whose output is displayed. If you specify more than one job, you must separate the job names with commas and enclose the entire list in parentheses. If there's more than one job with the same name, you must supply the job-id in parentheses.

NEWCLASS   Changes the output's SYSOUT class.

DEST   Changes the output's destination.

HOLD   Changes the output's HOLD status. HOLD means the output should remain in the
NOHOLD   SYSOUT queue until you release it for printing. NOHOLD means that held output should be released for printing.

CLASS   Limits the affected job output so that only those output data sets in the specified classes are processed. You must separate the SYSOUT classes with spaces.

DELETE   Deletes the output.

PAUSE   Interrupts the display between each SYSOUT data set and allows you to enter the OUTPUT subcommands shown in figure 11-7.

Figure 11-5   The OUTPUT command

Example 1

```
OUTPUT DLOWEA
```

Example 2

```
OUTPUT DLOWEA NEWCLASS(A)
```

Example 3

```
OUTPUT DLOWEA DEST(RMT193)
```

Example 4

```
OUTPUT DLOWEA NOHOLD
```

Example 5

```
OUTPUT DLOWEA CLASS(X)
```

Example 6

```
OUTPUT DLOWE CLASS(A M X) DELETE
```

Figure 11-6   Examples of the OUTPUT command

In example 1, I assume there's only one job named DLOWEA. If more than one job had the same name, I would have to enter a job-id, like this:

```
OUTPUT DLOWEA(JOB0403)
```

Here, JOB0403 uniquely identifies the job I want to display.

In example 2, I don't display the job output at my terminal. Instead, I change the SYSOUT class to class A. Since most installations define class A as output to the main system printer, you can use this command to print your job output.

Example 3 shows how to route job output to a remote printer. Here, the output is routed to a remote station identified as RMT193. When RMT193 signs on to the system, the

output will be delivered, assuming the output is assigned to a
SYSOUT class that's associated with RMT193.

In example 4, I specify the NOHOLD operand. That
causes any held output to be released for processing by
JES2/JES3. (Held output is not simply spooled output. It's
output that you've specified should not be printed until you
say otherwise.) If the output was originally directed to class A
but was held—for example, HOLD = YES was specified on the
DD statement—the output will be released for printing. Note,
however, that if the output class itself is reserved, saying
NOHOLD on an OUTPUT command won't cause it to be
printed unless you change the output class as well.

Example 5 shows how to limit the displayed output to
SYSOUT data of a specific class. Here, I want to display class
X output at my terminal. Any job output for DLOWEA that
isn't class X won't be displayed.

Example 6 shows how to delete output for three classes:
A, M, and X. In this case, the data isn't displayed. Instead,
it's deleted from the SYSOUT queues.

OUTPUT subcommands   As I mentioned earlier, the
OUTPUT command has several subcommands you can use
when you're displaying the contents of a SYSOUT data set.
Normally, when you display SYSOUT data, the data is sent in
a continuous stream to your terminal. Under normal TSO,
each screenful of data is followed by three asterisks (***),
signalling you to press the enter key to receive the next screenful of data.

You can interrupt the continuous display of SYSOUT data
in one of two ways: by pressing the attention key (PA1) or by
specifying PAUSE on the OUTPUT command itself. If you
press PA1, the output is immediately interrupted, and TSO
displays this mode message:

```
OUTPUT
```

That means TSO is waiting for an OUTPUT subcommand.
You can specify PAUSE on the OUTPUT command, like
this:

```
OUTPUT DLOWEA PAUSE
```

The CONTINUE subcommand

```
CONTINUE  [{BEGIN }
           {HERE  }]
           {NEXT  }

          [{PAUSE  }]
           {NOPAUSE}
```

The SAVE subcommand

```
SAVE   data-set-name
```

The END subcommand

```
END
```

Explanation

BEGIN HERE NEXT	Says what output should be displayed: the start of the current data set (BEGIN), the data following the current location (HERE), or the start of the next SYSOUT data set (NEXT). (NEXT is the default.)
PAUSE NOPAUSE	Says whether output should be interrupted between SYSOUT data sets. Overrides the corresponding operand on the OUTPUT command.
data-set-name	The name of the data set in which the output will be saved.

Figure 11-7 OUTPUT subcommands

Then, output will be interrupted between each separate SYSOUT data set. As a result, the OUTPUT mode message will be displayed after all the JCL messages have been displayed and after each separate SYSOUT data set has been displayed.

Once the display has been interrupted, you can enter one of the OUTPUT subcommands listed in figure 11-7. You use the CONTINUE subcommand to resume the display at the current location, at the beginning of the current SYSOUT data set, or at the start of the next SYSOUT data set. You use the SAVE subcommand to copy the current SYSOUT data set to a file. And you use the END subcommand to terminate OUTPUT.

To illustrate, suppose you enter an OUTPUT command to display output from a background job. As the job output is displayed at your terminal, you press PA1 to interrupt the display. TSO displays OUTPUT at your terminal, indicating it's waiting for an OUTPUT subcommand. At this point, if you enter:

```
CONTINUE HERE
```

the output display will continue at the point it was interrupted. If you enter:

```
CONTINUE NEXT
```

the output display will skip forward to the start of the next SYSOUT data set and continue displaying. If you enter:

```
CONTINUE BEGIN
```

the output display will skip backwards to the start of the current SYSOUT data set and continue displaying. If you enter:

```
SAVE JOBOUT
```

the current SYSOUT data set will be copied to a data set named DLOWE.JOBOUT.OUTLIST (assuming the user-id is DLOWE.) And if you enter:

```
END
```

the OUTPUT session will be terminated, and TSO will return to READY mode.

Discussion

Because managing SYSOUT data with the OUTPUT command isn't easy, I recommend a few simple techniques to control SYSOUT data. First, minimize the amount of SYSOUT data you create. For compile jobs, don't create a DMAP, PMAP, or XREF unless you really need them. Second, use the PAUSE operand on the OUTPUT command. That way, you can interrupt the output and skip over output you don't really need. And third, use the session manager if it's available. Then you can use scrolling and find operations to locate specific parts of your output listing, as described in topic 2 of chapter 8.

If you're using SPF, you may find that the SUBMIT, CANCEL, and STATUS commands are easier to use than the corresponding SPF options. However, for viewing SYSOUT data, SPF's outlist utility is superior to the OUTPUT command. So I recommend you use the outlist utility if it's available.

Terminology

job name
job-id
SYSOUT class
reserved class

Objective

Use the SUBMIT, CANCEL, STATUS, and OUTPUT commands to manage background jobs.

Part 4

How to use
command procedures
(CLISTs)

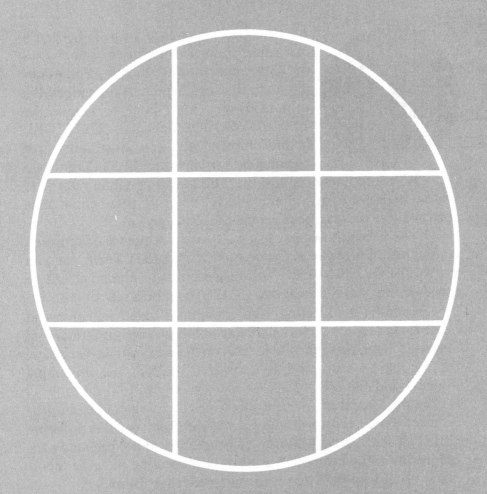

Chapter 12

Basic command
procedure facilities

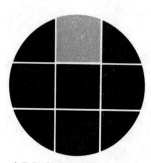

As you gain experience with TSO, you'll often find yourself entering the same series of TSO commands repeatedly. For example, in topic 2 of chapter 10 I described the commands you must issue to invoke the interactive COBOL debugger (TESTCOB). In the simplest case, you must issue three commands to invoke TESTCOB: two ALLOCATE commands and the TESTCOB command itself. If you're testing a program extensively, entering these commands for each test run can be a genuine inconvenience.

Under TSO, however, you can store a sequence of repeated commands in a *command procedure*, or *CLIST*. Then, you can invoke the CLIST by name to cause each of its commands to be executed. As you can imagine, a CLIST can be a real time-saver.

Besides just collecting TSO commands together, command procedures provide facilities similar to a high-level programming language. With these facilities, you can define symbolic variables, control the flow of execution within a CLIST, and do simple terminal and file I/O.

In this chapter, I present the basics of using command procedures. First, I describe how to create and invoke a simple CLIST. Then, I show you how to generalize your command procedures by using symbolic variables. I'll describe the other command procedure facilities in the chapters that follow.

348

```
ALLOCATE DDNAME(SYMDD) DSNAME(TEST.SYM(REORDLST))
ALLOCATE DDNAME(LOADLIB) DSNAME(TEST.LOAD)
TESTCOB (REORDLST:SYMDD) LOAD(REORDLST:LOADLIB)
```

Figure 12-1   A simple command procedure named ORDTEST in the library DLOWE.TEST.CLIST

HOW TO USE A SIMPLE COMMAND PROCEDURE

To illustrate the use of command procedures, suppose you're in the process of testing and debugging a COBOL program named REORDLST. As you proceed, you find yourself repeatedly issuing the same commands—in particular, the commands to compile, link-edit, and test your program over and over again. So, you decide to collect them together in a series of command procedures.

Figure 12-1 shows one of those procedures. It contains the three TSO commands necessary to invoke the interactive COBOL debugger to debug your program.

How to create a command procedure

You create a command procedure using your standard editing facility, whether it's SPF's edit option or some other editor like ROSCOE or an extended version of TSO's EDIT command. You simply enter the commands you want to include in the CLIST, keeping in mind that they'll execute in order. So you have to anticipate what TSO expects as you code each procedure line. For example, to extend the CLIST in figure 12-1, you would next code a TESTCOB subcommand because that's what TSO is expecting.

Whenever you create a CLIST, you have to decide if you want it to be a sequential data set or a PDS member. Usually, it will be a member of a partitioned data set whose standard type qualifier is CLIST. For example, the command procedure in figure 12-1 is a member named ORDTEST in a command procedure library named DLOWE.TEST.CLIST.

How to invoke a command procedure

To execute, or *invoke*, a command procedure, you use the EXEC command, whose format is shown in figure 12-2. As

Explicit form of the EXEC command

```
EXEC procedure-library-name(procedure-name) ['parameters']
```

Implicit form of the EXEC command

```
[%] procedure-name [parameters]
```

Explanation

procedure-library-name	The name of the library containing the procedure (a type qualifier of CLIST is assumed). May be omitted if the library name is user-id.CLIST.
procedure-name	The member name of the procedure to be invoked.
parameters	A list of parameter values as defined in the procedure's PROC statement. For the explicit form, the list must be enclosed in apostrophes.
%	For the implicit form, tells TSO to bypass the search of its command libraries.

Figure 12-2 The EXEC command

you can see, you can code the EXEC command in one of two forms.

In the *explicit form*, you specify the word EXEC followed by the name of the procedure library and member you wish to execute. To invoke the CLIST in figure 12-1 this way, you would code this EXEC command:

```
EXEC TEST(ORDTEST)
```

EXEC assumes that the type qualifier for the library is CLIST, so you shouldn't specify that in the command. And it will provide the current user-id, so usually you don't have to specify that either. In fact, for a library named user-id.CLIST, you can omit the library name entirely and just specify the member name, like this:

```
EXEC (ORDTEST)
```

In the *implicit form*, you don't specify the word EXEC or the name of the library that contains the procedure. Instead, you specify just the procedure name, like this:

```
ORDTEST
```

Here, the procedure named ORDTEST is invoked.

Notice that the implicit form of the EXEC command makes your command procedure look like another TSO command. In fact, it looks so similar that TSO has to search its own command libraries first to be sure it isn't a TSO command. Since you know it's not a TSO command when you enter it, you can save TSO the trouble by typing a percent sign in front of the procedure name, like this:

```
%ORDTEST
```

That tells TSO that ORDTEST is a command procedure, not a command, so TSO doesn't have to search its command libraries. Using a percent sign in this way can result in better execution time, since TSO will find your procedure more quickly.

As you can see in figure 12-2, both forms of the EXEC command let you pass parameters to the procedure you're invoking. Don't worry about that for now, though. I'll explain how and when to code parameters on the EXEC command later in this chapter.

Library allocation for the implicit form   When you use the implicit form of the EXEC command, TSO looks in the library allocated to the ddname SYSPROC to find your procedure. As a result, before you issue an EXEC command, you must allocate your command procedure library to SYSPROC with an ALLOCATE command similar to this one:

```
ALLOCATE DDNAME(SYSPROC) DSNAME(TEST.CLIST) SHR
```

SHR means that other TSO users can allocate this procedure library as well. If you omit SHR, you'll have exclusive control of the procedure library.

Usually, you allocate more than one data set to SYSPROC. For example, you might allocate three: a system command procedure library named SYS1.COMMAND.CLIST; a private command procedure library named DLOWE.COMMAND.CLIST;

and a library of command procedures being tested named
DLOWE.TEST.CLIST. To allocate all three of these libraries,
you'd issue an ALLOCATE command like this:

```
ALLOCATE DSNAME('SYS1.COMMAND.CLIST' COMMAND.CLIST +
TEST.CLIST) DDNAME(SYSPROC) SHR
```

The order in which you specify the procedure libraries on
the ALLOCATE command determines the order in which they
are searched when you invoke a CLIST. As a result, you
should specify the library you use most often first. That way,
you'll save search time.

You run into a problem here, though. When you
concatenate procedure libraries, you must follow this MVS
rule: the data set with the largest block size must be specified
first in a list of concatenated data sets. As a result, if
SYS1.COMMAND.CLIST has a block size of 6160 and
DLOWE.TEST.CLIST has a block size of 800, you *must* allocate
SYS1.COMMAND.CLIST before DLOWE.TEST.CLIST.

The easiest way around this problem is to use a model
data set—like SYS1.COMMAND.CLIST—when you create a
procedure library. That way, all of your procedure libraries
will have the same attributes, so you can concatenate them in
any order.

At most installations, if your procedure library is named
according to shop standards, it's automatically allocated when
you log on. Check with your supervisor to see if that's the case
at your shop. If so, you won't have to allocate your procedure
library since your logon procedure allocates it for you.

HOW TO GENERALIZE A COMMAND PROCEDURE

A command procedure like the one in figure 12-1 can save you
considerable time while you're testing and debugging a particular program. But, as you may already realize, the procedure
would be much more useful if it were generalized. In other
words, if the procedure weren't limited to a specific program,
you could use it to start a test of *any* COBOL program.

The command procedure

```
PROC 1 MEMBER LIBRARY(TEST) PARM()
ALLOCATE DDNAME(SYMDD) DSNAME(&LIBRARY..SYM(&MEMBER))
ALLOCATE DDNAME(LOADLIB) DSNAME(&LIBRARY..LOAD)
TESTCOB (&MEMBER:SYMDD) LOAD(&MEMBER:LOADLIB) PARM('&PARM')
```

Invoking the procedure

```
%COBTEST REORDLST LIBRARY(MASTER) PARM(MAY)
```

The actual commands executed

```
ALLOCATE DDNAME(SYMDD) DSNAME(MASTER.SYM(REORDLST))
ALLOCATE DDNAME(LOADLIB) DSNAME(MASTER.LOAD)
TESTCOB (REORDLST:SYMDD) LOAD(REORDLST:LOADLIB) PARM('MAY')
```

Figure 12-3 A command procedure named COBTEST that uses symbolic variables

Figure 12-3 presents a procedure named COBTEST that
does just that. As you can see, it consists of two ALLOCATE
commands and a TESTCOB command, just as in figure 12-1.
But these commands are coded a little differently than they
were before. And the procedure starts with a new statement,
the PROC statement.

In addition, the EXEC command to invoke this procedure
contains more information than the one for the ORDTEST
procedure did:

```
%COBTEST REORDLST LIBRARY(MASTER) PARM(MAY)
```

It invokes COBTEST for a program named REORDLST in a
library named MASTER. In addition, it causes a parameter
(MAY) to be passed to REORDLST.

The elements you see in the procedure's TSO commands,
the PROC statement, and the EXEC command all work
together to control the execution of COBTEST. I'm going to
explain those elements now so you'll know how to create and
use general-purpose procedures.

Symbolic variables

To make a procedure general-purpose, you use *symbolic variables*. Basically, a symbolic variable is a name that takes on a different value as the procedure executes. Since a symbolic variable's *real value* can change from one execution of the procedure to the next, a procedure can be processed differently with each execution.

A symbolic variable name consists of an ampersand (&) followed by up to 31 alphanumeric characters, starting with a letter. Thus, these are valid symbolic variable names:

```
&A
&MEMBER
&MEMB1
```

while these are not:

```
&1MEMBER
&MEMBER*
&(
```

In some cases, which I'll be sure to point out, you can omit the leading ampersand.

In figure 12-3, you can see that I used three symbolic variables in the ALLOCATE and TESTCOB commands: &LIBRARY, &MEMBER, and &PARM. For the procedure to execute properly, I have to provide real values for these variables in a PROC statement or an EXEC command.

The PROC statement

The PROC statement is one of many procedure statements that let you control the execution of a procedure. (A *procedure statement* is executed by the procedure interpreter, as opposed to a *command*, which is executed by TSO.) When you use a PROC statement, it must be the first statement in your procedure. It defines the symbolic variables in the procedure and relates them to parameters coded on the EXEC command.

The PROC statement

```
PROC   count   [positional-parms]   [keyword-parms[(values)]]
```

Explanation

count	Says how many positional parms follow. If none follow, you must code a zero.
positional-parms	Symbolic variable names for positional parameters, without the ampersands.
keyword-parms	Symbolic variable names for keyword parameters, without the ampersands.
values	Default values assumed by keyword parameters. If a null value is to be assumed, specify ( ).

Figure 12-4   The PROC statement

Figure 12-4 gives the complete format of the PROC statement. To code it, you enter symbolic variable names *without*
the ampersands to specify positional and keyword parameters.
A *positional parameter* is one that TSO recognizes because of
its position within a command; a *keyword parameter* is one
that TSO recognizes by its variable name.

As you'll see in a moment, the real values for positional
parameters must be coded in the EXEC command that invokes
the procedure; the real values for keyword parameters *may* be
coded there. If you want to assign a default value to a keyword
parameter, you enter the default in parentheses after the
variable name in the PROC statement.

Before the parameters themselves, though, you specify a
count of positional parameters. In other words, you tell TSO
how many of the variable names that follow should be treated
as positional parameters. If there are no positional parameters,
you must specify zero as the count.

In figure 12-3, then, the PROC statement defines only one
positional parameter—MEMBER. The other two—LIBRARY
and PARM—are keyword parameters, with their default values
in parentheses.

The effect of the PROC statement on the EXEC command

If you look back at the format in figure 12-2, you'll remember that you can code a list of parameters in an EXEC command. This is where you assign real values to the symbolic variables in a PROC statement. So you have to know what the PROC statement looks like before you can code a proper EXEC command for a procedure.

If there are positional parameters in the PROC statement, you must code their real values in the EXEC command immediately following the procedure name. You don't code the symbolic variable names at all—just the real values. When the command is executed, these values are matched up, in order, with the symbolic variable names for positional parameters in the PROC statement. If you leave out a value, TSO prompts you for it.

If there are keyword parameters in the PROC statement, you may assign real values to them in the EXEC command. To do this, you code the symbolic variable name *without* the ampersand (just as it is in the PROC statement). Then, you code the real value in parentheses.

I realize this may all seem confusing right now. But I think the examples that follow will clarify (1) how to code PROC statements and (2) how PROC statements work together with EXEC commands.

PROC examples   Figure 12-5 presents four examples of PROC statements. For each of these examples, assume the procedure name is TEST1.

Example 1 specifies one positional parameter, named MEMBER. If you invoke the procedure with an implicit EXEC command like this:

```
%TEST1 ORDTEST
```

the real value of the symbolic variable &MEMBER is ORDTEST. Throughout the procedure, then, wherever &MEMBER appears, TSO will substitute the name ORDTEST. Remember, positional parameters are always required. If you omit one when you invoke a procedure, TSO will prompt you to supply a value.

Example 1

```
PROC 1 MEMBER
```

Example 2

```
PROC 2 MEMBER1 MEMBER2
```

Example 3

```
PROC 1 MEMBER LIBRARY(TEST)
```

Example 4

```
PROC 0 LIB1(TEST) LIB2() LIB3
```

Figure 12-5   Examples of the PROC statement

Example 2 shows how to code two positional parameters, MEMBER1 and MEMBER2. Here, TSO will look for the first two parameters in the EXEC command and assign them to &MEMBER1 and &MEMBER2. So if you invoke the procedure like this:

```
%TEST1 ORDTEST NEWTEST
```

the real value of &MEMBER1 is ORDTEST and the real value of &MEMBER2 is NEWTEST.

Example 3 includes one positional parameter (MEMBER) and one keyword parameter (LIBRARY). In this example, the LIBRARY parameter is given a default value (TEST). So if you don't specify LIBRARY when you invoke the procedure, TEST becomes the real value of &LIBRARY.

To illustrate, suppose you invoke the procedure like this:

```
%TEST1 ORDTEST LIBRARY(MASTER)
```

Here, &MEMBER takes on a real value of ORDTEST, and &LIBRARY takes on a real value of MASTER. But if you omit the LIBRARY parameter, like this:

```
%TEST1 ORDTEST
```

the real value of &LIBRARY defaults to TEST. On the other hand, if you specify the keyword without a value, like this:

```
%TEST1 ORDTEST LIBRARY
```

TSO prompts you to supply the real value for &LIBRARY.

Example 4 illustrates three points. First, there are no positional parameters, so the count is zero. Second, the LIB2 keyword has a *null default value*. So if you don't specify LIB2 when you invoke the procedure, no value is assigned to &LIB2; it's as though &LIB2 doesn't exist. And third, the LIB3 parameter doesn't specify a default value.

When you code a keyword parameter like LIB3 without a default value, you *cannot* specify a real value when you invoke the procedure. Instead, the presence or absence of the keyword on the EXEC command determines the parameter's value. If you specify the keyword when you invoke the procedure, the parameter's value is set to the actual keyword name. If you omit it, the parameter's value becomes null. For example, suppose you invoke the procedure in example 4 like this:

```
%TEST1 LIB3
```

Then, the symbolic variable &LIB3 takes on a real value of LIB3. But if you omit LIB3 from the EXEC command, &LIB3 takes on a null value. Again, you *cannot* code any other value for &LIB3 in the EXEC command.

When do you use keywords without defaults? Generally, you use them to control processing within your procedure. Many TSO commands have operands whose presence or absence determines how the command works. For example, consider the DELETE command. On it, you can say PURGE to indicate that a file should be deleted even if its expiration date hasn't passed. But if you omit PURGE, the expiration date is enforced. In a similar manner, you can code keyword operands whose presence or absence on the EXEC command determines how your procedure executes.

With the examples in figure 12-5 as background, let's look again at the PROC statement in figure 12-3:

```
PROC 1 MEMBER LIBRARY(TEST) PARM()
```

Here, there's one positional parameter (MEMBER) and two keyword parameters (LIBRARY and PARM). The LIBRARY parameter has a default value of TEST, while the PARM parameter has a null default value. When the procedure is invoked by this EXEC command in figure 12-3:

```
%COBTEST REORDLST LIBRARY(MASTER) PARM(MAY)
```

&MEMBER takes on a value of REORDLST, &LIBRARY takes on a value of MASTER, and &PARM takes on a value of MAY.

Additional rules for coding EXEC parameters

So far, all the EXEC commands I've shown you have been pretty straightforward. But the coding rules are such that the commands can easily become complex and confusing, especially when you're using the explicit form.

First, when you use the explicit form, the entire list of parameters must be enclosed in apostrophes. So these are properly coded EXEC commands:

```
EXEC (TEST1) 'ORDTEST'
EXEC (TEST1) 'ORDTEST LIBRARY(MASTER)'
```

Second, if a keyword value contains spaces or commas, it must be enclosed in apostrophes, even in the implicit form:

```
%COBTEST UPDAT1 PARM('DIST1,PER1')
```

If the apostrophes were omitted, the comma would mark the end of the value and the data past the comma would be ignored.

However, for the explicit form, you have to distinguish between the apostrophes within the parameter and the apostrophes that mark the beginnning and end of the parameter list. So, in its explicit form, the previous EXEC command would be:

```
EXEC (COBTEST) 'UPDAT1 PARM(''DIST1,PER1'')'
```

As you can see, the apostrophes in the PARM parameter have to be doubled. Otherwise, the first apostrophe would mark the end of the entire list of parameters.

Third, if the keyword value itself contains an apostrophe, the apostrophe must be doubled, and the entire value must be enclosed in apostrophes. Here's an example using the implicit form:

```
DSN('''SYS1.COBLIB''')
```

In this example, the real value of &DSN is `'SYS1.COBLIB'`.

Of course, you're really in trouble if you try to code a value like this using the explicit form of EXEC. Since the entire list of parameters is enclosed in apostrophes, all of the apostrophes have to be doubled again. So you would code the keyword parameter like this:

```
'DSN('''''''SYS1.COBLIB''''''')'
```

Again, the real value of &DSN is `'SYS1.COBLIB'`.

Symbolic substitution

Whenever you specify a symbolic variable (including the ampersand) in the body of a procedure, TSO uses a process called *symbolic substitution* to replace the symbolic variable with its real value. To illustrate, assume the symbolic variable &DSN has a real value of TEST. Then, if a command procedure contains this statement:

```
ALLOCATE DSNAME(&DSN)
```

it's converted to this:

```
ALLOCATE DSNAME(TEST)
```

before it's executed.

That's the simple case. It gets more complicated when you want to combine the real value of a symbolic variable with another character or the value of another symbolic variable.

That process is called *concatenation*, and its rules are rather complex. Unfortunately, you need to know them well to use symbolic variables effectively.

Concatenation examples   To illustrate the rules of concatenation, figure 12-6 presents nine examples. In each of these examples, assume that the real value of &VAR1 is TEST and the real value of &VAR2 is LIST.

Example 1 doesn't look like a concatenation, but it is. Here, the characters DSN= are combined with &VAR1 to form DSN=TEST. I could have presented the examples in figure 12-6 without the leading DSN=. But since you almost always use symbolic substitution in conjunction with other TSO command text, I think it's clearer to present it as I have.

Example 2 is a more direct example of how a character string is concatenated with a variable. Here, the letter A is combined with &VAR1 to form ATEST. Notice in this example (and in example 1) that no special coding is necessary to combine text and the real value of a symbolic variable, provided the text comes first.

Likewise, adding text to the end of a symbolic variable isn't a problem as long as the text starts with a special character, as shown in example 3. Here, DSN=&VAR1(&VAR2) becomes DSN=TEST(LIST). The left parenthesis following &VAR1 causes no problem. Similarly, the right parenthesis following &VAR2 is concatenated as you would expect.

Adding text after a symbolic variable when the text begins with a letter or digit, however, is another matter. That's because TSO can't tell the start of the concatenated text from the symbolic variable name. For example, suppose you want to add the letter A to the end of a symbolic variable. If you coded this:

```
DSN=&VAR1A
```

TSO would look for a variable named &VAR1A.

To solve this problem, TSO uses a period as a *delimiter* between the symbolic variable name and the concatenated text, as shown in example 4. Whenever TSO encounters a period in a symbolic variable name, it marks the end of the variable name. Any text that follows is concatenated after the variable's

Example	As coded in CLIST	As interpreted during execution
1	DSN=&VAR1	DSN=TEST
2	DSN=A&VAR1	DSN=ATEST
3	DSN=&VAR1(&VAR2)	DSN=TEST(LIST)
4	DSN=&VAR1.A	DSN=TESTA
5	DSN=&VAR1..CLIST	DSN=TEST.CLIST
6	DSN=&VAR1&VAR2	DSN=TESTLIST
7	DSN=&VAR1..&VAR2	DSN=TEST.LIST
8	PARM='&VAR1,&VAR2'	PARM='TEST,LIST'
9	DSN=&&&&&VAR1	DSN=&&TEST

Note: In each example, the real value of &VAR1 is TEST; the real value of &VAR2 is LIST.

Figure 12-6 Examples of symbolic substitution

real value. Since the period doesn't become a part of the final text, &VAR1.A in example 4 becomes TESTA after symbolic substitution.

Unfortunately, the use of a period as a delimiter creates an exception to the rule that only alphabetic and numeric characters need the delimiter. If you want to contatenate a period following a variable, you must code the period twice, as shown in example 5. The first period is the delimiter; the second period is concatenated after the variable. So in this example, &VAR1..CLIST becomes TEST.CLIST. As you can imagine, this type of concatenation is common when forming data set names.

Example 6 shows that to concatenate two variables, you don't need a delimiter. Here, DSN=&VAR1&VAR2 becomes DSN=TESTLIST. You can use a period as a delimiter if you wish, but it's not necessary. So DSN=&VAR1.&VAR2 has the same result as example 6.

To concatenate two symbolic variables with a period in between, you still must use two periods, as shown in example 7. Here, &VAR1..&VAR2 becomes TEST.LIST.

Example 8 shows that apostrophes and commas cause no special problems. Here, PARM='&VAR1,&VAR2' becomes

PARM = 'TEST,LIST'. I included this example because many uses of concatenation in command procedures involve apostrophes and commas.

Finally, example 9 illustrates the special problem that's introduced when you want to include an ampersand in the final substituted text. To do this, you must code two ampersands in a row—otherwise, TSO thinks the ampersand marks the start of a symbolic variable name. And under standard MVS JCL, a temporary data set name must start with two ampersands. So to create such a name from a symbolic variable, you must code *five* consecutive ampersands as shown in example 9. The first four are converted to two ampersands in the final text, while the fifth marks the start of the variable name. As a result, DSN = &&&&&VAR1 becomes DSN = &&TEST.

That covers most of the possibilities for symbolic substitution and simple concatenation. In the next chapter, I'll introduce some new language elements and present some examples that are even more complicated. But now, look back to the CLIST in figure 12-3. If you study the symbolic variables coded in the ALLOCATE and TESTCOB commands, comparing them with the final text shown at the bottom of the figure, you'll get a good idea of how symbolic substitution works.

DISCUSSION

Using the command procedure facilities you've learned in this topic, you can now begin to write generalized command procedures of considerable complexity. In the next chapter, I'll present some advanced command procedure facilities that will give you even more control over a procedure's execution.

Terminology

command procedure
CLIST
invoke a procedure
explicit form
implicit form
symbolic variable
real value

procedure statement
positional parameter
keyword parameter
null default value
symbolic substitution
concatenation
delimiter

Objectives

1. Distinguish between *explicit* and *implicit* procedure invocation.

2. Create and invoke a simple command procedure that doesn't contain any symbolic variables.

3. Use symbolic variables and parameters to create and invoke a generalized command procedure.

Chapter 13

Advanced command procedure facilities

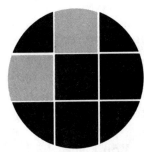

In this chapter, I present a variety of advanced command procedure facilities that let you create command procedures of considerable complexity. You'll find that these facilities together give command procedures some features that are normally associated with high-level programming languages—features like IF-THEN-ELSE structures and DO-WHILE loops. Before I present these features, though, a word of caution is in order: many CLIST features, though powerful, have a complicated and confusing syntax. As a result, consider carefully whenever you create a complex CLIST whether it would be better to implement it, if possible, as a COBOL or PL/I program.

Because these advanced facilities of CLIST are rather extensive, I've divided this chapter into two topics. Topic 1 presents a subset of the advanced command procedure facilities I think you'll use most often. Then, topic 2 expands that subset by presenting additional advanced CLIST features.

TOPIC 1   A subset of advanced command procedure facilities

In this topic, I present a variety of advanced command procedure facilities. In particular, I show you: how to use comments in a command procedure; how to write messages to the terminal; how to use advanced features of symbolic substitution, including expressions, built-in functions, and control variables; and how to control the execution of a CLIST using unconditional branching, IF-THEN-ELSE statements, DO-WHILE statements, and EXIT statements.

HOW TO USE COMMENTS

For simple command procedures like the ones I presented in chapter 12, there's really no need to provide documentation that explains how the procedures work; their operation is self-evident. But more advanced command procedures can easily become confusing. That's when you need to use *comments* in your procedures to explain what's going on.

Coding a comment in a CLIST is easy. You begin the comment with a slash and an asterisk (/*); you end it with an asterisk and a slash (*/). Between these delimiters, you can code any information you wish, with the exception of an asterisk-slash, since that would mark the end of the comment. For example, here's a valid comment:

```
/* THIS IS A COMMENT */
```

You can continue a comment to the next line, but you have to use a continuation character (- or +). Usually, I create a separate comment on each line to avoid the continuation characters.

Just how you use comments in your command procedures depends on shop standards and personal preference. It's usually a good idea to include a comment at the start of a CLIST to give the procedure's function as well as other

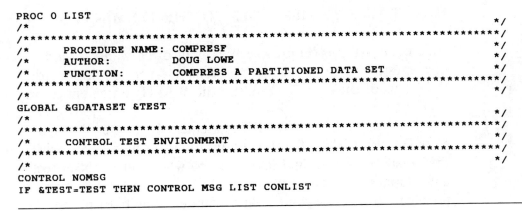

```
PROC 0 LIST                                                                    */
/*
/*****************************************************************************/
/*      PROCEDURE NAME: COMPRESF                                             */
/*      AUTHOR:              DOUG LOWE                                        */
/*      FUNCTION:            COMPRESS A PARTITIONED DATA SET                  */
/*****************************************************************************/
/*                                                                           */
GLOBAL &GDATASET &TEST                                                        */
/*
/*****************************************************************************/
/*        CONTROL TEST ENVIRONMENT                                           */
/*****************************************************************************/
/*
CONTROL NOMSG
IF &TEST=TEST THEN CONTROL MSG LIST CONLIST
```

Figure 13-1   A segment of a command procedure that uses comments

```
PROC 0 LIST                                                                    */
/*
/*****************************************************************************/
/*      PROCEDURE NAME: COMPRESF                                             */
/*      AUTHOR:              DOUG LOWE                                        */
/*      FUNCTION:            COMPRESS A PARTITIONED DATA SET                  */
/*****************************************************************************/
/*                                                                           */
GLOBAL &GDATASET &TEST
CONTROL NOMSG                                  /* CONTROL TEST ENVIRONMENT */
IF &TEST=TEST THEN CONTROL MSG LIST CONLIST
```

Figure 13-2   Coding a comment on the same line with other text

identifying information. It's also a good idea to use comments
liberally throughout your CLIST to identify major functions.

I like to set off my comments with lines of asterisks, as
shown in figure 13-1. Here, a group of seven comment lines
identifies the procedure's name, author, and function. Later
on, another group of comments indicates that the code that
follows controls the procedure's test environment. Again, shop
standards or personal preference may dictate a different format
for comments.

If you wish, you can code a comment on the same line as
a command procedure statement or TSO command. For
example, consider figure 13-2. Here, I placed the CONTROL
TEST ENVIRONMENT comment on the same line as the
CONTROL statement. Although this format uses less space, I
prefer the format in figure 13-1 because it makes the comments
more noticeable.

HOW TO WRITE MESSAGES TO THE TERMINAL

As a command procedure executes, you often want to send messages to the terminal user to indicate error conditions or the status of the CLIST. You use the WRITE statement to do that.

The format of the WRITE statement is simple. You just code the word WRITE followed by the information you wish displayed at the terminal. Contrary to what you might expect, apostrophes or quotes are *not* used to mark the text sent to the terminal. In fact, if you use apostrophes, they're displayed along with the rest of the message.

To illustrate the WRITE statement, consider this:

```
WRITE AN ERROR HAS OCCURRED
```

When this statement is executed, the following message appears at the terminal:

```
AN ERROR HAS OCCURRED
```

Symbolic substitution takes place in a WRITE statement, so you can also include symbolic variables. For example, suppose you code a WRITE statement like this:

```
WRITE AN ERROR(&LASTCC) HAS OCCURRED
```

Assuming &LASTCC has a value of 16, this message is displayed:

```
AN ERROR(16) HAS OCCURRED
```

As I said before, you use the WRITE statement most often to display status information or error messages as your procedure executes. In addition, the WRITE statement is useful when you're testing your CLIST. For example, suppose your procedure starts with a complex PROC statement. You might follow it with a WRITE statement, like this:

```
PROC 1 DATASET FG BG LIST SYSOUT(X) JOBCLASS(A) TEST
WRITE &DATASET &FG &BG &LIST &SYSOUT &JOBCLASS &TEST
```

Then, you can check the setting for each parameter before your CLIST continues. And, of course, you might use WRITE statements later in your procedure to make sure symbolic variables are set properly.

THE SET STATEMENT

In chapter 12, I showed you how a CLIST user can set the value of a symbolic variable by entering it as a parameter on the EXEC command that invokes the procedure. Now, I'll show you another facility—the SET statement—that lets you change a symbolic variable's value as your procedure executes. The SET statement is equivalent to the assignment statement in PL/I, BASIC, or FORTRAN, or the MOVE statement in COBOL.

The format of the SET command is simple:

```
SET variable-name = expression
```

On the left of the equals sign, you can omit the ampersand from the variable name; TSO knows it's a variable name by its location in the SET statement.

An *expression* can be a real value, like this:

```
SET COUNT = 1
```

or

```
SET DATASET = SYS1.COBLIB
```

Alternatively, an expression can be another symbolic variable:

```
SET VAR1 = &VAR2
```

Notice that on the righthand side of the equals sign, an ampersand is required to identify a symbolic variable name.

The spaces on either side of the equals sign are *not* required. In fact, they're ignored. So these three statements:

```
SET NAME=SMITH
SET NAME = SMITH
SET NAME=          SMITH
```

all have the same result: they set &NAME to SMITH. If you
need to set a variable to a value that starts with a space, you'll
have to use a special function, &STR, which I'll explain later
in this topic.

You can assign a *null value* to a symbolic variable like
this:

```
SET MIDDLE =
```

Here, &MIDDLE has no value. To illustrate how a null value
is used during symbolic substitution, suppose you code this:

```
WRITE &FIRST&MIDDLE&LAST
```

If &FIRST is ABC, &LAST is XYZ, and &MIDDLE is null,
this message is displayed:

```
ABCXYZ
```

Since &MIDDLE is null, nothing is substituted for it—not even
a space.

Arithmetic expressions   An expression in a SET statement
can also be an *arithmetic expression*—that is, a series of
symbolic variables and real values connected by *arithmetic
operators*, like this:

```
SET COUNT = &COUNT + 1
```

or

```
SET INDEX = &COUNT * 10 + 1
```

As you can see, arithmetic expressions in a command procedure look very much like arithmetic expressions in most high-
level programming languages.

Figure 13-3 lists the operators you can use in arithmetic
expressions. The first four provide the standard arithmetic
operations: addition, subtraction, multiplication, and division.
They should present no difficulties. The last two need some
explanation.

Function	Operator
Addition	+
Subtraction	−
Multiplication	*
Division	/
Exponentiation	**
Remainder	//

Figure 13-3   Arithmetic operators

The exponentiation operator (**) lets you raise a number to any power. For example, the value of 3 ** 2 is 9. CLIST doesn't support negative exponents; if you use a negative exponent, CLIST converts it to zero, yielding a value of 1 since any value raised to the power of zero is 1.

The remainder operator (//) gives the remainder resulting from a division operation. CLIST doesn't provide for fractional values; all of its numeric values are integers. As a result, the real value of 7 / 4 is 1, even though the exact result of the division is 1.75. To determine the remainder in that division, you code 7 // 4. Here, the real value of the expression is 3, since 7 divided by 4 is 1 with a remainder of 3.

The remainder operator is sometimes used for modulus arithmetic. Without going into the details of modulus arithmetic, suppose you want to convert any number to a value between zero and 11. You might code a SET statement like this:

```
SET MODVALUE = &VALUE // 12
```

Then, the real value of &MODVALUE will always be between zero and 11, since the remainder of &VALUE / 12 will never be greater than 11.

Within an expression, arithmetic operations are performed according to the rules of standard algebra. In other words, exponentiation is always performed first, followed by multiplication and division, followed by addition and subtraction.

Within that order, operations are performed from left to right. To illustrate, consider this expression:

```
1 + 2 * 3
```

Its real value is 7 because the multiplication (2 * 3) is performed before the addition.

You can change the standard order of evaluation by using parentheses. For example, this expression:

```
(1 + 2) * 3
```

has a real value of 9 because the parentheses specify that the addition be done *before* the multiplication.

BUILT-IN FUNCTIONS

Figure 13-4 lists five *built-in functions* that let you perform specific operations on an expression. The built-in function itself is a symbolic variable that's evaluated to a real value. You can use a built-in function anywhere you can use a symbolic variable, including in an expression.

The &DATATYPE function   You use the &DATATYPE function to determine an expression's data type: *numeric* or *character*. An expression is numeric if it consists only of digits with an optional leading sign. In that case, &DATATYPE has a real value of NUM. If an expression isn't numeric, it's character data, and the value of &DATATYPE is CHAR.

To illustrate, suppose the real value of &VALUE is AB34. Then, the real value of &DATATYPE(&VALUE) is CHAR. On the other hand, if &VALUE is 123, &DATATYPE(&VALUE) is NUM.

The &LENGTH function   The &LENGTH function determines the number of characters in the real value of an expression. The result of the &LENGTH function is numeric. For example:

```
&LENGTH(ABC)
```

Built-in function	Use
`&DATATYPE(expression)`	Returns the data type of the expression: NUM for numeric values, CHAR for character values.
`&LENGTH(expression)`	Returns the length of the expression.
`&EVAL(expression)`	Forces the expression to be evaluated when it normally wouldn't be.
`&STR(expression)`	Suppresses the evaluation of an expression when it would normally be evaluated.
`&SUBSTR(start:end,string)`	Extracts a substring from string starting at start and ending at end. Both start and end have numeric values. End is optional; if omitted, only the character in the position specified by start is extracted.

Figure 13-4   Built-in functions

is 3. Similarly:

```
&LENGTH(50 * 2)
```

is 3, since the result of the multiplication (100) is a three-digit number. The length of a null value is zero.

If the expression is numeric, leading zeros aren't counted in the length. As a result, the real value of this expression:

```
&LENGTH(00003)
```

is 1, since the four leading zeros aren't counted.

The &EVAL function   The &EVAL function causes an expression to be evaluated. For example, the real value of &EVAL(1 + 2) is 3, since the result of the expression 1 + 2 is 3.

You use &EVAL when you want to evaluate an expression even though the syntax of the CLIST statement doesn't call for an expression. For example, suppose you code this WRITE statement:

```
WRITE 1 + 2
```

Here, the following message is displayed at the terminal:

```
1 + 2
```

That's because the WRITE statement doesn't call for an expression, so the expression isn't evaluated. To display the result of the expression, you would code this:

```
WRITE &EVAL(1 + 2)
```

Then, the result of the expression (3) would be displayed.

The &STR function   The &STR function is the opposite of &EVAL; it suppresses the evaluation of an expression. For example, suppose you code this:

```
&STR(1 + 2)
```

Here, the real value is 1 + 2, not 3. That's because the expression 1 + 2 is *not* evaluated. Symbolic substitution takes place within the &STR function, though. So, if &VALUE is 1, this expression:

```
&STR(&VALUE + 2)
```

also reduces to 1 + 2.

You'll use the &STR function most for coding that might be confusing or even invalid without it. For example, suppose you want to test a variable to see if it's a slash (/). You couldn't code the expression like this:

```
&CHAR = /
```

because the slash is the division operator and that makes the syntax invalid. So you must code the expression like this:

```
&CHAR = &STR(/)
```

To the &STR function, the slash has no special meaning, so the syntax is correct.

The &SUBSTR function   You use the &SUBSTR function
to extract a portion of a character string. In its simplest form,
you extract a single character by specifying the character's
location and a symbolic variable that contains the character
string, like this:

```
&SUBSTR(5,&CHAR)
```

The real value of this expression is the fifth character in
&CHAR. So if &CHAR is ABCDEFG, the value is E.

You can use a symbolic variable or an expression to indicate the character location, as well. For example, suppose
&START is 4 and &CHAR is still ABCDEFG. Then, the real
value of this expression:

```
&SUBSTR(&START,&CHAR)
```

is D. And

```
&SUBSTR(&START + 1,&CHAR)
```

is E.

You can extract more than one character from a string by
specifying two locations—a starting and an ending location.
For example, suppose you set &ALPHABET like this:

```
SET ALPHABET = ABCDEFGHIJKLMNOPQRSTUVWXYZ
```

Then, you code this expression:

```
&SUBSTR(5:10,&ALPHABET)
```

This expression returns the fifth through the tenth characters in
&ALPHABET (EFGHIJ).

If you want to extract a given number of characters
starting at a particular location, you can code an expression
like this:

```
&SUBSTR(&START:&START + &LEN - 1,&ALPHABET)
```

Here, the starting location is &START, while the ending location is &START plus &LEN minus 1. If &START is 5 and &LEN is 6, this expression yields the fifth through the tenth (5 + 6 - 1 is 10) characters in &ALPHABET, again EFGHIJ.

CONTROL VARIABLES

Figure 13-5 lists 13 *control variables* that you can use in a CLIST to obtain system information. The meaning of each control variable is either self-evident or is explained later in this book, so I'm not going to describe them individually here. I just want you to be aware that these variables exist. They're automatically maintained by the system, but you can change the value of some of them if you wish.

To illustrate the use of a control variable, consider this WRITE statement:

```
WRITE JOB SUBMITTED AT &SYSTIME ON &SYSDATE
```

Here, the output generated by the WRITE statement would look something like this:

```
JOB SUBMITTED AT 13:45:20 ON 10/12/84
```

As you can see, TSO substitutes the current time for &SYSTIME and the current date for &SYSDATE.

HOW TO CONTROL
A COMMAND PROCEDURE'S EXECUTION

Like high-level programming languages, CLIST provides extensive facilities that let you change the flow of control through the procedure. Now, I'm going to show you how to branch unconditionally in a CLIST with a GOTO statement, test for conditions with an IF-THEN-ELSE statement, execute a loop repeatedly with a DO-WHILE statement, and terminate a procedure with an EXIT statement.

Control variables that contain information about the user who invoked the command procedure

&SYSUID   The user-id of the current user.

&SYSPROC   The name of the logon procedure used to start the current user's terminal session.

&SYSPREF   The default prefix added to the start of data set names for the current user.

Control variables that contain information related to the command procedure's execution

&LASTCC   The condition code returned by the last TSO command or CLIST statement. Should be zero unless an error condition exists.

&MAXCC   The highest condition code encountered during a command procedure.

&SYSICMD   If the user invoked the procedure implicitly, this variable contains the name of the member invoked. Otherwise, it's blank.

&SYSNEST   Contains YES if a procedure is nested; otherwise, contains NO.

&SYSPCMD   The name of the most recently executed TSO command.

&SYSSCMD   The name of the most recently executed TSO subcommand.

Control variables that contain information used for terminal I/O

&SYSDVAL   A special register that contains information entered by a user.

&SYSDLM   Used for terminal I/O when the TERMIN statement is used.

Control variables that contain the time and date

&SYSTIME   The current time in the form hh:mm:ss (two-digit hours, minutes, and seconds).

&SYSDATE   The current date in the form mm/dd/yy (two-digit month, day, and year).

Figure 13-5   Control variables

How to branch unconditionally

To branch unconditionally to another section of a command procedure, you must do two things. First, you must establish a command procedure *label*. Second, you must code a GOTO statement that refers to that label.

```
SET ALPHABET = ABCDEFGHIJKLMNOPQRSTUVWXYZ
SET COUNT = 1
LOOP: WRITE LETTER &COUNT IS &SUBSTR(&COUNT,&ALPHABET)
      SET COUNT = &COUNT + 1
      GOTO LOOP
```

Figure 13-6   Using a label and a GOTO statement to create a procedure loop

Figure 13-6 shows a short routine that prints the letters of the alphabet one by one using a label and a GOTO statement. The first statement assigns all the letters of the alphabet to &ALPHABET. The second statement assigns an initial value of 1 to &COUNT. The third statement is labelled. To label a statement, simply code a one- to eight-character alphanumeric label (it must start with a letter), followed by a colon and a TSO command or procedure statement. In figure 13-6, the label is LOOP, and it's followed by a colon and a WRITE statement. The next statement adds one to &COUNT. And the last statement branches to LOOP. As a result, this command procedure executes, writing output like this:

```
LETTER 1 IS A
LETTER 2 IS B
```

until an error occurs when the value of &COUNT is greater than the length of &ALPHABET.

The IF-THEN-ELSE structure

The IF statement shown in figure 13-7 provides for conditional execution within your command procedure. It's similar to equivalent statements in most high-level programming languages, so you'll have no difficulty understanding it.

Comparative expressions   The expression in an IF statement is usually a comparison of two symbolic variables or real values in a format similar to that found in most high-level languages. For example, to test if &A is greater than 10, you could code an IF statement like this:

```
IF &A > 10 THEN WRITE &A IS GREATER THAN 10
ELSE WRITE &A IS NOT GREATER THAN 10
```

The IF statement

```
IF expression THEN statement-1

[ELSE [statement-2]]
```

Explanation

expression   A comparative or logical expression.

statement-1   A single TSO command or procedure statement or a DO group that's executed if
                  the expression is true.

statement-2   A single TSO command or procedure statement or a DO group that's executed if
                  the expression is false.

Figure 13-7   The IF statement

Here, the first WRITE statement is executed if &A is greater
than 10; otherwise, the second WRITE statement executes. In
this example, &A > 10 is called a *comparative expression*.

Figure 13-8 lists the *comparative operators* you can use in
a comparative expression. Notice that you can use the normal
algebraic forms familiar to BASIC, PL/I, and COBOL, or you
can use the two-letter abbreviations commonly used in
FORTRAN. As a result, these two expressions are equivalent:

```
&A = &B
&A EQ &B
```

Note that if you use a two-letter operator, you *must* separate it
from the rest of the expression with spaces.

Logical expressions   Using the *logical operators* shown in
figure 13-9, you can combine two or more comparative
expressions to form a *logical expression*. If you use the AND
operator, all of the comparative expressions involved must be
true for the entire expression to be true. For example, this
expression is true:

```
50 < 75 AND 100 > 75
```

Function	Symbol	Abbreviation
Equal	=	E Q
Not equal	¬=	N E
Less than	<	L T
Greater than	>	G T
Less than or equal	<=	L E
Greater than or equal	>=	G E
Not greater than	¬>	N G
Not less than	¬<	N L

Figure 13-8   Comparative operators

As for this expression:

```
&A < &X AND &B < &X AND &C < &X
```

it's true if &A, &B, and &C are all less than &X; otherwise, it's false.

If you use the OR operator, only one of the comparative expressions must be true for the entire expression to be true. For example, this expression is true:

```
50 < 75 OR 80 < 75
```

because 50 is less than 75, even though 80 is not. However, this expression is false:

```
100 < 75 OR 80 < 75
```

since neither 100 nor 80 is less than 75.

If an expression contains both AND and OR conditions, TSO evaluates all of the AND's from left to right, then combines them with the OR's from left to right. I recommend you avoid mixing AND and OR, however, because the resulting expressions are often very confusing. For example, try to

Function	Symbol	Word
And	&&	AND
Or	||	OR

Figure 13-9   Logical operators

determine what's meant by this expression:

```
&A < &X AND &B < &X OR &C < &X OR &D < &X AND &E < &X
```

Even knowing the order of evaluation TSO will use doesn't make this expression any easier to follow.

Incidentally, you can use a double ampersand (&&) rather than the word AND. And you can use a double vertical bar (||) rather than the word OR. I prefer the words AND and OR because they indicate clearly what logical operation you're using. But if you prefer && and ||, that's fine. Of course, check to see if your shop has a standard dictating what form of the logical operators—and of the comparative operators as well—you should use.

Coding rules   There are a few rules you must follow when you code an IF-THEN-ELSE structure. First, the word THEN must appear on the same logical line as the word IF. (By logical line, I mean one or more lines connected by the continuation characters + or -.) Second, you can code only *one* statement to be executed if the expression is true, and it too must be on the same line as the word IF. Third, if you use an ELSE clause, the word ELSE must be on a separate line from the word IF. And fourth, you can code only *one* statement to be executed if the expression is false. In short, the IF-THEN-ELSE structure should be coded just as shown in figure 13-7.

DO groups   Obviously, limiting the THEN and ELSE clauses to a single statement is a severe restriction. Fortunately, there's a facility called a *DO group* that lets you code a series of statements on separate lines and have TSO treat them as if

```
IF expression THEN DO
      statement-1
      statement-2
      END
ELSE DO
      statement-3
      statement-4
      END
```

Figure 13-10   The basic format of a DO group within an IF-THEN-ELSE structure

they were a single statement. To code a DO group, enter the word DO, followed by TSO commands or procedure statements on separate lines, followed by the word END on a separate line, like this:

```
DO
      WRITE LETTER &COUNT IS &SUBSTR(&COUNT,&ALPHABET)
      SET COUNT = &COUNT + 1
END
```

Here, the WRITE statement and the SET statement are treated as if they were a single statement.

You use a DO group in an IF-THEN-ELSE structure as shown in figure 13-10. Here, statement-1 and statement-2 are executed if the expression is true. Otherwise, statement-3 and statement-4 are executed. In this example, I provided two statements for the THEN and ELSE DO groups. But there's no limit to how many statements you could code.

Figure 13-11 is an example of a DO group used in an IF statement. Here, the WRITE statement and the SET statement are executed together as a DO group if &COUNT is less than 27.

Notice in the examples I've given so far how I've indented the conditionally-executed statements from the main body of the procedure. That way, you can easily see the procedure's structure. In contrast, if no indentation is used, the procedure's structure becomes obscure and often misleading.

One other point about DO groups: Make sure each END statement has a previous DO statement. The reason is that the word END by itself is a TSO command that causes a procedure

```
IF &COUNT < 27 THEN DO
    WRITE LETTER &COUNT IS &SUBSTR(&COUNT,&ALPHABET)
    SET COUNT = &COUNT + 1
    END
```

Figure 13-11   Using a DO group in an IF statement

to stop executing. So although you would expect an unmatched END statement in a DO group to cause an error, it doesn't. Instead, it's executed as an END command, thus terminating your procedure with no apparent error. As you can imagine, a problem like this can take hours to isolate, unless you know to check for unmatched END statements. (By the way, don't use the END command to terminate a procedure. Instead, use the EXIT statement described later in this topic. It executes more efficiently and gives you more coding flexibility than the END command.)

Nested IF statements   Within an IF statement, or within a DO group under the control of an IF statement, you can code another IF statement. If you do, the IF statement is said to be *nested*. Within a nested IF statement, each ELSE clause is paired with the previous unpaired IF.

Since ELSE clauses are optional, nested IF statements can be coded in a variety of different forms. In all cases, however, indentation should be used to show the levels of nesting. In particular, you should align each ELSE clause with its corresponding IF statement so you can easily see how IF and ELSE statements are paired. But be careful. Your indentation doesn't affect how TSO interprets your CLIST. In other words, TSO always pairs an ELSE with the previous IF, regardless of what your indentation shows.

To illustrate, figure 13-12 shows some common variations for three levels of nesting. Note that in all cases the indentation corresponds to the way TSO interprets these statements.

Nested IF statements can be further complicated by the fact that the statement on an ELSE clause is optional. Thus, if you code just the word ELSE, you tell TSO to perform no action if the corresponding expression is false, but to move back one level in the nest so that the next ELSE clause is paired with the previous IF statement.

Example 1

```
IF expression THEN DO
    statements
    IF expression THEN DO
        statements
        IF expression THEN DO
            statements
            END
        END
    END
```

Example 2

```
IF expression THEN DO
    statements
    IF expression THEN DO
        statements
        IF expression THEN DO
            statements
            END
        ELSE DO
            statements
            END
        END
    ELSE DO
        statements
        END
    END
ELSE DO
    statements
    END
```

Example 3

```
IF expression THEN DO
    statements
    END
ELSE IF expression THEN DO
        statements
        END
    ELSE IF expression THEN DO
            statements
            END
        ELSE DO
            statements
            END
```

Figure 13-12 Some common examples of nested IF statements

```
IF expression THEN DO
    statements
    IF expression THEN DO
        statements
        IF expression THEN DO
            statements
            END
        ELSE
        END
    ELSE DO
        statements
        END
    END
```

Figure 13-13   Using a null ELSE in a nested IF statement

To illustrate, consider figure 13-13. Here, three levels of nested IF statements are coded, but only one of them—the second one—requires an action for the ELSE condition. Since ELSE clauses are always paired with the most recent IF statement, an ELSE clause with *no* action is coded for the third IF statement.

The DO-WHILE structure

The DO-WHILE structure provides an easy way to control looping within a CLIST. The basic format of the DO-WHILE structure is this:

```
DO WHILE expression
    statements
END
```

The statements in the DO-WHILE structure are executed repeatedly until the expression is false.

Figure 13-14 shows how a DO-WHILE structure can be used to refine the simple loop first presented in figure 13-6. The first two statements in figure 13-14 set &ALPHABET and &COUNT. Then, the DO-WHILE statement marks the start of a DO-WHILE structure. The expression, &COUNT < 27, says that the statements in the DO-WHILE structure are to be executed over and over again as long as &COUNT is less than 27.

```
SET ALPHABET = ABCDEFGHIJKLMNOPQRSTUVWXYZ
SET COUNT = 1
DO WHILE &COUNT < 27
    WRITE LETTER &COUNT IS &SUBSTR(&COUNT,&ALPHABET)
    SET COUNT = &COUNT + 1
END
```

Figure 13-14 Using a DO-WHILE loop in a refined version of figure 13-6

As soon as &COUNT is *not* less than 27, however, the DO-WHILE structure ends and control falls through to the next statement in sequence. The effect of the DO-WHILE loop in figure 13-14 is that each letter of the alphabet is displayed at the terminal.

In a DO-WHILE structure, the expression stated in the WHILE clause is evaluated *before* each execution of the loop. As a result, if the expression is false the first time, the statements in the loop aren't executed at all. Usually, that's the way you want the test to function.

The EXIT statement

You use the EXIT statement to terminate your command procedure. If you code just the word EXIT, your CLIST simply returns to TSO. If you also include a CODE operand, like this:

```
EXIT CODE(12)
```

your CLIST returns the *condition code* specified (in this case, 12) when it ends. This value goes into the control variable &LASTCC, where it can be examined by another procedure. Usually, a condition code greater than zero indicates that an error occurred during the execution of a statement or command.

In general, there are two places where you'll issue an EXIT statement. The first is at the end of your CLIST. Although you don't have to code an EXIT statement there, it's often a good idea. The second is where you detect an error condition and want to abort the CLIST immediately. In that

```
10 /*  &JOBCHAR HAS BEEN PREVIOUSLY SET TO THE LAST JOB CHARACTER */
20 SET CHARS = ABCDEFGHIJKLMNOPQRSTUVWXYZ0123456789A
30 SET COUNT = 1
40 DO WHILE &JOBCHAR ¬= &SUBSTR(&COUNT,&CHARS)
50     SET COUNT = &COUNT + 1
60 END
70 SET JOBCHAR = &SUBSTR(&COUNT + 1,&CHARS)
80 IF &BG = BG THEN DO
90     SUBMIT JCL(&MEMBER) JOBCHAR(&JOBCHAR)
100    WRITE JOB &SYSUID&JOBCHAR SUBMITTED AT &SYSTIME ON &SYSDATE
110    END
```

Figure 13-15 A segment of a command procedure that submits a job for background processing

---

case, you should issue an EXIT statement that sets an appropriate condition code.

A SAMPLE COMMAND PROCEDURE

Figure 13-15 presents a short section of a command procedure that submits a job for background processing. Although this is an incomplete example, it illustrates many of the command procedure facilities I've described in this topic.

As you know, if a submitted data set doesn't contain a JOB statement, the JOBCHAR operand of the SUBMIT command supplies a character that's appended to the user's user-id to form an appropriate job name. The code in figure 13-15 assigns a new value to JOBCHAR each time the procedure is run so the user's job names will be unique. You can assume that the variable &JOBCHAR has been previously set to the character used in the job name the last time the user submitted a job.

Lines 20 through 70 change &JOBCHAR to the next character in sequence. In other words, if the procedure starts with &JOBCHAR equal to A, these lines change &JOBCHAR to B. If &JOBCHAR starts out as M, it's changed to N. And the digits follow the letters, so if &JOBCHAR is Z on entry, it's changed to 0.

Line 20 sets &CHARS to a string that contains all of the possible characters to which &JOBCHAR can be set. Notice how the string ends with an A. That way, if &JOBCHAR is 9, it's changed to A, thus returning to the start of the list. Line

30 initializes a counter variable, &COUNT, to 1. Then, lines 40 through 60 set up a DO-WHILE loop that searches through &CHARS one character at a time until the character that matches &JOBCHAR is found. It does this by executing the loop repeatedly as long as this condition is met:

```
&JOBCHAR ¬= &SUBSTR(&COUNT,&CHARS)
```

In other words, the loop continues to execute as long as &JOBCHAR is *not* equal to the character at position &COUNT in &CHARS. The first time through the loop, &COUNT is 1. So the condition compares &JOBCHAR with the letter A (the first character in &CHARS).

    Assuming the condition is not true, &COUNT is incremented with this SET statement:

```
SET COUNT = &COUNT + 1
```

Then, the condition is tested again. This time, the next character in &CHARS is used in the test. This process continues until a character in &CHARS matches &JOBCHAR. At that point, the WHILE condition becomes false, and the loop ends with &COUNT indicating the position of the matching character within &CHARS.

    Since I want the next character in the sequence to be used as the job identifier, line 70 sets &JOBCHAR like this:

```
SET JOBCHAR = &SUBSTR(&COUNT + 1,&CHARS)
```

Thus, if the loop ends with &COUNT set to 10, this statement sets &JOBCHAR to the *eleventh* character in &CHARS. As a result, the proper job identifier is found.

    It's lines 80 through 110 that actually submit the job for background processing. Here, I assume that a symbolic variable, &BG, will have a real value of BG if the background job should be submitted. Though it's not apparent from the segment of code shown in figure 13-15, this variable is set as a keyword parameter when the procedure is invoked. For example, suppose the procedure starts with a PROC statement like this:

```
PROC 1 MEMBER BG
```

Then, if the procedure is invoked like this:

```
%TEST COMPRESS BG
```

&BG will be set to BG. (For the sake of the illustration, assume here that TEST is the name of the procedure and &MEMBER is the name of the member to be submitted for background processing.)

Assuming that &BG equals BG, line 90 submits the background job. The SUBMIT command specifies &MEMBER as the member name; the library name is user-id.JCL.CNTL. The JOBCHAR operand supplies &JOBCHAR, which was set in line 70, to use in the job name. Finally, line 100 writes a message to the terminal saying that the job has been submitted.

DISCUSSION

In this topic, I've presented command procedure elements that let you create complex expressions and control the flow of execution within your procedure. While these facilities raise CLIST to the status of a high-level programming language, I must again caution you to use them with discretion. Whenever possible, you should consider using a high-level programming language like PL/I or COBOL rather than using CLIST.

A COBOL or PL/I program has a couple of advantages over a command procedure. To begin with, both COBOL and PL/I are much easier to code than CLIST, because of their simpler syntax. And because they are compiled rather than interpreted, they will execute faster—perhaps dramatically faster—than a CLIST. So save the complicated command procedures for applications that require facilities only a command procedure can offer, such as dynamic file allocation, background job processing, and so on.

Terminology

comment
expression
null value
arithmetic expression
arithmetic operator
built-in function
control variable
label
comparative expression
comparative operator
logical operator
logical expression
DO group
nested IF statement
condition code

Objective

Given a problem requiring any of the command procedure facilities described in this topic, code a command procedure for its solution.

TOPIC 2   Expanding the subset

In topic 1 of this chapter, I presented a subset of the advanced features of command procedures. Now, I'll expand that subset by presenting additional command procedure facilities. Specifically, I'll show you how to use the CONTROL statement to control the command procedure environment, how to use DATA/ENDDATA statements to avoid a peculiar problem often encountered in a DO group, how to code exit routines to handle error conditions and attention interruptions, and how to nest procedures—that is, how to invoke one procedure from another.

HOW TO CONTROL THE CLIST ENVIRONMENT

The CONTROL statement is shown in figure 13-16. This statement turns on or off various options that affect how a command procedure executes. You normally place the CONTROL statement near the beginning of your command procedure. That way, the control options are in effect for the entire procedure.

Each option is controlled by one of the pairs of operands shown in figure 13-16. For example, if you code:

```
CONTROL MSG
```

you turn on the MSG option. To turn it off, code:

```
CONTROL NOMSG
```

To control more than one option, just list them on the CONTROL statement, like this:

```
CONTROL MSG NOFLUSH NOLIST
```

Here, the MSG option is turned on, but the FLUSH and LIST options are turned off.

The CONTROL statement

```
CONTROL     [{MSG  }]
            [{NOMSG}]

            [{FLUSH  }]
            [{NOFLUSH}]

            [{MAIN  }]
            [{NOMAIN}]

            [{LIST  }]
            [{NOLIST}]

            [{CONLIST  }]
            [{NOCONLIST}]

            [{SYMLIST  }]
            [{NOSYMLIST}]

            [{PROMPT  }]
            [{NOPROMPT}]

            [END(string)]
```

Figure 13-16   The CONTROL statement (part 1 of 2)

Now, I'll explain how each of the control options affects the way your command procedures execute.

The MSG option   The MSG option controls whether messages created by TSO commands are displayed. If you say MSG, the messages are displayed. If you say NOMSG, they're suppressed.

How you should set this option depends on the function of your procedure. If the user needs to see the TSO command output, you should activate the MSG option. (It's activated by default when a command procedure starts, so you don't need to say CONTROL MSG unless you previously said CONTROL NOMSG.) If your procedure invokes TSO commands that create output the user doesn't need to see, you should say CONTROL NOMSG.

The FLUSH and MAIN options   Normally, when an error condition occurs, your procedure is flushed—that is, removed from the system—even if you provide an error exit (a routine

Explanation

MSG NOMSG	If MSG is on, messages generated by commands are displayed at the terminal. Otherwise, they're suppressed. MSG is normally on.
FLUSH NOFLUSH	If FLUSH is on, the procedure is removed from the system when an error occurs and error exits are ignored. FLUSH is normally on. Note that the MAIN option overrides the FLUSH option.
MAIN NOMAIN	The MAIN option says that a procedure should not be deleted from the system because of an error or attention interruption. If you specify MAIN, NOFLUSH is assumed. MAIN is normally off.
LIST NOLIST	If LIST is on, TSO commands are listed before they're executed but after symbolic substitution has taken place. Otherwise, they're not listed. LIST is normally off.
CONLIST NOCONLIST	If CONLIST is on, command procedure statements are listed before they're executed but after symbolic substitution has taken place. Otherwise, they're not listed. CONLIST is normally off.
SYMLIST NOSYMLIST	If SYMLIST is on, TSO commands and command procedures are listed **before** symbolic substitution. Otherwise, they're not listed. SYMLIST is normally off.
PROMPT NOPROMPT	If PROMPT is on, the terminal user is prompted for missing information on TSO commands in the procedure. PROMPT is normally off.
END	Specifies an alternate string that's used to end a DO group.

Figure 13-16   The CONTROL statement (part 2 of 2)

to handle error processing). But if you code this CONTROL statement at the start of the procedure:

```
CONTROL NOFLUSH
```

your procedure won't be flushed when an error occurs, so your error exits will be processed. (I'll cover error exits in detail later in this topic.)

Alternatively, you can code this CONTROL statement:

```
CONTROL MAIN
```

The MAIN option is similar to the NOFLUSH option. But besides preventing your procedure from being flushed in the event of an error, the MAIN option also inhibits the attention key. As a result, the terminal user can't interrupt your procedure by pressing PA1 if you say CONTROL MAIN. Normally, you should use CONTROL NOFLUSH instead —especially during testing—so that you can interrupt your procedure whenever necessary.

The LIST, CONLIST, and SYMLIST options   You use the next three options, LIST, CONLIST, and SYMLIST, when you test your CLIST. The LIST option causes all TSO commands to be displayed before they're executed. They're displayed in their final form, after symbolic substitution. The CONLIST option causes all command procedure statements to be listed, again before execution but after symbolic substitution. And the SYMLIST option simply lists all TSO commands and procedure statements before any symbolic substitution is done.

I often provide a keyword parameter, TEST, on my PROC statements so I can establish a testing environment when I invoke my procedure for a test run. To do this, I include the statements shown in figure 13-17 at the start of my procedure. Here, I establish the production environment for my procedure—in this case, by turning off the MSG and the FLUSH options. Then, if the TEST keyword is specified, I issue another CONTROL statement so that the MSG, LIST, and CONLIST options will be in effect. As a result, during a test run I get the extra output I need to help me debug the procedure.

The PROMPT option   The PROMPT option determines whether TSO will prompt a user when required information is omitted from a TSO command in the procedure. Normally, the PROMPT option is off, so your procedure is terminated if it includes an incomplete command. If you say PROMPT, TSO prompts the terminal user to supply the missing information.

The END option   The last option controlled by the CONTROL statement is the string used to delimit a DO group. Normally, this string is the word END. But END has other meanings under TSO, such as indicating the end of an EDIT session. If you need to include END as a TSO command or subcommand—*not* as a command procedure statement—in a

```
PROC 0 TEST
CONTROL NOFLUSH NOMSG
IF &TEST = TEST THEN DO
    WRITE PROCEDURE EXECUTING IN TEST MODE
    CONTROL MSG LIST CONLIST
    END
```

Figure 13-17 Setting control options for test and production runs of a command procedure

DO group, you must change the END string, like this:

```
CONTROL END(ENDDO)
```

Then, you can code a DO group like this:

```
DO
    20 //SYSUT1 DD DSN=&DATASET,DISP=OLD
    END SAVE
ENDDO
```

Here, the ENDDO statement marks the end of the DO group. An alternative to this technique is to code the END SAVE command in a DATA/ENDDATA group, which I'll describe in a moment.

How to specify control options on the EXEC command   You can set two of the CONTROL options—LIST and PROMPT—on the explicit form of the EXEC command, if you wish. For example, you might invoke a procedure like this:

```
EXEC (COBTEST) 'REORDLST,LIBRARY(MASTER)',LIST,PROMPT
```

Here, the procedure will begin with the LIST and PROMPT options set. Since LIST and PROMPT aren't part of the parameter list sent to the procedure, they're coded outside the apostrophes that contain the parameters.

HOW TO USE A DATA/ENDDATA GROUP

As I mentioned before, you can use the CONTROL statement to change the END statement to another character string. That

```
DO
    EDIT JCL(TEST) CNTL
    40 //SYSUT1       DD   DSN=&&TEMPSET,
    50 //                  UNIT=SYSDA,
    60 //                  SPACE=(TRK,(10,1)),
    70 //                  DISP=,PASS
    80 //SYSIN        DD   *
    90   COPY OUTDD=DD1,INDD=DD2
    95 /*
    DATA
    END SAVE
    ENDDATA
END
```

Figure 13-18   A DATA/ENDDATA group

way, you can code END as a TSO command or subcommand without having it confused as a procedure statement. Another alternative is to use the DATA and ENDDATA statements. Basically, the DATA statement tells TSO that each line that follows is to be treated as a TSO command or subcommand until the word ENDDATA is encountered. Symbolic substitution is still done, but no procedure statements are interpreted.

To illustrate, consider figure 13-18. Here, I coded a DATA/ENDDATA group that includes an END subcommand to end an editing session. If it weren't for the DATA and ENDDATA statements, the END subcommand would have been interpreted as the end of the DO group that contains the entire editing session. As a result, the procedure would not have executed properly.

HOW TO CODE EXIT ROUTINES

An *exit routine* is a single statement—or, more commonly, a group of statements contained in a DO group—that's executed whenever an exit condition occurs. There are two types of exits that you can provide for in a command procedure: *error exits* and *attention exits*. You use an error exit to process error conditions that are encountered as your procedure executes. And you use an attention exit to invoke special processing when the terminal user presses the attention key (PA1).

To establish an error exit, you use an ERROR statement; to establish an attention exit, you use an ATTN statement. Since both statements have the same format, they're shown together in figure 13-19.

The ERROR statement

$$\text{ERROR} \quad \left\{ \begin{array}{l} \texttt{statement} \\ \texttt{OFF} \end{array} \right\}$$

The ATTN statement

$$\text{ATTN} \quad \left\{ \begin{array}{l} \texttt{statement} \\ \texttt{OFF} \end{array} \right\}$$

Explanation

statement   A single statement or a DO group that's executed whenever an error or attention interruption occurs.

OFF   Says that any previous error or attention exit should be deleted.

___

Figure 13-19   The ERROR and ATTN statements

Error exits

Normally, when a TSO command or procedure statement issues a return code greater than zero, TSO generates an error message and terminates your procedure. An error exit lets you anticipate possible errors and provide a more meaningful error message or perhaps provide special processing for the error so that your procedure doesn't terminate.

To establish an error exit, you must issue an ERROR statement *before* an error occurs. Then, any error causes control to transfer to your error exit (that is, your ERROR statement). When the statements in your error exit have been executed, control returns to the statement following the one that caused the error—unless your error exit terminates the procedure by issuing an EXIT statement or transfers control to another location with a GOTO statement. It's important to realize that the statements in an error exit are *not* executed when TSO first encounters the ERROR statement. They're not actually executed until an error occurs.

One common use of an error exit is to trap errors that may occur as a result of an ALLOCATE command. To illustrate, consider figure 13-20. Here, an ERROR statement establishes an error exit that consists of two statements. The first writes an error message to the terminal; the second

```
ERROR DO
    WRITE UNABLE TO ALLOCATE &DATASET--COMPLETION CODE &LASTCC
    EXIT CODE(12)
    END
ALLOCATE DSNAME(&DATASET) DDNAME(SYSUT1)
ERROR OFF
```

Figure 13-20   An error exit

terminates the procedure with a condition code of 12. Then, an ALLOCATE command attempts to allocate a data set. If the allocation fails, the statements in the error exit are invoked. If the allocation is successful, control falls through to the next statement in sequence—in this case, ERROR OFF. The ERROR OFF statement simply deactivates an error exit. So after an ERROR OFF statement, no error exit is in effect.

At any given point during the execution of a command procedure, only one error exit is in effect. So if you code several ERROR statements in a row, only the most recent one is in effect. As a result, it's not necessary to issue ERROR OFF statements if you're replacing one error exit with another. But if you don't provide a replacement error exit, you should use an ERROR OFF statement to clear the previous error exit.

Generalized error exits   If you wish, you can provide a generalized error exit like the one in figure 13-21. This simple routine displays the command that was executing, the condition code that resulted from the error, and exits with the highest condition code that was encountered. For example, if an error occurs during an ALLOCATE command, the terminal user might see this:

```
AN ERROR HAS OCCURRED DURING ALLOCATE
LAST CONDITION CODE WAS 12
```

Of course, a generalized exit routine can easily become very complicated, testing for specific error conditions and even trying to correct common ones.

The RETURN statement   In complicated error exits, it's often necessary to leave the error exit at several points. To do this, you use the RETURN statement. For example, consider the error exit in figure 13-22, used to trap errors from a

```
ERROR DO
    WRITE AN ERROR HAS OCCURRED DURING &SYSPCMD
    WRITE LAST CONDITION CODE WAS &LASTCC
    EXIT CODE(&MAXCC)
END
```

Figure 13-21   A generalized error exit

```
ERROR DO
    IF &LASTCC <= 4 THEN DO
        WRITE YOUR PROGRAM CONTAINS MINOR ERRORS
        RETURN
        END
    IF &LASTCC > 4 THEN DO
        WRITE YOUR PROGRAM CONTAINS SERIOUS ERRORS
        EXIT CODE(&LASTCC)
        END
END
```

Figure 13-22   An error exit that uses both RETURN and EXIT statements

COBOL command. When the condition code is four or less, an error message is written and a RETURN statement causes control to return to the statement following the command that caused the error. But if the condition code is greater than four, a different error message is written and the procedure terminates.

How to use error exits for conditions that aren't really errors
I want you to realize that an error exit is sometimes used for processing that you wouldn't normally consider error handling. To illustrate, suppose you want to determine if a data set exists. If it does, you'll allocate it as an existing data set. If it doesn't, you'll allocate it as a new data set. To determine which ALLOCATE command to invoke, you'll test a switch named &EXISTS. If the data set exists, &EXISTS will be Y; otherwise, it will be N.

To set the switch properly, you could code these statements (assuming the data set name is in &DATASET):

```
SET EXISTS = Y
ERROR SET EXISTS = N
LISTCAT ENTRIES(&DATASET)
ERROR OFF
```

This routine uses an error exit to determine if the LISTCAT succeeds or fails. If it succeeds, &EXISTS remains set to Y. But if it fails, the error exit sets &EXISTS to N. You would use a CONTROL NOMSG statement before these lines so the terminal user wouldn't see the output of the LISTCAT command.

Attention exits

When a terminal user presses the attention key (PA1), any processing currently active is terminated, whether it's a TSO command, a foreground program, or a command procedure. In many cases, you need to disable the attention key so that the user can't interrupt a procedure in the middle of an important series of steps. To do this, you use the ATTN statement to establish an attention exit. An attention exit works just like an error exit except that it's invoked by the attention key, not by an error condition.

Here's a simple attention exit:

```
ATTN WRITE YOU CANNOT INTERRUPT THIS PROCEDURE
```

If you issue this statement at the start of a procedure, the attention key won't interrupt the procedure. To restore the function of the attention key, issue this statement:

```
ATTN OFF
```

Then, the attention key can once again be used to interrupt the procedure.

Of course, you can make an attention exit as complex as you wish. You can allow the user to terminate the procedure under certain conditions. You can use the terminal I/O facilities I'll present in chapter 14 to verify that the user wants to terminate the procedure. Or you can perform any other type of special processing you wish.

One word of warning: Don't use an attention exit in a procedure that contains a loop. If you do, you'll be in trouble if your loop repeats indefinitely.

HOW TO USE NESTED PROCEDURES

When one procedure calls a second procedure, the procedures are said to be *nested*. The first procedure—that is, the one that does the calling—is an *outer procedure*. The procedure that is called is an *inner procedure*. Once the inner procedure has finished executing—either because all its statements have completed or because it issues an EXIT statement—control returns to the outer procedure. Execution then continues with the statement following the one that invoked the inner procedure.

You can nest many levels of procedures. In other words, one procedure can invoke a second procedure, which can in turn invoke a third procedure, and so on. As a result, a procedure can be both an inner and an outer procedure. Any given procedure is an inner procedure with respect to the procedure that invoked it, and an outer procedure with respect to the procedures it invokes.

Like many advanced command procedure facilities, however, you should limit your use of nested procedures. Two or three levels of nesting is acceptable, but if you need much more than that, you should consider using a high-level language like COBOL or PL/I instead.

How control options are passed among procedures

When you invoke a nested procedure, the environment set by any CONTROL statements in the outer procedure is passed to the inner procedure. Note, however, that the effect of any CONTROL statements in the inner procedure is *not* passed back to the outer procedure. When control returns to an outer procedure, the control options are restored to their status just before the inner procedure was invoked.

How variable values are passed among procedures

In many cases, an inner procedure needs to access symbolic variables that are set in the outer procedure. You can pass values on in one of two ways: as EXEC parameters or as

Procedure PROC1

```
.
.
.
%PROC2 REORDLST BG
.
.
.
```

Procedure PROC2

```
PROC 1 MEMBER BG
IF &BG = BG THEN DO
   .
   .
   .
```

Figure 13-23   Passing data among nested procedures as parameters

global variables. If you don't pass variable values on at all, the symbolic variables in the inner procedure will not have any values when the procedure's executed.

How to pass data as parameters   The easiest way to pass variable values is to use parameters on the EXEC command that invokes the inner procedure and provide a PROC statement within the inner procedure itself. Figure 13-23 shows how to do this. Here, PROC1 invokes PROC2, passing it two parameters: &MEMBER and &BG. PROC2 receives these parameters via its PROC statement.

How to pass data as global variables   Another way to pass variables among nested procedures is to define them as *global variables*. Figure 13-24 shows how a procedure named PROC1 defines two global variables, &MEMBER and &BG, using a GLOBAL statement:

```
GLOBAL MEMBER BG
```

PROC2 contains an identical GLOBAL statement. Then, both PROC1 and PROC2 can refer to &MEMBER and &BG. In short, the global variables are common to both procedures (in

Procedure PROC1

```
GLOBAL MEMBER BG
.
.
.
%PROC2
.
.
.
```

Procedure PROC2

```
GLOBAL MEMBER BG
IF &BG = BG THEN DO
    .
    .
    .
```

Figure 13-24   Passing data among nested procedures as global variables

fact, global variables are very similar to COMMON storage in FORTRAN).

There are a few rules that govern how you use the GLOBAL statement. To begin with, you must list all global variables on a GLOBAL statement *before* you refer to them in your procedure. That causes a special problem when you want a variable received as a parameter to be global. In short, you can't do it. For example, this sequence of statements is invalid:

```
PROC 1 MEMBER
GLOBAL MEMBER
```

To get around this problem, create another variable for global use, like this:

```
PROC 1 MEMBER
GLOBAL GMEMBER
SET GMEMBER = &MEMBER
```

Then, you can use &GMEMBER in your nested procedures.

It's important to realize the global variables listed in a GLOBAL statement are positional. The actual names you use

in the procedures that access the global variables don't matter.
To illustrate, suppose an outer procedure uses this GLOBAL
statement:

```
GLOBAL VAR1 VAR2 VAR3 VAR4
```

while its inner procedure uses this GLOBAL statement:

```
GLOBAL FIELD1 FIELD2 FIELD3 FIELD4
```

In this case, VAR1 in the outer procedure and FIELD1 in the
inner procedure refer to the same global variable even though
their names are different. That's because they appear in the
same position in the GLOBAL statements. Similarly, VAR2 in
the outer procedure and FIELD2 in the inner procedure refer
to the same global variable. As you can imagine, nested
procedures can become quite confusing if you refer to the same
global variable using two or more names.

To further complicate matters, an inner procedure doesn't
have to list all of its outer procedure's global variables in its
GLOBAL statement. For example, suppose a second inner
procedure needs to access only the first two global variables
defined above. You could code its GLOBAL statement like
this:

```
GLOBAL PARM1 PARM2
```

Now, VAR1, FIELD1, and PARM1 all refer to the same
global variable in three different procedures.

Frankly, global variables can cause you problems if you
use them excessively. But as long as you use them with
moderation, they're not overwhelmingly confusing.

How to restrict the use of a nested procedure

Sometimes, you need to restrict a procedure so that it can be
executed *only* as a nested procedure. In other words, you need
to make sure that a TSO user doesn't invoke the procedure

directly. To do this, include lines like these near the beginning of your procedure:

```
IF &SYSNEST = NO THEN DO
    WRITE YOU CANNOT INVOKE THIS PROCEDURE BY ITSELF
    EXIT
    END
```

&SYSNEST is a system control variable that contains YES if the current procedure was invoked from another procedure and NO if it was invoked directly by a TSO user. As a result, if &SYSNEST contains NO, this routine writes a message to the user and exits.

Terminology

exit routine
error exit
attention exit
nested procedure
outer procedure
inner procedure
global variable

Objective

Given a problem requiring the use of the command procedure facilities described in this topic, create a command procedure for its solution.

Chapter 14

Command procedure facilities for terminal and file processing

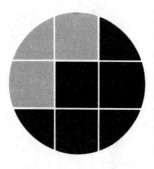

In this chapter, you'll learn how to use a variety of command procedure facilities that let you do simple input and output involving the terminal user and sequential files. First, you'll learn the basic elements for terminal and file I/O. Then, you'll learn two advanced I/O features: the READDVAL statement and the TERMIN statement.

BASIC CLIST ELEMENTS FOR TERMINAL AND FILE I/O

CLIST provides three basic statements for terminal I/O (WRITE, WRITENR, and READ) and four basic statements for file I/O (OPEN, GETFILE, PUTFILE, and CLOSFILE). After I explain how you code those statements, I'll present a complete command procedure that illustrates how the statements work together.

Terminal I/O features

Figure 14-1 summarizes the command procedure statements for terminal I/O. Since displaying messages to the terminal user is a critical function of just about any command procedure, I pre-

406

Statement	Function
`WRITE text`	Writes text to the terminal. Used to display error or informational messages.
`WRITENR text`	Writes text to the terminal but doesn't issue a carriage return. Used to prompt the user for input data.
`READ variables`	Reads values from the terminal into the variables listed. Used to accept data from a terminal user.

Figure 14-1   Command procedure statements for terminal I/O

sented the WRITE statement in chapter 13. In this section, then, I'll show you how to use the WRITENR and READ statements.

The WRITENR statement   The WRITENR statement works much the same way as the WRITE statement. The only difference is that the WRITENR statement doesn't generate a carriage return at the end of the line (the NR stands for No Return). As a result, the cursor stays on the same line as the displayed text instead of returning to the start of the next line.

You use the WRITENR statement most often to prompt the user for input that will be processed later by a READ statement. For example, suppose you code this WRITENR statement:

```
WRITENR PLEASE ENTER YOUR SELECTION:
```

Here, this message is displayed at the terminal:

```
PLEASE ENTER YOUR SELECTION:
```

and the cursor is positioned right after the colon.

The READ statement   The READ statement accepts one or more values from the terminal user and stores them in the symbolic variables you specify. For example, suppose you code this sequence of statements:

```
WRITENR PLEASE ENTER YOUR SELECTION:
READ SELECTION
```

Here, the WRITENR statement displays a prompting message. Then, the command procedure waits until the user keys in a value and presses the enter key. The READ statement then stores the value the user entered in &SELECTION.

You can specify more than one variable in a READ statement, like this:

```
WRITE ENTER PRINCIPAL, TERM, AND INTEREST:
READ PRINCIPAL TERM INTEREST
```

Here, the user is prompted to enter three values. The values can be separated by spaces or commas. So if the user replies like this:

```
75000,30,9
```

&PRINCIPAL is set to 75000, &TERM is set to 30, and &INTEREST is set to 9.

If the user enters more information than the READ statement requests, the extra information is ignored. For example, if you code a READ statement like this:

```
READ A B C D
```

and the user enters:

```
15,25,30,35,50
```

the last value (50) is ignored because there's no corresponding variable specified on the READ statement.

Similarly, if a user omits a value, the corresponding variable in the READ statement is assigned a null value. So, for the previous READ statement, suppose the user enters:

```
15,20,25
```

Here, &D is given a null value since the user didn't supply a value.

To give a null value to a variable other than the last one in the sequence, the user enters two commas, like this:

```
15,20,,25
```

Here, &A is set to 15, &B to 20, and &D to 25. &C is given a null value, since the double commas say to skip it.

In general, you should always code one or more WRITE or WRITENR statements before a READ statement. And the WRITE statements should fully identify the data requested. That way, the terminal user will always know what type of response the procedure expects.

File I/O features

The CLIST facilities for file processing let you do simple input and output operations on sequential (QSAM) files. To process a QSAM file in a CLIST, you must do four things: (1) use an ALLOCATE command to allocate the file; (2) use an OPENFILE statement to open the file; (3) use one or more GETFILE or PUTFILE statements to read or write records in the file; and (4) use a CLOSFILE statement to close the file. In addition, you may use a FREE command to deallocate the file when you're done with it.

Figure 14-2 summarizes these elements. You already know how to use the ALLOCATE and FREE commands. So now I'll describe the four procedure statements.

The OPENFILE statement   Before you can read or write records in a file, you must open the file using an OPENFILE statement. On the OPENFILE statement, you specify the ddname allocated to the file and a processing mode (OUTPUT or UPDATE) if the file isn't an input file. For example, this statement:

```
OPENFILE ORDLIST OUTPUT
```

opens the file whose ddname is ORDLIST for output processing. Similarly:

```
OPENFILE MASTER UPDATE
```

opens MASTER for both input and output processing. If you omit the processing mode, the file is assumed to be input.

Command/statement	Function
ALLOCATE DDNAME(ddname) DSNAME(data-set-name)	You use the standard TSO ALLOCATE command to prepare a data set for processing.
OPENFILE ddname mode	Opens the file. Mode is OUTPUT for output files, UPDATE for update files, or omitted for input files. If an output file already exists and you want to add the new records on to the end of it, you must code MOD as the file's disposition in its ALLOCATE command.
GETFILE ddname	Reads a record from the file and places it in &ddname.
PUTFILE ddname	Writes the record contained in &ddname to the file.
CLOSFILE ddname	Closes the file.
FREE DDNAME(ddname)	Frees the file so it can be processed by other users.

Figure 14-2 Commands and procedure statements for file I/O

Thus:

```
OPENFILE. ORDERS
```

opens ORDERS as an input file.

Normally, you code an ALLOCATE command just before an OPENFILE statement, like this:

```
ALLOCATE DDNAME(ORDERS) DSNAME(ORDERS.DATA)
OPENFILE ORDERS OUTPUT
```

Here, ORDERS is allocated and opened for output. For an output file that already exists, you must code a file disposition of MOD on the ALLOCATE command if you want to add new records at the end of the existing ones. Otherwise, the existing records will be overwritten by the new ones.

When you specify a ddname on an OPENFILE statement, that name becomes a symbolic variable whose real value represents the record area for the file. Thus, in the previous example, &ORDERS is used to store data written to the file.

The GETFILE statement   The GETFILE statement reads a record from a file. On it, you specify the symbolic variable that corresponds to the ddname for the file. For example:

```
GETFILE ORDERS
```

performs a read operation for the ORDERS file, placing the input record in &ORDERS.

After you read a record, you can use the &SUBSTR built-in function to extract data from specific fields in the record. For example, if the first five positions of the input record contain an item number, you might code a SET statement like this:

```
SET ITEMNO = &SUBSTR(1:5,&ORDERS)
```

to extract the item number from the record.

When an end-of-file condition occurs on a GETFILE statement, a condition code of 400 is generated. Thus, to continue processing after an end-of-file condition, you must supply an error exit, like this:

```
ERROR DO
    IF &LASTCC = 400 THEN SET EOF = Y
    ELSE EXIT
    END
```

Here, an IF statement tests to see whether the condition code is 400. If it is, a symbolic variable (&EOF) is given a value of Y. Then, control returns to the statement following the GETFILE statement, where &EOF can be tested. If &LASTCC is *not* 400, a genuine error has occurred, so the EXIT statement terminates the procedure.

The PUTFILE statement   The PUTFILE statement adds a record to a file. For example, this statement:

```
PUTFILE ORDERS
```

adds the record contained in &ORDERS to the ORDERS file.

Normally, you'll use one or more SET statements to build a record before you issue a PUTFILE statement. For example, these statements:

```
SET ORDERS = &ITEMNO&DESCR&QUANTITY
PUTFILE ORDERS
```

concatenate &ITEMNO, &DESCR, and &QUANTITY to form the record in &ORDERS before the PUTFILE statement transfers the record to the file.

If you opened the file in UPDATE mode, a PUTFILE statement overwrites the record read by the previous GETFILE statement. In other words, the file is updated in place. Unfortunately, all updates must be done sequentially. So to update the 50th record in a file, you must first issue a GETFILE statement for each of the first 49 records.

The CLOSFILE statement   After you've finished processing a file, you should close it by issuing a CLOSFILE statement. For example, here's a valid CLOSFILE statement for the ORDERS file:

```
CLOSFILE ORDERS
```

In addition, you may want to issue a FREE command to release the file.

A command procedure example

Figure 14-3 presents a simple command procedure that illustrates the terminal and file handling statements I've presented so far. This procedure is used to enter an order for one or more publications (such as IBM manuals or textbooks). First, it asks you to enter your employee number and department. Then, for each publication you wish to order, it has you enter the document id and quantity. Finally, when you've finished your order, it writes a record to a file named ORDER.

Figure 14-4 shows a sample execution of the procedure. Here, I invoke the procedure implicitly by entering %ORDER. Then, I provide my employee number (3822) and department

```
00010 ALLOCATE DDNAME(ORDER) DSNAME(ORDER.DATA) MOD
00020 OPENFILE ORDER OUTPUT
00030 WRITE PLEASE PLACE YOUR PUBLICATIONS ORDER
00040 WRITE
00050 WRITENR YOUR EMPLOYEE NUMBER:
00060 READ EMPNO
00070 WRITENR YOUR DEPARTMENT CODE:
00080 READ DEPTCODE
00090 WRITE
00100 DO WHILE &STR(&DOCID) ¬= END
00110     WRITENR DOCUMENT-ID, QUANTITY (ENTER END WHEN FINISHED):
00120     READ DOCID QUANTITY
00130     IF &STR(&DOCID) ¬= END THEN DO
00140         SET ORDER = &EMPNO &SYSUID &DEPTCODE &STR(&DOCID) &QUANTITY
00150         PUTFILE ORDER
00160         END
00170     END
00180 WRITE
00190 WRITE YOUR ORDER HAS BEEN PLACED
00200 CLOSFILE ORDER
00210 FREE DDNAME(ORDER)
```

Figure 14-3   The ORDER procedure

code (D10) and order two manuals (1 copy each of GC26-3841 and GC28-0692).

To be sure you understand how this procedure works, let's step through it line by line. Lines 10 and 20 allocate and open the ORDER file. The file is opened for OUTPUT, so records will be added to the file. But since I've coded MOD on the ALLOCATE command, existing records won't be overwritten; instead, the file is positioned after the last record when it's opened.

Lines 30 and 40 display the heading:

PLEASE PLACE YOUR PUBLICATIONS ORDER

Then, line 50 prompts the user to enter an employee number which is read into &EMPNO by line 60. Similarly, line 70 prompts the user for a department code, which is read into &DEPTCODE by line 80.

Line 100 sets up a loop that accepts orders until the user enters END as a document id. Lines 110 and 120 prompt the user and read two values: &DOCID and &QUANTITY. If &DOCID isn't END, line 140 builds the record containing &EMPNO, &SYSUID, &DEPTCODE, &DOCID, and &QUANTITY (it leaves a space between each of the fields) and line 150 writes the record to the file.

```
%ORDER
 PLEASE PLACE YOUR PUBLICATIONS ORDER

 YOUR EMPLOYEE NUMBER: 3822
 YOUR DEPARTMENT CODE: D10

 DOCUMENT-ID, QUANTITY (ENTER END WHEN FINISHED): GC26-3841,1
 DOCUMENT-ID, QUANTITY (ENTER END WHEN FINISHED): GC28-0692,1
 DOCUMENT-ID, QUANTITY (ENTER END WHEN FINISHED): END

 YOUR ORDER HAS BEEN PLACED
 READY
```

Figure 14-4   Executing the ORDER procedure

As a result, the sample execution shown in figure 14-4 causes these two records to be written to the ORDER file:

```
3822 DLOWE D10 GC26-3841 1
3822 DLOWE D10 GC28-0692 1
```

Since the ORDER file is allocated with a disposition of MOD, these records are added after any existing records in the file.

After the loop has finished, line 190 writes this message:

```
YOUR ORDER HAS BEEN PLACED
```

and lines 200 and 210 close and free the file.

HOW TO USE THE READDVAL STATEMENT

As I mentioned before, when you read a record from a file, the entire record is stored in the symbolic variable associated with the file. Then, you must use SET statements and the &SUBSTR function to extract individual fields from the record.

The READDVAL statement makes this process easier. Quite simply, the READDVAL statement reads one or more values from a system variable named &SYSDVAL. In &SYSDVAL, the values are separated by standard TSO delimiters—spaces or commas—just as if they had been entered by an operator. To illustrate, suppose &SYSDVAL contains this:

```
JONES 103
```

If you issue a READDVAL statement like this one:

```
READDVAL NAME EMPNO
```

&NAME is set to JONES and &EMPNO is set to 103. I'll show you how to get these values into &SYSDVAL in just a moment.

If one of the values in &SYSDVAL contains spaces, commas, or other special characters, it must be enclosed in apostrophes, or the READDVAL statement will treat it as two values. For example, suppose &SYSDVAL contains this:

```
'WILLIAM JONES, MD' 103
```

Then, the previous READDVAL statement will set &NAME to WILLIAM JONES, MD and &EMPNO to 103. Notice that although the apostrophes appear in &SYSDVAL, they're not a part of the value assigned by READDVAL.

If there are more variables in the READDVAL statement than values in &SYSDVAL, the extra variables are assigned null values. If there are fewer variables than values, the extra values are ignored.

For example, suppose you code a READDVAL statement like this:

```
READDVAL NAME EMPNO TITLE
```

and &SYSDVAL contains this:

```
JONES 103
```

Then, &NAME will be JONES, &EMPNO will be 103, and

&TITLE will have a null value. On the other hand, if &SYSDVAL contains this:

```
TAYLOR 1750 SUPERVISOR 'JUNE 12, 1984'
```

&NAME will be TAYLOR, &EMPNO will be 1750, &TITLE will be SUPERVISOR, and the last value—June 12, 1984—will be ignored. Note here that the READDVAL statement can extract values of varying lengths—like JONES and TAYLOR— with the same variable—in this case, &NAME.

How to assign and use the values in &SYSDVAL In general, there are two ways you'll assign values to &SYSDVAL so you can use the READDVAL statement. First, you can assign terminal input by coding a READ statement without any symbolic variables. Then, the entire text entered by the user is copied to &SYSDVAL.

A second, perhaps more useful, way to use &SYSDVAL is for file processing. For example, you might create a file whose records contain values separated by spaces or commas, as I did when I created the ORDER file in figure 14-3. Then, when you process the file in your CLIST, you assign it a ddname of SYSDVAL. That way, any GETFILE statements for the file transfer records to &SYSDVAL, so you can use the READDVAL statement to extract the individual fields from the record.

To illustrate this technique, consider the LSTORDER procedure in figure 14-5. It reads the file created by the CLIST in figure 14-3, formatting and listing each record at the terminal. Figure 14-5 also shows the terminal output from the procedure using the ORDER file given.

The key to understanding this CLIST is understanding the DO-WHILE loop in lines 150 through 220. In line 160, a GETFILE statement reads a record from the file. Since the ddname for the file is SYSDVAL, the record is placed in &SYSDVAL. Then, line 190 extracts five values from &SYSDVAL. Line 200 writes those five values with appropriate spacing so the report is formatted correctly.

The end-of-file logic is handled by the error exit in lines 110-140. Here, a symbolic variable (&EOF) is used to indicate the end-of-file condition. The error exit simply sets &EOF to Y

The LSTORDER procedure

```
00010 CONTROL NOFLUSH NOMSG
00020 ALLOCATE DDNAME(SYSDVAL) DSNAME(ORDER.DATA)
00030 OPENFILE SYSDVAL
00040 WRITE
00050 WRITE              PUBLICATIONS CURRENTLY REQUESTED
00060 WRITE
00070 WRITE EMP NO    USER ID    DEPT    DOCUMENT ID    QUANTITY
00080 WRITE
00090 SET EOF = N
00100 SET COUNT = 0
00110 ERROR DO
00120      SET EOF = Y
00130      RETURN
00140      END
00150 DO WHILE &EOF = N
00160      GETFILE SYSDVAL
00170      IF &EOF = N THEN DO
00180           SET COUNT = &COUNT + 1
00190           READDVAL EMPNO USER DEPTCODE DOCID QUANTITY
00200           WRITE &EMPNO      &USER      &DEPTCODE      &DOCID          &QUANTITY
00210           END
00220      END
00230 WRITE
00240 WRITE &COUNT RECORDS IN ORDER FILE
00250 CLOSFILE SYSDVAL
00260 FREE DDNAME(SYSDVAL)
```

Figure 14-5 Executing a procedure that uses &SYSDVAL for file processing (part 1 of 2)

and returns to statement 170, the statement following the
GETFILE that caused the error. &EOF is tested both by the
DO-WHILE statement in line 150 and the IF statement in line
170.

HOW TO USE THE TERMIN STATEMENT

The TERMIN statement is an I/O statement unlike the ones
found in other high-level programming languages. Basically,
the TERMIN statement returns control to the terminal user but
provides a way for the user to return control to the command
procedure. For example, suppose you code this statement:

```
TERMIN GO
```

When it's executed, control returns to the terminal user, who
can enter any TSO commands or subcommands. But once the

The contents of the ORDER file

```
4939 MURAC D10 GC28-4826 1
4939 MURAC D10 SC28-6652 2
4939 MURAC D10 GC30-5757 1
5037 STEVE A33 GC22-7746 1
5037 STEVE A33 SC22-7490 1
3822 DLOWE D10 GC26-3841 1
3822 DLOWE D10 GC28-0692 1
```

Resulting output

```
%LSTORDER

            PUBLICATIONS CURRENTLY REQUESTED

    EMP NO      USER ID      DEPT     DOCUMENT ID      QUANTITY

    4939        MURAC        D10      GC28-4826           1
    4939        MURAC        D10      SC28-6652           2
    4939        MURAC        D10      GC30-5757           1
    5037        STEVE        A33      GC22-7746           1
    5037        STEVE        A33      SC22-7490           1
    3822        DLOWE        D10      GC26-3841           1
    3822        DLOWE        D10      GC28-0692           1

    7 RECORDS IN ORDER FILE
    READY
```

Figure 14-5   Executing a procedure that uses &SYSDVAL for file processing (part 2 of 2)

terminal user enters the delimiter GO, control returns to the command procedure.

Figure 14-6 shows a portion of a CLIST that uses TERMIN along with a sample terminal session. If you'll follow the sample terminal session, comparing it with the command procedure statements, you'll see that control returns to the terminal user when the TERMIN statement is executed. The terminal user enters two ALLOCATE commands, which are processed by TSO. Then, the user enters GO, which returns control to the command procedure.

Command procedure statements

```
WRITE ENTER ALLOCATE COMMANDS FOR REQUIRED DATA SETS
WRITE ENTER 'GO' WHEN FINISHED
TERMIN GO
WRITE COMMAND PROCEDURE CONTINUING
```

Sample terminal session

```
  ENTER ALLOCATE COMMANDS FOR REQUIRED DATA SETS
  ENTER 'GO' WHEN FINISHED
  READY
ALLOCATE DDNAME(BFCRDS) DSNAME(BFCRDS.DATA)
  READY
ALLOCATE DDNAME(ORDLST) DSNAME(*)
  READY
GO
  COMMAND PROCEDURE CONTINUING
```

Figure 14-6   Using the TERMIN statement

If you wish, you can specify more than one delimiter on a
TERMIN statement, like this:

```
TERMIN GO CANCEL
```

Here, control is returned to the CLIST when the user enters
GO or CANCEL. You can find out which delimiter the user
entered by testing a system variable named &SYSDLM. After a
TERMIN statement, &SYSDLM contains a number that corresponds to the delimiter entered by the user. So in this example,
&SYSDLM would contain 1 if the user entered GO; if the user
entered CANCEL, &SYSDLM would contain 2.

Since the TERMIN statement gives the terminal user complete control under TSO, you should use it only with experienced TSO users. And since you can code anything you want as a delimiter, you should always use a WRITE statement before a TERMIN statement to tell the user how to return to the procedure.

DISCUSSION

I've presented just a brief introduction to the terminal and file handling capabilities of CLIST in this chapter. In general, I don't think you'll use these capabilities often. Interactive applications that involve extensive terminal and file handling are usually best implemented under CICS or some other advanced communications monitor. But for short, uncomplicated applications that must be implemented in a CLIST, the terminal and file handling features I've presented here are sufficient.

Objective

Given a programming problem involving simple terminal and file handling, code a command procedure for its solution using the terminal and file handling features presented in this topic.

Appendix A

SPF reference summary

This appendix summarizes the SPF options and commands you'll use most often. For each option or command, you'll find a complete format or brief description. For the elements covered in this book, you'll also find chapter references that will give you more detailed information. You can use this summary as a quick refresher on how to use a particular SPF feature.

SPF OPTIONS

0	SPF parms	
0.1	Specify terminal characteristics	
0.2	Specify list and log defaults	
0.3	Specify program function keys	
1	Browse	Chapter 3
2	Edit	Chapter 4
3	Utilities	
3.1	Library utility	Chapter 5, Topic 1
3.2	Data set utility	Chapter 5, Topic 2
3.3	Move/copy utility	Chapter 5, Topic 3

SPF OPTIONS (continued)

PROGRAM ACCESS AND PROGRAM FUNCTION KEYS

PA1	Interrupt a TSO command.	Chapter 1, Topic 3 Chapter 11 Chapter 13, Topic 2
PA2	Redisplay the current screen contents	Chapter 1, Topic 3
PF1/13	Help (tutorial).	Chapter 2
PF2/14	Enter split screen mode.	
PF3/15	End the current operation.	Chapter 2
PF4/16	End the current operation and return to the primary option menu.	Chapter 2
PF5/17	Repeat the previous FIND command.	Chapter 3, Topic 1
PF6/18	Repeat the previous CHANGE command.	
PF7/19	Move the window up.	Chapter 3, Topic 1
PF8/20	Move the window down.	Chapter 3, Topic 1
PF9/21	Alternate between split screens.	
PF10/22	Move the window left.	Chapter 3, Topic 1
PF11/23	Move the window right.	Chapter 3, Topic 1
PF12/24	Move the cursor to the command-area field on line 2.	

SCROLL AMOUNTS   Chapter 3, Topic 1

HALF   Move the screen window half a page (11 lines or 40 columns).

PAGE   Move the screen window one page (22 lines or 80 columns).

n   Move the screen window *n* lines or columns.

MAX   Move the screen window to the top, bottom, left, or right margin.

CSR   Move the screen window so data at the cursor position ends up at
             the top, bottom, left, or right of the screen.

BROWSE COMMANDS

Establish a label   Chapter 3, Topic 1

.label

The FIND command   Chapter 3, Topics 1 and 2

$$\text{FIND string } \left[\begin{Bmatrix}\underline{\text{NEXT}}\\ \text{PREV}\\ \text{FIRST}\\ \text{LAST}\\ \text{ALL}\end{Bmatrix}\right] \left[\begin{Bmatrix}\underline{\text{CHARS}}\\ \text{PREFIX}\\ \text{SUFFIX}\\ \text{WORD}\end{Bmatrix}\right] [\text{col-1 } [\text{col-2}]]$$

The LOCATE command   Chapter 3, Topic 1

$$\text{LOCATE } \begin{Bmatrix}\text{line-number}\\ \text{label}\end{Bmatrix}$$

EDIT COMMANDS

Line commands

Copying lines   Chapter 4, Topic 1

C   Copy this line.
Cn   Copy n lines starting with this line.
C C   Copy a block of lines.

A   Place the copied lines after this line.
An   Repeat the copied lines n times after this line.
B   Place the copied lines before this line.
Bn   Repeat the copied lines n times before this line.

Deleting lines   Chapter 4, Topic 1

D   Delete this line.
Dn   Delete n lines starting with this line.
D D   Delete the block of lines beginning with the first
        DD command and ending with the second DD
        command.

Excluding and redisplaying source lines   Chapter 4, Topic 3

X   Exclude this line.
Xn   Exclude n lines starting with this line.
X X   Exclude a block of lines.

S   Show one line of the excluded text.
Sn   Show n lines.

F   Show the first line of the excluded text.
Fn   Show the first n lines.

L   Show the last line of the excluded text.
Ln   Show the last n lines.

Inserting lines   Chapter 4, Topic 1

I   Insert a single line following this line.
I*n*   Insert *n* lines following this line.

Moving lines   Chapter 4, Topic 1

M   Move this line.
M*n*   Move *n* lines starting with this line.
MM   Move a block of lines.

A   Place the moved lines after this line.
A*n*   Repeat the moved lines *n* times after this line.
B   Place the moved lines before this line.
B*n*   Repeat the moved lines *n* times before this line.

Repeating lines   Chapter 4, Topic 1

R   Repeat this line.
R*n*   Repeat this line *n* times.
R R   Repeat a block of lines.
R R*n* Repeat a block of lines *n* times.

Shifting data   Chapter 4, Topic 3

Data shift command	*Column shift command*	*Meaning*
<	(	Shift this line left two positions.
<*n*	(*n*	Shift this line left *n* positions.
<<	((	Shift a block of lines left two positions.
<<*n*	((*n*	Shift a block of lines left *n* positions.
>	)	Shift this line right two positions.
>*n*	)*n*	Shift this line right *n* positions.
>>	))	Shift a block of lines right two positions.
>>*n*	))*n*	Shift a block of lines right *n* positions.

Other line commands   Chapter 4, Topic 2

TABS	Display a tab definition line.
COLS	Display a column line.
BOUNDS	Display a boundary line.
MASK	Display a mask line.

Primary commands

The AUTONUM command   Chapter 4, Topic 2

$$\text{AUTONUM} \quad \begin{Bmatrix} \text{ON} \\ \text{OFF} \end{Bmatrix}$$

The CANCEL command   Chapter 4, Topic 1

CANCEL

The CAPS command   Chapter 4, Topic 2

$$\text{CAPS} \quad \begin{Bmatrix} \text{ON} \\ \text{OFF} \end{Bmatrix}$$

The CHANGE command   Chapter 4, Topic 3

$$\text{CHANGE string-1 string-2} \left[\begin{Bmatrix} \underline{\text{NEXT}} \\ \text{PREV} \\ \text{FIRST} \\ \text{LAST} \\ \text{ALL} \end{Bmatrix} \right] \left[\begin{Bmatrix} \underline{\text{CHARS}} \\ \text{PREFIX} \\ \text{SUFFIX} \\ \text{WORD} \end{Bmatrix} \right]$$

$$\left[\begin{Bmatrix} \text{X} \\ \text{NX} \end{Bmatrix} \right] \text{[col-1 [col-2]]}$$

The COPY command   Chapter 4, Topic 3

COPY [member]

The CREATE command   Chapter 4, Topic 3

CREATE [member]

The FIND command   Chapter 4, Topic 3

```
FIND string [{NEXT  }] [{CHARS }] [{X }] [col-1 [col-2]]
             {PREV  }   {PREFIX}   {NX}
             {FIRST }   {SUFFIX}
             {LAST  }   {WORD  }
             {ALL   }
```

The HEX command   Chapter 4, Topic 2

```
HEX  {ON }
     {OFF}
```

The MOVE command   Chapter 4, Topic 3

```
MOVE [member]
```

The NULLS command   Chapter 4, Topic 2

```
NULLS  {ON }
       {OFF}
```

The NUMBER command   Chapter 4, Topic 2

```
NUMBER  {ON } {STD  }
        {OFF} {COBOL}
```

The PRINT command   Chapter 4, Topic 2

```
PRINT  {ON }
       {OFF}
```

The PROFILE command   Chapter 4, Topic 2

```
PROFILE [profile-name]
```

The RECOVERY command   Chapter 4, Topic 2

```
RECOVERY  {ON }
          {OFF}
```

The RENUM command   Chapter 4, Topic 2

```
RENUM  [{STD   }]
        {COBOL }
```

The REPLACE command   Chapter 4, Topic 3

```
REPLACE [member]
```

The RESET command   Chapter 4, Topic 1

```
RESET
```

The SAVE command   Chapter 4, Topic 1

```
SAVE
```

The STATS command   Chapter 4, Topic 2

```
STATS  {ON  }
       {OFF }
```

The TABS command   Chapter 4, Topic 2

```
TABS   {ON  } [tab-character] [ALL]
       {OFF }
```

The UNNUM command   Chapter 4, Topic 2

```
UNNUM
```

Appendix   B

TSO command summary

This appendix summarizes the TSO commands and command
procedure statements presented in this book. For each
command or statement, you'll find a complete format as well
as a chapter reference that will give you more detailed
information. You can use this summary as a quick refresher on
how to code a particular command or statement.

TSO COMMANDS

The ALLOCATE command   Chapter 9, Topic 2

For a new data set

```
ALLOCATE        DSNAME(data-set-name)

                DDNAME(ddname)

                ⎧KEEP    ⎫
                ⎨CATALOG ⎬
                ⎩DELETE  ⎭

                UNIT(device)

                VOLUME(volume-serial-number)

                SPACE(primary secondary)

                ⎧TRACKS   ⎫
                ⎨CYLINDERS⎬
                ⎩         ⎭

                DIR(directory-space)

                ⎧EXPDT(expiration-date) ⎫
                ⎨RETPD(retention-period)⎬
                ⎩                       ⎭

                DSORG(organization)

                RECFM(record-format)

                LRECL(record-length)

                BLKSIZE(block-size)

                LIKE(model-data-set-name)
```

The ALLOCATE command (continued)

For an existing data set

```
ALLOCATE    {DSNAME(data-set-name) }
            {DATASET(data-set-name)}

            {DDNAME(ddname)}
            {FILE(ddname)  }

            {OLD}
            {SHR}
            {MOD}

            {KEEP     }
            {DELETE   }
            {UNCATALOG}

            UNIT(device)

            VOLUME(volume-serial-number)
```

For terminal I/O

```
ALLOCATE    DSNAME(*)

            DDNAME(ddname)
```

For a dummy file

```
ALLOCATE    DUMMY

            DDNAME(ddname)
```

For SYSOUT output

```
ALLOCATE    DDNAME(ddname)

            SYSOUT(class)

            [{HOLD  }]
            [{NOHOLD}]

            [DEST(station-id)]
```

The CALL command
Chapter 10, Topic 1

```
CALL    data-set-name

        ['parameter-string']
```

The CANCEL command
Chapter 11

```
CANCEL     {job-name           }
           {job-name(job-id)   }

        [{PURGE   }]
         {NOPURGE }
```

The COBOL command
Chapter 10, Topic 1

```
COBOL      data-set-name

        [{LOAD(object-module-name)}]
         {NOLOAD                  }

        [{PRINT(print-file-name)}]
         {PRINT(*)              }
         {NOPRINT               }

        [{LIB(library-names)}]
         {NOLIB             }

        [compiler-options]
```

The COPY command
Chapter 9, Topic 1

```
COPY    old-data-set-name    new-data-set-name
```

The DELETE command
Chapter 9, Topic 1

```
DELETE    (data-set-names)

        [PURGE]
```

The DSPRINT command

Chapter 9, Topic 1

```
DSPRINT    data-set-name

           printer-name

          ⎧NUM(location,length) ⎫
        [ ⎨SNUM(location,length)⎬ ]
          ⎩NONUM                ⎭

          [LINES(start[:end])]

          ⎧SINGLE⎫
        [ ⎨DOUBLE⎬ ]
          ⎩CCHAR ⎭

          ⎧FOLD    ⎫
        [ ⎨TRUNCATE⎬ ]
          ⎩        ⎭

          ⎧EJECT  ⎫
        [ ⎨NOEJECT⎬ ]
          ⎩       ⎭
```

The EDIT command

Chapter 9, Topic 1

```
EDIT   library(member)   type   [⎧OLD⎫]
                                 [⎩NEW⎭]
```

EDIT subcommands

```
CHANGE   start-line   [end-line]   old-string   new-string   [ALL]

DELETE   start-line   [end-line]

END    ⎧SAVE  ⎫
       ⎩NOSAVE⎭

INPUT   line-number [increment]

LIST    [start-line] [end-line]

RENUM   [new-first-line] [increment]
```

The EXEC command

Chapter 12
Chapter 13, Topic 1

Explicit form

```
EXEC proc-lib-name(proc-name) ['parameters'] [control-options]
```

Implicit form

```
[%] proc-name [parameters]
```

The FREE command

Chapter 9, Topic 2

```
FREE      {ALL                     }
          {DSNAME(data-set-names)  }
          {DDNAME(ddnames)         }

          [{KEEP     }]
          [{CATALOG  }]
          [{UNCATALOG}]
          [{DELETE   }]

          [SYSOUT(class)]

          [{HOLD  }]
          [{NOHOLD}]

          [DEST(station-id)]
```

The HELP command

Chapter 8, Topic 1

```
HELP [command-name]
```

The LINK command

Chapter 10, Topic 1

```
LINK    data-set-name

        [LOAD(load-module-name)]

        ⎡⎧PRINT(print-file-name)⎫⎤
        ⎢⎨PRINT(*)              ⎬⎥
        ⎣⎩NOPRINT               ⎭⎦

        [LIB(library-names)]

        COBLIB
```

The LIST command

Chapter 9, Topic 1

```
LIST data-set-name
```

The LISTALC command

Chapter 9, Topic 2

```
LISTALC  [STATUS]

         [HISTORY]

         [MEMBERS]

         [SYSNAMES]
```

The LISTCAT command

Chapter 9, Topic 1

```
LISTCAT   ⎡⎧ENTRIES(data-set-names)⎫⎤
          ⎣⎩LEVEL(level)           ⎭⎦

          ⎡⎧NAME   ⎫⎤
          ⎢⎨HISTORY⎬⎥
          ⎢⎨VOLUME ⎬⎥
          ⎣⎩ALL    ⎭⎦
```

The LISTDS command

Chapter 9, Topic 1

```
LISTDS    (data-set-names)

          [MEMBERS]

          [HISTORY]

          [STATUS]

          [LEVEL]
```

The LOADGO command

Chapter 10, Topic 1

```
LOADGO    data-set-name

          ['parameter-string']

         ⎧PRINT(print-file-name)⎫
        [⎨PRINT(*)              ⎬]
         ⎩NOPRINT               ⎭

          [LIB(library-names)]

          COBLIB
```

The LOGOFF command

Chapter 1, Topic 2

```
LOGOFF
```

The LOGON command

Chapter 1, Topic 2

```
LOGON    user-id/password   ACCT(account-number)   [NONOTICE]
```

The OUTPUT command   Chapter 11

```
OUTPUT      {job-name          }
            {job-name(job-id)  }

            [NEWCLASS(class-name)]

            [DEST(station-id)]

            [{HOLD   }]
            [{NOHOLD }]

            [CLASS(class-names)]

            [DELETE]

            [PAUSE]
```

OUTPUT subcommands

```
CONTINUE    [{BEGIN}]
            [{HERE }]
            [{NEXT }]

            [{PAUSE  }]
            [{NOPAUSE}]

END

SAVE data-set-name
```

The RENAME command   Chapter 9, Topic 1

```
RENAME   old-name   new-name

         [ALIAS]
```

The STATUS command   Chapter 11

```
STATUS      [{job-name          }]
            [{job-name(job-id)  }]
```

The SUBMIT command

Chapter 11

```
SUBMIT    data-set-name

          [JOBCHAR(character)]
```

The TESTCOB command

Chapter 10, Topic 2

```
TESTCOB     (program-id:ddname1)

            LOAD(member:ddname2)

            [PRINT(ddname3)]

            [PARM('parameter-string')]
```

TESTCOB subcommands

```
AT    statement-list
      [(subcommand-list)]
```

```
DROP  [symbol]
```
(Use with EQUATE subcommand)

```
DUMP
```

```
END
```

```
EQUATE   symbol   data-name
```

```
GO [program-id][.statement-number][.verb-number]
```

```
IF (expression) {GO  }
                {HALT}
```

```
LIST     {identifier-list}
         {ALL            }

         [PRINT]
```

```
LISTFILE   file-name

           [PRINT]
```

TESTCOB subcommands (continued)

```
LSTBRKS

NEXT

OFF [statement-list]                          (Use, with AT subcommand)

OFFWN [identifier]                            (Use with WHEN subcommand)

RUN [program-id][.statement-number][.verb-number]

SET identifier-1 = {identifier-2}
                   {literal      }

        {line-1        }
SOURCE  {line-1:line-2} ddname

         ENTRY
        [PARA ]
TRACE   [NAME ]
         OFF

        [PRINT]

WHEN   identifier {data-name   }
                  {(expression)}
```

COMMAND PROCEDURE STATEMENTS

The ATTN statement
Chapter 13, Topic 2

```
ATTN   {statement}
       {OFF      }
```

The CLOSFILE statement
Chapter 14

```
CLOSFILE   ddname
```

The comment format
Chapter 13, Topic 1

```
/* [text] */
```

The CONTROL statement
Chapter 13, Topic 2

```
CONTROL   [{MSG      }]
          [{NOMSG    }]

          [{FLUSH    }]
          [{NOFLUSH  }]

          [{MAIN     }]
          [{NOMAIN   }]

          [{LIST     }]
          [{NOLIST   }]

          [{CONLIST  }]
          [{NOCONLIST}]

          [{SYMLIST  }]
          [{NOSYMLIST}]

          [{PROMPT   }]
          [{NOPROMPT }]

          [END(string)]
```

The DATA/ENDDATA statements

Chapter 13, Topic 2

```
DATA
commands
ENDDATA
```

The DO statement

Chapter 13, Topic 1

```
DO
        statements
END
```

The DO WHILE statement

Chapter 13, Topic 1

```
DO WHILE expression
        statements
END
```

The ERROR statement

Chapter 13, Topic 2

```
ERROR    {statement}
         {OFF      }
```

The EXIT statement

Chapter 13, Topic 1

```
EXIT [CODE(condition-code)]
```

The GETFILE statement

Chapter 14

```
GETFILE ddname
```

The GLOBAL statement

Chapter 13, Topic 2

```
GLOBAL variable-names
```

The GOTO statement   Chapter 13, Topic 1

```
GOTO label
```

The label format

```
label: statement
```

The IF statement   Chapter 13, Topic 1

```
IF expression THEN statement-1
[ELSE [statement-2]]
```

The OPENFILE statement   Chapter 14

```
OPENFILE   ddname   mode
```

The PROC statement   Chapter 12

```
PROC count [positional-parms] [keyword-parms[(values)]]
```

The PUTFILE statement   Chapter 14

```
PUTFILE ddname
```

The READ statement   Chapter 14

```
READ variables
```

The READDVAL statement   Chapter 14

```
READDVAL variables
```

The **RETURN** statement

RETURN

Chapter 13, Topic 2

The **SET** statement

SET variable-name = expression

Chapter 13, Topic 1

The **TERMIN** statement

TERMIN delimiters

Chapter 14

The **WRITE** statement

WRITE [text]

Chapter 13, Topic 1

The **WRITENR** statement

WRITENR text

Chapter 14

Index

Comment Form

Your opinions count

Your opinions today will affect our future products and policies. So if you have questions, criticisms, or suggestions, I'm eager to get them. You can expect a response within a week of the time we receive your comments.

Also, if you discover any errors in this book, typographical or otherwise, please point them out. We'll correct them when the book is reprinted.

Thanks for your help!

fold

Mike Murach, President
Mike Murach and Associates, Inc.

fold

Book title: MVS TSO

Dear Mike: _____

_____

_____

_____

_____

_____

_____

_____

_____

_____

_____

_____

fold   fold

_____

_____

_____

_____

_____

Name and Title _____

Company (if any) _____

Address _____

City, State, Zip _____

Fold where indicated and staple.
No postage necessary if mailed in the U.S.

fold

fold

NO POSTAGE
NECESSARY
IF MAILED
IN THE
UNITED STATES

BUSINESS REPLY MAIL

FIRST-CLASS MAIL   PERMIT NO. 3063   FRESNO, CA

POSTAGE WILL BE PAID BY ADDRESSEE

Mike Murach & Associates, Inc.

4697 West Jacquelyn Avenue
Fresno, CA 93722-9986

fold

fold

Order Form

Our Unlimited Guarantee

To our customers who order directly from us: You must be satisfied. Our books must work for you, or you can send them back for a full refund . . . no matter how many you buy, no matter how long you've had them.

Name & Title _____

Company (if company address) _____

Address _____

City, State, Zip _____

Phone number (including area code) _____

Qty	Product code and title	Price
OS Subjects		
____ TSO	MVS TSO	$25.00
____ MJCL	MVS JCL	32.50
____ OSUT	OS Utilities	15.00
____ OSDB	OS Debugging for the COBOL Programmer	20.00
DOS/VSE Subjects		
____ VJCL	DOS/VSE JCL	$30.00
____ ICCF	DOS/VSE ICCF	25.00
VM/CMS		
____ VMCC	VM/CMS: Commands and Concepts	$25.00
Assembler Language		
____ MBAL	MVS Assembler Language	$30.00
____ VBAL	DOS/VSE Assembler Language	30.00

Qty	Product code and title	Price
VSAM		
____ VSMX	VSAM: Access Method Services and Application Programming	$25.00
____ VSAM	VSAM for the COBOL Programmer	15.00
CICS		
____ CIC1	CICS for the COBOL Programmer: Part 1	$25.00
____ CIC2	CICS for the COBOL Programmer: Part 2	25.00
____ CREF	The CICS Programmer's Desk Reference	32.50
Data Base Processing		
____ IMS1	IMS for the COBOL Programmer Part 1: DL/I Data Base Processing	$30.00
____ IMS2	IMS for the COBOL Programmer Part 2: Data Communications and MFS	30.00
COBOL Language Elements		
____ SC1R	Structured ANS COBOL: Part 1	$25.00
____ SC2R	Structured ANS COBOL: Part 2	25.00
____ RW	Report Writer	13.50

☐ Bill me the appropriate price plus UPS shipping and handling (and sales tax in California) for each book ordered.

☐ Bill the appropriate book prices plus UPS shipping and handling (and sales tax in California) to my
_____VISA _____MasterCard:

Card number _____

Valid thru (month/year) _____

Cardowner's signature _____
(not valid without signature)

☐ I want to **save** UPS shipping and handling charges. Here's my check or money order for $_____. California residents, please add 6% sales tax to your total. (Offer valid in the U.S. only.)

To order more quickly,

Call **toll-free** 1-800-221-5528

(Weekdays, 9 to 4 Pacific Std. Time)

In California, call 1-800-221-5527

Mike Murach & Associates, Inc.

4697 West Jacquelyn Avenue
Fresno, California 93722
(209) 275-3335